W9-CLE-380

NATURAL RESOURCE ECONOMICS

About the Book and Editors

S. V. Ciriacy-Wantrup is widely recognized as a pioneer in the field of natural resource economics. During his lifetime, he made an indelible contribution as an economist and conservationist to the solution of increasingly complex global economic and natural resource problems.

This volume was assembled by two of Dr. Wantrup's students as a complement to his textbook, *Resource Conservation: Economics and Policies*. Wantrup's ideas on conservation economics continued to evolve in ways that were never fully reflected in that text, and although for the student of natural resource economics it is still essential reading, to stop there is to have missed some of his most valuable insights.

Richard C. Bishop is professor of agricultural and resource economics at the University of Wisconsin, Madison. **Stephen O. Andersen** is director of research at the Consumer Energy Council of America and is a professor of economics at College of the Atlantic in Bar Harbor, Maine.

Natural Resource Economics: Selected Papers

S. V. CIRIACY-WANTRUP
edited by Richard C. Bishop
and Stephen O. Andersen

WESTVIEW PRESS / BOULDER AND LONDON

All rights reserved. No part of this publication may be reproduced or transmitted in any form or by any means, electronic or mechanical, including photocopy, recording, or any information storage and retrieval system, without permission in writing from the publisher.

Copyright © 1985 by Westview Press, Inc.

Published in 1985 in the United States of America by Westview Press, Inc., 5500 Central Avenue, Boulder, Colorado 80301; Frederick A. Praeger, Publisher

Library of Congress Catalog Card Number: 85-40312
ISBN 0-8133-0064-9

Composition for this book was provided by the editors
Printed and bound in the United States of America

10   9   8   7   6   5   4   3   2   1

To Mary Rubo

TABLE OF CONTENTS

Part V: Natural Resources in Economic Development

Preface

In 1965, I enrolled in the graduate program in economics at Colorado State University. Given CSU's commitment to natural resource economics, it was not surprising that my new research assistantship involved water policy. There, and in my very first course in resource economics, taught by Ken Nobe, I encountered the written work of S. V. Ciriacy-Wantrup. This first encounter, it turned out, shaped my future dramatically.

The field of natural resource economics as it was emerging in the mid-1960's held much to fascinate me as a student, but Wantrup's work was especially interesting. No one else seemed so adept at placing day-to-day resource management issues in institutional, legal and historical perspective. No one else combined solid economics with such an intimate understanding of the physical and biological properties of natural resources. I must also admit that in those days I had what might be termed a love-hate relationship with theoretical optimization. On the one hand, much that I read in a theoretical vein seemed rigorous, tidy and even aesthetically pleasing. On the other hand, once I had mastered a new theoretical model the apparent shallowness of resulting policy prescriptions often left me restless and frustrated. When I read Wantrup's thinking on the usefulness and pitfalls of optimization, I knew that here was a kindred spirit.

It was thus not surprising that I moved on to Berkeley for Ph.D. study under Wantrup's guidance in 1967. It was also not without considerable uneasiness. One of my CSU professors, who knew him well, suggested that Wantrup would be "difficult but not impossible." That turned out to be a sound assessment. During the Berkeley years, I weathered some long tirades and occasional stunning blows to my ego. However, I now have no doubts about my choice of mentors. In Wantrup, I found a first-class economic mind combined with a firm commitment to improving natural resource management. Thinking of Wantrup always reminds me of a verse from Ecclesiastes (7:5, RSV): "It is better for a man to hear the rebuke of the wise than to hear the song of fools."

Wantrup was active in natural resource economics for nearly 40 years and some of his best work is buried in old journals or other less accessible places. I broached the idea of publishing a selection of his papers a year or two before his death in 1980. Wantrup was enthusiastic. However, the demands on the time of an assistant professor being what they are, the work did not really get under way until the summer of 1982. At that time, I asked Stephen

xi

Andersen, another Wantrup student, to help me select a cross-section of Wantrup's best papers. In addition to co-editing, Stephen researched and prepared the biographical sketch that appears as the second chapter. Other Wantrup students contributed introductory material for the various parts.

The book is intended for students and professionals in economics and other resource-oriented disciplines. Those who are already familiar with Wantrup's work will find it a useful compilation. But, Stephen and I hope for more than that. When we, as students, first read Wantrup we found both the inspiration for a life commitment to natural resource economics and the intellectual foundations for fulfilling that commitment. Our hope is that the papers we have selected will have similar effects on some newcomers to Wantrup's work.

This book would not have been possible without the help of Mary Rubo. Mary has had an active interest in Wantrup's work since she helped edit the first edition of his *Resource Conservation: Economics and Policies*, which was published by the University of California Press in 1952. Mary provided financial support to the Friends of the Earth Foundation, which in turn underwrote the preparation and publication of the present work. Mary also made me a guest in her home and provided access to Wantrup's files during the selection of the papers. Perhaps most important was Mary's moral support and patience as Stephen and I went through the process of selecting the papers, preparing related material, seeking a publisher, and finalizing the manuscript. For all these reasons, we gratefully dedicate this book to her.

We also gratefully acknowledge the financial support of the Friends of the Earth Foundation and particularly the help of its Executive Director, Jeffrey W. Knight.

The Department of Agricultural and Resource Economics at the University of California-Berkeley provided work space and access to the Giannini Foundation Library.

Cathy Walton's timely preparation of the manuscript on a word processor is appreciated. Special thanks are due to Mrs. Marcy Schoepp, my secretary at the University of Wisconsin, who coordinated the process of publication and whose careful proofreading helped us avoid many errors. The preparation of the camera-ready copy was done by Accent Graphics of Lincoln, Nebraska. Julie Williams and Sonja Lemmer were very helpful there.

Richard C. Bishop
University of Wisconsin

INTRODUCTION

by

Richard C. Bishop

S. V. Ciriacy-Wantrup is widely recognized as a pioneer in the field of natural resource economics. In private correspondence he once described his major field of interest in these terms:

> Topically, natural resource economics is mainly concerned with the economic analysis of public policy toward natural resources. It has closer relations with public finance, welfare economics, and neighboring areas of general economic theory than with marketing, farm management, and other subfields of agricultural economics. In methodology, natural resource economics is analytically oriented institutional economics with strong interests in quantitative approaches, such as the various forms of formal and informal benefit-cost analysis.

During Wantrup's lifetime, the world was increasingly confronted with natural resource problems that became ever more complex and global in character. He made an indelible contribution to a discipline devoted to better understanding the economic nature and origins of those problems and to designing public policies for their solution.

Perhaps his best known work is *Resource Conservation: Economics and Policies*. The enduring place of this work in the literature is well-established. However, the present volume was assembled on the premise that to have read only *Resource Conservation* is to have overlooked many of Wantrup's most valuable contributions. First, the literature on the so-called "common property problem" came to occupy its current place of prominence in natural resource economics only after the first edition of the book was published. Though Wantrup did address the same basic issues in the *Resource Conservation* book under the heading of "fugitive resources," he felt compelled late in his career to elaborate in some detail on the shortcomings of the theory of common property resources as developed by others. Second, over a large part of his career he examined issues relating to water which are given only very limited attention in his book. Also, his ideas on conservation economics continued to evolve and become clearer to a degree that was

1

never really reflected in later editions of his book. For the student of natural resource economics, *Resource Conservation* is still essential reading, but to a considerable degree it reflects Wantrup's thinking in 1952. To stop there is to have missed some of his most valuable insights.

Certain threads ran through Wantrup's work regardless of the specific topic. He has often been classed among the institutionalists. This is accurate to a certain extent. As the reader will soon see, he repeatedly emphasized the importance of institutions in natural resource economics. In his later writings, Wantrup conceived of economic decisions as occurring in a three level hierarchy. On the bottom or "operating" level, decisions are made which involve actual allocation of economic resources. The unit of decision making here may be a private individual, or a corporation, or a public operating agency such as a local water district. At the top of the hierarchy is the policy level where decisions are made about the goals and objectives of society. Here society may decide, for example, to seek full employment and to protect and enhance the environment. The middle, or "institutional," level was conceived as the level on which decisions are made about the links between stated goals (policy level choices) and actual resource allocation decisions (operating level choices). Appropriate institutions (including property rights, taxes, and regulations) are required if goals are to be achieved. This analysis was institutionalist.

On the other hand, Wantrup was a staunch defender of the theoretical value of optimization and equilibrium. As a preface to numerous references to this last point in the coming chapters, this quotation from an early unpublished manuscript (c. 1940) emphasizes the role of general equilibrium dynamic economics.

> The essential thing in equilibrium theory is not that it assumes a condition of equilibrium toward which economic adjustments move but it gives the student an organizing principle to guide him through the eternal ebb and flow of economic life. As such a tool of thought, the equilibrium theory has justified itself in the social sciences just as it has in the natural sciences, particularly biology. The analogy between equilibrium theories of the social sciences is not found in any external identity but in the internal unity of each science, in the fundamental interdependence of parts, and in the dependence of the part on the purpose of the whole. He who sees in equilibrium theory only a mechanical principle does not understand its scientific significance in the social sciences.

Had Wantrup's age been dominated by the institutionalists, one can imagine Wantrup arguing vehemently for the neglected virtues of optimization, but this was not to be. Instead, optimization under narrowly defined institutional assumptions held the stage, and he felt compelled to repeatedly emphasize the dangers of this approach to public policy-oriented economic analysis. Wantrup viewed theories based on optimization as useful scientific fictions. They are of greatest interest in analyzing decisions at the operating level, particularly in Western industrialized nations.

When one considers questions at the institutional level, serious doubts arise about the practical relevance of theoretical optima. For one thing, Wantrup took his welfare economics a whole lot more seriously than many of his contemporaries. No firm basis exists for transforming policy level decisions into a social welfare function which can be maximized in making institutional level decisions. To use market prices as criteria for institutional change would be like letting the tail wag the dog, since market prices are the result of operating level decisions within pre-existing institutional environments. To some degree at least, the purpose of institutional level decisions is to guide operating level decisions and not vice versa. Even where market prices are relevant on the institutional level, they are often absent altogether or badly distorted by market imperfections. Furthermore, decisions on the institutional level affect the distribution of property rights, wealth and income. This may affect prices and the optimum, thereby raising questions about what to maximize and whether Scitovsky paradoxes and other such inconsistencies may arise.

Then, too, there is uncertainty. In the coming chapters, Wantrup repeatedly emphasized that social optimization over time is made exceedingly difficult because the future course of critical parameters like technology, tastes, institutions, population, and income levels cannot be foreseen. Without knowledge of such future values how can one optimize over time, particularly given the irreversible implications of many natural resource decisions?

Confronted with all these difficulties, economists doing public policy-oriented research generally go one of three directions. Many mainstream economists plunge forward with applications of the optimization paradigm as if there is no problem. To them, this is the "economic viewpoint." If questioned, these economists freely acknowledge that society will no doubt want to consider "noneconomic viewpoints" in arriving at final decisions. Such "equity issues" are beyond the area of expertise of the economist, however. Perhaps society would do well to take economic optima as a starting point for policy choices and only depart from such optima where a clear "non-economic goal" will be satisfied.

The second direction that an economist can take is to completely abandon efforts to influence institutional and policy level decisions. Here the role of the economist *qua* scientist is limited to predicting the effects of alternative institutional level decisions. If a certain institutional change is proposed, this group would strive to predict how operating level behavior would be affected. Whether such a change *ought to be made* is outside the bounds of scientific economics. Among the proponents of this view are the "neoinstitutionalists" particularly Warren Samuels and Alan Schmid.

In the coming chapters, the reader will see Wantrup forging a trail between these two camps. He certainly had a great deal of sympathy for the neoinstitutionalists' view about the over-riding importance of institutions in economic affairs and the importance of accurately predicting how economic performance would change when institutions are modified. At the same time, however, he clearly used social optima as theoretical benchmarks. Consider, for example, his concept of the social optimum state of conservation.

This point of view carried over into practical applications as well. There he did not hesitate to embrace benefit-cost analysis, provided that it was competently done and properly interpreted. But, Wantrup parted company with the mainstream economists over the narrowness of their definition of what was within the economic purview. The economist must look at other social goals in addition to efficiency in analyzing decisions at the policy and institutional levels.

More specifically, granted the immense value of optimization for theory building and its more limited, but by no means negligible, value for practical applications, why not give its practical limitations explicit recognition and attempt to design practical decision criteria to deal with those limitations? His willingness to ask this question is what took him beyond both mainstream economists and neoinstitutionalists. The best known and best developed attempt to go beyond optimization was the safe minimum standard of conservation. Optimization is, he reasoned, inadequate to deal with irreversible loss of renewable resource because of uncertainty and extramarket values. The safe minimum standard was achieved when irreversibility was avoided. On a theoretical level, the safe minimum standard was integrated into the overall theoretical framework by treating it as an additional constraint in the optimization problem. Additional theoretical support was drawn from the theory of two-person zero sum games against nature. On a practical level, the distinction between objectives and constraints is often murky anyway, and the safe minimum standard was advocated as one possible objective (among many) of conservation policy. A less well-developed additional example of his attempt to deal with the limitations of optimization is his concept of survival value of institutions discussed in Chapter 4 of this volume.

Why should the modern day natural resource economist read Wantrup? Over the past thirty years, and at an accelerated pace since the first oil crises led to a tremendous resurgence of interest in natural resources among economists, the discipline of natural resource economics has placed heavy emphasis on increasingly sophisticated, rigorous theories developed in the context of restrictive, abstract assumptions. Much of great value has been learned in the process. Wantrup, however, continued to march to a different drummer. As we have just seen, he believed that it was more important to deal with the limitations of optimization than to build even more sophisticated models. He also felt that the rigorousness of much of modern natural resource economics was gained at the expense of abstractions that neglected essential social and natural relationships. In my view, many of his insights and criticisms are every bit as fresh, relevant, and unique to Wantrup himself as they were when they were first published ten, twenty, or more years ago.

The noneconomist too will find much of interest here. Wantrup continually strived to make his ideas practical and assessible to noneconomists. The result may well be that his work was more greatly appreciated by lawyers, biologists, conservationists, and engineers than by his colleagues from economics. Such noneconomists found in Wantrup a kindred spirit, well versed in the basic elements of their disciplines and more ready than many economists to embrace their views on policy issues as having economic relevance. Roughly a third of the papers selected for inclusion here originally appeared in noneconomic books and journals, and even those that were written primarily for economic audiences should not prove too difficult for those with limited economic backgrounds.

This volume begins with a biographical sketch. The selected papers by Wantrup are then presented in five separate parts. Part I deals with various aspects of the "commons" problems; Parts II and III focus on water-related issues; Part IV looks at recent writings in the conservation area, with particular emphasis on irreversibility and uncertainty; and the last part examines the role of natural resources in economic development.

Each part is introduced by one of Wantrup's former students in the hope that their special insights will help guide the reader toward the more significant of Wantrup's ideas. Except for these introductions, we will leave the reader to judge these papers for her/himself. Are the papers presented here merely of historical interest, once important building blocks which are now rightly buried in the debris of progress? Or do they represent a train of thought from which natural resource economics has recently departed, but to which it must soon return if it is to continue to expand in ways which will best help humankind deal with natural resource problems?

BIOGRAPHICAL SKETCH

by

Stephen O. Andersen[*][1]

Siegfried V. Ciriacy-Wantrup will be remembered both for his scholarly works, some of which are reprinted in this volume, and for his strong personality. This double reputation made him a legend in his own day, a legend characterized as Teutonic, brilliant, trenchant, confrontational, courageous, solitary, and stoic. This complex personality is best understood by considering his European upbringing, his professional years at the Giannini Foundation in Berkeley, and his private life as rancher and wildlife manager.

Professor Wantrup was born the son of a preacher in Langenberg Rheinland (today Velbert-Langenberg). Siegfried spent boyhood summers on his grandfather's farm, where he began the long process of learning to husband resources. He was a spirited youth who darted between academies while gaining a reputation as a genius and a free-thinker. His extraordinary grasp of the new science of genetics was soon recognized, and he was recruited by several institutes for advanced study. But he rejected these offers, in part because he abhorred the Nazi concept of the super-race, and chose instead to study agriculture.

His education included sojourns in Bonn, Berlin, Vienna, and at the University of Illinois, where he resided when the stock market crashed in 1929. Economists were perplexed by the world depression of the 1930's and Wantrup enjoyed the intellectual challenge of debates about trends whose results remained problematic. Discussion in his Illinois classes ranged from specific microeconomic relationships to the general condition of mankind. Wantrup had already mastered the economics that went into Keynesian formulations, and he was keenly aware of the very different perspectives of Marx, but he distilled his original view of economics from his own international background and experience of depression, war, and recovery.

*Director of Research for the Consumer Energy Council of America, Washington, D.C.

In 1932, the University of Bonn, in Germany, granted Wantrup a doctorate in economics. For a time he worked as a postdoctoral fellow, and then as Director of the Agricultural Department of Landtrehand A.G., with headquarters in Berlin. He then returned to the University of Bonn to teach until he left Nazi Germany with a temporary exit visa to present a professional paper in the United States in December of 1936. He worked briefly for the Rockefeller Foundation; from 1938 until retirement in 1974, he was in the Department of Agricultural Economics and at the Giannini Foundation on the University of California's Berkeley campus.

The Giannini Foundation had built a solid reputation in its field of agricultural economics. John Kenneth Galbraith worked there as a graduate student and teacher from 1931 to 1934 and later reflected on this experience in *A Life in Our Times: Memoirs* (1981).

> The University of California in those days existed in a unique political equilibrium in which my fellow agriculturalists played an important part. The instincts of the arts and sciences faculty members were generally liberal: the professors expressed sympathy for the migrant field workers, including the Oakies and Arkies who were now swarming into the state from the drought and depression of the southern Great Plains. My colleagues at Berkeley and Davis had gone on from the simple-minded empiricism of the early colleges of agriculture to a scientific and effective response to the numerous afflictions and opportunities of California agriculture...As Veblen had indicated, the agriculturalists at the University of California were, indeed, second-class citizens. But we protected the first-class citizens and never ceased to wish that we were better appreciated...Peach, prune, grape, avocado, artichoke, and citrus growers were told what they might expect as to prices, how in principle they might limit shipments to get higher prices, how they might better manage their cooperatives or farms.

Professor Wantrup had been hired for his proven talent as a "long cycle" business analyst, but he soon found that the obstacle of his German birth was hard to overcome. When America declared war five years after his arrival in the United States, he was automatically classified as an enemy alien and had to tolerate the anti-German attitudes fostered by the horrors of the war in Europe and by government propaganda. About once a month he ventured to the Berkeley police department to inspect and care for his prized sports rifles that were held there until the war's end. He was, of course, not allowed to travel freely and could not be an advocate of economic policy.

But the stress of these years as an "enemy alien" did not diminish Wantrup's appreciation of America. When he was granted citizenship in 1943, he wrote to a friend:

I cannot refrain from expressing a feeling of gratitude towards (the)... University where it was possible for me to continue my work...when I was legally an alien enemy. That in wartime all formalities and regulations could be satisfied...is not only personally gratifying but also a sign of freedom from national, racial, and religious prejudice in our democratic institutions. It is this freedom which is one of the greatest assets of this country. We all know that in practice it is not always applied as it should be. This is merely one more reason to stress its importance.

Even so, some damage must have been done by the enforced immersion in academic discipline, and by the frustrations of losing his original homeland only to be confronted by open hostility in America during the war years. In what way and to what extent, we shall never know.

In spite of these impediments, Wantrup pursued his research in business cycles and farm management with enough virtuosity to be elected to the Econometric Society in 1938. During the 1940s, he made the switch from agricultural problems to the broader field of resource use and conservation. It was during participation in benefit/cost analyses of Western irrigation projects—the traditional pork barrel projects—that he developed his critical approaches. For example, in 1947 he issued a dissenting opinion on a cost analysis for the Central Valley Project of California.

Other economists at Berkeley were either captivated by econometrics or, for other reasons, uninterested in the role of institutions. The conventional wisdom of that period was: rationality is better than wisdom; objective is better than subjective; quantitative is more objective than nonquantitative; and social and biological subtleties and complexities can be "solved" by simplifying assumptions. Respected economists devalued the role of natural resources in economic development and agreed that technological innovation and trade would eliminate concerns over scarcity. Agricultural economists knew no convenient way to reconcile Wantrup's holistic ideas with their own perspective; consequently, for the next twenty years his research colleagues were more often ecologists, lawyers, engineers, and political scientists.

In 1948, Wantrup articulated the following description of his own approach, which became a specialty:

Resource conservation is not merely a technological and educational problem. Resources are frequently misused not because resource users do not know any better but because they cannot help it under existing economic and social relations. A change of these relations is frequently essential for the success of public conservation policies...Public conservation policies cannot be discussed in the abstract. They are dependent on existing political and institutional arrangements.

This fresh approach won him Guggenheim Awards in 1947 and 1951, and membership at the Princeton Institute for Advanced Study in 1948. Although he occasionally mentioned his contact with Albert Einstein and other scientific masters at the Institute, we have no record of their interactions or the influence of these exchanges on his thinking.

Despite his reputation as a solitary worker, Wantrup made important contributions, locally and internationally, by showing others how to work together. At the University of California, he helped form the first interdisciplinary natural resources group. For the state of California, he created a curriculum for Fish and Game Department managers, served on the committee that drafted the coastal zone protection laws, and gave advice on water resources management. He consulted for numerous federal agencies and was influential in directing natural resources research. Internationally, he was a founding member of the Law of the Sea Conference, a frequent consultant to foreign governments, and he sponsored a dozen major research projects in South America, Africa, and India.

Outside the department that employed him, Professor Wantrup was becoming famous for his original work and for the success of his unorthodox approaches. Students began coming to Berkeley because, having read his work, they recognized his genius. One student who came to Berkeley for just this reason described Wantrup's "Resource Economics" in this way:

> Here, at last, was a field with some intellectual and policy content, where doing something seemed better than laissez faire. One could usefully bring to bear economic concepts of efficiency and distribution.

Although he served on only one doctoral committee between 1937 and 1950, Wantrup ultimately attracted a majority of the Ph.D. candidates at the Giannini Foundation. Between 1964 and 1975, the last decade of his career, he was chairman of 22 doctoral committees, and second member of four others.[2]

The students who chose Professor Wantrup as dissertation chairman are mostly loyal defenders of his ideas and his intensity. He was not initially patient or outwardly friendly, but once the student saw beyond his crusty manner, his compassion for economic science and his genuine affection for students became clear. A few students changed committees to avoid his demands, and a few report bitter experiences stemming from personality conflicts and difficulties in communication; but even these economists praise his greatness and acknowledge his influence on their careers. He was a loyal supporter of his students and a tireless assistant in their job searches. Unfortunately, once Wantrup broke with a student or colleague, he never took the initiative in effecting a reconciliation.

Graduate work with Wantrup involved a healthy combination of general theory and applied analysis. Most people do not think of him as particularly interested in, or possessing, empirical skills. The following story about one of his graduate students may shed a different light. In the early 1960's, he was concerned—perhaps incensed—that some economists were treating "the water industry" in too simplistic a fashion. He sent his student to the library to find out what amounts of water, in California and in the United States, were supplied by private, profit-maximizing firms. It turned out to be miniscule, but when the student returned with these industry figures, Wantrup asked what range of quality the figures encompassed. For example, was brackish water included? When the student returned once more, he was then asked if the figures included water for cooling uses which involve a substantially different consumption rate. This quest for precision continued until the student finally perfected a set of data that clearly and accurately defined these water uses. Wantrup almost always mingled sophisticated conceptual discussion expertly with the task-oriented research at hand. His mental ability was so keen that the full importance of his comments was seldom appreciated until hours after a short discussion ended.

Despite his success with graduate students, Wantrup was continually frustrated in his attempts to build a strong resource conservation program within the department. Emerging concepts in the social sciences can be promoted in two ways. The first and most successful method is to assemble a cadre of sympathetic young colleagues who will work together in developing the teaching of the new perspective. This has been the pattern for methodological breakthroughs, such as Leontief's input-output analysis, and for "schools" of economic thought, such as "the Chicago School." Of necessity, the initial critical mass of professionals is an inbred mix of close colleagues and their recent students. This option requires administrative support, but Wantrup was never accorded that; he was never allowed a leading role in departmental hiring. Such failures, of course, always pose a conundrum. His opponents at the administrative level could claim that he was uncooperative. It is obvious that in these intramural battles he took a track that would have frightened less assured individuals. He was direct and outspoken, and he documented his position with memos whose multiple copies filtered through the department and the university's administration. Adversaries bent on acting capriciously thought twice, and a petty bureaucrat whose decisions might otherwise have gone unnoticed would be shocked by inquiries from higher up. These bold tactics protected Wantrup and his allies from political reprisal on more than one occasion, but his efforts to build a strong natural resources specialty at Berkeley were nevertheless thwarted.

The second method for building up a program is to rely on students of the master architect to carry the tradition forward. This does not require administrative support, but it is fraught with uncertainties. Isolated students cannot pool their understanding, nor can they offer much constructive encouragement from a distance. Their exposure to the master may, in any event, have been insufficient during the distractions of graduate school to mold a strong disciple; and if they secure employment with another powerful economist, the original influence may have to be abandoned as they scramble for promotions and tenure. Being a disciple of Wantrupian conservation approaches has never been easy.

Wantrup contended that careful use of theory and its analytical design would enhance natural resources policy. Perhaps it was this conviction — conveyed to his students — that encouraged them to persevere with their research on resource policy within a department that championed mathematical economics and emphasized traditional areas of application that were frequently narrowly defined, and neglected concern for natural resources. Later, changes in departmental curricula vindicated Wantrup's conviction that sensible study of the economics of agriculture should entail an understanding of its natural resource base and the policies through which this base is made available for use. In his will, Professor Wantrup created a postdoctoral fellowship in natural resources economics. This perpetual fund will help support research that incorporates his broad interdisciplinary perspective.

Siegfried Wantrup's volatile personality is still well known. He was sometimes harsher with his close friends and respected colleagues than with economists he had no particular respect for. Those of us who count him a close friend had to adjust to this trait and accept occasional harsh encounters as a small price to pay for his friendship. Anti-German bias and personality conflict with colleagues in the field of economics do not satisfactorily explain the opposition Wantrup's work met. His popularity with graduate students and with other environmentally oriented economists is strong evidence that he was reasonable when treated with respect and constructive cooperation.

Part of his opposition may be a result of his diagnoses that serious deficiencies in economic theory and policy fostered depletion of resources at catastrophic rates. He was an early proponent of social economics, and he correctly described environmental protection and resource conservation as essential elements for long-term economic well-being. He broke with colleagues on these important conservation issues when the department's financial and political interests seemed to them better served by catering to big business.

Wantrup's radical views were, it now seems, not openly acceptable during much of the 1950s and '60s, and thus were particularly objectionable to those economists who sought personal advancement through the uneasy service of developmental interests. One must recall that Wantrup's career in California spanned that period when federal and state bureaucracies favored large farms over small, owners over workers, and producers over consumers.[3]

Wantrup was painfully aware of the costs of this controversy; and before he died, he predicted that his ideas would enjoy a renaissance, perhaps in a hundred years, when economists rediscover his work.

Wantrup, the outdoorsman, pursued the application of conservation principles in private life as much as in his professional endeavors. Having developed a keen understanding of ecological relationships, he bought and developed two important properties in California. A ranch on the Mendocino coast eventually became state parkland; his "Big Oak" ranch in Pope Valley, above the Napa Valley, is now a wildlife refuge of the Napa County Land Trust. In each case, he sought out, identified, and bought properties with unique wildlife habitat potential, which he then managed to develop and enhance this potential. He continued to acquire adjacent lands to round out his boundaries along ecological lines; he built access roads, watering ponds, and even small lakes; and he cleared ravines to restore springs and control erosion. When the land boom in coastal properties offered a fortune in profits in the 1960's, he stood firm and sold it to the state for use as a park. Later, when his inland ranch could have supported lucrative vineyards, he insisted that the bottomlands and their great California oaks be left as pasture to provide an important ecological complement to the uplands.

Wantrup was also an enthusiastic hunter. He was a member of the German marksmen's team at the 1936 Olympics, and never lost his skill. Those of us who watched him handling his hunting dogs saw the same firm guidance and reinforcement he gave his students. He regularly hunted deer, quail, pheasants, and ducks in California and he took occasional hunting vacations in Alaska, Europe, and Africa. He never hunted for trophies, nor did he hunt rare species. He was a superb tracker who also enjoyed sitting and studying the behavior of the animals he hunted. His ranches were equipped with benches made of log sections or suitable rocks placed at strategic locations to add this contemplative dimension to his walks. A sizeable collection of deer antlers was displayed at his ranch house, each neatly labeled with the year of kill, thus carrying a message of the lands productivity as well as of successful hunts and time spent in close association with nature.

Professor Wantrup kept his professional and personal life completely separated. He had several circles of friends and colleagues, and these rarely overlapped. In his later years, Mary Rubo, who edited his book for the University of California Press, was a source of important encouragement and advice for some three decades. She was especially influential in convincing him to donate the Pope Valley ranch to the public and she continues to assist with plans for its use as a trustee of the estate.

When friends visited the ranch, Wantrup was relaxed and gracious. He told stories and laughed at himself unreservedly. When his laughter threatened to get out of control, he chortled and turned away to recover his composure.

Much as he loved life on the ranch, however, Wantrup remained preeminently a research economist. He sought explanations for everyday economic phenomena, and he went on to tell us how to shape these passing events to serve society's long-term welfare. He taught a deeper truth, and he left what we believe will be a lasting influence on economic thought and on public policy.

[1]The author was a student of Wantrup's from 1970 to 1974 and received a doctorate under his chairmanship. As background to this essay, he surveyed the recollections of other students, colleagues, and friends of Professor Wantrup, and reviewed his correspondence files. Although the essay is largely impressionistic, the author is particularly grateful for the assistance of Richard Bishop, Mary Rubo, Hiroshi Yamauchi and Dr. Wantrup's younger sister, Hilde Kojetinsky.

[2]See Appendix I.
[3]Between 1875 and 1978, less than two percent of the human and monetary resources of the University of California Division of Agricultural Sciences were used for rural and community development. For a comprehensive history of these allocations, see Emmett P. Fisk, "The College and its Constituency: Rural and Community Development of the University of California 1875-1978." Dissertation, U.C. Davis, 1979.

Appendix I

Ph.D. Theses Completed Under the Supervision

of S. V. Ciriacy-Wantrup 1939-1975*

Chairman: 25 theses
?2nd Member: 4 theses

*Not including graduate work in departments other than Aricultural Economics and Economics.

1975

VEEMAN, Terrence Stanley. THESIS: Economic Consequences and Policy Implications of the "Green Revolution" in India with Particular Emphasis on Water Resources Policy in Punjab. S. V. Ciriacy-Wantrup, Chairman. (Degree awarded by Economics Department).

WENTZEL, Roland. THESIS: Aquaculture and the Conventional Fishery: The Salmon Case. S. V. Ciriacy-Wantrup, Chairman.

1974

ANDERSEN, Stephen Oliver. THESIS: Economics of Nuclear Power Plant Location with Emphasis on the Coastal Zone. S. V. Ciriacy-Wantrup, Chairman.

GUSTAFSON, Mark Rand. THESIS: An Analysis of Selected Economic Effects of Rural Subdivision Development Activity upon the Public and Private Sectors of Tuolumne County, California, 1970. S. V. Ciriacy-Wantrup, Committee Member.

WYETH, Peter Winthrop. THESIS: An Economic Evaluation of Trade Union Power in California Agriculture. S. V. Ciriacy-Wantrup, Chairman.

1973

CORUM, Kenton Rex. THESIS: The Demand for Human Resources in Agriculture in Relation to Government Price Policies in Economic Development: The Case of India. S. V. Ciriacy-Wantrup, Chairman.

GUSTAFSON, Gregory Clarence. THESIS: The California Land Conservation Act of 1965: Economic Analysis of a New Tool of Land Use Policy. S. V. Ciriacy-Wantrup, Chairman.

1972

CAMPBELL, David C. THESIS: The Economics of Environmental Policy with Respect to Offshore Oil Production. S. V. Ciriacy-Wantrup, Chairman.

GILL, Gurmukh Singh. THESIS: Demand and Supply of Wastepaper with Policy Implications for Quality of the Environment. S. V. Ciriacy-Wantrup, Chairman.

1971

BISHOP, Richard. THESIS: United States Policy in Ocean Fisheries: A Study in the Political Economy of Resoures Management. S. V. Ciriacy-Wantrup, Chairman.

BOLLMAN, Frank. THESIS: River Basin Development and the Management of Anadromous Fisheries: An Economic Analysis of the Columbia River Experience. S. V. Ciriacy-Wantrup, Chairman.

BRODIE, John. THESIS: Transitional Planning of Forest Management. S. V. Ciriacy-Wantrup, Committee Member.

GRAY, Edward Charles. THESIS: Economic Analysis of the Application of a New Technology: the Utilization of Hot and Saline Groundwater Resources in the Imperial Valley, California. S. V. Ciriacy-Wantrup, Chairman.

HUMPHREY, John. THESIS: Resource Allocation and Income Distribution in Agriculture: A Case Study of An Irrigation Economy in Northwest Mexico and its Implications for Development. S. V. Ciriacy-Wantrup, Chairman.

1970

MARASCO, Richard. THESIS: The Organization of the California Tuna Industry: An Economic Analysis of the Relations Between Market Performance and Conservation in the Fisheries. S. V. Ciriacy-Wantrup, Chairman.

SOLTANI-MOHAMMADI, Gholamreza. THESIS: Efficient Development of Irrigated Agriculture in Iran: The Problem of Choice Between Irrigation Techniques. S. V. Ciriacy-Wantrup, Committee Member.

UPDEGRAFF, Gail Eric. THESIS: The Economics of Sewerage Disposal in a Coastal Urban Area: A Case Study of the Monterey Peninsula, California. S. V. Ciriacy-Wantrup, Chairman.

1969

CHAPMAN, Lewis Duane. THESIS: Economic Aspects of Nuclear Desalination in California. S. V. Ciriacy-Wantrup, Chairman.

GATES, John Milton. THESIS: Repayment and Pricing in Water Policy: A Regional Economic Analysis with Particular Reference to the Tehachapi-Cummings County Water District. S. V. Ciriacy-Wantrup, Chairman.

WOOD, Lowell Dale. THESIS: An Economic Analysis of the Planning and Evaluation Procedures Emloyed by the U. S. Army Corps of Engineers with Particular Reference to the Proposed Dos Rios Project in Northern California. S. V. Ciriacy-Wantrup, Chairman.

1968

YAMAUCHI, Hiroshi. THESIS: An Economic Analysis of Cost Distribution Aspects of Groundwater Quality Conservation: Orange County Water District, California. S. V. Ciriacy-Wantrup, Chairman.

PHILLIPS, William Emerson. THESIS: Regional Development of the Owens Valley, California; An Economic Base Study of Natural Resources. S. V. Ciriacy-Wantrup, Chairman.

WAELTI, John Julius. THESIS: The Regional Economic Impact of Public Water Storage Through Recreational Development: A Case Study. S. V. Ciriacy-Wantrup, Chairman.

1964

BROWN, Gardner Mallard. THESIS; Distribution of Benefits and Costs From Water Development: A Case Study of the San Joaquin Valley-Southern California Aqueduct. S. V. Ciriacy-Wantrup, Committee Member.

LEONARD, Robert L. THESIS: Economic Analysis of Integrated Management of Ground and Surface Water in Relation to Water Importation. S. V. Ciriacy-Wantrup, Chairman.

TAYLOR, Gary Charles. THESIS: The Economic Planning of Water Supply Systems With Particular Reference to Water Conveyance. S. V. Ciriacy-Wantrup, Chairman.

1959

BREWER, Michael Fraser. THESIS: Water Pricing and Allocation with Particular Reference to California Irrigation Districts. S. V. Ciriacy-Wantrup, Chairman.

1954

SNYDER, John Herbert. THESIS: Factors Affecting the Ground-water Economy of the Antelope Valley, Los Angeles County, California. S. V. Ciriacy-Wantrup, Chairman.

1939

JOSEPHSON, Horace R. THESIS: Factors Affecting Costs and Returns of Timber Production in Second-growth Pine Stands of the Sierra Nevada Foothills. S. V. Ciriacy-Wantrup, Committee Member.

PART I
IS THE COMMONS A TRAGEDY?

INTRODUCTION TO PART I

by

Richard C. Bishop*

The scenario that Hardin (1968) so vividly characterized as "the tragedy of the commons" is now familiar to every student of natural resource economics. Using Hardin's own device for describing the basic principle, consider a pasture open to many herdsmen without limits on how many cattle are grazed. Focus on the stocking decision of the individual herdsman. The gains from stocking an additional animal can be totally appropriated by the herdsman himself. Stocking such an animal may cause overgrazing, but the resulting reductions in productivity of other animals will be born largely by other herders. Thus, quoting Hardin (1968, p. 20),

"...the rational herdsman concludes that the only sensible course for him to pursue is to add another animal to his herd. And another... But this is the conclusion reached by each and every rational herdsman sharing the commons. Therein is the tragedy. Each man is locked into a system that compels him to increase his herd without limit—in a world that is limited."

Wantrup found this view of grazing on the commons at odds with his own experience. Growing up in Western Europe, he had personally observed common forests and pastures in operation. Contrary to the Hardin scenario, the European commons had remained highly productive for centuries. Wantrup was also an avid reader in the social sciences, including cultural anthropology. He was fascinated by studies of primitive tribes showing that communal institutions played critical roles in their economic lives. Both the Europe of his youth and the experience of primitive tribes led Wantrup to ask, in effect, "Is the commons a tragedy?"

At the same time, the historical free-for-alls in resource exploitation,

*Professor, Department of Agricultural Economics and Center for Resource Policy Studies, University of Wisconsin—Madison.

including numerous instances of overfishing, destruction of wildlife populations around the world, and wasteful exploitation of oil pools could not be ignored. In fact, before Hardin and economists like Scott Gordon (1954) discovered the tragedy of the commons, Wantrup himself had devoted considerable attention to the problem of what he called "fugitive resources." This problem was addressed in detail in *Resource Conservation*, which was originally published in 1952. The theory of fugitive resources was summarized in Chapter 11 of this book under the heading of "Property Rights and Conservation." The conceptual problems in Wantrup's fugitive resources, Hardin's commons, and Scott's common property resources have many similarities.

How then was the sustained productivity of commons in some settings to be reconciled with the destructiveness of joint resource exploitation in others? In the three chapters in Part I of this book, this is the central issue. As it is addressed, the reader will get a clear view of Wantrup, the institutionalist. Wantrup would not suggest that joint exploitation of natural resources is necessarily trouble free. As already noted, the theory of fugitive resources shares much with the tragedy scenario. But—and here we come to the positive side of his argument with Hardin and the common property economists—in the European commons and other such situations, institutions evolved to prevent over-exploitation. This is important because such institutional innovations held clues for solving modern-day policy issues where private individual ownership is either physically difficult or otherwise undesirable.

Early in Chapter 1, Wantrup focused on definitional issues and the history of common resource exploitation. Then he turned to a broad review of what the historical experience with commons teaches about dealing with present-day water, land, and fishery problems. It was argued that common property management is an approach to solving resource problems rather than a source of problems. The correlative rights doctrine for groundwater, the public trust doctrine for both land and water, and fishing quotas were given as examples of such "commons solutions."

In addition to specific conclusions about common property institutions, the reader may wish to give close attention to Wantrup's institutional economic framework, his "hierarchy of decision systems." The concepts will be explicitly treated again in Chapter 2 and Chapter 5 and will be implicit in many of the other chapters. This way of explicitly describing his approach to economic institutions came to him only late in his career, after decades of work where it was implicit. The hierarchy is considered by many of Wantrup's students to be one of his most significant achievements, with implications far beyond the commons issue.

Chapter 2 is entitled "The Economics of Environmental Policy" and builds further on the hierarchy of decision systems. Other theoretical issues are addressed, too, including the role of welfare economics and economic optimizing in policy analysis. Marine resources are used as a case study. Chapter 3 is entitled "Criteria and Conditions for Public and Private Ownership of Range Resources." While it is much older than the first two chapters, having been published in 1958, Wantrup's thoughts will strike many readers as being quite timely, given the continuing debate over possible "privatization" of public grazing lands. Furthermore, the issues related to joint and individual exploitation of natural resources addressed in the two preceding chapters were very much on Wantrup's mind here as well.

REFERENCES

Ciriacy-Wantrup, S. V. 1952. *Resource Conservation: Economics and Policy*. Berkeley: University of California. (Later editions published by University of California Division of Agricultural Sciences.)

Gordon, H. Scott. 1954. "The Economic Theory of a Common Property Resources." *Journal of Political Economy* LXII(2):124-142 (April).

Hardin, Garrett. 1968. "The Tragedy of the Commons." *Science*, 162:1243-1248. Reprinted in *Managing the Commons*, edited by Garrett Hardin and John Baden. San Francisco: W. H. Freeman and Co., 1977. (Citations in text refer to reprinted version.)

Chapter 1

"COMMON PROPERTY" AS A CONCEPT IN NATURAL RESOURCES POLICY*[1]

Institutions based on the concept "common property" have played socially beneficial roles in natural resources management from economic pre-history up to the present. These same institutions promise help in solving pressing resources problems in both the developed and the developing countries. It is all the more important that these institutions be the focus of an economic study because they have been misunderstood by modern day economists: We refer to the so-called "theory of common property resources" or what is often termed the "tragedy of the commons."[2]

The extensive literature on the "theory of common property resources" accumulated over the past 20 years is summarized by the maxim "everybody's property is nobody's property." That is, when a given natural resource is physically and legally accessible to more than one resource user, the result is said to be a free-for-all, with users competing with one another for a greater share of the resource to the detriment of themselves, the resource, and society as a whole. At one time or another, this idea has been applied to an array of resources including fisheries, grazing lands, forestry, groundwater, oil, air, campgrounds, and even highways and the radio spectrum. Students of these resources maintain that the "common property condition" is largely to blame for a host of social ills including resource depletion, pollution, dissipation of economic surplus, poverty among resource users, backwardness in technology, and misallocation of labor and capital. Proposed solutions run in two directions. One is to make the "common property" resource in question the private property of individual resource users, who, via the "invisible hand," will manage the resource in society's best interest. Alternatively, the problem is to be solved by governmental intervention, through taxes or subsidies designed to bring private and social costs into balance or—that failing—by direct governmental controls of inputs or outputs or both.

*Reprinted, with permission, from 15 NAT. RES. J. 713–27 (1975), published by the University of New Mexico School of Law, Albuquerque NM 87131.

Is this an adequate picture of mankind's experience with commonly owned resources? We submit that it is not. One source of misunderstanding is that the term "common property" is used in a way often at odds with the long-standing meaning of the concept, sometimes to the point of being self-contradictory. To some extent, then, this paper necessarily involves the meaning of concepts, or the lack of such meaning. The paper goes beyond such a discussion of the concept of common property to an examination of its policy implications. These have been misinterpreted in economic literature in such a way as to discredit a concept that is a valuable tool in the economic analysis and solution of difficult problems of natural resources policy.

Common Property As
A Social Institution

"Property," as applied to natural resources, is a "primary" social institution[3] both because of its own importance and because several important "secondary" institutions, including taxation, credit and tenancy, are derived from it.[4] "Property" refers to a bundle of rights in the use and transfer (through selling, leasing, inheritance, etc.) of natural resources. Different rights (strands of the bundle) may be distributed in various combinations among natural and legal persons, groups, and several publics, including the many units of government.

The term "common property" as employed here refers to a distribution of property rights in resources in which a number of owners are co-equal in their rights *to use* the resource.[5] This means that their rights are not lost through non-use. It does *not* mean that the co-equal owners are necessarily equal with respect to the quantities (or other specification) of the resource each uses over a period of time. In other words, the concept as employed here refers to resources subject to the rights of common use and not to a specific use right held by several owners. In the legal literature this distinction appears as "common lands" on the one side and "tenancy in common" on the other.[6]

This meaning of the concept "common property" is well-established in formal institutions such as the Anglo-Saxon common law, the German land law, the Roman law, and their successors. It is also well-established in informal institutional arrangements based on custom, tradition, kinship and social mores.

Sometimes both the institution and the resources subject to the institution are called the "commons." It is helpful, however, to differentiate between the concept, the institution, which in many variations makes the concept operational in reality, and the particular resource that is subject to the institution. In any event economists are not free to use the concept "common property resources" or "commons" under conditions where no institutional arrangements exist. Common property is not "everybody's property." The concept implies that potential resource users who are not members of a group of co-equal owners are excluded. The concept "property" has no meaning without this feature of exclusion of all who are not either owners themselves or have some arrangement with owners to use the resource in question. For example, to describe unowned resources *(res nullius)* as common property *(res communes)*, as many economists have done for years in the case of high seas fisheries, is a self-contradiction. The problems of managing fisheries in territorial waters and those on the high seas have similarities— they are fugitive resources—but they are very different in actual and potential institutional regulation.[7]

On a broader scale, to lump problems associated with such greatly different resources as air—a ubiquitous resource—and fisheries—a fugitive resource— under the vaguely conceived concept of "common property resources" is to slur fundamental institutional relationships, an understanding of which is necessary if one wishes to study the social performance of an institution both in historical perspective and in the context of today's problems of resource policy. Such a study requires a conceptual framework.

Social Performance of Common Property Institutions: A Conceptual Framework

Institutions may be conceptualized as decision systems on the second level of a three level hierarchy of decision systems.[8] On the first or lowest level, decision-making relates to the determination of inputs, outputs, and the host of similar decisions made by the operating sectors of the economy, individuals, firms, industries, and public operating agencies such as water projects and irrigation districts. This level of decision systems may be called the "operating level." The decision systems on the next higher level comprise the institutional regulation of decision-making on the first level. One may call this level of decision systems the "institutional level." On the third level changes in institutions on the second level are the subject of decision-making. This level of decision systems may be called the "policy level."

Decision systems on each level can be analyzed with respect to structure, functioning, and performance. This paper is concerned with the decision systems on the second level. The purpose of decision-making on this level is not to determine directly inputs, outputs, etc., on the operating level of the economy nor to attain a path of welfare optima over time on the operating level. On the contrary, the welfare optima as defined in modern economics— even assuming that they are valid and relevant on the first level—can be shown to lack such validity and relevancy when applied to the institutional level. A discussion of the reasoning behind this conclusion is found elsewhere[9] and would take us too far afield here. Suffice it to say that the measure of performance of decision systems on the second level is not to achieve welfare optima, but rather to maintain and to increase welfare by continuously influencing decision-making on the lower level under constantly changing conditions that for any point in time cannot be projected, or can be projected only vaguely, and that are always uncertain with respect to actual occurrence.

What then has been the structure of common property institutions over the years? How have they functioned? And, most importantly, how well have they performed?

The Commons in Economic History

Let us begin to answer these questions by looking back into economic history. Mankind's experience with the common ownership of natural resources started with communal hunting and gathering societies. Did welfare decrease under common property institutions? In particular, was there a tendency for these societies to overuse their resources because of common ownership?

Hunting and gathering societies are interesting in themselves and also allow us to make inferences about our own economic history. Some anthropologists have shown renewed interest in these rapidly disappearing societies, and more adequate documentation is now available.[10] Obviously, within these societies the structure and function of resource-regulating institutions are based on customs, taboos, and kinship rather than on formal relations such as legislation and court decisions which characterize more "advanced societies." Still, these informal institutions confer the same rights, i.e., equality of the right to use for members of the group and exclusion of others, as the more modern formal institutions.

In communal hunting and gathering societies, without markets on which to sell surpluses, emphasis on sharing among members of the group tended to discourage accumulation.[11] The community coped with increasing population density through customs and taboos regulating marriage, lactation, and other forms of behavior. The most important process, however, was "fission." As group size grows, groups tend to split and become established in new areas. This process has been noted in enough situations to be regarded as a general characteristic of communal hunting and gathering societies.[12]

Some African communal hunting tribes have practices which are more familiar to us. The Acholi of Uganda, for example, enforced closed seasons.[13] In cases where depletion of resources would be tantamount to disaster, the headmen of South Africa's bushmen groups functioned as inventory keepers.[14]

Such institutions were effective in managing resources on a sustained-yield basis.[15] Population was not controlled by Malthusian scarcity. In fact, diets tended to be more than adequate. Some authors describe such societies as generally affluent, as that term is culturally defined for them.[16] Common ownership of resources must be regarded as the key factor in maintenance of this condition. Rules of sharing reduced the incentives to deplete resources for individual gain. The process of fission was facilitated because no individual property rights had to be settled. Many of these societies were either sedentary or moved only within definite geographic areas in accordance with seasonal changes affecting the availability of forage for game and for gathering by humans. Such societies were capable of existing over long periods in equilibrium with their resources unless disturbed by unusual environmental changes or interference from the outside.

The most important outside interference with these societies has been contact with the market economy and other aspects of western culture. In many cases resources were depleted as a result of this contact. Two points need to be made. First, the group depleting the resource was not always the communal hunters and gatherers, as exemplified by the fate of the American bison. Second, self-sufficient hunting and gathering societies have inherent weaknesses in adapting to contact with the market. These weaknesses are not related to common ownership. The scenario usually involves the hunters and gatherers overusing their resources in order to acquire market products.[17] Equally significant in many cases was the introduction of taxes to be paid in cash. Cash could only be acquired with overuse of resources in order to obtain a marketable surplus.[18] This raises an important question. Can common ownership of resources perform well in a market economy? To answer that question we will turn next to a discussion of the European commons, some of which have continued to the present day.

From pre-history until the present some grazing lands and forests in Europe have been managed as common property resources. Structure, functioning, and performance of these institutions have been studied over a much longer period than the institutions of hunting and gathering societies.[19]

Grazing on the commons under European conditions was seasonal, and the beginning and end of the grazing season were set uniformly for all co-equal owners in accordance with forage availability. Grazing was permitted only during the daylight hours. Strong controls on grazing were maintained by the simple requirement that each individual livestock owner have sufficient feed base at his command to support his stock in the nongrazing season and during the night. In cases where overgrazing was a threat even with the feed base restrictions, e.g., with an increase in aggregate feed base due to the intensification of agriculture, common users were assigned quotas of animals they could graze on the commons during the grazing seasons, e.g.,1 horse, 2 cows, 10 hogs, 6 geese, a process which the English called "stinting."[20]

The historical reduction of the commons in Great Britain is well-documented in the voluminous literature on enclosure.[21] Overgrazing was not a cause. One important factor was the increased profitability for the feudal lord of grazing sheep for commercial wool production. Much land which had previously been farmed by peasants to produce food and other products for home consumption, as well as the former grazing commons, went into direct management by the manorial estate. Another factor was breaking up of the open field system in response to agricultural progress. Different parts of the peasant economy are closely related. After harvest, livestock could be grazed on the fallow land and stubble in the open fields.[22] When agriculture intensified, through row crops and multiple cropping displacing the fallow and stubble fields, the open fields were enclosed, largely at the insistence of the feudal lord, and the peasants were displaced (often without compensation).[23]

England and Wales still contain 1.5 million acres of commons, the bulk of which is grazed much as it has been for centuries. In addition, these lands are playing a new role which becomes increasingly important with each passing year as a refuge for residents of crowded, polluted cities.[24]

Experience with the common forest lands on the European continent has been similar in many ways to that with grazing lands in Great Britain.[25] As forest lands became increasingly profitable as sources of timber for sale vis-a-vis their traditional role as sources of livestock forage, firewood for home consumption, and building material for the peasant village, the feudal lords changed from administrators and protectors to profit-seeking entrepreneurs. The feudal lord's rights in the common forests had been confined to hunting rights, which were vested solely in him, and his grazing and other rights, which he held as a co-equal with his villagers. When timber use became profitable, grazing and wood gathering became an impediment to timber production. The feudal lord was motivated to reduce and eliminate the grazing and other rights on the commons.[26]

In addition the same factors mentioned above in connection with the enclosures in Great Britain operated. Here also the result was a weakening of the village system and dispossession of the peasantry. The peasant was transformed from a co-equal owner on the commons with secure tenure to a landless worker on the feudal estate. This is the true "tragedy of the commons."

The feudal system never developed in some regions of the continent, such as portions of western Germany and Switzerland. With the increasing profitability of timber production some of the commons in these regions were divided among the villagers and became the woodlots of individual peasants. Frequently, however, the commons remained intact and formed the basis for modern municipal forests. The commons which remained intact became some of the best examples of progressive forest management. On the other hand, the commons that were divided into private woodlots were generally too small for efficient forestry and degenerated until government intervention through regulation, assistance, and education reversed the trend. Results were exactly the opposite of what the "theory of common property resources" would lead one to expect. The substitution of private ownership for common ownership is not in itself a socially desirable change.

Finally, we may mention the continued success of grazing commons in the highly productive Alpine meadows—for example, in Switzerland, Austria, and southern Bavaria. These are above the timberline and were, therefore, not affected by changes in the profitability of forestry under the expansion of the market economy. Here common property institutions have not changed significantly since the Middle Ages. Seasonal grazing and the necessary home feed base are still key features. The only difference from the feudal grazing system described above is that the movement to and from the commons takes place only once a year because travel is longer and more difficult.

The continued operations of commons both in England and on the continent answers the question raised earlier about the viability of common property in the market system. Common property, with the institutional regulation it implies, is capable of satisfactory performance in the management of natural resources, such as grazing and forest land, in a market economy.

The Common Property Concept in the Solution of Problems of Natural Resource Policy

If the conclusions of the preceding historical sketch of the social performance of common property institutions are correct, one may ask whether such institutions might be helpful in the solution of present problems of natural resources policy. We believe that the answer is in the affirmative. In fact, it can be shown that the common property concept is already being employed to help solve important resource policy problems in the twentieth century. Groundwater and the fisheries may serve as illustrations.

Riparian institutions regulated the use of water from surface streams in England and on the continent long before formal riparian law was developed in Anglo-Saxon common law and German land law. The notion that the users of a common surface source were co-equal in right was anchored in customs and traditions long before a codified and legally enforceable riparian law existed. One of the factors favorable to this development was the long experience with the commons in grazing and forest resources.

While the solution of problems of surface water use through riparian institutions is old, the problems created by groundwater use are recent. To be sure, use of groundwater is also old, as, for example, in most countries of the Middle East. But pumping with the Persian wheel did not create problems because of the shallow depth and the low capacity of this system. The situation changed radically with the advent of modern pumping technology based on the deep well pump and electric and internal combustion power. Resource depletion, increasing costs of pumping, and overinvestment in wells were the result.

These problems were first solved in California by applying what is known as the Correlative Rights Doctrine, implemented through adjudication. As shown elsewhere, the Correlative Rights Doctrine must be regarded as a direct descendant of riparian law, which as we have seen is based on the common property concept.[27]

All pumpers of a given groundwater basin are regarded as co-equal in right but adjudicated within the limits of the safe yield of the basin in proportion to their historical use. In the process of adjudication, small, essentially domestic uses are usually not considered, and new uses of this kind are permitted. There is no "limitation of entry" for the small user.

Procedures similar to adjudication based on the common property concept and resulting in quantitatively defined "quotas" of the resource also exist for fisheries. The fisheries situation is of interest not only in its own right but also because the "theory of common property resources" traces its origins to the literature on fisheries economics.[28] Overfishing has occurred with increasing frequency over the last century. The bulk of the literature blames this problem on the common property condition. In reality, common property institutions are much in evidence in the evolution of institutions to remedy overfishing.

The fishing season, for example, has been a widely applied tool of fishery regulation. Ideally, the season is open long enough to allow the fishermen to take the maximum sustainable yield from a given fish stock and then closed until another cropping becomes desirable. The parallels between fishing seasons and grazing seasons on the European commons are easily seen.

An important part of the evolution of the European commons was the determination of boundaries of the grazing land of each village and the determination of who had and who did not have co-equal rights to graze. Extension of exclusive national fishing zones (and in some cases territorial waters) to as much as 200 miles from the coast is analogous. While broad exclusive fishing zones raise many important issues, they do constitute one alternative institutional basis for better fisheries management.

Another interesting parallel between the historical commons and recent developments in fishery regulation is found in the establishment of national quotas. Such a system has been in effect for many years under the Convention for the Protection and Extension of the Sockeye Salmon of the Fraser River System, where the catch, which is predetermined on the basis of estimated maximum sustainable yield, is divided equally between fishermen of the United States and Canada. More recently a system of national quotas for certain species has been implemented by the International Commission for Northwest Atlantic Fisheries. Both of these management measures run parallel to the long-standing practice of stinting grazing commons.[29]

As the prices of fish products have increased and the technology of capturing fish has improved, problems have developed with trying to regulate the fisheries through fishing seasons alone. In the extreme, the entire maximum sustainable yield may be taken in a few weeks, leaving men and gear idle for at least part of the rest of the year. This may also place great strain on processing facilities. The fishermen apply political pressure on regulatory agencies to extend the season and to allow the taking of protected species outside the regular season as "incidental catch," while exploiting other species. As a result of these pressures, the resource may become depleted. The common property approach suggests a potential remedy: to assign catch quotas to individual fishers in such a way as to make the aggregate of the quotas equal to the desired total catch, which, in the long run, would normally equal maximum sustainable yield. Just as in the groundwater case, small operators could be excluded from the quota system in fisheries where they take a sufficiently small share of the total catch. It might even be desirable to make the quotas salable. The details of implementation would vary from case to case. Just to define who is a "fisherman" and hence entitled to a quota would require careful study of each individual situation.

There are some similarities between such a quota system and limitation of entry as it is discussed in the more theoretical literature in fisheries economics. In practice, however, limitation of entry programs are emphasizing restrictions on inputs. In British Columbia, for example, the restrictions apply to the tonnage of vessels. This reflects the emphasis which most economists have placed on the misallocation of capital and labor that they believe exists between fishing and the rest of the economy. Thus, the goal of limitation of entry is to get capital and labor out of fishing and into other industries until an efficient balance is reached. Under the quota system suggested above, the emphasis is on outputs, not inputs, although some reduction in inputs might well occur. This reflects the conclusion that in a grossly imperfect economy like that of the United States the problem of misallocation between the fishing industry and the rest of the economy is insignificant, especially if fishing resources are as immobile as available data indicate that they are.[30] A quota system would place the emphasis exactly where it needs to be: on protection of the resources and, if desired, on security of tenure for fishermen, especially those with low incomes and few employment alternatives.

There is much yet to be done before the world's commercial fisheries are adequately managed. These examples, however, do show that the common property approach is already fulfilling an important role. Following those who believe that the high seas fisheries should be treated as the common heritage of all mankind, one might well wonder if the ultimate solution is to treat these resources as a giant commons managed as a trust by some international agency such as the United Nations.

In summary, overgrazing, overfishing, permanent depletion of groundwater, air pollution, and the like are serious present-day problems which deserve the attention of economists. But the "theory of common property resources," as interpreted in the economic literature, is an inadequate conceptual tool for the solution of such problems. The problems discussed in this literature involve resources which are either "ubiquitous" or "fugitive." Ubiquitous resources are resources which, at least up to some stage of economic development, are not scarce. Nobody is excluded from their use. Examples are air, solar radiation, precipitation, and wind. Institutions regulating their use and allocation are not needed before that stage of economic development is reached. In the case of air that stage has been reached, and institutions regulating use are developing. Fugitive resources are resources which are mobile and must be captured (reduced to possession) before they can be allocated to groups and individuals. Such capture and allocation always pose the problem of exclusion and, thus, institutional regulation tends to develop early. Common property institutions, as interpreted here, are the most important means of regulation.

Common Property, Public Trust, and Public Property

The suggestion of the preceding section, that the concept of common property facilitates rather than hinders the solution of present problems of resource policy associated with the fugitive nature of resources (as illustrated by groundwater and fisheries), may now be broadened. We refer to the application of what is known as the "public trust doctrine" to a wide spectrum of resource policy problems.

While we fully appreciate the important role of the judiciary in developing and applying the public trust doctrine in the United States,[31] there is little doubt that the basic doctrine as embodied in Roman and Anglo-Saxon law is derived from the common property concept as interpreted in this essay. Some legal scholars even maintain that the public trust doctrine "is really the common lands concept, which has and continues to express communal interest and right to land resources."[32]

Public trusteeship in the United States is already extensive. With some exceptions Indian land is held in trust by the federal government in accordance with the communal traditions of Indian tribes, although the Bureau of Indian Affairs has often acted as if it were public land.[33] Water resources, shorelines, parklands, fish and game, and other natural resources are held in trust by many states.[34]

For purposes of natural resources policy such public trust resources must be differentiated from public property resources. First, legal restrictions on disposition of trust resources and on changes in their use are more stringent than on public property resources not subject to the trust doctrine. Second, resources under the public trust doctrine are subject to government regulation without the legal obstacle of "taking for a public purpose" and therefore without involving the issue of compensation. The latter point is frequently not appreciated and may be illustrated by a recent case.

The navigable waters of Wisconsin are held in trust by the state.[35] This principle was involved in a court test of the Wisconsin Shoreline Protection Act.[36] Passed in 1966, this act requires local governments to develop shoreline zoning. The case in question was *Just v. Marinette County*.[37] The plaintiff was prevented from filling some wetlands by Marinette County under its shoreland zoning ordinance and asked for compensation, claiming that his private property had been taken for a public purpose. The court ruled to the contrary. It stated that the ordinance was a legitimate use of the police power. One of the key points in the case has been stated by Bosselman, Callies, and Banta as follows:

> The court noted that the lakes and rivers were originally clean and said that the State of Wisconsin has an obligation in the nature of a public trust to "eradicate the present pollution and to prevent further pollution." It found that the regulation sought to prevent harm to "the natural *status quo* of the environment," and was not designed to produce a public benefit for which compensation would be required.[38]

From a standpoint of natural resources policy the public trust approach offers important advantages over the public property approach. Frequently public property resources are disposed of or their use is changed as a result of the influence of rather narrow interests on governmental bureaucracies. The Army Corps of Engineers, the Bureau of Reclamation, the Bureau of

Land Management, and the highway departments of the states are examples. Application of the public trust doctrine would force these bureaucracies to take broader public interests—i.e., those of *all* common owners—into account.

Even more important, the public trust doctrine can be applied to many problems of "quality" in resource use for the solution of which the public property approach would be ineffective or too costly. The problems of water and air quality are well-studied examples.[39] Beyond these some even broader public interests in the environment can be protected through application of the public trust doctrine. Protection of endangered wildlife species and of the scenic beauty of a landscape may be mentioned in this connection.[40] Such application is still in the first tentative stages. But some optimism for the future is warranted in view of the durability of the common property concept and the viability and social performance of the institutions that make it functional.

[1]Co-authored by Richard C. Bishop. Originally published as a Giannini Foundation Research Paper and by the *Natural Resources Journal* 15:713-727 (October, 1975). Richard L. Barrows, Daniel W. Bromley, Peter Dorner, Melvin Sabey, Stephen C. Smith, Hiroshi Yamauchi, and Douglas Yanggen were helpful in a variety of ways during the preparation of this paper.

[2]The literature in economics is large. Recent examples, some of which provides extensive references to the earlier literature include:

Bell, *Technology Externalities and Common Property Resources: An Empirical Study of the U. S. Northern Lobster Fishery*, 80 J. Pol. Econ. 148-58 (1972); Haveman, *Efficiency and Equity in Natural Resource and Environmental Policy*, 55 Am. J. Ag. Econ. 868-78 (1973); A. Freeman, R. Haveman, & A. Kneese, The Economics of Environmental Policy 77-9 (1973); Dales, *Rights and Economics*, in Perspectives in Property 151 (Wunderlich and Gibson eds. 1972). Two contributions from outside of economics but expressing the same views are: Hardin, *The Tragedy of the Commons*, 162 Sci. 1243-48 (1968); and Crowe, *The Tragedy of the Commons Revisited*, 166 Sci. 1103-7 (1969).

[3]Institutions have been defined elsewhere as social decision systems "that provide decision rules for adjusting and accomodating, over time, *conflicting* demands (using the word in its more general sense) from different interest groups in a society." Ciriacy-Wantrup, *Natural Resources in Economic Growth*, 51 Am. J. Ag. Econ. 1319 (1969). (Chapter 17 in this volume.)

[4]*See* S. Ciriacy-Wantrup, Resource Conservation: Economics and Policies (3rd. ed. 1968).

[5]It should be noted that the concept, as employed here, refers to the right *to use* the resources, but not to transfer. Heirs of a common owner become co-owners themselves only through their membership in the group (tribe, village, etc.).

[6]Jurgensmeyer & Wadley, *The Common Lands Concept: A "Commons" Solution to a Common Environmental Problem*, 14 Nat. Res. J. 368-81 (1974).

[7]For further discussion, *see* Ciriacy-Wantrup, *The Economics of Environmental Policy*, 47 Land Econ. 36-45 (Feb. 1971). (Chapter 2 in this volume.)

[8]For more detailed discussions *see* Ciriacy-Wantrup, *Water Policy and Economic Optimizing: Some Conceptual Problems in Water Research*, 57 Am. Econ. Rev. 179-89 (1967) (Chapter 4 in this volume.) and Ciriacy-Wantrup, *supra* note 7, at 40-45; and Ciriacy-Wantrup, *supra* note 3, at ch. 10 and elsewhere.

[9]See material cited in note 8 *supra* for more detailed treatment.

[10]Man the Hunter (R. Lee & I. DeVore eds. 1968).

[11]Lee, *What Hunters Do for a Living, or, How to Make Out on Scarce Resource* in *Id.* at 30-43. *See also* M. Sahlins, Stone Age Economics 46-47 and elsewhere (1972).

[12]*Supra* note 10, at 9. The Mbuti Pygmies are an example and are described by C. Turnbull in Man the Hunter, *supra* note 10, at 132-37 and also in a book by Turnbull, Wayward Servants (1965). Other groups displaying this characteristic are discussed in Man the Hunter, *supra* note 10, by Lee & by R. Woodburn, *Stability and Flexibility in Hazda Residential Groupings* at 103-10.

[13]Parker & Graham, *The Ecological and Economic Basis for Game Ranching in Africa*, The Scientific Management of Animal and Plant Communities for Conservation 394 (1971).

[14]D. Fraser, Village Planning in the Primitive World (1968).

[15]We should note, however, that some authors suspect that hunting and gathering societies were instrumental in the extinction of some species during distant pre-history. *See* Long & Martin, *Death of the Ground Sloth*, 186 Sci. 638-60 (1974).

[16]Parker and Graham, *supra* note 13 and Sahlins, *supra* note 11.

[17]A. Firth, Primitive Polynesian Economy (1966).

[18]*See, e.g.*, Behannan, *Impact of Money on African Economy*, 19 J. Econ. Hist. 499-500 (1959).

[19]B. Slicher Van Bath, The Agrarian History of Western Europe, 500-1850 (1963).

[20]W. Tate, The English Village Community and the Enclosure Movements, 162-3 (1967) and W. Hoskins & L. Stamp, The Common Lands of England Wales, 36-7, 50, and elsewhere, (1963). An analogous system in the United States exists for stocking of the public range under Forest Service and Bureau of Land Management grazing permits. Here also grazing permits are allocated in accordance with the home feed base of the permittee and the availability of forage.

[21]A recent collection of works which include references to the previous literature is Studies of Field Systems in the British Isles (A. Baker & R. Butlin, eds. 1973).

[22]N. Neilson, Medieval Agrarian Economy (1936).

[23]For more de tail on the political economy of enclosure in England see Tate, *supra* note 20.

[24]*See* Hoskins and Stamp, *supra* note 20, at 3 and elsewhere.

[25]We do not consider the French case explicitly here but the interested reader may consult S. Herbert, The Fall of Feudalism in France 47-50 and elsewhere (2nd ed. 1969).

[26]One writer described developments in France as follows: "As the commercial and manufacturing activity increased, there was a concomitant rise in the market value of forest products and the struggle was on. The increased economic value of forest holdings led the seigneurs and the king to become covetous of the community rights and to devise various ways and means for usurping them." F. Sargent, Land Tenure in the Agriculture of France, (1952 unpublished Ph.D. thesis in library of University of Wisconsin, Madison).

[27]Ciriacy-Wantrup, Some Economic Issues in Water Rights, 37 J. Farm Econ. 875-85 (Giannini Foundation of Agricultural Economics Paper 148, 1955).

[28]Gordon, The Economic Theory of a Common Property Resource: The Fishery, 62 J. Pol. Econ. 1240-42 (1954).

[29]The economics of commercial fishing, including the institutional aspects, is discussed in more detail in R. Bishop, U. S. Policy in Ocean Fisheries: A Study in the Political Economy of Resources Management 1971 (University Microfilms No. 12-21, 623) (unpublished Ph.D. thesis in the library of University of California, Berkeley).

[30]See Bishop, Limitation of Entry in the United States Fishing Industry: An Economic Appraisal of a Proposed Policy, 49 Land Econ. 381-0 (1973).

[31]Sax, The Public Trust Doctrine in Natural Resource Law: Effective Judicial Intervention, 63 Mich. L. Rev., 471- 565, (1970).

[32]Jurgensmeyer and Wadley, supra note 6 at 379.

[33]Dorner, Needed: A New Policy for The American Indians 37 Land Econ. 162-73, (1961); see also Jurgensmeyer and Wadley, supra note 6, at 371-74.

[34]See Sax, supra note 31.

[35]H. Ellis, et. al., Water-Use Law and Administration in Wisconsin 140 and elsewhere (1970).

[36]Wisc. Stat. Ann. Section 144.26, Section 59.971.

[37]56 Wis. 2d 7, 201 N.W.2d 761 (1972).

[38]F. Bosselman, D. Callies, & J. Banta, The Takings Issue, 218-19 (1973).

[39]See Ciriacy-Wantrup, Water Quality: A Problem for the Economist, 43 J. Farm Econ. 1133-44 (1961). (Chapter 7 in this volume.)

[40]Ciriacy-Wantrup & Phillips, Conservation of the California Tule Elk: A Socioeconomic Study of a Survival Problem, 3 Biological Conservation 23-32 (Oct. 1970); Bishop, Conceptual Economic Issues in Conserving the California Condor, 1972 W. Agricultural Econ. Ass'n. Proc. 119-22.

Chapter 2

THE ECONOMICS OF ENVIRONMENTAL POLICY*[1]

Economics and Ecology

The fact that the terms ecology and economics stem from the same root that they deal with whole systems, and that some quantitative scientific tools—such as a maximizing calculus, input-output analysis, and simulation—can be used to advantage in both fields may suggest that there are substantial identities and analogies. Such a suggestion should be received with caution in the very interest of better understanding and cooperation between the two scientific fields. Let us put it this way: An economic system contains the interrelations constituting an ecosystem in the same sense as an ecosystem contains the interrelations representing the system of an individual organism or that of a cell. But for the scientific understanding of an ecosystem, cell biology is no more useful than ecology is for a scientific understanding of an economic system.

There would be little use in presenting here a variant of definitions of an economic system that have been advanced in the literature—except to say that economics is not concerned only with monetary valuation of costs and benefits and with maximizing net economic yields. I am partial to Jacob Viner's "definition" that "economics is what economists do." In so "doing," I shall attempt to show that economics as an analytical system can contribute to conceptual clarification and more effective public action in the important area where the concerns of ecology and economics meet. This area is environmental management or, as I shall call it here, "environmental policy."

The Meaning of Environmental Policy

The term *policy* is used with many different meanings, both in scientific and in popular language. For the present purpose, its meaning is restricted to interrelated actions (action systems) real or hypothetical, or organized

*Reprinted, with the permission of The University of Wisconsin Press, from *Land Economics*, Volume XLVII, No. I, pp. 36–45, (February, 1971).

publics, such as international agencies and federal, state, and local governments. This restriction of meaning is in accordance with the etymological origin of the term. Any private individuals, firms, or industries may have opinions, attitudes, and proposals pertaining to policy; they may aid or hinder the formation and implementation of policy; and they are always affected by it. The term itself, however, will be used here in the restricted sense of *public* policy.

The unifying principle that transforms a number of individual public actions into a system termed policy is supplied, first of all, by the viewpoint of the scientific observer interested in the kinds of relations that exist between individual actions in objectives, criteria, execution, and effects. In this sense, policy is both a conceptual tool of analysis—a construct—and a field of scientific inquiry.

Ideally, a second unifying principle is supplied by the objectives and criteria of the public undertaking or considering actions; ideally, individual actions constitute a segment of a purposefully coordinated system. In actuality, however, the objectives and criteria of actions by different publics and of the same public at different times are frequently not coordinated. Such lack of coordination and multiplicity of objectives is an important subject in the study of policy.

In environmental policy, it is helpful to differentiate between conservation and allocation. In political reality, actions in these two spheres are closely related. In economic analysis, it is useful to separate them. The term conservation policy refers to public actions affecting the distribution of physical yields (use rates) of the environment in different instants of time. The term allocation policy refers to public actions affecting the distribution of given physical yields and their benefits and costs among different users— such as countries, regions, industries, firms, and households. In technical terms, conservation policy refers to the length and the direction of use vectors with respect to time; allocation policy refers to the direction of these vectors and their benefits and costs with respect to users.[2]

Environmental Policy and Welfare Economics

In identifying the economic objectives and criteria of environmental policy, one encounters the problem of unity of science—in this case the unity of economics as an analytical system. Environmental policy cannot, in principle, be divorced from policies relating to housing, working conditions, family and racial relations, and many others. Although sometimes forgotten by present day environmental activists, such policies are interrelated, and criteria are, in principle, no different in environmental policy than in other fields of public action. In an attempt to identify such criteria, economists have developed a branch of normative economics called "welfare economics." More recently this branch has become known as the "new" welfare economics to emphasize its development in England and the United States since the 1930's. Its essential problems were recognized and its relevant theorems developed in the 1890's by Pareto.[3]

In formulating policy criteria, welfare economics takes explicit account of differences in individual preferences and incomes and of the resulting problems in aggregating individual utilities. It is an economic axiom that the marginal utility of individual income decreases with increasing income. There is no agreement among economists on whether and in what sense— ordinally or cardinally—individual utilities can be compared but welfare criteria that avoid interpersonal comparisons are generally preferred.

Classical and neoclassical economists were well aware of these problems.[4] They, however, focused on an increase of real aggregate national income as the main criterion of economic welfare.[5] Pareto's views were not in conflict with this emphasis because he believed—supported by historical experience as he saw it—that an increase of national income and greater equality of income distribution tended to be associated. In this case an increase of national income means also an increase of economic welfare according to Pareto's criterion, at least under some generally accepted assumptions.

The Pareto criterion says that a change that makes at least one individual better off and leaves no individual worse off represents an increase of welfare. This criterion is usually interpreted to mean that welfare is increased by a change rendering it "possible" to make at least one individual better off and leave no individual worse off by compensating the losers. Most of the discussion in the new welfare economics deals with this compensation principle.

The Pareto criterion "without" compensation is so restrictive that it has little relevance for an appraisal of public policies—even if it could be practically applied. There are scarcely any policies which make nobody worse off. Furthermore, if there were such policies, the criterion would be ineffective for choosing between more than one alternative to the status quo.

The Pareto "with" criterion is conceptually not identical with the criterion "increase of national income." But the latter criterion may be regarded as a practical, first approximation to the former, provided that the policy under consideration does not appreciably increase inequality of income distribution and provided further that there are other policies in operation which work independently and continually in the direction of greater equality of income distribution. Such policies are, for example, progression in income and property taxes, high inheritance taxes, and social-welfare legislation in the narrower sense (relating to old age, invalidity, unemployment, minimum wages, public health, education, and so on). In some practically important cases, these two conditions can be regarded as fulfilled when considering resource policies in modern western societies.

The contribution of welfare economics has been a clarification of the theoretical difficulties in arriving at a social-welfare function and social indifference curves and of the operational difficulties in applying the Pareto criterion in actuality. The disservice of welfare economics has been that its terminology is used without pointing out these theoretical and operational difficulties. The false impression is created that a simple criterion is available that can be used for legislation, court decisions, administrative regulation, and other applications of policy.

Environmental Policy and Economic Optimizing

After this sketch of welfare economics, we may now raise the question of what is the conceptual meaning of economic optima. In other words, is it conceptually at all useful to make the maximization principle the basic criterion for environmental policy? The maximization principle is applied in normative economics, first as efficiency criterion for limited operations under restrictive assumptions and second as the assumed overall objective of public policy.

As efficiency criterion, the maximization principle is used, for example, in finding the optimum output under given cost and revenue functions and also in determining minimum costs for each output under given production functions and given price schedules of productive factors, that is, in determining a cost function. For these and similar purposes, the maximization principle is necessary. There can be no disagreement on the usefulness of such operations. One may call this application of the maximization principle "efficiency economics" or, more appropriately in some cases, "efficiency engineering."

If applied as the assumed overall objective of public policy, on the other hand, the maximization principle is a construct—a scientific fiction.[6] A fiction is permissible in science if its character is clearly understood. A fiction is a deliberate, conscious deviation from reality. A fiction, however, is not a hypothesis or theory. By itself, a fiction is not intended to be validated by testing with empirical evidence. But a scientific fiction should be useful as a stimulus for or as a part of hypotheses and theories which can be tested. Hence, the test of a scientific fiction is its conceptual usefulness, its expediency in understanding, explaining, and predicting reality. A fiction becomes mere dogma and therefore unscientific if its two characteristics (consciousness of its fictional nature and conceptual usefulness) are obliterated. There are many examples in the history of science of fictions changing into dogma. One may wonder whether or not the maximization principle, as applied to policy, has become dogma in economics. There is increasing emphasis on techniques which facilitate greater numerical accuracy in the determination of optima with no conceptual gain and at the expense of "assuming away" essential economic relations.

It was suggested in the preceding section that, under certain conditions, an increase of national income may be accepted as a criterion for policy. This is the approach of benefit-cost analysis which, originating in the field of water policy, is increasingly applied to all kinds of public action affecting the environment. Limitations on the general applicability of benefit-cost analysis are imposed by a number of theoretical and practical difficulties. Some of these are the following.[7]

The quantities of goods and services making up the national income must be evaluated (weighted) in order to be aggregated. The weights used—

market prices and unit values derived indirectly from prices and in other ways—are affected by the host of social institutions which influence income distributions (and thereby demand) and market form. The policies to be appraised may change income distribution and market form. Such an appraisal deals with the future. Over time, individual preferences and technology (both affecting value weights and quantities of national income) change, and these changes are highly uncertain. Again, the policies to be appraised affect these changes. Besides such "structural" changes, there are changes connected with economic fluctuations of various amplitude and duration. These, likewise, are related to the policies to be appraised.

Practical approximations to a solution of some of these difficulties are possible but only under restrictive assumptions with respect to social institutions, preferences, technology and time periods. For policies of broader scope, these restrictive assumptions weaken validity and relevancy of results. This is true for most environmental policies. In appraising such policies, it is useful to analyze their effects upon significant conditions which influence the *direction* and the *rate* of changes of national income and income distribution rather than to focus on quantitative changes themselves. Among these conditions, two deserve special attention in environmental policy both in the spheres of conservation and allocation. One is the institutional system which influences the use of the environment by man; this will be discussed in the following section. The other is whether or not such use leads to avoidable irreversibilities.

There is no need to go into the technical aspects of reformulating the objectives and criteria of environmental policy from the viewpoint of avoiding irreversibilities. These aspects are treated in uncertainty economics and game theory.[8] Suffice it to say that the objectives of environmental policy can often be compared to the objectives of an insurance policy against serious losses that resist quantitative measurement. There the objective is not to maximize a definite quantitative net economic yield but to choose premium payments and benefits in such a way that maximum possible losses are minimized. As a special case of this strategy, "a safe minimum standard" is frequently a valid and relevant criterion for conservation policy.

With this reformulation of objectives and criteria of environmental policy, we are mainly interested in the order of magnitude of maximum possible losses and, compared with that, of the "insurance premium" that must be paid to guard against them. As a general rule, if action is taken in time the maximum possible losses which would result from not adhering to a safe minimum standard of conservation are large in relation to the costs which must be expended in order to guarantee such a safe minimum standard.

The emphasis of this approach is on avoiding overuse rather than on achieving optimum use, on establishing base levels rather than on locating peaks, on not entering dead-end streets and on keeping direction rather than on computing the shortest distance, and on mobility and adaptability of productive factors rather than on their optimum combinations. This approach does not pretend to establish criteria for optimizing social welfare. But it offers effective direction signals turn by turn for public actions in environmental policy to increase social welfare.

Social Institutions as Decision Systems

There is scarcely need to emphasize the fundamental importance of social institutions for conservation and allocation policy as differentiated in an earlier section. In particular, the impact of the various legal forms of property institutions and, derived from them, of resource tenure, taxation, and credit are well established. This impact operates through what may be called "indefiniteness," "instability," and "imbalance" of property rights.[9]

On the other hand, in economics as an academic discipline, the once great concern with social institutions has been pushed into the background during recent decades in favor of quantitative optimizing models. In these models, social institutions, if considered at all, are treated as constraints in the same way as technological conditions and resource availability. Partly, at least, institutional economics itself is to blame for this setback because it had become descriptive-historical rather than analytical in orientation, without a body of viable theory and burdened by traditions and value judgements. It is the proposition of this section that, in the field of resource economics in general and of environmental policy in particular, an analytically oriented institutional economics is by no means obsolete as an aid in clarifying and directing policy.

When social institutions are used as constraints in optimizing models, they become conceptually indistinguishable from policy objectives. In reality, however, they are more frequently means than ends in the sense both of policy tools and of obstacles to be removed or modified. In other words, failure to realize the conceptual difference between technological and institutional constraints results in blurring and distorting the distinction between the part of the model that constitutes the objective function to be maximized or minimized; the part that constitutes the constraints describing the structure of the operation; and the part that identifies the variables and their interrelations.

When social institutions are used as constraints in optimizing models, a new optimum must be calculated for each combination of constraints; the optima calculated for different sets of constraints must then be compared. A considerable literature has grown up around this problem, known as the Theory of Second Best.[10] This term indicates that there is at least one constraint additional to the ones existing in the Pareto conditions discussed earlier. The exponents of this theory maintain that the major conclusion is a negative one: If a deviation from one of the Pareto conditions prevails, the best course of action is not to attack this deviation. On the contrary, a second-best solution is usually obtained by departing from all other Pareto conditions. To apply only a part of the Pareto conditions would change social welfare away from rather than toward a second-best position.

If this criticism of "piecemeal welfare economics" is valid—I believe it has some merit—does it not point to a basic weakness in the logic of using social institutions as constraints? If one tries to avoid the futility of piecemeal welfare economics and strives for bold changes in the combination of constraints, can one be sure that the resulting optima are comparable in a meaningful way? Is it not unavoidable that such bold changes affect some structural elements of the model, especially technology, preferences, and motivation of human agents? Are we not confronted with a problem of identification in the econometric sense on a large scale?

In view of these questions, a different analytical approach to social institutions may be considered: Social institutions may be conceptualized as decision systems on the second level of a three-level hierarchy of decision systems. On the first level, the lowest, decision-making relates to the control of inputs, outputs, and the host of similar decisions made by the operating sectors of the economy, namely, firms, industries, and public operating agencies such as water projects and irrigation districts. This level of decision systems may be called the operating level. The decision systems on the next higher level, the second, comprise the institutional framework of decision-making on the first level. One may call this level of decision systems the institutional level. On the next higher level, the third, changes of institutions on the second level are the subject of decision-making. This level of decision systems may be called the policy level.

Decision systems on each level can be analyzed with respect to structure, functioning, and performance. Performance need not be measured in pecuniary terms even on the first level, where this yardstick is most frequently employed. So far, economists have concerned themselves largely with the structure, the functioning, and the performance of decision systems on the first level. However, some studies on the second level are available. They are concerned with water institutions, especially the systems of water rights.[11] Similar studies are needed concerning the law of the sea, the laws governing pollution, the systems of resource taxes, land tenure systems, and many other social institutions which are of interest to environmental policy. This is a promising field for the "new" institutional economics.

The purpose of decision-making on the second level is not to directly control inputs, outputs, etc., on the operating level of the economy nor to obtain a path of welfare optima at various points in time under projected conditions for these points. Rather, the purpose is to maintain and to increase welfare by continuously influencing decision-making on the lower level under constantly changing conditions that, for any point in time, can be projected only vaguely; not only is it uncertain when given anticipated conditions will occur but it is even always uncertain whether they will ever actually occur.

Decision systems on the second level therefore can be appraised only by viewing them as they function over time under various economic conditions. It is inadequate to appraise these systems by studying temporal cross-sections for particular conditions and points in time. Performance criteria need not be the same as those on the lower level. What is needed on the second level are criteria that could serve as conceptually and operationally meaningful proxies for increasing national income. They may be called intervening criteria in analogy with intervening variables. Proposals for such criteria in the appraisal of water institutions have been made elsewhere.[12]

Some Implications for the Ocean Environment

In conclusion, some implications may be drawn from the preceding analysis for the world oceans—the part of the environment which is of special interest at this juncture. There is a close similarity, if not identity, of the basic economic issues of all environmental policies, whether concerned with land, air, upland game, inland waters, or oceans.

Because of space limitations, this discussion will be confined to the living resources of the sea and especially to fisheries. These resources are economically by far the most significant ones and, as just suggested, the basic economic issues of environmental policy are very similar for living and non-living resources and for those of the sea and those of the seabed.

Since the middle of the 1950's, fisheries policy has received considerable attention from economists.[13] All of these writers have blamed the same cause for the economic problems of the fisheries and have come to the same conclusions and policy recommendations. This cause is the alleged "common property" character of fisheries resources. The effect is said to be overexploitation of the resource, overinvestment in the fishing industry, suboptimization of net economic yield, and low per capita income of fishermen. The remedy recommended appears simple: reduce the investment in the fishing industry through limitation of entry until net yields are maximized on a sustained basis. These recommendations are repeated in the recent report of the Commission on Marine Science, Engineering and Resources appointed by the President of the United States.[14] The two recommendations regarding the "principles of fishery management" read as follows:

"The Commission recommends that fisheries management have as a major objective production of the largest net economic return consistent with the biological capabilities of the exploited stocks."

"The Commission recommends that voluntary steps be taken—and, if necessary, Government action—to reduce excess fishing effort in order to make it possible for fishermen to improve their net economic return and thereby to rehabilitate the harvesting segment of the U. S. fishing industry."

The notion that the common-property character of resources is the main cause of environmental depletion has spread recently from the fisheries to other fields of resource use and has been termed "the tragedy of the commons."[15] This catchy phrase has created much confusion. Some clarification is needed in the light of our previous discussion.

Common property of natural resources in itself is no more a tragedy in terms of environmental depletion than private property. It all depends on what social institutions—that is, decision systems on the second level—are guiding resource use in either case. Effective social institutions to conserve common-property resources have been developed for the administration of public forests in many countries. The same is true for the conservation of game and fish whether by primitive tribes in pre-Columbian America or modern game-management departments. Agricultural land held in common by villages in medieval Europe was conserved by institutions based on custom and law before private property and the profit motive broke up these decision systems.[16] During the colonial period of the 18th and 19th centuries the spread of private property rights in resources did not prevent serious depletion of forests, range, and agricultural land in many parts of the world.

The term "common property" in itself is a misnomer when applied to fishery resources outside of territorial waters. If no institutional decision system is devised (through effective bilateral or multilateral international treaties), these resources are *res nullius*—one class of fugitive resources—rather than *res communes*—a different class. Examples of the latter class are fishery resources in territorial public waters, upland game, and public range and forests. Another class of fugitive resources is oil, gas and, in some cases, groundwater. In this class, private property rights exist but are indefinite among a limited number of resource users. Because of the existence of three classes of fugitive resources (to only one of which the term common property can be applied), synonymous use of common-property resources and fugitive resources is misleading.[17]

Common property as an institution usually facilitates devising a regulatory system that conserves and allocates resources. If fisheries are labeled a common-property resource when no such institutional basis for regulation exists, this becomes a barrier to understanding and public action. Conceptual and terminological clarification is the first step toward adequate environmental policy.

With respect to conservation policy, "maximum sustained yield" is accepted as a general objective by fisheries biologists and, in principle, by most countries. This is a higher state of conservation than the safe minimum standard discussed above, and it is more costly to maintain. But in practice, the former state of conservation is easier to define and to administer with less biological information than is needed to diagnose with certainty at what point of exploitation irreversibility will be reached.

While maximum sustained yield constitutes a relevant, operational, and noncontroversial objective of conservation policy, this cannot be said of the objective of "maximum net economic yield"—even if its realization through limitation of entry could be agreed upon by the fishing industry.

Besides the conceptual and operational difficulties of economic optimizing discussed earlier, it can be shown that maximum net economic yield, if realized through limitation of entry, will generally lead to a decrease in social welfare.[18] Results will be similar to those under a private monopoly. Output will be lower and prices will be higher than under competition. In addition, costs of administering this scheme must be considered. There may also be other costs which are more difficult to express in monetary terms: fishermen who are "limited out" may have difficulties in finding employment elsewhere. Other fishermen may not be interested mainly in monetary returns but may enjoy fishing as part-time or seasonal work, even if they do not much more than break even. Compared with these social costs of limiting entry, the alleged overinvestment in the fishing industry—for which reliable quantitative estimates have not been given by the economists mentioned above—is probably of the second order of smalls.

Turning to allocation policy, it is here that international decision systems on the second level are needed most. Admittedly, the conservation argument is frequently used in defense of exclusive fishing zones (such as the 200-mile limit) and other devices to give the fishermen of one sovereign state preference over those of others. I have had occasion to discuss these devices informally on a man-to-man basis with officials of several South American countries. My impression is that the conservation argument is largely a rationalization. The real concern is with allocation, that is, with greater participation by an individual country in the economic benefits from fisheries. For this concern it does not matter very much whether fishing is close to shore or further out or even whether it is done by a domestic fleet or by those of other nations. In the presently popular terminology, nations who do not belong to the "haves" in fisheries benefits want "a larger piece of the action."

There are many bilateral and multilateral institutional decision systems affecting the international allocation of benefits from ocean fisheries. Examples of these decision systems are given by Chapman and Schaefer.[19] There is a demand by a considerable number of "have not" nations (in terms of fisheries benefits)—especially in the developing world—for modification of the existing decision systems and for entirely new ones. This demand, I believe, will increase. Before such modification and replacement is attempted, it would be worthwhile to appraise the existing decision systems in their structure, functioning, and performance. There is some indication that the allocative performance of these systems has been better from the standpoint of developing nations than one might expect. But no systematic comparative appraisal is available. Such an appraisal would require a major interdisciplinary effort in which research workers from biology, international law, and economics should cooperate. While economics is best qualified to appraise performance, appraisal of structure and functioning is best undertaken by experts in international law. The biologist, in turn, is needed to appraise these systems in terms of conservation objectives.

In view of the increasing demand for an international regime of the oceans, and in order to incorporate the best and to avoid the worst of past experience in any new regime, such as appraisal may well be given a high priority by research foundations and international agencies.

[1]Giannini Foundation Paper No. 314. Reprinted from Land Economics, Feb. 1971, Vol. XLVII, Numver 1, pp. 36-45

[2]For a more detailed discussion of the economic meaning of conservation and of conservation policy see, S.V. Ciriacy-Wantrup, *Resource Conservation: Economics and Policies* 3d ed.; Berkeley, California: Division of Agricultural Sciences, University of California. 1968. pp. 1-397.

[3]Vilfredo Pareto, *Cours de Economique Politique*, F. Route, Libraire-Editeur, Lausanne, 1897. An excellent bibliography of welfare economics is apended to, E. J. Mishan, "A Survey of Welfare Economics, 1939-1959," *Economic Journal*, June 1960, pp. 197-265.

[4]The first edition of Alfred Marshall's *Principle of Economics* appeared in 1890 seven years before publication of Pareto's main work in French. Marshall mentions Pareto only in passing and in a different connection.

[5]When comparing national income at different points of time and for different countries, per capital figures are used. In appraising alternative policies, it is more useful to focus on aggregate income.

[6]Next to mathematics and law, economics is the discipline in which scientific fictions are most common. But the natural sciences, especially modern physics, frequently employ fictions.

[7]For greater detail see, S. V. Ciriacy-Wantrup, "Benefit-Cost Analysis and Public Resource Development," in, Stephen C. Smith and Emery N. Castle, editors, *Economics and Public Policy in Water Resource Development* (Ames, Iowa: Iowa State University Press, 1964). pp. 9-21. *See* also, other papers in this book.

[8]*Idem, Resource Conservation: Economics and Policies, op. cit.*, Chapters 17 and 18.

[9]*Ibid.*, Chapters 10-14.

[10]R. G. Lipsey and Kelvin Lancaster, "The General Theory of Second Best," *Review of Economic Studies*, Vol. XXIV (1), No. 63 (1956-57).

John V. Krutilla, "Welfare Aspects of Benefit-Cost Analysis," in, Stephen C. Smith and Emery N. Castle, editors, *Economics and Public Policy in Water Resource Development* (Ames, Iowa: Iowa State University Press, 1964), pp. 22-23.   O. A. Davis and A. B. Whinston, "Welfare Economics and the Theory of Second Best," *Review of Economic Studies*, January 1965, pp. 1-14.

[11]S. V. Ciriacy-Wantrup, "Some Economic Issues in Water Rights, *Journal of Farm Economics*, December 1955, pp. 875-885.

Idem, "Concepts Used as Economic Criteria for a System of Water Rights," *Land Economics*, November 1956, pp. 295-312.

Idem, "Water Policy: Relations to Law and Policy," Robert Emmet Clark, editor-in-chief, *Waters and Water Rights*, Vol. 1 (Indianapolis, Indiana: The Allen Smith Company, 1967), pp. 397-430. (Reprinted as Chapter 5 of this book.)

[12]*Op. cit.; see also, idem*, "Water Policy and Economic Optimizing: Some Conceptual Problems in Water Research," *American Economic Review*, May 1967, pp. 179-189. (Reprinted as Chapter 4 of this volume.)

[13]J. A. Crutchfield and A. Zellner, "Economic Aspects of the Pacific Halibut Fishery," *Fishery Industrial Research*, Vol. 1 No. 1 (Washington, D. C.: United States Government Printing Office, 1963).

F. T. Christy, Jr. and A. Scott, *The Common Wealth in Fisheries* (Balitmore, Marlyand: The Johns Hopkins Press, 1965), pp. 1-281.

H. Scott Gordon, "The Economic Theory of a Common-Property Resource: The Fishery," *Journal of Political Economy*, April 1954, pp. 124-142.

Ralph Turvey, "Optimization and Suboptimization in Fishery Regulation," *American Economic Review*, March 1964, pp. 64-76.

[14]Commission of Marine Science, Engineering and Resources, *Our Nation and the Sea: A Plan for National Action* (Washington: United States Government Printing Office, 1969), pp. 92 and 93.

[15]G. Hardin. "The Tragedy of the Commons," *Science*, December 1968, pp. 1243-1248; also, Beryl L. Crowe, "The Tragedy of the Commons Revisited," *Science*, November 1969, pp. 1103-1107.

[16]S. V. Ciriacy-Wantrup, "Soil Conservation in European Farm Management," *Journal of Farm Economics*, February 1938, pp. 86-101.

[17]For a definition of fugitive resources and for more detail on this point, see, *idem, Resource Conservation: Economics and Policies, op, cit.*, Chapter 10.

[18]For evidence on this point, see, Richard C. Bishop, "United States Policy in Ocean Fisheries: A Study in the Political Economy of Resource Management." Unpublished Ph.D. dissertation, University of California, Berkeley, 1970.

[19]Wilbert McLeod Chapman, "The Theory and Practice of International Fishery Development-Management," and Milner B. Schaefer, "Investigation, Conservation and Management of the Fisheries of the High Seas with a Case Example of the Tuna Fisheries." *In Maribus I*, Vol. 5: *The Ocean Environment; Proceedings of the Preparatory Conference on Ecology and the Role of Science, April 1970*, (Malta: The Royal University of Malta Press, 1971).

Chapter 3

CRITERIA AND CONDITIONS FOR PUBLIC AND PRIVATE OWNERSHIP OF RANGE RESOURCES*[1]

When Does the Issue of Public Ownership Arise?

By way of introducing a complex and controversial subject, one may raise the question why it is that in range resources—and also in forest resources—public ownership is a live and hotly debated issue in a country which, in its basic ideology and institutions, relies on private ownership. Public ownership of agricultural or mineral resources, on the other hand, is not a controversial issue in this country.

In range and forest resources, public ownership is not only an issue, but most people would concede that public ownership should play at least some role. Is this attitude determined only by the momentum of historical experience, by the fact that, in the relatively short history of this country, public ownership has played such an important role in range and forest resources? Without denying this influence, there are more important reasons for the attitude toward public ownership of range and forest resources.

In order to get at these reasons, one has to clarify certain basic assumptions with respect to the over-all role of ownership in natural resources. For the purposes of this paper, a particular form of ownership—public or private—will be regarded not as an *end* of community welfare nor as a necessary condition for the development of that society one usually calls "Modern Western," but as a *means* for public policy to increase welfare or as a variable in economic development (Ciriacy-Wantrup, 1956).

Our first question, then, may be answered by saying that public ownership of natural resources becomes an issue under conditions which create doubt as to the superiority of private ownership as a means to increase community welfare. For range resources these conditions prevail more frequently than for agricultural resources. But there are cases when they prevail for agricultural

*Reprinted, with permission, from the *Journal of Range Management*, Volume 11, No. 1, pp. 10–13, (January, 1958).

resources also. In California, for example, considerable areas of agricultural land of high per-acre value have been transferred from private to public ownership; they are intensively cultivated to sustain the waterfowl of the Pacific Flyway. Such transfer is an important policy tool for decreasing crop damage on surrounding private agricultural lands and for perpetuating and distributing benefits from waterfowl.

Let us inquire what are the criteria for identifying such conditions in range resources. Two interrelated criteria will be discussed. For short, one will be called the "social-benefit" and the other the "conservation" criterion. Only a short sketch of these two criteria can be given here. A more detailed treatment is found elsewhere (Ciriacy-Wantrup, 1952).

Social Benefits from Range Resources

Range resources yield several products jointly. Besides livestock, the most important are water, protection of the soil against erosion by water and wind, and outdoor recreational opportunities, especially those provided by fish and game. Except the first, these products are generally not sold in the market and are difficult to evaluate in monetary terms. Potentially they are of benefit to others besides the private owner of range resources, but both their production and their distribution are affected by private range management decisions. Largely for economic reasons, these effects are not and cannot be taken into account by the private owner to the same extent as they would be from the standpoint of welfare economics.

Such "extra-market" products by themselves do not distinguish range resources from agricultural resources. Wildlife and other recreational opportunities are also produced on corn belt farms. There, however, the social benefits derived from them—this means benefits received not only by the owner but also by other members of society—are generally small relative to the social benefits derived from crops and livestock. Social benefits from the latter products are evaluated through the market and taken into account in private management decisions.

The concept "welfare" in economics has reference to both the aggregate volume and the distribution of social benefits. Hence, both the production and the distribution of social benefits from range resources must be considered here. In the future, the problem of distribution may become even more important than the problem of production. There are three major reasons for this expectation.

First, there is a trend for wildlife and other recreational opportunities yielded by range resources to become marketable products. This is exemplified by leasing hunting and fishing rights to individuals and groups, by fees charged for trespass permits, by taking in "paying guests" and by outright "dude" ranching. In view of such trends, production per acre of opportunities for outdoor recreation may not be smaller under private than under public ownership of range resources. But the distribution of these benefits is quite different under the two forms of ownership. Under private ownership these benefits are distributed to those who are able to pay for them; they are distributed on the basis of money incomes, as are most other products in our society. Under public ownership these benefits are distributed free. Where rationing becomes necessary, this is generally accomplished on a "first come, first served" basis. (The relatively small fees for hunting and fishing licenses are paid also by those who use private lands.)

Second, through education, through public assistance in habitat improvement, stocking and patrolling, and through taxation, zoning, and land-use regulations, public policy can exercise considerable influence upon the production of wildlife and other recreational opportunities on private land. Such policy tools can also be used to influence distribution. This latter influence, however, is likely to remain minor. Let me illustrate the basis for this conclusion by an example. Public assistance to private landowners can be given under the condition that at least a portion of the land is open to public hunting and fishing. This approach is taken in the cooperative hunting areas in California. In these, the major advantage to the private landowner is that a portion of the land (not more than 20 percent) is reserved for him, his family and guests, and that the posting and patrolling is done by the state (Harper, Metcalf, and Davis, 1950).

This interesting and worthwhile attempt to influence distribution of benefits from wildlife is endangered by the trend, just noted, for wildlife to become a paying crop. If a private landowner knows that his hunting rights have a market value, when sold by him directly or through some community organization, he will be reluctant to join a cooperative hunting area. As a consequence, the state may have to acquire hunting rights through payments to private landowners or through other ways if free public hunting is to be provided.

Third, it would not be realistic to expect that in this country distribution of social benefits from range resources will be exercised *entirely* through the market mechanism on the basis of money incomes. Here, in contrast to some European countries, the tradition of free hunting and fishing is strong. Furthermore, the provision of some forms of outdoor recreation, for example, in parks and playgrounds, is generally regarded as a public responsibility.

This is not to imply that the provision of free hunting and fishing for everyone to his heart's content should be made a public responsibility. The trend toward sale of recreational opportunities has just been mentioned. This trend favors a greater aggregate volume of such opportunities available for use. In this sense, one may regard the trend toward marketability as being in the interest of welfare. The point is that, in view of and in addition to an increasing sale of outdoor recreational opportunities, there is an increasing demand for a public program in order to distribute these opportunities in the interest of community welfare. Efficient administration of such a program may require public ownership of the land and not merely acquisition of certain use rights.

If these three points are accepted, it follows that, in applying the social-benefit criterion for public and private ownership of range resources, one must consider recreational opportunities provided in relation to the production of livestock. Computation of a precise numerical ratio between the net value of these two types of products on a given acre of range land presents difficulties, but is not always necessary. Such a ratio would be relevant only under constraints: minimum requirements of wildlife management, such as balance of summer and winter range and suitable administrative units, must be met. More importantly, public policy must look toward the future. On the basis of fairly clear trends in total United States population, age distribution, occupational patterns, per-capita income, and residence, one can predict that the demand for outdoor recreational opportunities will increase much faster than the demand for livestock. At present, the criterion under discussion may seem more important for range resources in a fast-growing state like California with a large urban population. But in the future it may become important also for range resources in areas like the Northern Great Plains which, at present, are less urbanized.

Although no attempt is made here to define the social-benefit criterion numerically, it can be applied on a considerable acreage without difficulty and certain consequences that would follow from its application can be spelled out. It would seem sound public policy to deal with those areas first where the ratio which is being considered here as a criterion clearly is either very large or very small. In some parts of this country, such as the Northern Great Plains, there are range resources presently in public ownership which now and in the future have little significance for outdoor recreation. In terms of the social-benefit criterion, therefore, there would be no objection against a transfer to private ownership. On the other hand, there are range resources presently in private ownership that have great significance for outdoor recreation. This is especially true for some critical winter ranges of deer and elk. In terms of the social-benefit criterion, such range resources should be in public ownership. The State of California, for example, has recently bought from private owners a large acreage of this type of range in the foothills of the Sierra Nevada.

Conservation of Range Resources

Let us turn now to the second criterion. The classical argument in favor of public ownership of range resources is based on the criterion of conservation. The argument in favor of this criterion points out that under some conditions private owners do not practice conservation and that such conservation is in the public interest. Before one can apply this criterion, the meaning of conservation must be clear. Then one needs to ascertain whether the conditions that prevent conservation under private ownership can be changed without changing the form of ownership. Let us look somewhat more closely at these requirements.

Range conservation by itself has no clear meaning in terms of a certain level of range productivity that should be preserved indefinitely. Range productivity is increasingly manmade. This raises the question what productivity level should be aimed at and to what extent productivity variations over time should be tolerated—for example, in periods of drought or economic depression. Furthermore, in an attempt to connect range conservation with the public interest, the question arises which level of productivity is regarded as the social "optimum."

A detailed discussion of the meaning of conservation in the light of these questions cannot be undertaken here. It is sufficient to say that a minimum standard of conservation defined in terms of range management practices, or physical results of such practices appears more relevant and useful for public policy than defining as the objective of range conservation a status quo of productivity or a social optimum of productivity (Ciriacy-Wantrup, 1952, chapters 4, 17, 18; Ciriacy-Wantrup and Schultz, 1957).

If this point regarding the meaning and objective of range conservation is accepted, the requirements for advocating public ownership on the basis of the conservation criterion are, first, that a minimum standard of range conservation is not adopted under private ownership because range operators are not sufficiently informed about appropriate practices or are not able for economic reasons to adopt them; and second, that these factors cannot be changed more effectively through education, land-use regulations, zoning, subsidies, and other policy tools than through public ownership.

Conditions under which these requirements are fulfilled still exist. But insufficient information and economic inability are much less important now than during the history of the range industry even as late as in the 1930's. Today, and probably also in the future, another economic factor is more important. This is the short-run private profit that can be made in regions with high climatic hazards but fairly level topography by plowing up range lands, which in the public interest should remain permanently in grass. This factor operated especially during and shortly after the two world wars and the Korean War.

Zoning and land-use regulations by grazing districts or other units of government are tools of public policy to prevent such privately profitable but socially costly plowing up of range lands. Experience shows, however, that these tools are not always acceptable to the owners of range resources and to the people as a whole. To the extent, then, that such tools are politically not acceptable or administratively too expensive, public ownership may be the safest and most economical way to guarantee a minimum standard of range conservation.

It is possible to outline certain consequences if the conservation criterion is applied in a decision on whether in particular areas private or public ownership is superior. In the more mountainous areas of the West, where topography precludes plowing up of range lands, considerable areas could be safely transferred from public to private ownership. Most range managers know of areas where range conservation is practiced on private lands to the same or even to a higher degree than on similar public lands. On the other hand, in the arid or semi-arid plains, expansion of public ownership may become necessary if other tools of public policy remain insufficient.

After saying this, a word of caution would seem appropriate with respect to the relation between the two criteria. The argument in favor of public ownership may be strong according to the social-benefit criterion and weak according to the conservation criterion, or vice versa. As a matter of geographical fact, there is a tendency for the two criteria to operate in opposite directions when applied jointly. This is explained by the habitat requirements of the presently important wildlife species and the characteristics of the demand for outdoor recreation. This complexity brings us to the last major point of the paper.

Need of More Research in the
Economics of Range Policy

In discussing the form of ownership and related problems of range policy, one is handicapped by lack of scientific facts. Some of this lack is in the field of natural sciences. For example, more information is needed on how far and under what conditions livestock and game compete for feed; far too little is known about the deferred effects—as distinguished from the more immediate effects—of management practices on range productivity. But much of the lack of scientific facts is in the field of the social sciences, especially economics. There is a great need for more research in economics of range policy.

The social-benefit criterion points to the need for more research in the economic evaluation of extra-market products, especially of recreational opportunities. Whether one likes it or not, their evaluation and also the dismissal of such evaluation are already a part of the political process. Reports of fish and game departments and other public agencies illustrate many attempts to evaluate these products. One may have professional doubts about some of the procedures used. Still these attempts should be encouraged. Otherwise, social benefits from these products may fail to receive due attention in policy decision.

Not all social benefits from these products can be evaluated. Partial measurement, however, is possible by using market values indirectly—for example, through analyzing data on leases, fees, and real estate transactions. Values of additional physical units of use can be approached through questionnaires and similar procedures. These and related problems of benefit-cost analysis have been more thoroughly explored for water resources than for range resources (Ciriacy-Wantrup, 1955).

The conservation criterion points to the need for more research in the response by private range operators to economic forces and government policies. In studying the response to variations in prices and price supports of products and cost factors, special attention should be given to shifts from grass to cultivated crops. In studying the response to economic uncertainty and the reaction to the actual incidence of drought and other extreme variations in the physical and economic environment, one should focus on fluctuations of livestock numbers. The type and the degree of response in terms of livestock numbers frequently gives rise to social costs. From the standpoint of conservation, responses to variations in institutional arrangements such as tenancy, taxation, credit, and subsidies are no less important than responses to price variations and weather fluctuations. Knowledge about these responses is needed in order to decide whether or not range policies other than transfer to public ownership guarantee a minimum standard of conservation.

But the usefulness of such studies is not confined to this decision. The response of private operators using public range resources to various forms of tenure and to other economic forces is of great interest for the administration of the public range. More research in the economics of range policy is needed, not only to identify in terms of criteria and conditions where the margin between public and private ownership should lie, but also to improve the use of public range resources by private enterprise.

[1]Giannini Foundation Paper No. 164. Presented at the 11th Annual Meeting of the American Society of Range Management, Great Falls, Montana, January 29 to February 1, 1957. Reprinted from the Journal of Range Management, Volume 11, No. 1, January 1958, pp. 10-13.

Literature Cited

Ciriacy-Wantrup, S. V. 1952. Resource conservation: economics and policies. Univ. Calif. Press: Berkeley. 397 pp.

————. 1955. Benefit-cost analysis and public resource development. Jour. Farm Econ. 37:676-689.

————. 1956. Policy considerations in farm management research in the decade ahead. Journ. Farm Econ. 38:1301-13ll.

————, and A. M. Schultz. 1957. Problems involving conservation in range economics research. Jour. Range Mangt. 10:12-16.

Harper, Harold T., George Metcalf and John Davis. 1950. Upland game cooperative areas. Calif. Fish and Game 36:404-432.

Part II

WATER POLICY

INTRODUCTION TO PART II

by

Hiroshi Yamauchi*

The four papers in this part were published in the 1960's, culminating over two decades of water research. In the field of water economics S. V. Ciriacy-Wantrup distinguished between the economics of water policy and the economics of water development. The latter included benefit-cost analysis and was only a small part of the former in spite of the unbalanced attention to the contrary in the literature. The scope of these four papers conforms to the broader concerns of water policy.

Wantrup's articles on water policy are as valuable now to economic understanding as they were when first published. The analysis resembles what came to be called systems control theory. The first step in the study of water policy is to identify the characteristics of the water resources system with which water policy is concerned. This seemingly simple determination is, Wantrup submitted, at the root of some of the most serious conceptual problems in contemporary research.

Confusion, he said, results if the distinction between the descriptive, the functional, and the theoretical is ignored. He advocated benefit-cost analysis but considered it as only one aspect of the much broader subject he called the economics of water policy. He insisted that economic research can only be successful when it is conducted in the context of a full understanding of water policy. For the most part, his concepts and principles remain as valid today and for the future as they were at the time of his writings.

The first paper, "Water Policy and Economic Optimizing: Some Conceptual Problems in Water Research" (1967), explains problems of system identification for resource policy decisions. It includes the first published version of his three level hierarchy of decision-making. Wantrup describes an integrated water resources system as a mix of groundwater and surface water uses at the operational level. The operating level is controlled by institutional decision systems at the second level which, in turn, are the subject of policy level decision-making at the third and highest level.

*Professor, Department of Agricultural and Resource Economics and Research Associate, Water Resources Research Center, University of Hawaii.

Wantrup developed the hierarchy model at a time when other economists were trying unsuccessfully to substitute sophisticated econometric models for fundamental understanding. He turned to the scientific criterion common to all disciplines concerned with human ecology: survival under the pressure of selection as measured by economic growth and welfare. This construct is complementary to other scientific systems modeling and brings to focus relevant institutional decision systems. In rapidly changing dynamic economies such as the world is currently experiencing, Wantrup's perspective is vital.

The usefulness of the survival value criterion is demonstrated using water district taxation and water rights in California as illustrations. This seemingly simple construct allows readers to understand some of the more difficult ideas which he so painstakingly hammered out in the remaining three papers in this part.

The second, "Water Economics: Relations to Law and Policy" (1967), presents a detailed analysis of water law. It was originally intended for legal audiences and follows Wantrup's tradition of taking the time to explain his perspective to lawyers, hydrologists, biologists, and others in addition to economists. An introduction to water rights is appended to this introduction for readers who are not familiar with water law.

In keeping with his quest for criteria to evaluate institutional performance, Wantrup suggested the twin criteria of security and flexibility. The criterion of security reflects the fact that both public and private investors need assured rights to water in the future as a precondition to expensive capital investment in water development. Flexibility, on the other hand, is concerned with decision rules that affect the ability to legally transfer water rights and, therefore, the reallocation of scarce water supplies among competing uses and users as economic circumstances change.

"Philosophy and Objectives of Watershed Policy" (1960) is a transition from his conceptualization of the economics of water development to the more comprehensive economics of water policy. The paper first appeared in *Land Economics* (August, 1959) and was immediately recognized as a significant contribution. It was selected for the lead-off chapter in *Economics of Watershed Planning*, edited by Tolley and Riggs.

This explanation of concepts and principles reinforces the previous papers. The conditions that cause the economy to diverge from the fictional welfare optima deserve careful reading. Among other useful insights, he elaborates on why the theory of "externalities" is of little help for understanding the malfunctioning of the price system and for formulating policy decisions. The complication arises because it is necessary to ascertain what kind of externality is involved in order to trace its incidence and incentive effects at the operating level.

Wantrup's critique of the so-called "new" benefit-cost analysis literature of that time notes that no progress had been made in the important areas of treating extra market values, offsite and indirect benefits and costs, consumer sovereignty, income distribution, market organization, and institutional influences. These are all serious shortcomings of benefit-cost analysis connected with the reliance on market prices for the evaluation of benefits and cost streams. In his view, the contribution of economics as an operationally significant policy science is potentially greater in the areas of repayment and pricing than in evaluation.

The fourth paper in Part II, "Water Quality, A Problem for the Economist" (1961), is one of the earliest attempts by an economist at systematizing the general problem of water reuse. More than a decade before the Federal Water Pollution Control Act Amendments of 1972 (PL 92-500), Wantrup called attention to the fact that water quality standards might be adopted as a policy objective but their success, at least social cost, requires that controls be directed at the sources of pollution. Of particular current interest in this paper in a uniquely Wantrupian view on the relative economic merits of standards and charges.

The approach in this paper, highlighting the imbalance in allocation and incidence of social costs and revenues, contrasts with the malfunctioning of the price system approach in the previous watershed management paper. Imbalances in the social benefits and costs at the operating level result from institutional conditions. The consequences of such imbalances are the lack of incentives to change production functions (broadly interpreted to include consumption) to employ technology for water reuse.

In the formulation of such controls, Wantrup justified direct and indirect controls at the institutional level at a time when sanitary engineers were debating the issue of stream versus effluent standards and well before environmental economists began debating the issue of standards versus effluent charges.

Throughout these four chapters, some common threads are prominent. Wantrup repeatedly emphasized the importance of understanding the physical and hydrological aspects of water resources as a prerequisite for studying economic issues. He focused on the relative importance of ground water, on the interrelationships between ground and surface water, and on the links between water quality and quantity.

A second research prerequisite, according to Wantrup, is an in-depth knowledge of water institutions. He cogently reminded his readers that institutions, including those governing water, should not be judged on their performance at any particular point in time, but rather over time under changing economic conditions that cannot be adequately forecast in advance. Wantrup the institutionalist continually sought criteria to evaluate existing institutions and design new ones. In the paper, "Water Policy and Economic Optimizing," he explored survival under the pressure of selection as one such criterion. In "Water Economics" he developed the twin criteria of security and flexibility of water rights. In "Water Quality" he considered modifications of his safe minimum standard as a criterion for institutional performance in that area.

The qualities that attract students interested in water resources to Wantrup are clearly evident in these chapters. He combined an interest in theory with a no-nonsense practical orientation. He seemed—and still seems—to be so much broader than most contemporary economic researchers, insisting on the relevance of historical factors and institutions to understanding water policy. He had a genuine interest in water resources themselves and their wise management, rather than viewing them as a convenient subject for another application of his model. He was a staunch critic of the conventional wisdom in the water policy field—a quality that students always find exciting— but he was more than a critic. In the coming pages, the reader will find a fertile field of original, thought-provoking ideas on the topic of water policy.

APPENDIX

NOTE ON WATER RIGHTS[1]

Water Right

An irrigation water right is a right, granted by law, to take possession of water occurring in a natural source of water supply and to divert the water and put it to a beneficial use on or in connection with land.

Water rights may be impaired or lost because of certain processes that are recognized by law. In the following definitions, it is assumed that the water right came into being unimpaired and that it suffered no impairment or loss after it was acquired.

Riparian right. The owner of land that is contiguous to or borders a natural stream or lake is entitled to take water from that source for use upon that contiguous land. This right is called a riparian right. The land to which it relates is called riparian land.

The riparian right exists solely by reason of location of the land with respect to the water supply.

Appropriative right. A person may acquire a right to the use of water for the irrigation of a particular tract of land, or for other beneficial purposes, by performing certain acts required by law. These acts include taking or diverting the water from a stream or other source and applying it to use on or in connection with the land. If the source of water is a surface or underground

[1]This note on water rights is taken from Wells A. Hutchins *Irrigation Water Rights in California*, Circular 452, revised (February, 1967) of the California Agricultural Experiment Station Extension Service, in order to provide the uninitiated reader an introduction to the legal concepts that are referred to in Wantrup's article on "Water Economics: Relations to Law and Policy" (1967). The details of such water rights concepts vary from state to state and also are modified over time to adjust to changing economic conditions. The overall structure of water rights as it existed in California at the time of Wantrup's writing serves as a useful base of reference since the dynamic economic functions that he saw in water institutions are typified in the progressively changing case of California.

65

watercourse, certain formalities for acquiring the right are prescribed by statute.

The person who performs these acts appropriates the water, or makes an appropriation of the water. Such person is an appropriator. The right that he acquires is called an appropriative right.

The land to which the appropriative right relates may either be contiguous to the stream, or may be located at a distance from it. In some instances, it may lie in a different watershed.

When a supply of water to which several appropriative rights have attached is not enough for them all, the earlier rights have preference over rights of later date. Each right is entitled to its full quantity of water before any water may be taken for rights that are later in time. This superiority over later rights is called the priority of an appropriative right.

Correlative right. A person who owns land overlying a body of percolating ground water is entitled to extract water from the ground for use upon his overlying land. This right is called a correlative right.

The correlative ground water right exists solely because the percolating ground water in question underlies the land of the holder of the right.

Prescriptive right. A person may possibly divert to his own uses water to which riparian or overlying landowners or appropriators have prior claims, thereby depriving them of the use of water to which they are entitled. If he does this without interruption for a period of five consecutive years prescribed by the State statute of limitations, and if he fulfills certain other legal requirements, he gains a prescriptive right against the parties whose rights he has invaded.

The perspective right gives the holder a valid right, so far as the parties he has dispossessed are concerned, to continue diverting and using the water to the extent that he has been doing throughout the five-year period.

Under the usual circumstances prescriptive rights can be acquired against downstream parties only.

Pueblo right. A California city that succeeded a Spanish or Mexican pueblo (municipality) has the paramount right to the use of water of a stream that flowed through the old pueblo limits, for the use of the inhabitants of the city. This is called the pueblo water rights.

Chapter 4

WATER POLICY AND ECONOMIC OPTIMIZING: SOME CONCEPTUAL PROBLEMS IN WATER RESEARCH*[1]

I. Water Policy and Water-Resources Systems

For the purpose of this discussion, I should like to view water policy from the standpoint of decision theory: water policy may be regarded as a set of decision rules in a multistage decision process. In this process, a sequence of decisions extends over time and space in an "open" system.

The first step in such a study of water policy[2] is to identify the system or systems in the control of which decision rules are sought. In other words, what are the characteristics of the water-resources system with which water policy is concerned? This seemingly simple issue of system identification is, I submit, at the root of some of the most serious conceptual problems in contemporary water research.

The large and still expanding literature on water economics during the last decade is mainly concerned with one particular class of a water-resource system; namely, the public multipurpose development of surface water through storage dams, canals, and other large engineering structures. The term "public" usually refers to the federal government, and economic analysis focuses on the efficiency of federal investment in water resources. This is the same class with which the earlier discussion of benefit-cost analysis was concerned—exemplified by the Green Book, the controversy about the TVA, and the various critiques of the Army Engineers and the Bureau of Reclamation. The Green Book used the term river-basin project for this class, but later the terms water-resources system and water development became synonymous with it.

Such terminology is not helpful for several reasons. First, this particular class is less significant in inputs and outputs than other classes. Second, this

*Reprinted, with permission, from *The American Economic Review*, Volume LVII, No. 2, pp. 179–189, (May, 1967).

class is always closely related to others as a part of an integrated system; it is merely a subsystem. Third, the decision rules suggested in the literature for this subsystem under constraining assumptions are neither valid nor relevant for the integrated system as a whole. The last point will be elaborated presently (Section II), but first let us ask what are the characteristics of an integrated water-resources system as understood here?

Such a system is a mixed groundwater-surface water system. Groundwater use is quantitatively at least as significant as surface-water use, and integration of the two uses raises some of the most important issues for water policy. The design of such a system does not necessarily involve large engineering structures. Appropriate institutional structures, on the other hand, are a necessary and frequently sufficient condition for its functioning. Such institutions relate to water law influencing water development, water allocation, and water quality; to water district law controlling the establishment, organization, and operation of public water districts; and to state and federal administrative agencies affecting water development, allocation, and quality. For short, these structures will be called here "water institutions."

Groundwater is developed largely by private rather than by public investment. The public investment that is involved is by water districts rather than by federal and state governments. Private firms and water districts are also active in multipurpose, multiunit surface-water development. Some of the federal developments and the California State Water Plan outrank private and district developments in size of individual projects; but in the aggregate, water development by private firms and water districts exceeds that by federal and state governments.

We may say, then, that the water-resource system with which we are concerned consists of operating sectors which are private firms, public districts, and projects of federal and state governments.[3] In aggregate quantity of water developed, private firms—households, farms, industrial corporations, and public utilities—are the most significant group of operating sectors. In second place are public water districts such as irrigation districts, municipal water districts (and departments), and conservancy districts. Federal projects are in third place and state projects are last.[4]

II. Water Policy and the Hierarchy of Decision (Optimizing) Levels

In order to find decision rules for such an integrated water-resource system I should like to differentiate three levels of decision making. These levels constitute a logical pyramid similar to the levels of conceptualization differentiated in formal logic.[5] For the present purpose, this pyramid will be called "the hierarchy of decision levels."

On the first level, the lowest, the decision-making process relates directly to the control of inputs, outputs, and other quantitative characteristics of the water-resource system. These characteristics may be deterministic or stochastic; they may be in physical or in value terms. Decision making on the next higher level, the second, controls the institutional framework of the decision-making process on the first level. On the third level, the framework of the decision-making process on the second level is the subject of decisions.

Decision levels may also be conceived as optimizing levels. This term will not be used here because it requires interpretation of optimizing as a fictional construct or scientific fiction.[6] On each level, decision rules are sought for making the best decision on that level. Although decision-making processes differ from level to level, they are interrelated because the effects of each decision can be traced through all lower levels. From the observation of these effects on the water-resources system, decision-makers can learn how to make improvements in decision-making processes on all levels. Such learning—or in computer jargon "feedback"—is the essence of a multistage decision process. The decision-making process on each level can be studied in its structure, its functioning, and its performance.

We can now proceed to the application of these general concepts. As we know, an integrated water-resource system is composed of private and public operating sectors (Section I). The decision making on the level of these operating sectors constitutes the first level of our hierarchy. Decision rules for this level are familiar to economists because they are identical with "the" rule generally suggested for decision making in economic literature. This rule was originally postulated for a calculative economic man and for the private profit-seeking firm. It was later modified for public decision making in order to take account of problems involved in aggregating individual utilities and in dealing with externalities. The recent revival of the concept of social time preference may be regarded as a special case of these two problems. The public maximizing agent striving to obtain such Pareto optima in water-resources development by internalizing externalities has been dubbed the "river basin firm."[7]

The common decision rule for private and public operating sectors specifies maximization of an objective (profit or welfare) function under constraints regarding institutions, technology, and resource availability. In terms of formal criteria, maximization is accomplished through fulfilling the necessary and sufficient conditions and other qualifications given by the first and second derivatives of the objective function and, for maximization over time, by the calculus of variations.

Little needs to be said here about this decision rule itself. The conceptual and operational limitations of quantitative optimizing in private and in public decision making have been discussed elsewhere.[8] There is, however, one aspect of these limitations that is of interest here because it points to the next higher decision level. This aspect is the treatment of institutions as constraints in quantitative optimizing. Such treatment does not create conceptual problems in private decision making. In social decision making, however, institutions correspond conceptually more to independent or dependent variables than to constraints.

The latter treatment of institutions has received critical review in welfare economics through "the theory of second best."[9] This critique has cast serious doubts on the validity of Pareto optimizing under institutional constraints. Whether or not one agrees with the entire reasoning of this critique, the main result can well be accepted; institutional conditions are conceptually different from technological conditions and resource availability. To look at the former as constraints views their appearance only on the first decision level. On the second level, they appear as the operational parts in the decision-making process.

The purpose of decision making on the second level is not to control directly inputs, outputs, and other quantitative characteristics of the water-resources system nor to obtain a path of quantitative welfare optima at various points in time under projected conditions for these points. Rather, the purpose is to maintain and to increase welfare by continuously influencing decision making on the lower level under constantly changing conditions that for any point in time cannot be projected—or only vaguely—and that are always uncertain with respect to actual occurrence.

In order to fulfill such a purpose, each water institution may be regarded as a decision-making system that functions as a whole with a particular pattern of change. Under the constitutional organization of the United States and other Western democracies, the system is modified through actions by the three branches of government—the legislative, judicial, and executive—each with a different range over which modification can be accomplished. Modification takes place on the federal, the state, and the local levels; generally the state level is the most important for water institutions.

Performance of such a decision-making system can be appraised only by viewing the system as it functions over time under various economic conditions. It is conceptually inadequate to appraise performance by studying temporal cross-sections of the system for particular conditions and points in time. Criteria for performance must be sought on the system's own level. They need not be the same as those on the lower level discussed previously. Neither need the criteria on the lower level be those that economists suggest they should be. What we seek for the second level are criteria that could serve as conceptually and operationally meaningful proxies for the fictional construct of optimizing welfare. They may be called intervening criteria in analogy with intervening variables. The search for such criteria will be undertaken in the following section (Section III).

While the second decision level is the most significant one for the study of water policy, it does not complete our hierarchy. A third decision level was implied by the reference to the constitutional organization of the United States, which sets the basic framework for water policy as for all other policies. Water institutions, however, are not confined to modern Western democracies. Highly developed water institutions existed in ancient feudal societies and city states in the Old and in the New World. They exist in primitive tribal communities in Africa no less than in modern authoritarian states. Time does not permit sketching the differences between water institutions in different societies. Although the causal connection is controversial, the basic organization of a society is always closely interrelated with water institutions. Accordingly, this organization may be regarded conceptually as a social decision-making process on the next higher, the third, level of our hierarchy. Discussion of this level would lead away from water policy and need not be undertaken here.

III. Criteria for the Performance of Water Institutions

Decision-making processes on the second and third levels are a part of the political process. When economics was understood as political economy, it encompassed the political process in the study of decision-making. Later, emphasis shifted toward the quantitative optimizing model almost to the exclusion of other decision-making processes. However, there are some nonconformists. For example, Lindblom and his coauthors in several books, especially in the last one, argue that the political process is the only valid and relevant general model of decision-making.[10] He applied his central theme of "mutual accomodation of partisans" to private as well as to public decision-making. Others have suggested that the political process should merely supplement quantitative optimizing in the solution of specific technical difficulties: for example, to determine trade-off values between different objectives of public investment.[11] Multidimensionality of the objective function has long been a major conceptual and operational difficulty in quantitative optimizing

These and similar suggestions are a refreshing change from reiterating over and over the goal of quantitative optimizing—often with little regard for the operational possibility of fulfilling the necessary and sufficient conditions and other qualifications. There are, however, two provisos which I should like to make: First, one must recognize the differences between decision-making processes on different levels: the political process must be brought in at the second level; it cannot be relied upon to solve *ad hoc* the many technical difficulties of quantitative optimizing. Second, conceptually satisfactory criteria must be provided to differentiate a "good" from a "bad" situation.

By the authors mentioned and by others, agreement based on mutual accomodation of partisans is specified as the main criterion. Such a criterion has strong appeal in a Western democracy. But its application involves several conceptual difficulties. The criterion requires a careful definition of the meaning of political agreement and a specification of the means of bringing it about. While the criterion is operational in the sense that "feasible" decisions are always selected, it does not enable one to make a selection between alternative decisions for all of which agreement is attainable. Agreement may fluctuate over relatively short periods of time for substantially identical decisions; this would not make the criterion inoperative at any point in time, but differentiation between good and bad decisions would have little meaning under these conditions. Finally, and most importantly, the agreement criterion is not useful in appraising performance for the purpose of scientific analysis.

To find a more satisfactory criterion is not easy. But since the social sciences may be regarded as an extension of human ecology, performance criteria used in our sister sciences may offer a suggestion.

Geneticists, studying genotypes, populations, and species, differentiate between favorable and unfavorable gene variants, mutations, traits, and other characteristics.[12] Students of animal behavior differentiate between favorable and unfavorable instincts and other habit patterns of behavior with various degrees of openness to learning.[13] These and similar appraisals of characteristics—from molecular to social—are based on a common criterion; namely, survival under the pressure of selection. One might explore the possibility of applying a similar criterion to characteristics of economic behavior, in our case to the performance of water institutions. Here, survival must be interpreted in economic terms; that is, not in physical growth and numbers but in economic growth and welfare.

The first step in such an exploration is to note some relevant conceptual implications of survival value as a criterion of performance. Survival value indicates only direction, even though highly quantitative methods may be used in determining it; it cannot be employed, therefore, for obtaining optima. It has no normative connotation; it is useful for scientific analysis; but for political decision-making, its usefulness is indirect and uncertain. Knowledge of structure and functioning of a system is required before performance of its individual characteristics can be appraised. Appraisal is valid only for a specified environment or sequence of environments.

None of these implications render the criterion unsuited for our purpose. It will be recalled that quantitative precision and optimizing are not involved on the second level of decision-making. Further, a criterion is desired that is useful for scientific analysis. For political-decision making, such a criterion can only be a supplementary one, its significance depending on the influence of scientific understanding on political agreement.

Survival value can be applied in various ways. Sometimes it is the performance of water institutions as it affects the viability of operating sectors (in the sense of Section I) that is of interest; for example, how water-district law affects the viability of water districts during economic depressions or their growth in underdeveloped regions. Sometimes it is the water-resources system itself that is of interest; for example, to what extent are water institutions responsible for the growth, stagnation, and decay of irrigation systems in many parts of the world? Usually, however, scientific interest is focused on how water institutions—especially water law—are related to the welfare of a whole region in various periods of its development.

IV. Illustrations and Conclusions

In order to bring the conceptual analysis (Sections I-III) closer to applied water research, some of these examples may be spelled out further.

Among the most difficult problems of water policy is the allocation of costs of water development among beneficiaries for the purpose of repayment.

For water districts, solution of this problem is crucial for viability because they cannot rely on the resources of the federal and state treasuries. Water research can use two approaches: First, through various computational techniques of benefit-cost analysis one can project benefits accruing to different groups of beneficiaries and allocate costs and repayment more or less in proportion. The second approach focuses on alternative characteristics of water-district law. The objective of this approach is to appraise the allocative performance of these characteristics and to select those with survival value in terms of viability of districts.

Since the Wright Act of 1887, California has had a great deal of experience in employing district taxation and water prices in various combinations. With some modification in 1907, the original taxation provisions of the Wright Act have stood up well under the test of cyclial and structural economic change. Conversely, the difficulties of water districts in other states, in Canada, and elsewhere are largely due to the absence of similar provisions in water-district law. The details are of great interest for institutional analysis, but time does not permit discussing them here.[14] In summary, one may suggest that as a basis for repayment to water districts, computation of indirect benefits and of optimum cost allocation has yet to demonstrate their superiority over the results of institutional characteristics tested over some eighty years. In other words, a decision-making process on the second level, by controlling decision-making on the first level, has performed in a way that is conceptually and operationally more acceptable than ad hoc sophisticated computations. One might call the taxation provisions of the Wright Act an institutional characteristic with survival value.

By far the most significant of water institutions are the systems of water rights that function in great variety in the fifty states and in most organized communities all over the world. Here, also, California offers interesting material for appraising performance under a sequence of different economic environments.

Starting in the 1850's, when industrial use of water—for placer mining— was more important than agricultural use in a pastoral, nonurban region, water rights have controlled water development, allocated water, and influenced water quality up to the present day, when agricultural use of water is dominant in one of the most highly industrialized states of the union.[15] This adaptability of water law in responding to and influencing a rapidly changing economic environment can be explained largely by the functioning side-by-side of two legal systems, one based on riparian, the other on appropriative rights. Over time, they have come to a workable blend. For groundwater, this blend can be regarded as a specific system, that of correlative rights.[16]

To the superficial observer, the California "mix" of water-right systems appears as utter confusion. It is often criticized by economists who have made it responsible for retardation of water development, misallocation of water, cross-hauling of water, and other inefficiencies. Instances of this kind exist, although other factors are frequently more responsible for them than water law. Even if water law were solely responsible, economic inefficiencies under particular conditions at particular points in time are not sufficient for an indictment of the whole institution. As we have seen (Section II), the function of water institutions is not to maximize economic efficiency for particular conditions and points in time but to structure decision making on the lower level under various and constantly changing conditions.

In studying the performance of water-right systems in fulfilling this function, a dichotomy of criteria has been developed.[17] They are security against legal, physical, and tenure uncertainties and flexibility in various legal and economic categories. Applying these criteria to California water law gives a fairly good "fit." California water law has performed relatively well— as compared with other water-law systems—in stimulating water development, allocating water, and protecting water quality over more than a century of profound changes in the economic environment. To be sure, some structural characteristics, such as the system of preferences, have lost survival value and are largely neutralized by others.

The purpose of such a general evaluation is not to defend California water law but to suggest that in the perpetual process of legal adaptation, economists could be more helpful by making careful institutional analyses of the performance of water law than by reiterating the criticism that water law has failed to optimize water development and allocation for particular conditions and points in time. Such criticism is neither valid nor relevant because its criteria are not applicable to a system operating on the second decision level.

If I may draw a conclusion for water research, it is that comparative analysis of water institutions is a promising field for economists. Like all institutional analysis, it is closely related to the political preferences, the emotions, and the social conditioning of the investigator—witness what some investigators have called the "rape" of Owens Valley. This challenge to scientific attitude must be faced. Even though some material is slanted and some merely descriptive, much is available in economic history, political science, law and engineering that is valuable for an analytical treatment of the structure, the functioning, and the performance of water institutions. In this treatment, theoretical constructs and their testing are no less needed than in the analysis of the marketplace. The hierarchy of decision levels is the most important of such constructs. From it follows the basic difference between decision rules (criteria) on the first and second levels.

As to criteria for decisions on the second level, the approach suggested here focuses on what we called intervening criteria as proxies for optimizing welfare; namely, on institutional characteristics that have demonstrated favorable or unfavorable effects on welfare. Examples were given for two of the most important water institutions. Other institutions would lend themselves to the same approach.

This approach is greatly interested in economic history and in relating one time period to another but not necessarily through increasing the number of variables and equations in mathematical models. It relies heavily on theoretical constructs but less on the maximization principle. Emphasis is on determining conditions for economic growth rather than on locating peaks, on avoiding dead-end streets rather than on computing the shortest distance, and on adaptability rather than optimum adjustment. This approach does not pretend to establish criteria for economic optimizing, but it offers a basis for water policy at successive stages of decision-making.

[1]This was published as Giannini Foundation Paper No. 272.

[2]In the terminology of decision theory, policy refers to the decision rules; that is, the criteria of decision-making. But the study of policy includes the whole decision-making process and the implementation and the effects of decisions.

[3]It should be noted that a differentiation is made here between projects of federal and state agencies and those agencies themselves. This is in accordance with procedures of economic optimizing. Thus, optimizing procedures are applied to projects of the Bureau of Reclamation and not to the Bureau itself or the laws regulating its establishment, organization, and operation. A parallel differentiation is made here between public water districts and the state water district laws controlling the establishment, organization, and operation of such districts.

[4]In recent decades, water districts have changed in part from water developers in their own right to retailers of water developed by federal and state projects. In some states—for example, California—federal and state projects are intertwined. Statistical separatiion of quantities of water developed by districts, federal projects, and state projects has become increasingly difficult. For a more detailed discussion of the relative significance of the various groups of operating sectors in the above sense, see S. V. Ciriacy-Wantrup, "Water Policy," *Handbook of Applied Hydrology: A Compendium of Water-Resources Technology,* Editor-in-Chief, Ven Te Chow (McGraw-Hill Book Co., 1964), Sec. 28, pp. 28-1 to 28-25.

[5]For an application of levels of conceptualization to the concept: "resources," see Ciriacy-Wantrup, *Resource Conservation: Economics and Policies* (2nd ed. rev., Div. of Agric. Sci., Univ. of California, 1963), Chap. 3. It scarcely needs to be mentioned that the logical pyramid referred to here carries no connotation of social or ethical ranking.

[6]For a discussion of this interpretation, see Ciriacy-Wantrup, "Policy Consideration in Farm Management Research in the Decade Ahead," *J. of Farm Econ.,* Dec., 1956, pp. 1301-11.

[7]Allen V. Kneese, *The Economics of Regional Water Quality Management* (Johns Hopkins Press, 1964).

[8]Ciriacy-Wantrup, "Philosophy and Objectives of Watershed Policy," *Economics of Watershed Planning,* ed. G. S. Tolley and F. E. Riggs (Iowa State Univ. Press, 1961), pp. 1-12; and "Conservation and Resource Programming," *Land Econ.,* May, 1961, pp. 105-11. (Reprinted as Chapters 4 and 14, respectively, in this book.)

[9]R. G. Lipsey and R. K. Lancaster, "The General Theory of Second Best," *Rev. of Econ. Studies,* Vol. XXIV (1), No. 63 (1956-57), pp. 11-32; John V. Krutilla, "Welfare Aspects of Benefit-Cost Analysis," *Economics and Public Policy in Water Resource Development,* ed. Stephen C. Smith and Emery N.

76 Water Policy and Economic Optimizing

Castle (Iowa State Univ. Press, 1964), pp. 22-33; and O. A. Davis and A. B. Whinston, "Welfare Economics and the Theory of Second Best," *Rev. of Econ. Studies*, Jan., 1965, pp. 1-14.

[10]Robert A. Dahl and Charles E. Lindblom, *Politics, Economics, and Welfare: Planning and Politico-Economic Systems Resolved into Basic Social Processes* (Harper, 1953). David Braybrooke and Charles E. Lindblom, *A Strategy of Decision: Policy Evaluation as a Social Process* (London: The Free Press of Glencoe, Collier-Macmillan Limited, 1963). Charles E. Lindblom, *The Intelligence of Democracy: Decision Making Through Mutual Adjustment* (The Free Press, 1965).

[11]Arthur Maass, "Benefit-Cost Analysis: Its Relevance to Public Investment Decisions," Q.J.E., 1966, pp. 208-26.

[12]Curt Stern, "The Genetic Resources of Man," *Natural Resources: Quality and Quanity*, ed. S. V. Ciriacy-Wantrup and James J. Parsons (Berkeley: Univ. of California Press, 1967). Ernest Mayr, *Animal Species and Evolution* (Harvard Univ. Press, 1963).

[13]Konrad Lorenz, *On Aggression* (Harcourt, Brace and World, 1963). N. Tinbergen, *The Study of Instinct* (Oxford: Clarendon Press, 1951).

[14]For details, see Michael F. Brewer, *Water Pricing and Allocation With Particular Reference to California Irrigation Districts* (Univ. of California, Giannini Found. Mimeo. Report No. 235, 1960).

[15]For comparing different uses quantitatively, two factors are frequently not sufficiently considered: (1) whether conveyance losses are included or excluded for agricultural use and (2) whether water use by steam-electric plants—the quantitatively most significant one among industrial uses—is included or excluded for industrial use. In California, for example, agricultural use is 87 percent; industrial use, 5 percent; and domestic use, 8 percent of total use, if conveyance losses are included and steam-electric plants are excluded. Agricultural use is 67 percent; industrial use, 25 percent; and domestic, 8 percent, if conveyance losses are excluded and steam-electric plants are included. In terms of water consumption, the former is a more appropriate comparison, provided that double counting is avoided. Some conveyance losses are used via groundwater and counted then. There is considerable interfirm reuse of water both in aricultural and in industrial use; the quantitative extent of such reuse is not known. Steam-electric plants use, largely, cooling water that is not usable for other purposes and, in any event, is not consumed. Potentially, of course, most domestic use can be made nonconsumptive.

[16]Ciriacy-Wantrup, "Some Economic Issues in Water Rights," *J. of Farm Econ.*, Dec., 1955, pp. 875-85.

[17]Ciriacy-Wantrup, "Concepts Used as Economic Criteria for a System of Water Rights," *Economics and Public Policy in Water Resource Development*, ed. Stephen C. Smith and Emerey N. Castle (Iowa State Univ. Press, 1964), pp. 251-71; and "Water Economics: Relations to Law and Policy," *Waters and Water Law in the United States*, ed. Robert Emmet Clark (Chicago: Allen Smith and Co., 1967). (Reprinted as Chapter 5 in this book.)

Chapter 5

WATER ECONOMICS: RELATIONS TO LAW AND POLICY*[1]

Introduction to Economics, Law, and Policy

Economics in the law

It would be presumptuous for an economist to attempt a definitive statement of the content, the criteria, and the objectives of the law's norms. But he may submit as a proposition that economics is a major, if not dominant, concern of the law. Water law, the focus of this treatise, is a good illustration.

Most of the content of water law relates to establishing a normative framework for the economic behavior of individuals and groups with respect to one of their most pressing economic wants. Most of the water law's criteria, such as "reasonable," "beneficial," "adequate," "waste," and "surplus" require an economic interpretation. Most of the water law's objectives such as "maximum development of water resources," "safeguarding the public interest," and "protection of private property rights" have an economic meaning and are closely related to the objectives of economic policies.

The law in economics

In economics, on the other hand, the law is one of the most significant institutional constraints, both conceptually (that is, in economics as an academic discipline) and in actuality (that is, for the economic behavior of individuals and social groups). But the law is also one of the most important institutional variables when economic policy is considered in hypothetical terms as a field of scientific inquiry, when economic policy is implemented in the political arena through the various branches (legislative, judicial, and executive) and on the various levels (federal, state, and local) of government,

*Ciriacy-Wantrup, S. V., "Water Economics: Relations to Law and Policy." Chap. 5 in *Waters and Water Rights: A Treatise on the Law of Waters and Allied Problems*, edited by Robert Emmet Clark, Vol. 1, 397–430. Indianapolis: The Allen Smith Company, 1967. Reprinted by permission of the publisher.

and when economic policy is discussed or proposed by interested private individuals and organizations.

Water policy and the objectives of this chapter

These general relations between law and economics suggest that there is a broad area where both are intimately involved. This area will be called here "water policy." It is the central theme of this chapter.

First, this chapter intends to explore the meaning, the objectives, and the criteria of water policy in order to give members of the legal profession an insight into the approaches and conceptual tools of economics.[2]

Second, an attempt will be made to explain economic criteria for the structure, the functioning, and the social performance of water law in the implementation of water policy. Such implementation, we believe, depends to a large extent on understanding and co-operation between law and economics.

Third, it is hoped that an increase in such understanding and co-operation will stimulate the creative development of water law and water economics as two sister disciplines among the social sciences.

Meaning of Water Policy

Definition of terms

The word "policy" is used with many different meanings, both in scientific and in popular language. For the present purpose, it is helpful to restrict its meaning to interrelated actions (action systems), real or hypothetical, of organized publics such as federal, state, and local governments, including public districts. This restriction of meaning is in accordance with the etymological origin of the word. Any private individuals, firms, or associations may have opinions, attitudes, and proposals pertaining to policy; they may aid or hinder the formation and implementation of policy, and they are always affected by it. The word itself, however, will be used here in the restricted sense of *public* policy. Accordingly, the term "water policy" refers to actions of governments at various levels and in various branches affecting the development and allocation of water resources.

The unifying principle that transforms a number of individual government actions into a system termed policy is supplied, first of all, by the viewpoint of the scientific observer interested in the many kinds of relations that exist between individual actions in objectives, planning, execution, and effects. In this sense, water policy is both a conceptual tool of analysis—a construct— and a field of scientific inquiry.

Ideally, a second unifying principle is supplied by the purposes of the governments undertaking or considering actions; ideally, individual actions constitute a segment of a purposefully co-ordinated system. In actuality, however, the purposes of actions by different governments and different branches of the same government are frequently not co-ordinated. Furthermore, objectives of an individual action may be disconnected with, or contrary to, those of others by the same government agency. Such lack of co-ordination and multiplicity of objectives is an important subject in the study of water policy.

Reference was just made to the words *development* and *allocation* of water resources. In political reality, actions in these two spheres are closely related. In economic analysis, it is useful to separate them. The term "water-development policy" refers to actions affecting the increase of quantities of water available for distribution and use. The term "water-allocation policy" refers to actions affecting the distribution of given quantities of water among different uses, such as domestic, industrial, agricultural, and recreational, and among users, such as farms, industrial firms, and households. This terminology follows common usage that generally, although sometimes rather vaguely, employs the words "development" and "allocation" in connection with natural resources. In technical terms, water-development policy refers to actions affecting the length of the water-use vector; water-allocation policy refers to actions affecting the direction of this vector.[3]

Water policy and water projects

It is implied in the definition of terms just given that water policy includes, but is not limited to, public investment in water projects. The study of water policy is far more comprehensive than the study of public water projects. The economics of public water projects—such as benefit-cost analyses, formal programming, and other techniques of evaluating such projects and the whole problem of efficiency in government investment—constitutes only a segment, and sometimes only a small segment, of water policy.

Reasons for this statement are not far to seek. In the United States—and this is true also for most countries of western society—water is largely developed and allocated through decentralized decision-making of self-supplying farms, industrial corporations, and nonprofit water organizations. These water firms are the operating subsectors in the water economy. Federal and state projects may be regarded as subsectors in this sense, subject to rules of the game not greatly different from those applying to other subsectors. These rules of the game and their modifications are the domain of water policy.

The significance of self-supply is so great for the economic and political issues of water policy that a few quantitative data on the relative importance of various types of subsectors in the above sense may be helpful.[4]

According to the 1950 census, 47% of the irrigated acreage in the United States was supplied by single-farm irrigation enterprises. Of the industrial use of water in the United States, 97% was supplied by individual company systems.

The second largest part of aggregate water use was supplied by water users themselves co-operatively, through nonprofit water organizations such as mutual water companies and public districts. In the United States, 28% of irrigated acreage was supplied by mutual water companies and 18% by public districts. Regarding domestic water use, 87% of a population of 79 million in communities of more than 25,000 covered by a survey of the United States Public Health Service in 1957 was supplied by water systems owned by municipalities or municipal water districts. In the formation, operation, and growth of all of these water organizations, water consumers have a direct and significant influence that is outside the demand-supply mechanism of a market. In many respects, the factors affecting decision-making in these organizations are similar to those affecting self-supplying firms.

Only a small part of the aggregate water supply is produced for sale by profit-seeking firms. Most of these, in turn, are regulated by state public-utility commissions. In the United States, only 3% of the irrigated acreage is supplied by such firms and only 5% of industrial water use. The data in the above-mentioned survey indicate that only 13% of the population surveyed is supplied for municipal water use by privately owned systems.

The significance of ground water

The significance of self-supply in the water economy is related to that of ground water. Ground water is largely developed through investment by self-supplying water firms and not by state and federal investment. Furthermore, in the development of ground water, private investment is more significant than the investment by public districts.

The significance of ground water is especially great for agricultural use. For industrial and municipal use, in the United States as a whole, surface water is quantitatively more important than ground water. For industry, the locational attraction to surface water is partly based on the adequacy of "free" brackish water and seawater for steam-electric plants—the largest industrial users. Other locational attractions to surface water for industry and urban communities alike are the effects of navigable water on costs of transportation and the suitability of large bodies of water for waste disposal. In the arid and semarid basins of the West, on the other hand, ground water is no less significant for industrial and domestic use than for agricultural use.

The significance of ground water for agricultural use may be illustrated with a few figures. Ground-water development has been responsible for 67% of total public and private irrigation development in the seventeen western states since 1940. If federal water development is excluded, this figure rises to 89 percent. The share of ground-water development by decades is also interesting. Before 1900, ground water was responsible for only 1% of total public and private irrigation development in the seventeen western states. Between 1900 and 1909, the groundwater portion was 8%; from 1910 to 1919, 27%; from 1920 to 1929, 52%; from 1930 to 1939, 42%; from 1940-49, 63%; and from 1950 to 1958, 69 percent.[5]

The increasing significance of ground water is one of the reasons for the above emphasis on the differentiation between public water policy and public water projects. Ground-water development, being based largely on private investment, is highly sensitive to changes in general economic conditions for investment. For example, during the depression decade 1930 to 1939, ground-water development decreased absolutely; it decreased even more relative to surface-water development. During this decade, public investment in water development, consisting largely of surface-water development, showed a strong increase.

The significance of ground-water development and the increasing need for integrating ground-water development and surface water development poses important issues for water policy that are different from those of public investment. Recent economic literature focusing exclusively on the efficiency of public investment in water projects must be diagnosed as myopia that overlooks some of the most important issues of water policy.

Water policy and the water market

Present-day economics in western countries is largely concerned with the analysis of markets and market prices. Accordingly, economic policy is to a large extent price and market policy.

Subsection *water policy and water projects* showed that decisions about production and use of water are largely internal within self-supplying water firms. In other words, such decisions are not expressed through the firm's behavior in a water market. Neither are they coordinated through such a market. Hence, market-oriented economic concepts have more limited analytical significance for explaining and evaluating the behavior of water-producing and water-consuming firms than in many other fields of economic inquiry.

In water economics, the price per unit—for example per acre-foot—is only a part of the total payment complex. Costs of water development are covered through various forms of taxes, special assessments, and fees. While there is an upward trend in the portion covered by prices, and some economic argument for continuation of this trend, a major portion of the water bill will continue to be met in other ways than through prices. Furthermore, as already implied, water prices are always under strong institutional influence, such as the rules of a public district, contracts with the United States Bureau of Reclamation and other public agencies, or the regulation of a public-utility commission.

Seasonal and permanent transfers of water between water firms occur. In special cases—for example, if water consumers are owners of mutual water companies—seasonal water transfers show market characteristics. Permanent transfer is generally in terms of water rights and is governed by water law. Water exchanges (water for water, differentiated in terms of time and location) are not uncommon. They are individual transactions, usually not involving pecuniary considerations. But they are potentially important for increasing efficiency of water allocation with respect to time, location, and uses. More research is needed on the social performance of these transfer mechanisms. But it is already fairly clear that there is little meaning in speaking of a water market in which water-supplying and water-demanding industries meet.

The challenge of institutional analysis

It is evident from what has been said so far that, as compared with other economic policies, water policy is less concerned with markets and prices and more with the laws, regulations, and administrative structures under which self-supplying individual firms and nonprofit organizations make decisions. This situation poses a challenge to scientific inquiry that must be faced squarely: institutional influences are so diverse, so pervasive, so widely distributed over time, so difficult to isolate and quantify, so resistant to controlled experiment, and so closely related to the social conditioning of the political preferences and the emotions of the investigator that the temptation is great to remain on the descriptive level instead of proceeding toward analysis.

Over many years, the descriptive approach to water institutions has yielded much valuable material, contributed largely by noneconomists. This material is now available to the social sciences for analysis focusing on the structure, the functioning, and the performance of water institutions. Water policy as a field of scientific inquiry is analytically oriented institutional economics. In such an economics, theoretical constructs and their testing are no less needed than in the economics of the market place.

In order to take up this challenge, we must explore next the economic objectives and criteria of water policy.

Economic Objectives and Criteria of Water Policy

Water policy and welfare economics

In identifying the economic objectives and criteria of water policy, one encounters what might be called the problem of unity of objectives and criteria. Objectives of water policy cannot, in principle, be divorced from the objectives of other policies. Such objectives are interrelated, and social-welfare criteria are no different in water policy than in other fields of public policy.

, In an attempt to develop criteria for public policy, economists have developed a branch of normative economics called "welfare economics." More recently this branch has become known as the "new" welfare economics to emphasize its development in England and the United States since the 1930's. Its essential problems were recognized and its relevant theorems developed in the 1890's by Pareto.[6]

In formulating policy criteria, welfare economics takes explicit account of differences in individual preferences and incomes and of the resulting problems in aggregating individual utilities. It is an economic axiom that the marginal utility of individual income decreases with increasing income. There is no agreement among economists on whether and in what sense—ordinally or cardinally—individual utilities can be compared; but welfare criteria that avoid interpersonal comparisons are generally preferred.

Classical and neoclassical economists were well aware of these problems.[7] They, however, focused on an increase of real aggregate national income as the main criterion of economic welfare.[8] Pareto's views were not in conflict with this emphasis because he believed—supported by historical experience as he saw it—that an increase of national income and greater equality of income distribution tended to be associated. In this case an increase of national income means also an increase of economic welfare according to Pareto's criterion, at least under some generally accepted assumptions.

The positive correlation between changes of national income and of equality of income distribution—sometimes called "Pareto's law"—was challenged by Pigou[9] and others; but Pareto's welfare criterion is independent of his law. This does not imply that the correlation noted by Pareto does not exist, or that Pareto's criterion is of greater significance for economic theory than his law. Quite the contrary, one may wonder whether the great intellectual effort of the last thirty years which has been invested in developing Pareto's criterion might not have yielded greater dividends, in terms of knowledge as well as welfare, if it has been employed for further investigation of Pareto's law and of the problems associated with the increase of national income.

The Pareto criterion says that a change that makes at least one individual better off and leaves no individual worse off represents an increase of welfare. This criterion is usually interpreted to mean that welfare is increased by a change rendering it "possible" to make at least one individual better off and, by compensating the losers, to leave no individual worse off. Most of the discussion in the new welfare economics deals with this compensation principle.

The Pareto criterion "without" compensation is so restrictive that it has little relevance for an appraisal of public policies—even if it could be practically applied. There are scarcely any policies which make nobody worse off. Furthermore, if there were such policies, the criterion would be ineffective for choosing between different alternatives to the status quo. The Pareto criterion "with" compensation is not so restrictive, but its application is even less practical.

The Pareto "with" criterion is conceptually not identical with the criterion "increase of national income." But the latter criterion may be regarded as a practical, first approximation to the former, provided that the policy under consideration does not appreciably increase inequality of income distribution; and provided further that other policies in operation are working independently and continually in the direction of greater equality of income distribution. Such policies are, for example, progression in income and property taxes, high inheritance taxes, and social-welfare legislation in the narrower sense (relating to old age, invalidity, unemployment, minimum wages, public health, education, and so on). In some practically important cases, these two conditions can be regarded as fulfilled when considering natural-resource policies in modern western societies.

Accepting an increase of national income as an economic criterion for public water policy does not imply that application of this criterion faces no theoretical and practical difficulties, or that it is the most useful criterion under conditions where economic change and uncertainty are the central problems. We shall return to these problems in subsection *water policy and economic optima*.

The contribution of welfare economics has been a clarification of the theoretical meaning (or absence of it) of a social-welfare function and social-indifference curves and of the difficulties (or impossibility) of applying the Pareto criterion in actuality. The disservice of welfare economics has been that its terminology is used by economists and others without pointing out these theoretical and practical difficulties. The false impression is created that a simple criterion is available that can be used for legislation, court decisions, administrative regulation, and social planning in general.

Water policy and economic optima

After this sketch of the problems of welfare economics, we must now raise the question of the conceptual meaning of economic optima. Is it conceptually useful to make the maximization principle the basis of economic criteria for pursuing the public interest? Much has been written lately, both by economists and engineers, on the need for and the statistical procedures of "optimizing systems" in water-resources development.

The maximization principle is applied in normative economics, first as an efficiency criterion for limited operations under restrictive assumptions, and second, as the assumed over-all objective of individuals and groups.

As an efficiency criterion, the maximization principle is used, for example, in finding the optimum output under given cost and revenue functions and also in determining minimum costs for each output under given production functions and given price schedules of productive factors—that is, in determining a cost function. For these and similar purposes, the maximization principle is necessary. There can be no disagreement on the usefulness of such operations. One may call this application of the maximization principle "efficiency economics" or, more appropriately in some cases, "efficiency engineering."

If applied as the assumed over-all objective of individuals and groups, on the other hand, the maximization principle is a construct—a scientific fiction.[10] It is useful in economics, especially in modern western culture, if employed in connection with another construct—the "firm." Frequent references in recent economic literature to maxima of individual and social satisfaction indicate that the maximization principle is more and more applied as a fiction.

A fiction is permissible in science if its character is clearly understood. A fiction is a deliberate, conscious deviation from reality. A fiction, however, is not a hypothesis or theory. By itself, a fiction is not intended to be validated by testing with empirical evidence. But a scientific fiction should be useful as a stimulus for or as a part of hypotheses and theories which can be tested. Hence, the test of a scientific fiction is its conceptual usefulness, its expediency in understanding, explaining, and predicting reality. A fiction becomes mere dogma and, therefore, unscientific if its two characteristics— consciousness of its fictional nature and conceptual usefulness—are obliterated. In the history of science there are many examples of fictions changing into dogma.

One may wonder whether the maximization principle has sometimes become dogma in economics. There is increasing emphasis on techniques which facilitate greater numerical accuracy in the determination of optima for the firm. These same techniques are then used for maximizing social satisfaction of whole groups with no conceptual gain and at the expense of "assuming away" essential economic relations.

It was suggested in subsection *water policy and welfare economics* that under certain conditions an increase of national income may be accepted as a criterion for resource policies. The Pareto welfare criterion is suited only for ascertaining whether an increase of social welfare has occurred, but not for determining a maximum.

The criterion "increase of national income" can be employed in appraising water policies of more limited scope, for example, in appraising an individual water-development project or in deciding a particular controversy in water allocation. This is the approach of benefit-cost analysis.

Limitations on the applicability of the national-income criterion are imposed by a number of theoretical and practical difficulties. The quantities of goods and services making up the national income must be evaluated (weighted) in order to be aggregated. The weights used—market prices and unit values derived indirectly from prices and in other ways—are affected by income distribution and by the host of institutions which influence this distribution. Institutional and economic influences present difficulties in the following ways:

(1) Both value weights and quantities are affected by market form. The policies to be appraised may change income distribution and market form. Economists differentiate two principal market forms: pure competition and monopolistic conditions. The latter includes monopolistic competition, oligopoly, duopoly, monopoly, and the parallel phenomenon on the buyer's side, monopsonistic conditions. The term "workable competition" has recently become popular for the state of competition prevailing in most industries under United States law.

(2) An appraisal of policy deals with the future. Over a period of time, individual preferences and technology (both affecting value weights and quantities of national income) change, and these changes are uncertain. Again, the policies to be appraised affect these changes. Thus, one could scarcely have assumed a few years ago that technology

in the use of nuclear power and desalinization methods would have progressed enough to make it economically feasible to erect a huge desalinization plant in southern California; clearly, federal policies of encouraging research and peaceful uses of nuclear power have played a large role in these changes.

(3) Besides such "structural" changes, there are changes connected with economic fluctuations of various amplitude and duration. These, likewise, are related to the policies to be appraised.[11]

All these problems are of interest for benefit-cost analysis, input-output studies of the Leontieff type, and other systematic attempts at a quantitative economic appraisal of policy.

Practical approximations of a solution of some of these difficulties are possible but only under restrictive assumptions with respect to institutions, preferences, technology, and time periods. Frequently, these assumptions are not made explicit when public water-development projects are appraised through benefit-cost analysis, or when judicial decisions and arguments before the courts involve equity of water allocation and the interpretation of "reasonable" and "beneficial" water use.

For policies of broader scope, the restrictive assumptions needed for benefit-cost analysis become too burdensome. In appraising such policies, it is useful to employ as criteria their effects upon significant conditions which facilitate or impede an increase of national income rather than focus on such an increase itself. This approach to policy criteria relies heavily on economic theory but less on maximization. This approach is greatly interested in economic history and in relating one time period to another but not necessarily through increasing the number of variables and equations in mathematical models. This approach is especially suited for natural-resources policies and has been discussed in detail elsewhere.[12] An illustration for this approach in the area of immediate concern to this chapter is given in section *Implementation of Water Policy: Economic Criteria for Water Law*, below.

The emphasis of this approach is on minimum standards in resource use rather than on the optimum use; on establishing base levels rather than on locating peaks; on avoiding dead-end streets and on keeping direction rather than on computing the shortest distance; on mobility and adaptability of productive factors rather than on their optimum combinations; and on reducing institutional obstacles to water development rather than on maximum development.

This approach does not pretend to establish criteria for maximizing social satisfaction. But it offers effective direction signals for pursuing the public interest turn by turn.

Economic criteria and water institutions

Before discussing in detail some of these criteria and their application to water law (section *Implementation of water policy: economic criteria for water law*), a few words may be helpful about such application to water institutions in general.

It was stated in subsection *water policy and water projects* that water policy is concerned with the rules of the game. These rules, however, cannot be understood by taking them one by one and introducing them into an economic optimizing calculus as constraints. Rather, these rules are structured systems that function as wholes, each with a particular pattern of change over time. These systems can be studied in structure, functioning, and performance. They are created by men and can be modified through the legislative, the judiciary, and the executive branches of government, each with a different range over which such modifications can be accomplished.

The purpose of these systems is *not* to obtain quantitative optima of welfare at given points in time under given conditions projected for these points in time. Instead, their purpose is to maintain and to increase welfare continuously under constantly changing conditions that at any point in time can be projected only vaguely and are always uncertain with respect to actual occurrence.

It follows from their purpose that it is inadequate to appraise the performance of these systems by introducing arbitrary temporal cross-sections of them, either actual or hypothetical, as alternative combinations of constraints in a quantitative optimizing calculus. Performance can be appraised only by criteria applied to a whole system as it functions over time. Such criteria need not be pecuniary—as will be shown in section *implementation of water policy: economic criteria for water law*.

To put the foregoing in somewhat different terms, implementation of the objectives of water policy involves programming of water institutions rather than programming (in the technical sense of linear programming) of water resources themselves. Resources programming must be pragmatic; that is, it must regard institutions as means (tools) or as ends (objectives), depending on the purposes of the analysis.[13] In the analysis of water policy, water institutions must be regarded as means, and the criteria under discussion must be applied to them. Water allocation may serve as an illustration.

In the arid and semiarid regions in the United States and elsewhere, water allocation among uses and users has always been a policy problem under greatly changing conditions affecting the aggregate quantity of water and the quantitative relations between uses. In the beginning of water development—for example, in the gold-rush days in the mother-lode country of California—water allocation was such a problem when all uses, including agricultural, were small, but when industrial use—namely, hydraulic mining—was dominant. In present-day California, water allocation is such a problem even though other uses are a fraction of a quantitatively dominant agricultural use.[14] Since water allocation is always vital for societies in arid and semiarid regions, institutional arrangements have been developed which govern it. The result is an allocative system which cannot be understood in its structure, functioning, and performance by taking its legal provisions one by one.

In making an economic appraisal of the allocative performance of this system, one cannot be content with appraising quantitative allocation prevailing at a particular point of time. The purpose of the system is not to optimize water allocation in particular instants of time. What needs to be appraised is the direction and speed of reallocation. Incremental improvements in these respects are the main policy objectives. The first step toward such improvements is an understanding of the existing system and of the process of its change. Each state is a laboratory in which this system has developed and is still developing. When individual provisions are modified, such changes must be fitted into the whole system. If the system as a whole is judged inadequate, a better substitute must be offered. Only too often, criticism of water allocation at a particular point of time is voiced by economists without regard to the nature of the decision problems that water allocation poses for policy. Optimizing as a fictional construct is confused with an actual policy objective.

Implementation of Water Policy:
Economic Criteria for Water Law

A dichotomy of criteria

Among water institutions, water law is by far the most significant. No attempt can be made here to deal with all aspects of water law as a means of water policy. Our purpose is to illustrate the discussion of the preceding section through focusing on economic criteria which might be used to appraise the structure, the functioning, and the performance of water law in the implementation of water policy. As we know, such criteria must be applied to a whole system of law as it functions over time.

For our present purpose, we may differentiate between three such systems in the United States. First, in the eastern states, water rights are based on the riparian doctrine—with modifications in some states, as for example, North Carolina. Second, in the Great Basin and mountain states, water rights are based on appropriation. Third, around the fringes of this heartland of the appropriation doctrine, the prevailing system of water rights is a blend exhibiting features of both doctrines—although in secular perspective the appropriation doctrine appears in the ascendancy; this blend prevails in the Pacific Coast and the High Plains states.

In appraising these systems of water rights, a dichotomy of criteria is used. One criterion is exemplified by a set of concepts such as "security," "protection," and "rigidity" of water rights. The other criterion is represented by concepts like "flexibility," "adaptability," and "insecurity." No one familiar with the literature can fail to become impressed by the vagueness, plasticity, and contradiction which characterize the use of these concepts. An examination of their economic meaning is needed.

This dichotomy of criteria (security and flexibility) is applied jointly. In examining its application, one must explore the gradations on the logical axis between the two poles and the resulting compromise in institutional arrangements. But also one must examine the extent to which the two criteria can be applied together without such a compromise.

The consequences of institutional arrangements, if viewed over time, are complex. Applying a logical polarity to relations in reality does not always give a perfect "fit." Although it frequently happens—examples will be given in subsection *security of water rights*—that a change in institutional arrangements results in an increase in terms of one criterion and a decrease in terms of the other, this does not always happen. In other words, that the two criteria are at opposite poles logically does not preclude the possibility of a change in institutional arrangements that results in increases in terms of one criterion without change in terms of the other, or that results in increases or decreases in terms of both. In this and in other aspects, our dichotomy is similar to that of "order" and "freedom," which has occupied students of jurisprudence for a long time and is not being neglected by economists of quite different "schools."[15]

The two criteria imply a problem area which is one of the most important and difficult, both for economic theory and for policy; this is the problem area of economic change and dynamics versus statics in economic discourse. This area is also the one in which the relations between law and economics raise some of the most acute and baffling issues.[16] Thus, focusing on these two criteria brings us to the core of the main theme.

In examining concepts as criteria, we may repeat that the emphasis here is on functional relations in economics, not on legal history or on normative meanings in law. The significance of case law in this country is impressive— especially to one, as the present writer, who grew up in the legal climate of the Code Napoleon and its successors. But tracing historically the interpretation of economic concepts through the maze of case law is more a task for a student of law than for an economist. Likewise, it would be presumptuous for an economist to suggest how economic concepts should be interpreted in law.

The functional relations to be studied may be indicated by two closely connected questions. First, one may ask, what are the economic implications—in the sense of logical and probable factual consequences—if concepts used as criteria for water law are interpreted and applied in certain ways? Second, one may ask, how far and why are these implications helpful or obstructive if certain objectives are sought? The economic interpretations and objectives selected should, of course, have relevance for actual problems of water policy.

Although indicated by these questions, it may be well to point out explicitly at this time that the problem at hand will be viewed as one of positive rather than normative economics.[17] The consequences of this approach for the relations between economics and law will become apparent later.

Security of water rights

To the economist, "security" of water rights means something different and much broader than their "protection" means to the student of law. The latter concept merely means protection against *unlawful* acts by others—as such acts are construed by the law. Such protection is always subject to the two major categories of "legal uncertainty," that is, to "rule uncertainty" and to "fact uncertainty."[18] Legal uncertainty, in this sense, is a characteristic of judicial decisions. Like other types of uncertainty, it also affects economic decisions.

Economists are inclined to disregard or underestimate the significance of legal uncertainty. For them, security of a water right connotes (1) protection against what I propose to call "physical uncertainty," that is, against variability over time of the quantity of water usable under the right due to seasonal or annual variability of "natural" runoff and ground-water recharge, and (2) protection against what I shall call "uncertainty of water tenure"[19] or, for short, "tenure uncertainty," that is, protection against variability over time of the quantity of water usable under the right due to *lawful* acts of others— who may be individuals or groups, private or public.

We are concerned here with the relative degree of security resulting from different types of rights. Absolute security, that is, transformation of probabilities into single-valued expectations, cannot be obtained through water law. Furthermore, we are not concerned with the many other types of uncertainty which affect economic decisions—for example, uncertainties connected with variability over time of wants, technology, prices, and incomes. A few examples may illustrate differences between water rights if "security" is interpreted in the way just indicated.[20]

Under natural conditions a senior appropriative right is more secure than a junior appropriative right against physical uncertainty but not necessarily against tenure uncertainty; if there is a shortage of water, the owner of a senior right has a better chance of getting his share than the owner of a junior right, but the two are equally subject to prescription. A water right in a high-preference class is more secure than one in a low-preference class against tenure uncertainty but not necessarily against physical uncertainty. A water right in a high-preference class (such as domestic use) is more secure against physical uncertainty than one in a low-preference class (such as recreational use). A water right restricted by reservations in favor of other users (for example, a right for agricultural use that is subject to a reservation for future domestic use) is less secure than these other rights against tenure uncertainty but not against physical uncertainty.

An appropriative right is more secure against tenure uncertainty than is a riparian right or a ground-water right under the correlative-rights doctrine— assuming that only one system of rights applied to a water resource. Against physical uncertainty, however, an appropriative right is not necessarily more secure than a riparian or correlative right; this holds especially (but not solely) for a junior appropriative right.

In all these examples, the two main categories of legal uncertainty are also present. The degree of legal uncertainty may be quite different for different water-right systems and individual water rights. It is meaningful, however, to proceed "as if" the degree of legal uncertainty were approximately the same.

If one speaks of "quantity of water usable" under a water right, one implies certain characteristics with respect to water quality. Over time, water quality is also subject to legal, physical, and tenure uncertainties. When water rights are defined in quantitative terms—as under appropriation and through adjudication under the riparian and correlative rights doctrine—reference should always be made to water quality.

Security of water rights in terms of quality is no less significant economically than security in terms of quantity. Frequently, the higher water uses—in terms of value product—require a higher quality of water than the lower uses. Furthermore, quality and quantity are directly interrelated in that water of high quality—in terms of low mineral content, especially sodium and sulphates—can be reused, sometimes for more than one cycle. Such water can also be used to upgrade surface and ground water of low quality which could otherwise be used only for lower uses or not at all.

These interrelations of quality and quantity are especially significant when water must be transported over great distances. Such transport may be economically feasible only for high-quality water. It follows, from the interrelations of quantity and quality just explained, that in setting minimum standards for water quality, problems of reuse of the same water and upgrading of other waters need to be considered. Minimum standards based on suitability for one cycle of direct ("unmixed") use alone may be, economically speaking, too lenient.

Sometimes the only security of water rights in terms of quality is their protection against unlawful acts of water pollution (including contamination and nuisance). In many states, antipollution laws are being strengthened. More federal action is also being considered. Dealing specifically with the economics of water quality would lead us too far afield.[21]

Physical uncertainty can be significantly reduced through physical means, mainly through storage of water—above *and* below ground—from season to season, from year to year, and over a period of years. A reduction of physical uncertainty in this sense produces benefits for water users and others. Whether these benefits are "net" depends on the costs of constructing, maintaining, and managing storage.

A system of water rights may impede construction of storage facilities by limiting development to a vaguely defined "safe yield" of a water resource and by making cyclical management of storage capacity and co-ordination of surface and subsurface storage more difficult.

The appropriation doctrine can easily be used to limit water development. In several western states this doctrine has actually been used with this objective and result in the case of ground water.[22] With respect to surface water, the actual facts are somewhat different. Most western surface waters are over-appropriated. Sometimes, appropriation covers a multiple of the average flow during the season of use.

After storage capacity has been provided and is managed with a view to reducing physical uncertainty, the relative economic status of appropriative rights changes without changes in their relative legal status. Priority in time, in conjunction with the quantitative definition of appropriative rights, limits the number of rights that can be served with the regulated flow. Rights exceeding this flow become, economically speaking, less meaningful the better the flow is regulated. For rights that can be served with the regulated flow, the new situation, in terms of economics, is not greatly different from that prevailing under a water-delivery contract where a limited number of users are equal in right—although the quantities to which their contract entitles them may differ.

With the development of storage facilities, the differentiation of water rights, so characteristic of the appropriation doctrine, has undergone a shift in its economic implications: Within limits a junior right is no longer less secure against physical uncertainty than is a senior right. Increasingly, storage is provided by large public or semipublic projects and managed by government agencies—public districts, state water departments and boards, and federal bureaus.

In contrast to appropriation rights, riparian rights are coequal in law.[23] An economic implication of this equality is that the legal status of riparian rights is not a cause for differentiation with respect to their security against physical uncertainty. This holds both for the riparian right to surface water, as it is generally applied in the eastern states, and for the application of the riparian right to ground water through the correlative-rights doctrine as, for example, in California.

This lack of differentiation on the basis of legal status does not necessarily mean that there are no differences between individual riparian or correlative rights in security against physical uncertainty. Applying legal equality through adjudication to a given stream system or ground-water basin is a time-consuming and costly process. For a while, at least, individual riparian and correlative rights may differ in security against physical uncertainty. Such differences are caused not by legal differentiation but by physical facts such as relative location of diversions along a surface stream or the location of wells with respect to the source of recharge and to the geologic characteristics of a ground-water basin.

Differences between individual water rights (and between water-right systems where they exist side-by-side in the same general area) in security against physical uncertainty may obstruct or retard construction and co-ordinated cyclical management of storage. Individuals and groups who have greater security may be reluctant to join those who have not if they must bear a portion of the costs of reducing physical uncertainty. Thus, the holder of a senior appropriation right on a year-round stream may not expect to suffer during dry years and, hence, may be unwilling to share the cost of building storage facilities.

Turning now to security of water rights against tenure uncertainty, it was mentioned earlier that appropriative rights are more secure in this respect than riparian rights or groundwater rights under the correlative-rights doctrine. Appropriative rights are clearly defined in priority, quantity, period of use, points of diversion, and in other ways. Riparian and similar rights are coequal, and quantitative definition depends on adjudication; this adjudication is in terms of shares and subject to the restriction that there shall be reapportionment if the conditions upon which the original apportionment was made change sufficiently to justify it.

There are, however, several factors which modify such a general comparison of water-right systems. The first factor is prescription, which operates under all water-right systems—with some differences in economic significance as shown below. The second factor is differentiation of preference classes based on purpose (kind and type) of water use. This factor also operates under all water-right systems but under appropriation only *before* rights are vested and under emergencies. Customary preference classes are "natural" and "artificial" under the riparian doctrine and "domestic," "municipal," "industrial," "agricultural," and "recreational" under appropriation. The third factor is a restriction (reservation) on water rights to yield to future water demands by others. This factor operates only under appropriation and affects future (not already vested) rights. Water reservations are frequently used in favor of certain preference classes. But the connection with preference classes is not a necessary one. In California, water reservations in favor of whole regions are in force regardless of preference class.

There can be little argument, on economic or any other grounds, with the proposition that domestic and municipal uses deserve special consideration as far as security against tenure uncertainty is concerned. This type of use can frequently prevail over other uses by eminent-domain proceedings. Still, the highest preference ranking and water reservations in favor of this use are desirable because other uses, for example agricultural use, may also be organized as public districts. By adequate requirements for the treatment of sewage, domestic and municipal use can be made largely nonconsumptive. Agricultural use, on the other hand, is largely consumptive.

An economic argument can be made in favor of abolishing the usually lower preference rating of industrial uses relative to agricultural use. The average value product of consumptive use is higher in industry than in agriculture. Furthermore, in the western states total consumptive use in industry—although increasing—is still relatively small as compared with that in agriculture.

In ascertaining the value product of recreational uses—which are largely nonconsumptive—one faces the difficult problem of extramarket values. There are cases, however, in which the economic argument suggests a change in the present preference ranking of recreational uses. Generally, this ranking is the lowest. Under some statutes, recreational uses are not even recognized as "reasonable and beneficial."

In spite of the existence of a favorable economic argument for abolishing the usual statutory raking of industrial and agricultural uses and for other changes in preference classifications, inferences with respect to water policy would be premature without considering the criterion of flexibility jointly with that of security. The economic implications of water reservations likewise cannot be fully appraised without considering the criterion of flexibility. An interpretation of this criterion will be undertaken in subsection *flexibility of water rights*. Before this can be done, our interpretation of security of water rights must be related to "protection of investment" in water-resources development.

Security of water rights and protection of investment

The relations between security of water rights and investment in water-resources development are generally the main point of emphasis when the economic implications of differences in individual water rights and whole water-right systems are discussed. This emphasis is justified. Most economic implications of security are in this area.

In economic theory, "investment" and its corollary "disinvestment" refer to value changes in total capital of individuals or whole social groups as a result of differences between income and consumption. This is not what is meant here. In the present context, "investment" refers to what the economist would call the value of particular durable physical assets.[26] This value depends on the flow of net income which the assets are expected to yield over time.[27] Assets are described in terms of the present; the future income flow which determines their value is subject to a time discount and an allowance for uncertainty. Thus, we are concerned here with the protection against physical and tenure uncertainties to which this income flow is subject. The degree of such protection differs greatly for water rights with different security—as explained.

At first glance, it might be expected that, other things being equal, a greater or smaller security of water rights will result in an increase or decrease of investment (that is, value of durable assets) in water-resources development. This inference needs some scrutiny.

Frequently a greater degree of security for some water rights necessarily entails a smaller degree of security for other rights. For example, dividing appropriative rights on a given surface stream into senior and junior rights increases security against physical uncertainty for the senior but decreases it for the junior. If a certain type of use such as municipal use receives a higher-preference ranking than another such as agricultural use, or if the rights of the lower-preference use are restricted by water reservations in favor in a higher-preference use, security against tenure uncertainty is increased for water rights held under the higher preference but decreased for rights held under the lower preference. It may be valid to say that *individual* investment (value of durable assets) is increased or decreased by this increase or decrease in security against tenure uncertainty in this situation. But this principle should not be applied to *aggregate* investment in water-resources development of a given surface stream, ground-water basin, or region. From the standpoint of public water policy, such aggregates of investment are important.

The statement was made above that generally (that is, without taking account of modification through prescription, preferences, reservations, and physical factors) appropriative rights give greater security against tenure uncertainty than do riparian and correlative rights. This comparison refers to all water rights on a surface stream, in a ground-water basin, or in a region. In this case, therefore, the inference that investment varies in relation to tenure security is valid for aggregates of investment. This justifies the conclusion that the appropriation doctrine favors investment in water-resources development as compared with the riparian and correlative-rights doctrines. One should keep in mind, however, that only protection against tenure uncertainty in the defined sense is involved.

When one compares different water rights and water-right systems in terms of implications for investment, one touches on aspects of the concept "adequate compensation." This occurs, for example, if the degree of protection against tenure uncertainty is affected by prescription, preferences, and reservations. Prescription does not involve compensation according to law. Preferences and reservations involve compensation under some laws but not under others.[28] Regardless of the legal aspects, one may raise the question whether and under what conditions compensation might be considered in public policy as a problem of economics.

Let us assume that a municipality holds a reservation on the flow of a surface stream but will not need the water for twenty years. During this period the water is available for temporary appropriation by other users. Let us assume that the only alternative use is agricultural. Let us assume further that such use involves considerable expenditure for diversion and storage dams, main canals, a distribution system, land leveling, and other durable improvements. A private user will make these expenditures only if they seem warranted by the income flow that the durable assets are expected to yield. From the standpoint of the private user, the duration of the income flow is uncertain because of the nature of his tenure. Under these conditions, the expenditure may not be forthcoming, and the water may go unutilized for twenty years.

In such a situation a guarantee of compensation for nonrecovery of expenditures (because of termination of water tenure) plus a sufficient profit margin would offset the reservation's deterrent effect on private development of the available water on a temporary basis. Whether "protection of investment" in this sense would be economically warranted from the standpoint of public water policy is not self-evident but can be ascertained by benefit-cost analysis.[29]

In such an analysis some benefits are considered which the private user must leave out of account. Such benefits may, for example, result from flood control or ground-water recharge. Benefits yielded after twenty years are also considered. For example, dams and other facilities may be usable by the municipality although it may not be legally required to pay for them. Further, some costs of construction which the private user must consider appear smaller in benefit-cost analysis—for example, labor costs of construction in a period of unemployment under sticky wage rates.

The foregoing argument in favor of "protection of investment" in water-resources development in based on two necessary conditions: (1) that expenditures for durable assets are in the public interest although they may not be economical for private water users, and (2) that the most economical alternative for public policy to develop water resources is a guarantee just sufficient to induce private development. There is no implication in this argument that "protection of investment" per se is in the public interest.

Flexibility of water rights

In interpreting flexibility of water rights one thinks first of all of "legal flexibility." This is a corollary to "legal uncertainty," the two main categories of which were mentioned in the first paragraph of subsection *security of water rights*.

Legal uncertainty may be regarded as the price that must be paid for obtaining legal flexibility. There has been considerable discussion within the legal profession on whether the product—a law responsive to the needs of the community—stands in fair relation to its price. During the twentieth century, the trend in legal thinking has been to answer this question in the affirmative. To be sure, there are differences among prominent legal thinkers with respect to the desirable degree of flexibility in particular areas of law—such as property rights; but all (including non-American jurists) agree that flexibility is necessary and that the American development of the Anglo-Saxon common law is better suited than other legal systems for approaching the most desirable degree of flexibility through trial and error and step by step. Within jurisprudence the degree of flexibility at a given time and place will remain the subject of perpetual discussion, reappraisal, shifting of emphasis, and ambivalent attitudes. Far from being a weakness, such a condition would appear normal or even necessary for an effective contribution by the law to "social engineering"—to use a term popular with Roscoe Pound[30] and more recent writers.

Within economics we are concerned not so much with legal flexibility as with the needs themselves to which the law responds. In economics, therefore, the interpretation of "flexibility of water rights" differs from that of "flexibility of water law" as discussed in jurisprudence and an increase in flexibility of water rights is not necessarily incompatible with an increase in their security—as stated earlier. The needs of particular interest in connection with flexibility of water rights are created by economic change.

The impact of economic change upon water use may be divided conceptually into two parts—which in reality, and for water policy, are not independent: (1) a change in aggregate development of water resources within a region (country, state, watershed, and ground-water basin), and (2) a change in allocation of water resources between regions, uses (municipal, agricultural, industrial, and recreational), and users (individuals, firms, public districts, and government agencies). The criterion "security of water rights" is significant for the change in aggregate development—as discussed in subsections *security of water rights* and *security of water rights and protection of investment*. The criterion, "flexibility of water rights," as interpreted here, focuses on those aspects of water rights which facilitate or obstruct changes over time in the allocation of water resources between regions, uses, and users. Several such aspects must be considered.

There is first the "transferability" of water rights. Water rights like other property rights, can be transferred in various ways. Voluntary transfer of water rights through buying and selling—with land if they are "appurtenant" or without land if they are not—is not uncommon. Appropriative rights are better suited for such transfer than riparian rights because appropriative rights are clearly defined in quantity, priority, points of diversion, and other ways. Transfer of riparian and correlative rights generally requires also transfer of land.[31] Furthermore, these rights are not clearly defined quantitatively and are insecure against physical and tenure uncertainties. With respect to transferability, therefore, the appropriation doctrine favors flexibility of water rights in the course of economic change.

Involuntary transfer may, first of all, be accomplished through condemnation for public use. This process, by constitutional provision, involves compensation. Appropriative rights are better suited for this process than riparian and correlative rights for the reasons mentioned in connection with voluntary transfer. Furthermore, it is usually sufficient to condemn only a few appropriative rights with high priority. Under the riparian doctrine it is frequently necessary to condemn *all* riparian rights. In this comparison, we assume of course that only one system of rights applies to a water resource.

Second, involuntary transfer can be accomplished through prescription. This process of transfer does not involve compensation. Prescription operates under all water-right systems; but there are differences in its economic significance under various systems.[32] Prescription takes time—from three to twenty years, depending on the statute of limitations—to ripen into a vested prescriptive right. Adverse and open beneficial use, the condition for prescription, is more likely to persist unobjected to for such a period against downstream riparian rights and correlative rights than against appropriative rights. A prescriptive right can in turn be lost through prescription by others. Prescription, therefore, is not irreversible but a potentially always present and economically interesting process of transfer.

Abandonment and forfeiture of water rights—operating only under appropriation—may also be regarded as processes of transfer. Their present over-all significance for flexibility of water rights is minor. However, through defining conditions of forfeiture—for example, through legislative, judicial, and executive defining and redefining of "beneficial" use—the economic significance of this process could be increased.

Voluntary and involuntary transfer of water rights is only one aspect of flexibility. There is fairly general agreement that, aside from the aspect of transferability, a water-right system based on the riparian and correlative rights doctrines contains elements of greater flexibility than does a system based on appropriation. Under the riparian doctrine, new uses created by economic change compete on an equal legal basis with older uses and obtain rights that are no less secure against physical uncertainty than older rights. This is a corollary to the tenure uncertainty so characteristic of riparian and correlative rights. Under the appropriation doctrine, on the other hand, new uses can obtain only inferior rights in terms of security against physical uncertainty. As just noted, however, the economic significance of such flexibility, inherent in riparian and correlative rights, is reduced over time for a given region through prescription.

Preferences and reservations are important for flexibility because of their obstructive influence. They tend to continue into the future the favorable treatment of certain uses or users on the basis of present economic conditions. Preferences and reservations do not obstruct all growth; quite the contrary, they are designed to facilitate growth. They facilitate, however, only the growth of that use which is deemed to deserve preferential treatment on the basis of present economic conditions; they obstruct the growth of other uses.

Economic change may well require a change in the ranking of uses. As already suggested, preferential treatment is unobjectionable for domestic and municipal uses. On the other hand, extension of preferences to other uses—for example, in favor of agricultural against industrial—or extension of reservations to all users of one region against users of another—for example, in favor of counties and watersheds of "origin" against those of "destination"[33]—obstructs changes over time in the allocation of water resources.

The aspects of flexibility discussed so far relate to statutory water law. It would be a serious mistake to overlook the great significance of case law for flexibility. There is considerable scope to the judicial development of water law through decisions in individual cases of controversy. Concepts like "reasonable" and "beneficial" use, "waste," "surplus" of water, "maximum utilization" are interpreted and reinterpreted by the courts continuously in the light of changing economic conditions. Over time, the result has frequently been a change in the allocation of water resources between uses and, through it, between users.

Besides taking economic change into account in deciding controversies, the courts are directly concerned with the transfer of water rights through eminent domain. Condemnation of water rights for public use is well established in all states. Going much further than that, the state of Washington permits any person to condemn a lower water use for a higher use.[34] For this purpose any beneficial use is declared to be a public use. The courts determine which use is higher.

Under the American form of government, the contribution of flexibility by the executive branch of government is probably smaller than that of the legislative and the judiciary because of the constitutional restrictions on delegation of power. In some states, however, the executive agency charged with the administration of water-appropriation statutes is given considerable discretion in granting and conditioning appropriation permits. Such discretion has been upheld by the courts.[35]

Conclusions regarding the relations between law and economics in the implementation of water policy

The preceding subsections of this section attempted to show in what sense security and flexibility can be regarded as economic criteria for the structure, the functioning, and the performance of water law in the implementation of water policy. Both criteria relate to significant conditions which facilitate or impede an increase of national income in a world of persistent but uncertain change. It was suggested in subsection *economic criteria and water institutions* that criteria of this type are best suited for the implementation of public policies of a broader scope — such as water policy.

It was shown that the security criterion is especially significant for the performance of those portions of water law that are concerned with water development. The same holds for the flexibility criterion in the area of water allocation. We also saw that the logical polarity of these criteria does not necessarily imply that they are competitive if applied in an economically meaningful way. This is a corollary of the economic interdependence of policies concerned with water development and those concerned with water allocation (subsection *definition f terms*).

The criteria of security and flexibility were studied because they seemed especially suited for a socioeconomic appraisal of water law. No claim is made here that the same criteria would be especially suited for the appraisal of other social institutions. It is quite possible, however, that further study will show that the same criteria are meaningful in the appraisal of other institutions as well.

What are the conclusions from this for the relations of law and economics — taken as two important social-science disciplines — in the implementation of water policy? A great deal is being written on the "integration" of law and economics. If by this term it is meant that students in the two disciplines need greater understanding for each other's problems, tools, and limitations, one can wholeheartedly agree. If it is suggested by this term that concepts and processes of concept formation employed by economists should be transplanted to law (and vice versa), the prospective benefits would seem dubious. On the other hand, emphasis on the functional relations of concepts used as economic criteria for water law may help in clarifying areas of co-operation and in pointing out some limitations and potentialities.

Economics cannot define social optima which the law — as "social engineering' '—should aim to realize. What economics can do, however, is to explain why and how far certain conditions, which are decisively influenced by the law, facilitate or impede an increase of national income. Economics can point out the essential features of conflict situations and the probable consequences of changes in statutory provisions, judicial decisions, and administrative regulations. Sometimes these consequences can be shown in quantitative terms under restrictive assumptions. More often the consequences can be indicated merely in terms of direction and in terms of relative magnitudes and rates of change.

Economics need not be passive in fulfilling this function. Frequently, a conflict situation can be identified in economic terms before it has arisen in law as a controversy. After it has arisen as a controversy, the essential economic features may not be clear to the contestants themselves.

A first, but necessary, step toward implementing such a relation between economics and law is mutual understanding with respect to the interpretation and application of key concepts used as economic criteria. In the area of water law, such concepts are security and flexibility of water rights.

To such an understanding, both normative and positive economics can make a contribution. If a value judgment is permitted, one may add that the contribution of positive economics has been far greater, and this will probably hold also in the future. The law, on the other hand, is essentially a normative discipline. But in spite of—or possibly because of—differences in basic orientation, positive economics and law have many complementary relations. To explore and to strengthen these relations will benefit both social-science disciplines.

[1]*Waters and Water Law in the United States*, ed. Robert Emmet Clark (Chicago: Allen Smith and Co., 1967) pp. 397–430.

[2]Within the limitation of a single chapter, only a beginning in the diretion of this and the following two objectives can be made. A more detailed discussion of water economics has been presented in earlier publications. Some of these are mentioned in footnotes. The present chapter draws heavily on the author's "Water Policy," in *Handbook of Applied Hydrology: A Compendium of Water-Resources Technology,*, pp. 28-1 to 28-25 (Ven Te Chow, editor-in-chief, 1964); and "Concepts Used as Economic Criteria for a System of Water Rights," in *The Law of Water Allocation in the Eastern United States*, pp. 531-552 (Haber and Bergen, editors, The Ronald Press Company, New York, 1958).

[3]For an explanation of these terms, see Ciriacy-Wantrup, Economics of Joint Costs in Agriculture, 23 J. Farm Economics 771 (1941).

[4]For sources and statistical methodology concerning these data, see Ciriacy-Wantrup, "Conceptual Problems in Projecting the Demand for Land and Water," in *Modern Land Policy*, ch. 3 (Halcrow, ed., 1960). (Chapter 9 in this book).

[5]Computed from data given in United States Congress, Senate Select Committee on National Water Resources, Water Resources Activities in the United States: Future Needs for Reclamation in the Western States, Committee Print No. 14, 86th Congress, 2d Sess., 1960, pursuant to S. Res. 48.

[6]Vilfredo Pareto, *Cours de Economique Politique,* F. Route, Libraire-Editeur, Lausanne, 1897. An excellent bibliography of welfare economics is appended to Mishan, A Survey of Welfare Economics, 1939-1959, 70 Economic Journal 197 (No. 278, June 1960).

[7]The first edition of Alfred Marshall's *Principles of Economics* appeared in 1890, seven years before publication of Pareto's main work in French. Marshall mentions Pareto only in passing and in a different connection.

[8]When comparing national income at different points of time and for

different countries, per capita figures are used. In appraising alternative policies, it is more useful to focus on aggregate income.

[9]A. C. Pigou, *The Economics of Welfare* (London, Macmillan & Company, Ltd., 1939).

[10]Next to mathematics and law, economics is the discipline in which scientific fiction is most common. But the natural sciences, especially modern physics, frequently employ fictions.

[11]For a detailed discussion on the relations between economic fluctuations and resource development, see Ciriacy-Wantrup, Resource Conservation and Economic Stability, 60 Q. J. Economics 412 (1946).

[12]Ciriacy-Wantrup, *Resource Conservation: Economics and Policies* (2d ed. rev., 1963).

[13]On the schism between "orthodox" and "pragmatic" attitudes toward institutions, see Sargent, A Methodological Schism in Agricultural Economics, 8 Canadian J. Agric. Econ. 45 (No. 2, 1960).

[14]For comparing different uses quantitatively, two factors are frequently not sufficiently considered: (1) whether conveyance losses are included or excluded for agricultural use, and (2) whether water use by steam-electric plants—the quantitatively most significant one among industrial uses—is included in or excluded from industrial use. In California, for example, agricultural use is 87%, industrial use 5%, and domestic use 8% of total use, if conveyance losses are included and steam-electric plants are excluded. If conveyance losses are excluded and steam-electric plants are included, agricultural use is 67%, industrial use 25%, and domestic 8%. In terms of water consumption, the first method gives a more appropriate comparison, provided that double counting is avoided (some conveyance losses are used via ground water and counted then). On the other hand, there is considrable interfirm reuse of water both in agricultural and in industrial use. The quantitative extent of such reuse is not known. Steam-electric plants use, largely, cooling water that is not usable for other purposes and, in any event, is not consumed. Potentially, of course, most domestic use can be made nonconsumptive.

[15]Commons, *Institutional Economics* (1934); Knight, *The Economic Organization* (1951) and *Freedom and Reform* (1947); and Robbins, "Freedom and Order," *Economics and Public Policy*, Brookings Lectures, pp. 131-157 (The Brookings Institution, Wash. D.C., 1955).

[16]Ciriacy-Wantrup, Some Economic Issues in Water Rights, 38 J. Farm Economics 875-885 (1955).

[17]For a discussion of this differentiation, see Friedman, *Essays in Positive Economics* (1953).

[18]This terminology has been popularized by Frank. See Frank, *The Law and the Modern Mind* (6th ed., 1948).

[19]Tenure uncertainty is not confined to water—and other "fugitive" resources—but is one of the most important economic forces affecting resource use. See Ciriacy-Wantrup, Capital Returns from Soil-Conservation Practices, 29 J. Farm Economics 1181 (1947).

[20]For these examples, one assumes, of course, "other things being equal";

that means in this case physical conditions and legal features other than those under consideration being the same.

[21]Ciriacy-Wantrup, Water Quality, A Problem for the Economist, 43 J. Farm Economics 1133 (1961). (Chapter 7 in this book).

[22]For illustrations, see Ciriacy-Wantrup, Some Economic Issues in Water Rights, 37 J. Farm Economics 875 (1955).

[23]They are coequal within the two traditional preference classes of "natural" and "artificial" uses—except that an upstream user need not share with downstream users if the flow of the stream is only sufficient to satisfy his own natural uses.

[24]Significant exceptions occur, for example, in Texas.

[25]We are using the word "average" because each of the two preference classes covers water development by different users for different products in different time intervals. In the present context, we refer, of course, to future "additional" water development. A change in preference classification does not affect already vested appropriative rights. Under the riparian doctrine, industrial and agricultural uses are both "artificial" and, therefore, coequal.

[26]One may differentiate between three forms of assets: (1) physical assets (natural resources, improvements, equipment, and inventories); (2) money assets (securities, loans, and cash); and (3) personal assets (labor, skills, and "goodwill" of the individuals or groups who hold assets).

[27]The resale or "scrap" value of durable physical assets at the time they are sold or scrapped may be formally included in this flow.

[28]The constitutions of Idaho and Nebraska grant preferences in time of scarcity of water, first to domestic uses, second to agriculture, but make exercise of the right contingent on payment of compensation. The Colorado Constitution grants similar preferences without mention of compensation but the Colorado Supreme Court has held that, despite that provision, full compensation is required. Statutes of Oregon and Utah give similar preferences in time of scarcity without mention of compensation. In Texas, reservation does not involve compensation, although there is a difference of opinion as to the validity of the statute granting blanket reservations to municipalities. In California, a municipality holding a reservation must compensate the temporary appropriator. For these and other differences in state laws, see Hutchins, *Selected Problems in Western Water Law,* Dept. Agric. Misc. Pub. No. 418, especially pages 337-358 (1942).

[29]Ciriacy-Wantrup, Benefit-Cost Analysis and Public Resource Development, 37 J. Farm Economics 677 (1955). (Chapter 8 in this book).

[30]Roscoe Pound, *The Spirit of the Common Law* (1921).

[31]Riparian rights may be waived by a grant to nonriparians. Such grant is not effective against other riparians and is not really a transfer of the riparian right. But from the economic standpoint, it is just as effective. It frequently happens that riparian rights are bought up or condemned.

[32]The differences suggested here do not involve the legal problem of whether or not a prescriptive title "good against the world" can be established without the necessity of valid statutory appropriation. For different conclusions

on this point, see Kletzing, Prescriptive Water Rights in California: Is Application a Prerequisite?, 39 Calif. L. Rev. 369 (1951); Trowbridge, Prescriptive Water Rights in California: An Addendum, 39 Calif. L. Rev. 525 (1951); and Craig, Prescriptive Water Rights in California and the Necessity for a Valid Statutory Appropriation, 42 Calif. L. Rev. 219 (1954).

[33]Cal. Water Code, 10505. 11460. See also Ciriacy-Wantrup, Some Economic Issues in Water Rights, 37 J. Farm Economics 875 (1955).

[34]Wash. Rev. Code, @90.03.040.

[35]Sections 1253 and 1254 of the California Water Code provide that the department of public works shall allow appropriations under terms and conditions which "in its judgment" will best serve the public interest in water conservation. However, in acting upon applications the department shall be guided by the policy that domestic use of water is highest and irrigation next highest. The California Supreme Court, in East Bay Municipal Utility Dist. v. Department of Public Works, 1 Cal. 2d 476, 479, 35 P.2d 1027 (1934), upheld the action of the state agency in inserting in a permit, pursuant to these statutory provisions, the following condition: "The right to store and use water for power purposes under this permit shall not interfere with future appropriations of said water for agricultural or municipal purposes." In a more recent decision, Temescal Water Co. v. Department of Public Works, 44 Cal. 2d 90, 99, 280 P2d. 1 (1955), the court held that the cumulative effect of statutory changes had been to create a type of proceeding greatly different from that considered in some earlier decisions. In carrying out its present duty, held the court, the department of public works exercises a broad discretion in determining whether the issuance of a permit will best serve the public interest. That determination requires an administrative adjudication. If issuance of the permit is protested as the statute authorizes, the administrative decision may be made only after a hearing of the protest. The decision is subject to judicial review by way of writ of mandate. These two decisions were called to my attention by Wells A. Hutchins.

Chapter 6

PHILOSOPHY AND OBJECTIVES
OF WATERSHED POLICY*

The Watershed as a Unit in the Social Sciences

Having no claims to the status of philosopher—being a mere economist—I have puzzled a little about my assignment. I propose to focus on some of the essential concepts and principles that underlie the economics of watershed development and that need to be considered in public policy. Consequently, a number of topics are touched upon which will be treated more thoroughly in subsequent parts of this volume.

A watershed has clear conceptual unity in hydrology, physical geography, and other natural sciences.[1] It is not self-evident that, as a corollary, a watershed is a logical unit in a social-science context. There are many examples when rivers and swampy valleys have been barriers to social intercourse rather than arteries of communication. Frequently the upstream part of a watershed is occupied by a social group different from the one occupying the downstream part, and political boundaries bisect watersheds at the piedmont zone. In some parts of the world, the struggle between lowland people and mountain people has continued for centuries.

As a proposition, one may submit that the watershed has emerged rather recently in the social sciences as a unit of understanding and policy-making. This emergence appears connected with technological change and with shifting demands for the main products of a watershed in the course of economic development.

A most significant technological change was the discovery of large-scale uses for electric energy and of the role of falling water and producing such energy. A second change was the invention—or, possibly, rediscovery—of concrete and of its reinforcement through steel rods. These two changes made high dams both technologically possible and economically feasible. The experience with the construction of high concrete dams, together with

*Reprinted, with permission, from *Economics of Watershed Planning*, Eds. G. S. Tolley and F. E. Riggs, (Ames: Iowa State Univ. Press, 1961), pp. 1-14.

the development of large earth-moving machines, led to the use of high earth-filled dams where they were cheaper or more suitable—for example, in earthquake areas—than concrete dams. All these technological changes took place during the last quarter of the nineteenth and the first quarter of the twentieth centuries. During the same period the demand for the main products of a watershed—hydroelectric power, water, timber, livestock, agricultural crops, and recreation—increased greatly. This increase in turn gave new significance to the control of floods, to soil erosion, to sedimentation of reservoirs and canals, to salinity, and to drainage—in other words, to the pervasive problems of water-quality, in contrast to water-quantity, management. Water-quality management becomes increasingly important as the demand for products of watersheds increases. This is a special case of the over-all problem of waste disposal when a population of organisms increases in size and density. The atomic age will pose this problem on a gigantic scale. These physical and economic interrelations force consideration of the watershed as a unit in economic understanding and policy.

From this sketch of the emergence of the watershed as a concept in the social sciences, two conclusions may be drawn.

First, the physical and economic interrelations that make the watershed a unit in the social sciences operate largely on the side of production and not on the side of consumption. Consumption of the products of a watershed may largely take place outside of it, and such consumption need not be interrelated. To regard a watershed as a unit in consumption is not required by the physical and economic interrelations just observed. Policies based on this misconception may hinder rather than facilitate watershed development. Let me give a few illustrations.

Important parts of water law implicitly regard the watershed as a unit in the use and consumption of water. The riparian doctrine, in contrast to the appropriation doctrine, is generally opposed to water export from the watershed in which the water originates. Ground-water laws in many states and the areas- and counties-of-origin laws in California permit water export only as long as it can be regarded as "surplus" water. The California laws require a reservation of all potential future water requirements for the watershed.[2] Sometimes it is claimed that the watershed should have the first rights to the hydroelectric energy that is produced within it boundaries.

My second conclusion is that a watershed as a helpful conceptual unit in the social sciences is not immutable. It is a concept of economic dynamics and not of statics. By dynamics I do not mean reference to time merely by dating, but an explicit consideration of changes in technology, preferences, and institutions. In the same way that the concept of a watershed has emerged in the social sciences in the course of technological and general economic change, so its significance may well be affected by similar changes in the future. A presently forseeable technological change that may have such results in artificial modification of precipitation. In weather-making, a single watershed may not be an appropriate unit for understanding and policy-making. The boundaries of individual watersheds, which may be different for surface and ground water, change over time through geologic forces and drastic action by man.

It may be objected that the self-sufficient irrigation cultures that have existed during long periods of history prove the watershed concept to be of early origin, to be static over time, and to include interrelations in consumption as well as production. However, existing knowledge about the early irrigation cultures tends to confirm my proposition and conclusions. In these cultures the modern watershed concept did not exist, and this absence may well be related to some of the difficulties they encountered.

The early irrigation cultures were located in the alluvial plains of major river basins. They relied on periodic flooding and low diversion dams. While levees and water distribution systems were highly developed, high storage dams and upstream water management—especially quality management such as silt control, salinity control, and drainage—were absent. Physical difficulties caused by this absence were not the only ones. The actual destruction of some irrigation cultures was caused by military attack from outside. But such an attack came generally from the less civilized people, the "barbarians," in the upper watershed, attracted by relatively high economic development downstream. In this sense, one may regard the attacks as a consequence of the absence of economic and political unity in the watershed.

Watershed Policy and Watershed Projects

When tracing the emergence of the watershed as a unit in the social sciences, I referred to public policy rather than public projects. The difference between watershed policy and watershed projects is not merely semantic. The economics of watershed projects, including benefit-cost analysis and other quantitative techniques for evaluating projects, comprises only a segment—and sometimes only a small segment—of the economics of watershed policy. In such project analyses, significant aspects of watershed policy are mentioned, if at all, as "institutional constraints." I submit that variation of the constraints should be one of the most important parts of the economics of watershed development. In other words, are the constraints to be *means to* or *obstacles to* social welfare?

In modern Western society, watershed development is accomplished largely through decentralized decision-making of many individual agents, both private and public. The public agents are, for example, flood control, drainage, irrigation, and conservation districts; municipalities; also federal and state forests. The private agents range from small subsistence farms to large commercial forest holdings, public utilities, and industrial corporations. These agents are subsectors in organizing and operating Western economies.

The "rules of the game" under which subsectors make decisions become operational largely through property institutions and the price system. These two systems are, therefore, of special interest in the social sciences. The ground rules and their continuous adjustment are the domain of policy decisions. Individual public watershed projects may be regarded as subsectors

subject to ground rules not greatly different in principle from those applying
to other subsectors.

Objectives and Criteria of Watershed Policy

In proceeding to the objectives of watershed policy, one encounters a
problem of unity of social objectives and criteria. The objectives of watershed
policy cannot be divorced from those of other economic policies. Such
objectives are interrelated. Social welfare criteria are no different in watershed
policy than anywhere else.

Since Pareto,[3] economists have taken a special interest in optimizing
social welfare and in the criteria for such optimizing. Optima of social
welfare and formal criteria for optimizing are constructs in the sense of
useful scientific fictions.[4] Optimizing is not and cannot be an actual policy
objective. These fictional constructs are useful as organizing principles for
the variables and relations that must be considered in welfare economics—to
decide which ones to bring into the analysis explicitly, which ones to neglect,
which ones to combine with others, and which ones to take into account as
constraints. Information about variables and relations is insufficient for
projecting an optimum expansion path of social welfare over time in a
dynamic framework. The actual objective of policy decisions involves successive
incremental improvements of the existing state of welfare, considering a
limited number of alternatives. The Pareto criterion, likewise, is suited only
for appraising whether an increase of social welfare results, but not for
projecting an optimum.

For policy decisions of more limited scope—for example, evaluating
individual watershed projects—incremental improvements in social welfare
can be determined cardinally. This may be done by comparing hypothetical
changes in income that can be attributed to projects. For policy decisions of
broader scope incremental improvements in social welfare can be appraised
only ordinally in terms of *direction* of changes, the relative *speed* of changes,
and their *sequence in time*. The issues involved in optimizing versus
incrementally improving social welfare will be taken up in more detail later
when quantitative analytic techniques are considered as an aid in watershed
policy.

Having stressed the unity of objectives and criteria in public policies, I
must now make a suggestion which may appear at first sight inconsistent: In
natural resource economics, and particularly in watershed development,
there tend to be characteristic divergencies in the actual welfare performance
of the economy from the fictional welfare optima.

The conditions leading to these divergencies may be systematized in a
number of ways. In what follows I shall try to systematize them in a way that
brings out the relation of watershed development to the market economy
and the price system.[5] It is frequently argued that market prices provide the
signalling system that steers Western economies toward the social welfare
optimum. An examination of the extent to which the price system fulfills this

function helps to reveal conditions where public policy may need to find substitute or supplementary or countermanding systems.

Watershed Policy and the Price System

Three major types of breakdown and malfunctioning of the price system may be mentioned. The first two are of special significance in watershed policy:

1. Price signals do not exist.
2. Price signals are not received by the agent who makes decisions but are received by others.
3. Price signals are "distorted."

Price signals do not exist for that part of benefits and costs of watershed development which I call "extramarket." Some of them are collective benefits in the sense that they are not divisible in consumption. The scenic values of a watershed unmarred by soil erosion, destructive logging, billboards, and slums are an example. Collective costs are the damage by floods, and the risk therefrom, to the general economy of a watershed rather than to individual properties, and threats to public health, such as malaria, related to drainage conditions.

Some benefits of watershed development, on the other hand, are divisible in consumption. In other words, a price could be charged for their enjoyment by individuals. Many of these goods, however, are free or nearly free institutionally. Recreational facilities offered by public reservoirs and public hunting and fishing are examples of extramarket benefits that are divisible in consumption but are public goods institutionally.

For some time, resource economists have been emphasizing the importance of extramarket benefits and costs without reference to particular stages of economic development. Recently, John Kenneth Galbraith has called special attention to them with reference to affluent societies.[6] Great emphasis is given the increasing lack of what is called "social balance" between the products supplied by the market economy and products such as education, defense, parks, and playgrounds, which are publicly supplied and financed by general taxation rather than sale. Galbraith reasons that the supply of extramarket goods has an inherent tendency to lag behind the supply of market goods because modern advertising and emulation, which are largely responsible for demand shifts in affluent societies, operate in favor of market goods.

While in substantial agreement on these points, I should like to note that the problem of social balance between market and extramarket goods is not confined to affluent societies. Furthermore, there are many examples of societies—not excluding contemporary ones—for which social balance might be regarded as threatened by the preponderance of public-supplied goods.

The historical fact of a great many ratios between the supply of market and extramarket goods raises the question of what is the criterion of an optimum social balance. Galbraith rejects the traditional criterion, namely, that the utility from a marginal increment of productive services devoted to the production of extramarket goods should be equal to the utility of the same increment devoted to the production of market goods. This criterion is rejected because the utility of market goods is what is called "synthesized," whereas utility from extramarket goods is not. A precise optimum in the social balance is regarded as unimportant. The direction in which policy should move to correct this condition is regarded as plain and the distance to be traversed considerable.

It has been suggested above that direction is frequently an acceptable criterion for incremental improvements in social welfare through policy decisions of broad scope. For individual watershed projects, one may well consider going further. Whether the economist likes it or not, evaluation of extramarket benefits and costs—and also dismissal of such evaluation—is already a part of the political process. Reports of fish and game departments and other public agencies illustrate these attempts at evaluation. One may have professional doubt about some of the procedures used. Still, the economist may well take an interest in them in order to develop better substitutes. Otherwise, the arguments of well-organized groups interested in market values alone, who dismiss extramarket benefits and costs as "intangible," might receive disproportionate attention in policy decisions.

This is not to suggest that *all* benefits of recreational resources could be evaluated. In connection with many such resources, however, market values can be used indirectly—for example, through analyzing data on fees, leases, and real estate transactions. In other cases, measurement in terms of physical units of use—for example, man-days—can be accomplished fairly easily. Values of additional units of use can be approached through questionnaires and the study of behavior in other experimental choice situations. Even such crude and partial measurement is more useful than disregarding these values altogether, or substituting for them some figure based on the expenditures of users for transportation, room and board, guns, fishing tackle, and similar items.

Proceeding now to the second major type of breakdown or malfunction of the price system, what is meant by "price signals are not received by the decisions-making agent but by others"? In traditional economics these problems appear as external economies and diseconomies. In watershed economics these externalities are discussed largely under the labels "offsite" and "indirect" benefits and costs.

External economies and diseconomies are of many kinds. They may be market or extramarket, pecuniary or nonpecuniary, static or dynamic, reversible or irreversible. In spite of an early article by Ellis and Fellner,[7] there is still much confusion between externalities that are merely transfer items in an international, national, regional, or local framework and those that are not. By some authors the terms "pecuniary" and "nonpecuniary" are employed in order to differentiate between transfer and nontransfer items. This is confusing because externalities may be either market or extramarket benefits and costs. If there are multiple decision levels in the same firm, price signals may affect these levels differently. In farming, for example, the tenant may be affected but not the landlord, or vice versa. The term "externality" becomes inapplicable, although the breakdown of the price system is of the same type as in other kinds of externality. For public policy it is necessary to ascertain in each particular case what kind of externality is involved. The term itself is of little help for understanding and policy-making.

The origin and the incidence of off-site benefits and costs can be influenced through property institutions—especially resources law and taxation. Taxation is used here in a broad sense as including "negative taxation," that is, tax bonuses. Such bonuses may consist of depletion or depreciation allowances, reduction of taxes, or outright supports and subsidies. Tax bonuses may be made dependent on fulfillment by the taxpayer of certain requirements regarding his use of resources.

Public districts can be employed effectively to make the influence of resources law and taxation operational. This is a vital area for cooperative research between economics and other social sciences, especially law and public administration. The last part of this volume considers this area. When supplemental and countermanding systems were mentioned previously, I had in mind especially resources law and taxation. It is difficult to see, for example, how the relations between upstream and downstream interests and upland- and bottom-land landowners could be adequately taken into account by the price system.

The problems of indirect benefits and costs in watershed policy have been analyzed elsewhere.[8] It may be mentioned, however, that transfer items deserve consideration in benefit-cost analysis. For example, they are relevant to project repayment, interpreted broadly as including cost-sharing and financing. This may be in an international, national, regional, or local framework. Transfer items are also relevant to project evaluations, provided the transfer is "out of" the framework considered.

Turning now to distortions of the price system, the first difficulty is to define "distortions." Most economists may agree that, for the following four basic reasons, distortion exists. However, few would deny that value judgments are involved and that some qualification is needed with respect to degree of distortion.

The first distortion was indicated earlier when the synthetic nature of market demand in affluent societies was mentioned. That is the problem of the interpretation of and divergencies from consumer sovereignty. Consumer sovereignty is a basic assumption in any attempt to employ market prices in an economic analysis of alternative states of social welfare.

The second distortion is more often explicitly considered in welfare economics than the first. It occurs when the income distribution that generated the market prices employed in welfare statements diverges from an income distribution regarded as the "ideal."

The third distortion occurs in the absence of the necessary conditions regarding market organization which must be fulfilled if the price system is to steer the economy toward a welfare optimum. The effects of monopoly, duoply, oligopoly, and other divergencies from pure competition have been discussed by economists over the last several decades.

Last and not least, the price system may be called distorted if social institutions have lost the identity of "concept" and "structure," to use Sumner's terms.[9] Social institutions affect market prices not merely through income distribution and market organization, but in many other ways, both on the side of demand and on that of supply. It was noted previously that social institutions are brought into welfare economics as constraints. Usually, no attempt is made to ascertain whether they have lost identity of concept and structure.

Watershed policy is concerned with all these distortions, but no more so than other public policies. Watershed policy can work in the direction of correcting for these distortions. On the other hand, existence of these distortions suggests caution when market prices are used in quantitative economic analysis.

These points lead me to the last part of my assignment, namely, to appraise the merits and limitations of benefit-cost analysis for evaluating public investment in watershed development projects.

Benefit-Cost Analysis and Watershed Policy

The literature on benefit-cost analysis and related techniques has increased by leaps and bounds. At one time the professional contributions in this field consisted of a few articles. Now contributions are counted in books. In 1958 alone, three such books were published.[10] This literature is widely quoted and a flattering review article has appeared.[11] A careful and critical stock-taking will soon become necessary in order to ascertain where we stand and in what direction we should push forward. This is not the occasion for a detailed critique, but a few comments are called for by my assignment.

The claim of the "new" benefit-cost analysis is that evaluation of public investment in water resources projects is viewed for the first time as a problem of optimizing social welfare under budgetary constraints. Much space is devoted to formulating criteria for optimizing and to stressing the insufficiency of traditional benefit-cost ratios as such a criterion.

There is little awareness in this literature that economists in governments and universities who have worked critically with benefit-cost analysis over many years have frequently pointed out the insufficiency of benefit-cost ratios as an optimizing criterion. This insufficiency is rather obvious. Why, then, was use of these ratios not opposed more vigorously? There are several reasons.

First, to those familiar with the operational aspects of benefit-cost analysis, it seems naive to identify optimizing of social welfare, as a useful fictional construct in the sense explained above, with actual policy objectives. In time and uncertainty economics, such objectives must be formulated, as we know, in terms of incremental improvements in social welfare. The "new" benefit-cost analysis gives much attention to the numerical value of interest rates and uncertainty allowances that should be used in optimizing. But the real challenge of time and uncertainty economics—namely, how changes of technology, preferences, and institutions are to be taken into account through formulation of objectives and identification of variables and constraints—receives little consideration.

Second, even if optimizing of social welfare is assumed an operational policy objective, the shortcomings of the traditional ratios as a criterion for this purpose may well be regarded as of the second order of significance when considering other shortcomings of benefit-cost analysis. These other shortcomings are connected with the reliance on market prices in evaluating benefit and cost streams. The new benefit-cost analysis is little concerned with these other shortcomings. In other words, there is no progress in the treatment of extramarket values, offsite and indirect benefits and costs, consumer sovereignty, income distribution, market organization, and institutional influences. More is needed here than translating economics into the jargon of operations research or renaming externalities "spillover effects" or substituting a multiplicity of opportunity cost rates of interest for a multiplicity of market rates.

Third, the particular budgetary constraint that is emphasized by the new benefit-cost analysis, namely, that a water resources budget must be assumed as "given," is by no means the only one that can be selected. This constraint is merely similar to the one imposed by the present federal administration. Theoretically, optimizing of social welfare for the budget as a whole—not item by item—and relating investment expenditure to other expenditure and taxation is desirable. Operationally, especially in terms of political decision-making in the legislative branches of federal and state governments, it would seem more relevant to assume that water resources appropriations are actually made project by project, and that the total water resources budget is to some extent dependent on the size and number of projects that can muster the necessary political support in the legislatures. Under this assumption, benefit-cost analysis has the more modest but still highly important functions of ruling out, or at least stigmatizing, projects that do not make an incremental contribution to social welfare, and of selecting for each project, not necessarily the best alternative, but at least one of the better ones. For these purposes, ratios can serve.

Project selection is only one of three areas in which benefit-cost analysis may be useful. The other two areas comprise the broad problems of repayment of project costs, including problems of cost sharing and financing, and the related problems of pricing those products that are sold. The new benefit-cost analysis pays little attention to the problems of repayment and pricing. This is in accordance with the emphasis on optimizing and optimizing criteria. One may submit that the contribution of economics as an operationally significant policy science is potentially greater in the areas of repayment and pricing than in that of evaluation. My reason for this proposition is that problems of repayment and pricing remain important after a project has been selected and constructed. This means that benefit-cost analysis can operate in the areas of repayment and pricing with a more complete and better identified set of conditions that can be assumed as "given."

Present trends are toward substitution of linear programming for benefit-cost analysis. The programming techniques presently in use are static even though dating may be employed. The basic mathematics of dynamic programming have been known for some time. They have been used in the conceptual clarification of conservation economics.[12] As yet, no operational applications of dynamic programming are available in watershed economics. It will be interesting to see, when actual results become available, whether the particular advantages of the technique are sufficient to overcome its particular limitations.

Benefit-cost analysis is essentially an informal but flexible programming technique. The informal technique leaves considerable latitude to the user in exercising judgment, professional competence, and integrity—or absence of these qualities—in selecting and stating his assumptions. In formal programming, the assumptions are largely "built in" and concealed from those who are not familiar with the technique—like most legislators. Formal programming is superior to benefit-cost analysis in the sense that it can determine cheaply and precisely an *optimum optimorum*. As already implied, the significance of this superiority in time and uncertainty economics is at least doubtful. The numerical precision in determining optima may actually become harmful it if induces greater confidence in them. Calculation must be projected for fifteen to twenty years in the future. Such a gestation period is unavoidable between the planning stage and operation. The subsequent pay-out period cannot well be set at less than forty years. Programming for subsectors in the above sense necessitates great detail in "activities" and "processes." While the conceptual defects of optimizing for subsectors are less than for broader policy decisions, the problems posed by the availability of data for smaller statistical aggregates are usually greater.

Turning now to policies of broader scope, we noted that they can often be appraised only ordinally and in terms of direction of changes, the relative speed of changes, and their sequence in time. Before concluding, one aspect of such an appraisal may be mentioned because it is of particular interest to watershed policy.

It is important for public policy to know whether a change sets in motion corrective counterchanges tending over time toward a balance of the initial change, or whether it sets in motion other changes that are circular and cumulative and tend to reinforce the initial change.[13]

For example, there is evidence that in the United States during the first half of the twentieth century relations between prices of land, prices of agricultural inputs other than land, and technological change in agriculture can be regarded as a corrective system.[14] On the other hand, Myrdal's well-known thesis about the nature of economic change is an example of a circular and cumulative system.[15] There is also evidence that the relation between soil erosion, income, population, and technology is frequently such a system.[16] Such a system, if operating in the upstream portion of watersheds, has physical and economic consequences downstream which have circular and cumulative effects upon the whole watershed.

Watershed policy may make allowance for the risks involved in this circular and cumulative system, but it cannot be made by adding a few percent to the interest rate used in benefit-cost analysis. Rather, the approach is that of establishing minimum standards in resources use through a variety of institutional approaches. In this way, allowance for uncertainty is built into the formulation of policy objectives itself.[17]

This is merely an illustration for the generalization suggested above that objectives of policy of broader scope may well focus on conditions that cause characteristic divergencies in the actual welfare performance of the economy from fictional welfare optima. For the pursuit of these objectives, benefit-cost analysis and related quantitative techniques must be supplemented by a type of analysis that takes cognizance of research in economic history, in the sociology of value systems, and in the change of social institutions, especially the law. This type of analysis relies heavily on theory, but not on economic theory alone. It focuses on time and uncertainty economics, but not necessarily through increasing the number of variables and equations in optimizing.

[1]Sometimes only the dividing ridges are defined as the watershed. This narrow definition is now generally replaced by a definition that includes the whole area between dividing ridges.

[2]For details on these laws, see S. V. Ciriacy-Wantrup, "Some Economic Issues in Water Rights," *Jour. Farm Econ.,* Vol. XXXVII, No. 5, Dec., 1955, pp. 875-85.

[3]Vilfredo Pareto, *Cours d'Economique Politique*, (Lausanne: F. Rouge, Libraire-Editeur, 1897).

[4]"A fiction is permissable in science if its character is clearly understood. A fiction is deliberate, conscious deviation from reality. A fiction, however, is not a hypothesis or theory. By itself, a fiction is not intended to be validated by testing with empirical evidence. But a scientific fiction should be useful as a stimulus for or as part of hypotheses and theories which *can* be so tested. That means the test of a scientific fiction is its conceptual usefulness, its expediency, in understanding, explaining, and predicting reality. A fiction becomes mere dogma and, therefore, unscientific if its two characteristics— consciousness of its fictional nature and conceptual usefulness—are obliterated. There are many examples in the history of science of fictions changing into dogma." S. V. Ciriacy-Wantrup, "Policy Considerations in Farm Management Research in the Decade Ahead," *Jour. Farm Econ.,* Vol. XXXVIII, No. 5, Dec., 1956, pp. 1301-11.

[5]An alternative way of systematizing is to differentiate between various classes of benefits and costs—explaining why their allocation to decision-making agents and the incidence among members of a social group lead to

characteristic divergencies from a social welfare optimum. See S. V. Ciriacy-Wantrup, *Resource Conservation: Economics and Policies* (Berkeley: University of California Press, 1952), especially Chaps. 16-18.

[6]J. K. Galbraith, *The Affluent Society* (Boston: Houghton Mifflin Co., 1958).

[7]H. S. Ellis and William Fellner, "External Economics and Diseconomics," *Amer. Econ. Rev.,* Vol. XXXIII, No. 3, Sept., 1943.

[8]S. V. Ciriacy-Wantrup, "Cost Allocation in Relation to Western Water Policies," *Jour. Farm Econ.,* Vol. XXXVI, No. 1, Feb., 1954, pp. 108-29; and by the same author, "Benefit-Cost Analysis and Public Resource Development", *Jour. Farm Econ.,* Vol. XXXVII, No. 4, Nov., 1955, pp. 676-89.

[9]William G. Sumner and Albert G. Keller, *The Science of Society* (New Haven: Yale University Press, 1927), 4 Vols.

[10]Otto Eckstein, *Water-Resource Develoment: the Economics of Project Evaluation* (Cambridge: Harvard University Press, 1958); John V. Krutilla and Otto Eckstein, *Multiple Purpose River Development: Studies in Applied Economic Analysis* (Baltimore: Johns Hopkins Press, 1958); Roland N. McKean, *Efficiency in Government Through Systems Analysis with Emphasis on Water Resources Development* (New York: John Wiley and Sons, 1958).

[11]Julius Margolis, "The Economic Evaluation of Federal Water Resource Development: A Review Article," *Amer. Econ. Rev.,* Vol. IL, No. 1, Mar., 1959, pp. 96-111.

[12]S. V. Ciriacy-Wantrup, "Private Enterprise and Conservation," *Jour. Farm Econ.,* Vol. XXIV, No. 1, Feb., 1942, pp. 75-96.

[13]The common terms, "equilibrium" and "disequilirium," are not too well suited for describing these two systems. A corrective system has at best only a tendency toward equilibrium. A cumulative system, under some conditions, is more likely to realize and maintain equilibrium.

[14]S. V. Ciriacy-Wantrup, *Conceptual Problems in Projecting the Demand for Land and Water.* Presented before the Land Economics Institute, University of Illinois, June 24, 1958. Giannini Foundation Paper No. 176, Berkeley, California, May, 1959 (Processed). (Chapter 9 in this volume.)

[15]Gunnar Myrdal, *Rich Lands and Poor* ("World Perspectives," Vol. XVI New York: Harper and Brothers, 1957).

[16]S. V. Ciriacy-Wantrup, "Resource Conservation and Economic Stability," *Quart. Jour. Econ.,* Vol. XL, May, 1946, pp. 412-52.

[17]Ibid., Chap. 18.

Chapter 7

WATER QUALITY,
A PROBLEM FOR THE ECONOMIST*[1]

It is with some diffidence that I approach a problem area which, with respect to private and public investment and to effective public policies, is one of the most significant underdeveloped areas in the economics of natural resources. This is true no less domestically than abroad. In the terminology of my assignment, this is the area of managing the quality of natural resources or, for short, the problem of quality management. I prefer this broader concept to the more usual term "pollution control."

Quality Management in Natural Resource Economics

A few words need to be said about the meaning of quality in this context. It is well known that use of natural resources by man frequently does not involve an irreversible decrease of physical quantities of stocks and flows through consumption and transformation but, rather, a reversible decrease in suitability for *reuse*. For some important resources, such decrease of quality is restored through natural processes—provided that intensity of use is held within certain limits. Regardless of whether quality is restored by natural processes, man can prevent, reduce in degree or duration, or reverse a decrease of quality at the expense of some use benefits foregone or some additional costs incurred; he can do so even if a decrease of quality is due not to his own use but to natural causes, such as erosion and deposition. Thus, the problems of quality management are not merely technological but, to a large extent, economic and political.

Reuse is an especially intriguing problem for the economist because different uses of the same resource commonly have different effects on quality and, in turn, have different quality requirements. Thus, quality management has to deal with a multiple-use problem of a particular sort, namely, with the sequence of different uses over time. Some problems of the quantitative allocation of resources among different uses appear in a new

*Reprinted, with permission, from the *Journal of Farm Economics*, Vol. XLIII(5):1133–1144 (December, 1961).

light if differences in quality effects and quality requirements are taken into account.

The economics of quality management are significant problems for many natural resources. This paper is confined to water resources by assignment. A closely similar economic analysis, however, can be applied to other natural resources—especially to soil, air, and recreational resources.

All major water uses, except irrigation, are largely nonconsumptive. This is true for uses by households (domestic), manufacturing, including steam electric plants (industrial), transportation on rivers and canals, recreation (boating, swimming, fishing), hydroelectric plants, and, last but not least, waste disposal. Even in irrigation, less than two-thirds of total wateruse is consumptive—through evapo-transpiration. In arid and semiarid climates, at least one-third of total water use, and frequently more (depending on its quality and on the soil), is needed for leaching harmful salts into the ground water. Drainage of such ground water through streams and canals is becoming a crucial problem for the continuity of irrigated agriculture. The economic problems created by agricultural pollution are no less important than those created by industrial, domestic, and recreational pollution.

What was just said about quality effects and quality requirements of different uses is applicable especially to water resources. For example, some important industrial uses, such as cooling, have practically no quality requirements, and the quality effects are merely increases of temperature. But other industrial uses, for example, in the chemical industry, and most domestic uses have strict quality requirements, and the quality effects are great. Irrigation use has an intermediate position between these extremes.

In an economics of natural resources that focuses on use rates, on their complementarity, competitivenes, or neutrality in benefits and costs, and, especially, on the time aspects of these relations, reuse is conceptually integrated into the economic analysis. Such an analysis has been presented elsewhere.[2] It may be helpful, however, to restate here the main economic problems and conclusions with explicit reference to water quality management.

Only too often, water is treated in economic analysis as if physical quantities of a homogenous commodity were under consideration. Concern is expressed over the increasing competition between agricultural and industrial uses even when they have different quality requirements and are, therefore, "noncompeting groups." In input-output analysis, technical coefficients of water use for different sectors—expressing acre-feet of water required per dollar output of product—are developed without taking into account differences among sectors in quality requirements and intersector reuse of water. Aggregate quantities "required" by all sectors are computed on this basis and projected. In linear programming studies of quantitative optima in water development and allocation, problems of waste disposal and reuse are neglected. Although the past and present extent of reuse is one of the least satisfactory parts of water statistics, it is certainly significant, not constant over time, and greatly affected by water policy.

Referring to problems in quantitative water economics might create the impression that problems of quality management are less amenable to quantitative measurement. Such as impression is not justified. The semantics of the words "quantity" and "quality"—like that of many dichotomies—are unfortunate, and some possible confusion must be guarded against.

The technological aspects of water quality are no less amenable to precise quantitative measurement than the volume, weight, or flow rate usually employed to measure water quantity. Rather, different quantitative dimensions are involved when water quality is considered. These dimensions are measurable with a degree of precision not greatly different from the traditional dimensions. The "new" dimensions are water temperature, dissolved oxygen (D.O.), biochemical oxygen demand (B.O.D.), total dissolved solids (T.D.S.) in parts per million (ppm)—or as milligrams per liter (mg/l)—and many similar ones for particular dissolved solids—such as chlorides, toxins, synthetic organics—that are important for particular kinds of reuse.

Difficulties of quantitative measurement arise frequently when these dimensions are to be evaluated in social economics. If evaluation is one-dimensional, for example, in pecuniary terms, a problem of "quality" is present in the sense that precise quantitative measurement may become meaningless or misleading. This problem of the relevant degree of quantification in science is not peculiar to water quality management; it is present in all attempts to identify social optima in water development and allocation and has been discussed elsewhere.[3] We shall return later to the problems of evaluation in connection with the formulation of policy objectives in water quality management.

Time does not permit going into the technological aspects of water quality management. The very complexity of these aspects makes the literature in this field of great interest to the economist. Suffice it to say that a thorough study of the technology of water quality management is a necessary condition for dealing with the economic and political problems associated with them. No attempt is made here to treat these problems exhaustively. They will be ordered according to their relevance for water policy. Emphasis will be placed on the reasons why in a market economy investment in water quality management has an inherent tendency to fall short of a conceptual social optimum and on the possibilities for water policy to remedy this situation.

The first step in this analysis is a study of the incidence of social costs and benefits in water quality management. This is the key economic problem. We shall then proceed to an analysis of how the incidence problem is related to a conceptually and operationally helpful formulation of policy objectives.

Incidence of Social Costs and Benefits in Water Quality Management

In a regulated market economy like that of this country, the extent to which decreases of water quality are taken into account as costs by planning units making production decisions that cause pollution, is determined not by the interplay of economic forces in the market place but by laws and similar social institutions. In other words, if economic forces alone were operative, the social costs of decreases in water quality would not be incident on the polluters but on the pollutees—if you permit. By the same token, the social benefits of pollution abatement would not accrue to the planning unit that could prevent pollution at the source. Water pollution has long been the classical example of real external economies and diseconomies.[4] By "real," I mean externalities that are not merely income transfers among sectors of the economy through offsetting increases and decreases of values due to price changes. At least in degree, real external social costs and benefits are more important in water quality than in water quantity management. Several economic consequences are especially relevant for water policy.

First, at a given state of technological development, individual planning units—industrial firms, farms, households, cities, and public districts—select production functions without regard to the effects of quality, quantity, and timing of their discharge on the quality of receiving water resources, such as ground water, streams, lakes, and tide water. Timing needs to be stressed because, owing to variations of flow rate, temperature, dissolved oxygen, turbidity, and other conditions, water resources vary over time in their capacity to receive discharge. The term "production function" is interpreted here broadly. Households are regarded as processing firms using water for production. Some household production functions, for example, those involving detergents, have significant effects on the quality of discharge. Similarly, city sewer departments and public sewer districts may be regarded as processing firms with alternative production functions available to them for collecting, treating, and discharging sewage.

Second, and more important over time, planning units have no economic incentive to undertake and support research with the objective of pushing technological change into directions that would help to control their discharge in the interest of reuse by others. Experience in recent decades indicates that the potentialities for technological change in this area are great. The technology of waste treatment in this country and abroad has advanced in spite of a relatively small over-all research effort. One important direction of technological change which should be emphasized in the future is finding substitutes for especially harmful but stable materials that enter discharge. Some detergents and pesticides are examples. The industries producing these are on the front line of technological change and, in the past, have reacted effectively when private of public needs called for the development of new products. Another important direction of technological change in the future is reclamation of wastes into salable products. Fuel, fertilizer, feed, and fish are important by-products of modern sewage treatment plants in some European countries. A study we are making of water policy in Soviet Russia points to economic incentives through administered prices and large resulting investments for producing ethyl alcohol from the wastes of the pulp and paper industry.[5] Many wastes of the chemical and oil industries could be reclaimed with proper incentives. Pollution abatement is a joint product. All these industries are characterized by rapid technological change.

Third, a given standard of water quality which, as discussed in detail below, may be adopted as a policy objective for the water resources receiving discharge is not likely to be realized with minimum total social costs if quality management is not applied at the source; that is, *before* discharge. Technologically, the same quality standard can be realized through dilution and treatment *after* discharge. As an extreme, individual reusers can refine water at their intake to any degree of quality desired. But minimum total social cost combinations of technological alternatives for realizing a given standard of quality are usually unobtainable if discharge remains uncontrolled.

The three foregoing consequences could be avoided by inducing planning units to take external social costs into account in their decision making. The many laws and regulations that apply to quality, quantity, and timing of discharge have this objective. Economic soundness of this policy objective of water quality management depends on several important conditions.

First, when regulations regarding discharge are imposed in order to force planning units to take external costs into account, external benefits produced by such units should be considered. It is possible, for example, that costs necessitated by legal requirements regarding quality of discharge prevent a pulp and paper industry from locating in a certain region or bring about migration to other regions or force it out of business altogether. If such an industry creates external *net* economies, it may be in the interest of regional or national welfare that an appropriate portion of the costs of discharge control be taken over by the public.

Second, the sound policy objective of forcing planning units to take external costs into account does not necessarily mean that each planning unit should be forced to control its own discharge. For some industrial firms and some farms, for example, dairies, this approach may be the one with minimum total social costs. For other industrial firms and most farms, the economies of scale of treatment plants and economies based on technological advantages in treating a discharge-mix from different industries will argue for unified collection and treatment at strategically located points of a river basin. In irrigated agriculture, large master drains known as wasteways take the place of unified collection and treatment of city sewage.[6] In unified water quality management, the economic incentive of internal costs may still be realized by distributing costs among individual planning units through a sewer service rate system based on studies of the effects of quantity, quality, and timing of individual discharges on the costs of collection, treatment, and disposal. Such rate systems exist in this country and abroad.[7] They deserve further refinement and general application. Frequent or, better still, continuous checking of discharges and of the quality of the receiving water resources is a prerequisite of an effective application and adjustment over time of such rate systems. A water intelligence service is one of the most important components of water quality management. Electronic recording and transmitting instruments are effective tools of such a service.[8]

For households, however, checking of individual discharges would be too expensive. For households, therefore, economic incentives to change production functions must be applied at the manufacture and distribution stages. Several countries—among them, Great Britain and West Germany—are considering prohibition of manufacturing, or at least of domestic distribution, of some detergents.

Third, when attempting to force planning units to take external costs into account, one must recognize that cities, counties, public districts, and State and Federal agencies are in a different economic and legal position from private firms and farms with respect to decisions making. Decision making in private planning units is sensitive to economic and legal incentives. The management of a city or county sewer department, on the other hand, may have the best understanding and intention to cooperate in the elimination of external costs, but investment decisions depend on city and county Governments. Financing of investment in pollution abatement is generally by bond issues, which usually require a two-thirds majority of the electorate. Local governments and electorates are not easily convinced that taxes should be increased for public resource development, the benefits of which will largely accrue to other communities. Furthermore, it is difficult to enforce laws and regulations against public bodies.[9] Some courts, for example, treat the right of a municipality to use streams for waste disposal as a public right that has priority over other water uses.[10] The system which is developing, therefore, in this country and abroad, is one of large-scale Federal and State grants, wherever possible on a matching basis, and of low-interest loans, to help local governments reduce on a voluntary basis the external costs of pollution caused by their jurisdictions.[11] Potentially, such Federal and State grants and loans could be used to coordinate quality management throughout a river basin. Efficiency in Government expenditures requires such coordination.

The last point leads me to a conclusion—or prediction if you like—which follows from the analysis of problems of incidence of costs and benefits just presented. I should like to submit that water quality management will become a stronger force toward unified river basin development than water quantity management has proved up to now. In water quantity management, the incidence of costs and benefits is such that it is economical for groups of beneficiaries to undertake partial development themselves. Most of California water development took place on this basis. In water quality management, the polluters as well as the beneficiaries of pollution abatement must participate. On the other hand, through the economics of dilution, water quality management is intimately related to quantity management, especially storage. The most completely unified river basin I know of—that of the Ruhr, comprising the industrial heartland of Germany—is one with quantitatively abundant water resources in a humid region. The driving force for unified development came from the quality side. Some aspects of this example have a bearing on the formulation of policy objectives in water quality management. This problem will be considered next.

Formulation of Policy Objectives
in Water Quality Management

At first glance, one might conclude from our discussion of the incidence problem that policy objectives in water quality management might be conceptualized as "the optimum waste disposal system" taking account of externalities, of alternatives in abatement, of interdependence with water quantity management, of cyclical and stochastic aspects, of uncertainty, and of changes over time in all of these elements. The term "watershed firm" or "basin firm" has become popular for the fictitious entity that optimizes. Some authors contend that the optimum waste disposal system can be quantitatively specified through formal programming techniques.

One may wonder a little about the helpfulness of such a formulation. The conclusion reached above, that the need for water quality management is a strong force toward unified river basin development, does not mean that policy objectives should be formulated within a basin framework. The two major policy objectives mentioned above—changes of industrial, agricultural, and household production functions and changes in the state of technology over time—transcend a river basin.

An optimizing basin firm is not a helpful construct for conceptualizing the relations between water policy and individual planning units. The basin firm cannot, even conceptually, take the place of individual planning units as optimizers. Neither can the basin firm undertake to optimize changes in technology in a conceptually meaningful way.[12]

In the past, economic incentives have operated to *increase* pollution. Even if this influence were reversed through water policy along the lines suggested, there would be no assurance that all planning units would respond to the same extent and at the same time. Serious types of pollution are caused by a single polluter sometimes during a very short time. In addition to this uncertainty, a change of economic incentives will increase uncertainties related to technological change. Thus, while a reversal of the direction in which economic incentives have operated in the past can be expected to solve a major part of the pollution problem over time, these incentives must be applied in such a way that a definite *minimum* response by individual planning units is assured. This, as we know, can be achieved through regulations regarding quantity, quality, and timing of individual discharges, through prohibition of certain production functions, through unified collection and treatment of wastes with appropriate distribution of costs, or through a combination of all three.

The question now arises: how far should water policy go with these measures? In other words, what is the particular minimum standard of quality in the receiving water that should be the policy objective? At present, this standard is determined on the basis of considerations in the fields of public health, sanitary engineering, and other applied natural sciences. Economic considerations come in by the back door in the political process through which quality standards are enacted in laws and regulations.

There is also some argument among experts in public health and sanitary engineering on whether emphasis should be on standards of quality in individual discharges or on standards of quality in the receiving water. Both types of standards are needed. As previously mentioned the former are usually the most economical means of obtaining the latter. If treatment is applied after discharge, varying degrees of treatment will be needed to conform with stream flow variations. Under these conditions, treatment plants cannot operate at maximum efficiency. For example, a plant designed to remove 90 percent of the B.O.D. will not operate efficiently when removing 50 percent of the B.O.D., and, of course, the reverse is impossible. Yet, variations in stream flow will be considerable, whereas the waste being treated will probably not vary greatly in degree of pollution at a particular treatment plant. Dilution, which has been the major tool of pollution abatement in the past is of decreasing importance as the pollution problem increases. In the future, emphasis should be placed on other alternatives. This would avoid many of the problems posed by variations in stream flow.

Determination of a minimum quality standard in terms of economics is not simple. First, I should like to suggest that the distribution of the costs of maintaining such a standard—with a view to providing incentives in the two directions discussed—appears no less important than a particular standard and the quantitative level of the abatement investment associated with it. Second, while I do not believe that economics has the tools to specify an optimum standard which would change over time and which would be different for different streams and different sections of the same stream, economic arguments can be advanced for a minimum standard that would be stable over time for all normal streams and sections of streams. By "normal," I mean streams and sections of streams that are not deliberately set aside for waste disposal. The economic aspects of such stream specialization will be considered presently.

An economic argument for the general adoption of minimum standards as policy objectives in the field of natural resources has been offered elsewhere.[13] This argument is based on the need to make allowance for uncertainty, on the desirability of avoiding irreversibilities, and on the relatively small costs of minimum standards.

For the present purpose, additional arguments may be offered for a particular minimum standard of water quality. This standard is one that would maintain a healthy habitat for fish life. Such a standard can be defined with respect to the well-known quantitative dimensions of quality within a narrow range. Dissolved oxygen, for example, is not to drop below 5 ppm.[14] In addition, fish life is a sensitive indicator for a wide spectrum of quality dimensions, the standards for which are not yet fully established. For example, the *cumulative* effect of certain pollutants on aquatic life is still uncertain.

From the viewpoint of the economist, the minimum standard suggested here does not avoid all arbitrary elements, but it defines a point of the external cost function of pollution that is of great economic interest. External cost functions of pollution are conspicuously discontinuous. In other words, over a certain range of pollution, external costs are small. At a critical level of pollution, however, external costs become large.

The critical point of discontinuity in pollution damage to fish is economically relevant not merely for commercial and sport fishing. Recreational uses, such as swimming, boating, water skiing, hiking along the shores, and mere aesthetic enjoyment, suffer critically if this minimum standard is not maintained. Likewise, agricultural uses and some natural and artificial processes of purification are seriously affected. Furthermore, this minimum standard has economic relevance for other uses. Although it is too low for domestic, municipal and some industrial uses, costs of special treatment for these uses are decreased because the supplying water resources are free of toxic and other substances that are no less harmful to fish than to humans. On the other hand, it would be very costly to impose quality standards applicable to domestic water on water resources generally.

The "fishy" standard suggested here avoids the most difficult aspects of benefit-cost analysis, namely, the evaluation, in quantitative, pecuniary terms, of extramarket and collective benefits of pollution abatement. Economic calculation, however, is not pushed to the sidelines. The problem of realizing the standard with minimum total social costs remains but it has become more manageable. General adoption of the minimum standard does not mean that a higher standard may not be economical for particular streams or sections of streams. The additional costs of a higher standard can be compared with the resulting additional benefits in each case. Here, also, the economic problem has become more manageable.

The last point brings me to the special case that was previously alluded to, namely, the zoning of a stream or a section thereof as open sewer without quality standard. For technological reasons, an open sewer has certain advantages over a closed one. The economies of such stream specialization are best discussed with reference to an actual example which I studied 2 years ago.

Water quality management in the Ruhr basin is based on the concept of stream specialization. Water quality of the Ruhr is maintained at the minimum standard just discussed. A large portion of the wastes of the Ruhr basin, one of the largest industrial centers of the world, is transferred to the neighboring, parallel basin of the Emscher. The Emscher is intensively managed as a large, open sewer with up-to-date treatment plants at strategic points, making full use of the economies of scale. The Emscher basin, like that of the Ruhr, is under unified management. The two managements are so closely linked that functionally, although not legally, they can be regarded as one organization.

The results are impressive. The Ruhr and its man-made lakes form an attractive body of water that serves not only as the main water supply for the many municipalities and industrial complexes that make up the Ruhr district but also serves effectively the recreational needs of a large industrial population. All water sports are possible. The shores are intensively developed for recreation and residential purposes.

Stream specialization is sometimes recommended for this country. Some aspects of our example should be noted before it is imitated. Because of the small distances involved, the water supply and the recreational opportunities of the Ruhr basin are fully accessible to the Emscher basin—which has lost these assets. Further, a sewer system must discharge somewhere. The Emscher discharges into the Rhine, the large flow of which was for many years sufficient for dilution. In recent years, however, demands on the Rhine for waste disposal have become so great that dilution is no longer sufficient. The problem is international in scope because the Rhine flows from Germany into Holland below the point of discharge of the Emscher. At this point a very large treatment plant is now under construction to bring the discharge from the sewer stream up to the quality of the receiving stream. Thus, before the concept of stream specialization is applied elsewhere, one should consider whether substitutes are available for those water uses which are irreversibly eliminated from the sewer stream and whether the discharge from the sewer stream will not create diseconomies that offset the economies made possible through stream specialization.

Time is running short, and I have not given a quantitative estimate of what the minimum standard suggested here would cost. I confess that there is no figure which I would regard as valid. The main reason is the uncertainty about the effects on this figure of changes in productive processes affecting the origin and disposal of wastes. Water policy itself will increase this uncertainty if it provides appropriate incentives along the lines suggested.

Fortunately, however, there are economists who are less skeptical than I am about long-range quantitative projections in water policy. Professor Wollman and his collaborators, for example, have undertaken such a study for the Select Committee on National Water Resources of the United States Senate.[15] They estimate that an additional abatement investment of $99.6 billion will be needed in this country between their base year (1954) and the year 2000 to maintain a quality standard of 4 ppm of dissolved oxygen in all streams. In this estimate, the interdependence of quality and quantity management is taken into account. Annon of the wastes of the Ruhr basin, one of the largest industrial centers of the world, is transferred to the neighboring, parallel basin of the Emscher. The Emscher is intensively managed as a large, open sewer with up-to-date treatment plants at strategic points, making full use of the economies of scale. The Emscher basin, like that of the Ruhr, is under unified management. The two managements are so closely linked that functionally, although not legally, they can be regarded as one organization.

The results are impressive. The Ruhr and its man-made lakes form an attractive body of water that serves not only as the main water supply for the many municipalities and industrial complexes that make up the Ruhr district but also serves effectively the recreational needs of a large industrial population. All wat can be achieved are a subject for another paper.

[1]Giannini Foundation Paper No. 212, reprinted from *Jour. Farm Econ.*, Proceedings Issue, Vol. XLIII, No. 5, December, 1961, pp. 1133-1144.

[2]Ciriacy-Wantrup, S. V., *Resource Conservation, Economics and Policies* (Berkeley: Univ. of Calif. Press, 1952), 395 p.

[3]Ciriacy-Wantrup, "Projections of Water Requirements in the Economics of Water Policy," *J. Farm Econ.*, Vol. XLIII, No. 2, May 1961, and "Philosophy and Objectives of Watershed Policy," *Economics of Watershed Planning*, ed. Tolley, G. S. and Riggs, F. E. (Ames: Iowa State Univ. Press, 1961). (Chapter 6 in this book.)

[4]The term "spill-over effects" that has become popular recently adds nothing to the analysis.

[5]This study is being undertaken by M. Gucovsky under a grant from Resources for the Future, Inc.

[6]Such a master drain is being proposed for the San Joaquin Valley in Calif. See: Calif., Dept. of Water Resources, Div. of Resources Planning, *Lower San Joaquin Valley Water Quality Investigation*, Div. of Resources Planning Bul. No. 89 (Sacramento, Dec. 1960).

[7]Laboon, John F. and Dougherty, R. J., "Setting Fair Sewer Services Rates for Sewage and Industrial Wastes," *Wastes Engineering*, Vol. 31, No. 2, Feb. 1960, pp. 92-94 and 113. An even more elaborate rate system than the one discussed in this article for Allegheny County in Pa. is in use by the "Ruhrverband," the Metropolitan Water District responsible for the unified quality and quantity management of the water resources of the Ruhr in West Germany.

[8]To illustrate, the 1960 annual report of the Ohio River Valley Water Sanitation Commission mentions that they will have 40 electronic instruments located along the Ohio River. These will record and report data on dissolved oxygen, chloride content, hydrogen ion contentration, specific conductants, biochemical oxygen demand, temperature, and solar radiation. The Ohio River Valley Water Sanitation Commission is a regional authority in which nine states are cooperating. See: Ohio River Valley Water Sanitation Commission, *Chronicle of the 12th Year, 1960* (Cincinnati, 1961), p. 15.

[9]The same problem exists in air pollution. California had to enact a special law in 1961 to give the Bay Area Air Pollution Control District authority over State and municipal jurisdictions.

[10]Beuscher mentions a Wisconsin case in which an irrigation permit was denied because stream flow might be reduced to a point where it was not sufficient to dilute sewage from a downstream municipality. Beuscher, J. H., "Appropriation Water Law Elements in Riparian Doctrine States," *Buffalo Law Review*, Vol. 10, No. 3, Spring, 1961.

[11]California started this system with a $90 million grant in 1946 under the Construction and Employment Act. Under later legislation, a Water Pollution Control Fund was set up for the purpose of low-interest loans. See: Calif., *Statutes of Calif.* (1946-1947), pp. 30-39. "Construction and Employment Act"; Calif., *Statutes of Calif.* (1949), pp. 2793, 2794; Calif. *Statutes of Calif.* (1953), pp. 1361-1362.

In the Federal government, the 1956 Water Pollution Control Act was amended this year and appropriations increased to $570 million. This bill fixes the Federal share of any single antipollution project at $600,000 or 30 percent of the total cost, whichever is smaller. See: U. S. Public Laws, Statutes, etc., an act to amend the Federal Water Pollution Control Act to provide for a more effective program of water pollution control, Washington, D.C., July 24, 1961 (Public Law 87-88).

[12]In programming, technology is included in the constraints and not in the objective functions.

[13]Ciriacy-Wantrup, *Resource Conservation,....,* Ch. 18, and "Conservation and Resource Programming," *Land. Econ.*, Vol. 37, No. 2, May 1961. (Chapter 14 of this book.)

[14]Most experts regard 4 ppm as the minimum (sublethal) figure for aquatic life and feel that at least 5 ppm is needed for normal reproduction.

[15]U. S. Congress, Senate, Select Committee on National Water Resources, *Water Resources Activities in the U.S.*, 86th Cong., 2d Sess., 1960, Comm. Print No. 32, 131 p.

Part III

WATER DEVELOPMENT ECONOMICS

INTRODUCTION TO PART III

by

Michael F. Brewer*

Water development has been a theater of activity in which many basic topics of natural resource economics have been identified and illuminated. Public investment in water projects stimulated the evolution of benefit-cost analysis. It also prompted critical discussion and debate about the economic implications of natural resources, related institutions, and policies that guide their development. The three papers that follow provide examples of how practical analytical problems have stimulated conceptual, methodological and interpretative advance.

Drawing from public investment, public utility and business cycle theory, as well as from the analytical constructs of production economics, Wantrup illuminated the field of natural resources policy with original ideas, closely reasoned dicta about the propriety of concepts and the relevance of microeconomic analysis to this field. The papers in this section treat an array of issues—some relating to the proper quantification of benefits and costs, others pertaining to the efficacy of public policies. Wantrup saw both an opportunity and obligation for economists to address these questions.

Public water resource development policy was a principal paradigm within which he worked. He recognized both the holistic and dynamic character of public policy, and through his papers he engaged the array of issues to which his examination of policy leads. Though the argument often is at a high level of abstraction, his analysis is "applied" in a very real sense. The "so what?" question that punctures so many virtuoso performances in economics never begs to be posed.

The stage of natural resource policy remains a broad one. Wantrup clearly hasn't exhausted it, but his work displays exemplary intellectual rigor for those who continue in this line of work.

Concern with water development is natural for a Californian. In the semi-arid West, water often is the limiting resource for agricultural and non-agricultural development. This concern was especially natural for Wantrup

*Land and Water Consultant, Washington, D.C.

131

who had been an active participant in the lively dialogue about the Federal government's role in developing water resources in the state's Central Valley.

The first of the three papers that follow makes the important distinction between the economic justification of a public water development project and its financial feasibility. It demonstrates the different applications of cost-benefit analysis appropriate for each. Wantrup explicitly recognizes the flexibility afforded the analysis through such elements as "secondary benefits." In examining the relevancy of such benefits, he raises basic questions about accounting stance and inclusiveness of the accounting system employed. The ample opportunities for error in these areas notwithstanding, Wantrup concludes that benefit-cost analysis remains a valid and important tool for informing those who formulate water policy.

The second paper on cost allocation provides an opening to explore a potpourri of policy topics—an opportunity of which Wantrup takes full advantage. Equity matters, the importance of assorted repayment institutions, water rights, and the concentration of administrative authorities of the Commissioner of Reclamation are among the subjects considered. On the title subject of allocating joint costs, Wantrup candidly acknowledges that current formulations contain an arbitrary element, and thus he finds no purpose in trying to rank them by preference. Wantrup sees some advantage in this arbitrariness, reasoning that it permits affected parties a chance to argue their comparative merits, and ultimately to negotiate, and thereby generate a supporting consensus for water development.

The third paper also uses the nominal subject as a window for viewing underlying issues. In contrast to the previous piece, however, these issues are primarily methodological. Commencing with well-taken caveats about the slipperiness (and often sloppiness) of the language with which the subject is discussed, Wantrup explores differences and similarities between analyses of qualitative vs. quantitative phenomena. He remained concerned with this distinction for some time, and considers it elsewhere in his writings. The paper reprinted here treats an array of philosophical issues relating to the properties of theory and the meaning of models, projections, predictions and prophecies.

The principal contribution is to point out inadequacies of projections of natural resource supply and demands that are made within the comparative static framework. In detailing a number of these shortcomings, he implies the need for truly dynamic models—a need he expresses more directly in subsequent work. Recognizing that quantitative projections for a parameter at some point in future time hold policy implications that may trigger behavioral change in the meantime, Wantrup expresses skepticism of analyses that assert behavior and extrapolate conditions to the end of some planning interval. He considers "end-state" projections of limited value for policy purposes.

Throughout his pioneering work in water resources development, and despite the force of his arguments, Wantrup has modest ambitions for economic science. He recognizes that political criteria often will supercede economic ones. Yet, he sees a major opportunity for resource economics to develop in this area of application. Indeed, Wantrup maintains that a principal benefit of cost-benefit analysis is its utility for focussing professional disagreement and debate, thereby enhancing the likelihood of economics making more explicit and more significant contributions to natural resource development policy in the future. Though he emphasizes its current shortcomings, he clearly has high hopes for applied economic analysis of natural resource problems.

The evolutionary character of policy-oriented analysis leads Wantrup repeatedly to the contention that by careful use of theory and by its analytical design, the contribution of economics to policy can best be enhanced. He perceives economists engaged in such work as vitally important human resources for advancing the productivity of natural resources through improved policies.

Chapter 8*

BENEFIT-COST ANALYSIS AND PUBLIC RESOURCE DEVELOPMENT*[1]

1. A Crucial Question

Decisions by the government regarding resource development are essentially political rather than economic. This holds for their substance, for the social process by which they are reached, and for the institutions through which they are implemented. This, in itself, is merely a commonplace observation of reality, neutral in terms of value judgments. But in connection with my topic, it gives rise to a crucial question.

There is fairly general agreement that benefit-cost analysis is subject to many weaknesses. There is also recognition that benefit-cost analysis can be and has been distorted and abused.[2] One may ask then: Is it worthwhile investing considerable effort and expense in benefit-cost analysis if the risk of misleading results is great and—even though this risk is avoided—if the results are of relatively minor significance as compared with political factors in actually affecting public resource development?

This question has been answered in the negative by individuals and groups with quite different attitudes toward public resource development. Some regard benefit-cost analysis as merely a waste. Others feel that economic measurement—being allegedly "static"—understates the "induced" benefits. Benefit cost analysis thus tends to hold public resource development at a lower level than is desirable. Therefore, instead of benefit-cost analysis, some feel that the political process should be relied upon. Still others fear that inflated benefit-cost ratios may be a pretext for the government to propose projects that are economically unsound, to be undertaken mainly for empire building of a particular agency, or to satisfy a pressure group. Alternatively, if the projects are economically sound, they should be paid for by beneficiaries. Thus, instead of benefit-cost analysis, many feel that "willingness to repay" a portion of the costs should be made the criterion for public resource development.

I should like to submit—and at this point of my paper, it is meant merely as

*Reprinted, with permission, from the *Journal of Farm Economics,*Vol. XXVII(4):676–689 (November, 1955).

proposition—that this question can be answered clearly in the affirmative. This means that benefit-cost analysis by the government appears worthwhile *in spite* of its weaknesses, its risks, and its relatively small, direct influence upon the actual course of events.

2. Abuse of Benefit-Cost Analysis

The first point mentioned in support of this proposition relates to distortion and abuse of benefit-cost analysis. One must keep in mind that economic and pseudoeconomic arguments are by far the most important weapons in the arsenal of opposed regional, industrial, and occupational interests contending in the political arena for or against a public project. Hence, distortion and abuse of benefit-cost analysis would not disappear if the government were to stay out of it. Quite the contrary. There would then be no calculation in which the general public could have confidence and that could be used as a standard to measure various claims. Furthermore, there would be no calculation easily open to public scrutiny in every detail. Such a standard can be provided only by a government. Even if this standard is not simon-pure, compared with an ideal standard conceived through economic theory, it still serves a worth-while purpose *to restrain the abuse of economic arguments in the political process.*

One may admit that abuse of government benefit-cost analysis is more dangerous in its consequences than abuse of private calculations because of the greater confidence placed in the government by the general public. In this country, however, abuse of the government standard is made more difficult by the variety of government institutions.

In benefit-cost analysis, as in other fields, this government is not a monolithic structure. Besides the federal government, state governments are highly important in resource development. In all these governments there is division between the executive and the legislative branches. In the federal government alone, the agencies engaged in benefit-cost analysis comprise at least four major executive departments (some of them with several fairly independent bureaus), the Federal Power Commission, and, of course, the Bureau of the Budget. Many of these government agencies have their own traditions and objectives in benefit-cost analysis. Some of them compete directly or indirectly for public funds and, therefore, take a lively interest in each other's calculations. The rivalries and duplications among various agencies are well known. From the standpoint of benefit-cost analysis, however, the results have not been all bad. Inconsistencies and conflicts are brought into the open. Mutual review and criticism encourage improvements.

3. Quantifying in Benefit-Cost Analysis

Benefit-cost analysis requires quantification both in physical and economic terms. Quantifying in economic terms involves evaluating on the basis of a common denominator or weight. In practice this means money, although other denominators are conceivable and are used in economic theory.

The necessity of quantifying in terms of money is frequently pointed out as a weakness of benefit-cost analysis. One may wonder whether or not this necessity does have a positive side. Economics and the social sciences in general do not stand alone in dealing with important problem areas in which quantifying is difficult or irrelevant. On the other hand, an attempt to overcome these difficulties and to determine the relevance of quantification is an important stimulus of scientific progress. In economics, particularly, an attempt at evaluation compels the student to face and take into account his own preferences, to scrutinize whether or not he has considered all relevant variables, and to get some idea of the relations among the variables and the institutional restrictions in economic measurement.

An attempt to quantify in one science frequently has stimulating effects upon others. This holds for benefit-cost analysis. Engineers, hydrologists, ecologists, and other physical scientists who furnish the necessary basic data for benefit-cost analysis, have sometimes regarded the social scientist as an irritant if not a nuisance. But would they deny that his persistent quest for additional quantitative information has stimulated research in the physical problems of flood control, reclamation, and land management?

One may argue, therefore, that the mere necessity of quantifying makes benefit-cost analysis worthwhile *because of its stimulating effects in expanding scientific understanding of the physical as well as social problems involved in public resource development.* This role of benefit-cost analysis, like the preceding one of restraining the abuse of economic arguments in the political process, exists even if some weaknesses could not be overcome and if direct influences upon policy decisions should remain relatively minor.

After dealing with the two most frequent general objections against benefit-cost analysis, let us now attempt to appraise some of its weaknesses and to consider potentialities for reducing them. If these potentialities could be realized, the influence of benefit-cost analysis would be greater.

4. Extramarket Benefits and Costs

When the necessity of quantifying is cited as a weakness of benefit-cost analysis, two types of benefits and costs are usually mentioned or implied, "intangible" and "indirect" or "secondary." The evaluation problems posed are theoretically intriguing and of considerable practical significance. Next to problems of cost allocation,[3] such evaluation raises the most controversial problems of benefit-cost analysis among students and government agencies.

In this paper, I should like to focus on these two problems. The problem of "intangibles" is considered first because its discussion touches upon the more basic weaknesses of benefit-cost analysis.

At first glance, one portion of benefits and costs appears rather obvious and simple to evaluate. Such items are usually called "tangible." Examples are the value of cotton produced by an irrigation project and the costs of the cotton, the dam and the productive agricultural areas flooded by the reservoir. On the other hand, if the project water is to be used to rehabilitate wintering grounds for waterfowl such as the "grasslands" in the western San Joaquin

Valley, if the dam interferes with anadromous fisheries as in most rivers of the Pacific Slope, and if a reservoir floods a canyon, a "product" of which is impressive scenery as in the Upper Colorado Storage Project as presently proposed, these benefits and costs are usually called "intangible."

The price of cotton, of course, is reported every morning in the newspapers. Similarly, the current prices of raw materials, the wages, and the interest rates, used in computing the costs of the cotton and of the dam can easily be ascertained. The same holds for the price of an acre of agricultural land that is flooded. However, if such unit values yielded directly by the market are to be used in public resource development, such use is by no means obvious and simple. At this point, I do not refer to the problems connected with elasticities of demand and supply, with economic fluctuations, with changes over time of preferences and technology, and with the uncertainties attaching to all these estimates. Solution of these problems is not simple, but practical approximations can be found. More basic difficulties are created by the fact that the functioning and results of the price system itself are profoundly affected by aggregate income, income distribution, and market form. These, in turn, are affected by a host of social institutions having an important and highly complex status in individual preference systems.

For some purposes, it makes sense in economic analysis to regard properly defined institutional conditions as dependent or independent variables. For example, relations among the systems of tenure, taxation, and credit on one side, and resource development on the other, may usefully be discussed in this way. Similarly, the effects of changes in particular statutes or government organization can be studied.[4] On the other hand, for purposes of benefit-cost analysis—which comprises only a small part of economic analysis—most social institutions can only be brought into the calculation as logical restrictions (constraints). This means that benefit-cost analysis has relevance for an economic criterion of public resource development only under "given" institutional conditions. The investigator should be clear about this even if he does not state the significant institutional conditions explicitly.

Institutional restrictions on the validity and relevance of values directly yielded by the market are far more severe than the additional restrictive assumptions that become necessary if evaluation is extended to those benefits and costs not evaluated directly in the market place. One may wonder whether or not economists are justified in placing great confidence in the validity and relevance of the price of cotton, for example, in evaluating water resource development, and rejecting the evaluation of recreational opportunities as belonging to the field of metaeconomics.

The implied conclusion is not that benefit-cost analysis of "tangibles" should be given up. Rather, in accordance with the over-all role of benefit-cost analysis suggested above, evaluation procedures should be tightened but not necessarily confined to goods whose values are directly yielded by the market. The semantics of the terms "tangible" and "intangible" reflect and strengthen confusion and emotional attitudes in matters of evaluation. Various evaluation procedures range from those that use market values directly to those that use market values with considerable adjustments, or only indirectly.

In public resource development in this country at the present juncture, recreational opportunities in a broad sense—including fish and game, wilderness areas, and national and state parks—are some of the items among extramarket values that may well be considered in benefit-cost analysis. Whether the economist likes it or not, evaluation of these items (and also dismissal of such evaluation) is already a part of the political process. Reports of fish and game departments and other public agencies illustrate many attempts to evaluate these resources. One may have professional doubts about some of the procedures used. Still, these attempts should be encouraged. Otherwise, the arguments of well-organized groups interested in market values alone, who dismiss these resources as "intangible" might receive disproportionate attention in policy decisions.[5]

This is not to suggest that *all* benefits of recreational resources could be evaluated. In connection with many such resources, however, market values can be used indirectly—for example, through analyzing data on fees, leases, and real estate transactions. In other cases, measurement in terms of physical units of use—for example, man-days—can be accomplished fairly easily. Values of additional units of use can be approached through questionnaires and the study of behavior in other experimental choice situations. Even such crude and partial measurement is more useful than disregarding these values altogether, or substituting for them some figure based on the expenditures of users for transportation, room and board, guns, fishing tackle, and similar items.

5. Primary (Direct) and Secondary (Indirect)

Benefits and Costs

Let us now turn to the problem of indirect benefits and costs. Although this problem is sometimes confused with that of "intangibles"—the terms "indirect" and "intangible" are even used interchangeably—there is little relation between the two. Most indirect benefits and costs considered in benefit-cost analysis are evaluated in the market place. But this is not the issue. The issue is whether or not, and for what purpose, indirect benefits and costs should be considered and added to direct ones.

First, what is the meaning of direct and indirect benefits and costs? We may adopt the definition and terminology of the Subcommittee on Benefits and Costs of the Federal Inter-Agency River Basin Committee.[6] According to this definition, direct costs are the value of the goods and services needed for the establishment, maintenance, and operation of the project and to make the immediate products of the project available for use or sale.[7] Direct benefits are the value of the immediate products and services for which the direct costs were incurred. Indirect benefits are the values added to the direct benefits as a result of activities "stemming from or induced by" the project. Indirect costs are the costs of further processing and any other costs (above the direct costs) "stemming from or induced by" the project. The Subcommittee prefers the terms "primary" and "secondary," instead of "direct" and "indirect," presumably because in the economics of flood control the terms "indirect" or "incidental" have for sometime been used in connection with products (other than the prevention of direct flood damage) which, in the terminology of the Subcommittee, must be regarded as "immediate."

Three problem areas are as important in appraisal of secondary benefits and costs as in discussion of cost allocation.[8] The first problem area is the selection of the "best" project; the second is the repayment by beneficiaries to the government; the third is the pricing of those immediate products of a project that are sold. These problem areas are connected in benefit-cost analysis through economic concepts, some common basic data, and existing statutory provisions. But the potentialities and limitations of benefit-cost analysis differ among these three areas, the concepts and basic data needed are not all the same, and the statutory provisions that connect them are neither precise nor unchangeable. This paper is concerned mainly with the two problem areas of project selection and repayment. The problem area of pricing is excluded because of space limits, not because it is less important.

For purposes of project selection, benefits or costs that constitute transfer items among regions, among industrial or occupational groups, and among individuals, should not be considered. Whether or not such transfers are desirable is a separate issue in public policy. Considerations concerning income distribution will appear in clearer focus if they are separated from the problems of increasing real national income. An account in which transfer items are not considered may be called a "national" account.

On the other hand, repayment of net benefits to certain regions, to industrial or occupational groups and to individuals may well be considered even if they are transfer items. Such repayment accounts will generally be on the basis of regional, industrial, or occupational groupings. For that reason, they may be called "regional" or "industry" accounts. The significance of differentiating among these various accounts will appear presently.

6. Secondary Benefits "Stemming from" a Public Project

The many kinds of secondary benefits (and costs) considered in the literature[9] and practice of benefit-cost analysis may be divided into two major classes. The first comprises those alleged to accrue in connection with the processing of the immediate products; this class is referred to by the term "stemming from." The second class comprises those benefits (and costs) alleged to accrue because expenditures by the producers of the immediate products stimulate other economic activities; this class is referred to by the term "induced by."

Let us start with secondary benefits from processing.[10] Under competitive markets, net benefits arising from processing (above all corresponding costs of processing) quickly find expression in the demand by processors for the immediate products of a project. In connection with public resource development, a demand function may be identified with a marginal benefit function. An estimate of the demand function for the immediate products of a public project is, therefore, the most essential basic step in considering primary benefits.[11] Hence, if by some more or less arbitrary accounting procedure secondary net benefits from processing are determined and added to the primary net benefits, a portion of primary benefits is counted twice.[12]   If "abnormal" profits would be derived from processing the products of a public project under monopsonistic or monopolistic markets, there are several possibilities. This situation can sometimes be avoided by expanding the "project." Processing facilities—for example, for transporting power— may be included as a part of public resource development. In other cases, competition may be encouraged by appropriate public policies. Many opportunities for such action exist because the government either is the producer or has considerable influence with the producers to set up processing facilities on a cooperative basis.

If this approach is not chosen, correction for these market conditions may be made in benefit-cost analysis. If the problem area is project selection, such correction should be made through the demand function used as the basis for computing primary benefits. In such a computation quantities and values used "as if" markets for the immediate products were competitive. To construct such a demand function, data are required on revenues and costs in processing. But such data are also required for identifying "secondary benefits" from processing.

If the problem area is repayment, net income in processing industries "stemming from" the public project may be identified as secondary benefits in regional or industry accounts. However, benefit items in these accounts should not be added to benefit items in the national account.

Identification of secondary net benefits in industry or regional accounts stimulates a better understanding of regional effects of public resource development. Such identification has practical significance as a preliminary step toward broadening the repayment base—which is sometimes rather narrow if confined to primary benefits—toward obtaining dependable repayment contracts from groups of beneficiaries, and toward making special taxes socially more acceptable. The term "preliminary" is used because the problem area of repayment is dominated by social institutions. Benefit-cost analysis in itself can only call attention to their economic aspects and thereby facilitate changes.

Sometimes people argue[13] that secondary net benefits from processing arise from the fact that the goods produced by a public project may lower market prices. Since the immediate products are available to processors at lower prices, the project should then receive a credit for secondary net benefits equal to the price differentials times the quantities produced. Some question may be raised about this argument.

The quantities produced by a public project of course may be large enough to have effects upon prices; but such a situation in itself does not indicate additional profits from processing. At best, such additional profits are short-lived. The quantities produced by the project should be evaluated with the prices at which these quantities can be absorbed.

On the other hand, the project should not be debited with the effects of price decreases of "intramarginal" quantities—that is, of quantities that would be produced without the project. Such price effects of a project, both through products supplied and services demanded, are transfer items among producers and consumers that should not be considered in benefit-cost analysis for purposes of project selection. For purposes of repayment, on the other hand, net income resulting from such effects may be considered as secondary benefits in industry or regional accounts.

7. Secondary Benefits "Induced by" a Public Project

Next, let us consider the other major class of secondary benefits, namely, those from an expansion of economic activity "induced by" the public project. This is a more complex and more important problem than the preceding one.

The argument for including this class of secondary benefits is supported on the academic level through analyses based on Keynesian economics. In the practice of benefit-cost analysis, however, this class of benefits is computed regardless of underemployment among productive services, in the course of general fluctuations of investment, saving, and income. First, therefore, it is advisable to deal with this class under the assumption that there is no "cyclical" underemployment.

This assumption does not mean that there is no unused capacity. In reality, an economy is in constant change even if aggregate investment, saving, and income are assumed constant. In such an economy, there is always unused capacity, not only in industries in a state of stagnation or decay but also in those in a state of growth, because growth rates are different in interrelated activities. Furthermore, such "structural" underemployment is generally concentrated in particular industries and regions. Public resource development can, under some conditions, help in making use of such underemployed services.

The most logical and practical way to take such effects into account for benefit-cost analysis is through evaluation of primary costs—not through secondary benefits. Under competitive markets, the fact that productive services are underemployed is reflected in the prices at which they are available—in situ or including costs of movement—to the public project. Under monopolistic markets, this may not be true. In such cases, appropriate corrections can still be made through the supply functions of productive services used as a basis for computing the primary costs. If data are not sufficient to estimate prices of productive services "as if" their market were competitive, an "offset" to primary costs may be calculated in connection with cyclical underemployment. This procedure is indicated for the problem area of project selection.

For the problem area of repayment, such effects may be identified as secondary benefits through income statistics. But again, care should be taken that such benefits are not counted twice—that is, are taken into account both on the cost and on the benefit side. Besides income statistics, some new techniques of economic analysis—for example, Leontieff's input-output model—may become helpful in the *ex ante* identification of such induced secondary benefits.

People frequently argue that secondary benefits are induced regardless of underemployment of productive services, cyclical or otherwise. Public resource development—for example, irrigation development in an arid region—may certainly induce many new economic activities. Under the assumptions of no underemployment and no change in technology and preferences, one may doubt that this increase is "net" for the national account. In other words, such increases are offset by decreases elsewhere in the economy. Hence, the increase may be considered for repayment but not for project selection.

On the other hand, public resource development may, over time, induce economic change in a broader sense. That is, it may change technology and preferences and thereby induce shifts of supply and demand schedules for the immediate products of a project. Some argue that such changes should be taken into account in benefit-cost analysis through secondary benefits (or costs) and that otherwise such analysis would remain "static."

Admittedly, the instantaneous supply and demand schedules used as basis for benefit-cost analysis involve highly restrictive assumptions with respect to future economic change. Far too little is known about the conditions of economic change to trace in practice a continuous "path" over time in terms of expected benefits and costs functionally related to public resource development. On the other hand, benefit-cost analysis may well be undertaken within discrete consecutive time periods—each involving different but interrelated assumptions. I have shown elsewhere that such time-period analysis and explicit consideration of the future are basic issues in resource economics.[14] The "pay-out schedules" commonly used in benefit-cost analysis may well be refined with respect to expected shifts in supply and demand for the immediate products of a project.

Only a part of the change in these assumptions from period to period will be related to the effects of public resource development itself. In this country especially, the effects of other forces are far more important. There are practical limits on the number and extent of periods and assumptions considered. Still, the fact remains that long periods of gestation—at least ten and usually closer to twenty years from the time of project selection—make emphasis on future rather than past conditions of supply and demand a necessity in public resource development. Improvements in the direction of a period analysis of primary benefits and costs would seem more meaningful than attempting to make benefit-cost analysis "dynamic" through a more or less arbitrary addition of secondary benefits and costs—which are "static" in the same sense as alleged for primary ones.

Finally, there is fairly general agreement that public resource development can have secondary beneficial effects under the assumption of cyclical underemployment and should be considered from the standpoint of integration with other more direct and more effective anticyclical policies. The possibilities and difficulties of such integration need not be considered here.[15] In connection with the present topic, the issue is: How much should these beneficial effects be taken into account in benefit-cost analysis?

As in the case of structural underemployment discussed above, the most logical and practical way to take such effects into account is through evaluation of primary costs—especially construction costs—not through secondary benefits. Public resource development is most effective in reducing cyclical underemployment during the construction period. By taking the state of employment into account in the evaluation of construction costs, public projects will appear economically more attractive during depressions and less attractive during booms. This is because no corresponding adjustment should be made in benefits. As just emphasized, benefits from a public project start to flow only after a long period of gestation. Even if this start does not coincide with the next boom phase, it can be assumed that the flow continues over several "cycles."

Under competitive markets, cyclical underemployment of productive services is reflected in the prices of such services. Under monopolistic (monopsonistic) markets, this is not likely. Still, adjustments can often be made in the computation of construction costs by using prices for productive services "as if" their markets were competitive. Alternatively, a sliding-scale "offset" to primary costs may be calculated.

The Panel of Consultants suggested that such an offset be added to construction costs. This offset is calculated by multiplying construction costs with a plus (full employment) or minus (unemployment) factor which is "the percentage of the resources used in construction of this project which is estimated will be drawn from unemployment rather than diverted from other uses."[16]

Although this method seems in need of clarification, there is no conflict in logic between it—if properly used—and the method that tries to take underemployment into account directly through prices of productive services used in the evaluation of construction costs. The method suggested by the Panel may be regarded as a first approximation to the other method. Care should be taken, however, that underemployment is not taken into account twice—that is, through prices used in evaluating construction costs *and* through the offset factor. Because of this danger, I prefer the more direct method. Also, practical advantages in obtaining basic data are probably in favor of this method—except in the case of labor costs.

8. Conclusions

When one tries to draw conclusions from this analysis of secondary benefits and costs, one is forced to suggest that all classes of secondary net benefits be dropped from consideration if the problem area is project selection. This is the most important problem area in which benefit-cost analysis is presently used.

This suggestion may seem to reflect an overly conservative if not negative attitude toward public resource development. This is not at all the case. But the effort presently invested in justifying the inclusion of secondary benefits and costs in the national account could be employed to greater advantage in a more careful evaluation of primary benefits and costs.

This advantage would accrue to the twofold over-all role of benefit-cost analysis indicated above, especially the first one of restraining the abuse of economic arguments in the political process (Section 2). Secondary benefits and costs have for some time been suspected by legislative bodies as facilitating double counting and other forms of "padding" benefits.[17] If the foregoing analysis is correct, these suspicions are not unfounded. Elimination of secondary benefits and costs in the national account would make benefit-cost analysis more straightforward, not only for the professional economist but also for the layman. The influence of benefit-cost analysis with legislative bodies and the public at large may thereby be increased.

Beyond that, advantages may accrue to the second over-all role of benefit-cost analysis, that of stimulus to scientific understanding (Section 3). There are few issues in benefit-cost analysis that force the student to ask more searching questions regarding public resource development than a critical appraisal of secondary benefits and costs in their relation to primary ones.

Another conclusion to be drawn is the need for a clear differentiation among problem areas, or purposes, of benefit-cost analysis (Section 5). Some items that should not be considered for project selection may well be considered for repayment. For other items, the reverse may be true. For example, recreational benefits should be considered for project selection (Section 4), but as a matter of policy or practical expediency they may be omitted for repayment.

The twofold over-all role of benefit-cost analysis appears no less important for repayment than for project selection. Most of the economic arguments by interested regional, industrial, and occupational groups are concerned with repayment. A government "standard" in the above sense (Section 2) is especially needed in this problem area.

Establishing regional and industry accounts, as discussed for benefit-cost analysis of repayment (Section 6), stimulates research in the regional effects of public resource development, in the factors affecting the economic growth and location of industries, and in the social institutions—as variables and as restrictions (Section 4)—that dominate the criteria, the form, and the assessment of repayment.

Practical influences of benefit-cost analysis—in broadening the repayment base, in obtaining dependable repayment contracts, and in making public districts and special taxes more acceptable—exist insofar as appropriate changes of social institutions are facilitated. The latter influences are largely educational and must operate through the political process.

Such indirect and modest influences may seem to give support to the proposal mentioned in the beginning (Section 1), to adopt "willingness to repay" as a more direct and effective substitute for benefit-cost analysis. If this "willingness" were affected primarily by economic factors, ascertaining it would require an effort similar to that for benefit-cost analysis. But "willingness to repay" is more akin to "requirement to repay" as determined by statutory provisions, precedent, and political influence of beneficiaries. It makes little sense to employ or even to define "willingness to repay" as an economic criterion. Through benefit-cost analysis, on the other hand, an economic upper limit of "willingness to repay" can be determined. Furthermore, through benefit-cost analysis, the political lower limit of "willingness to repay" may be raised through the indirect and modest influences suggested above.

We conclude that there is no substitute for benefit-cost analysis in public resource development. Its role in the actual course of affairs may be unspectacular but properly used the effort is worthwhile. Furthermore, there are potentialities for improvement that may render the practical influence of benefit-cost analysis considerably more potent.

[1]Giannini Foundation Paper No. 146, *Journal of Farm Economics*, Vol. XXXVII, No. 4, (November, 1955), pp. 676-689. An earlier version of this paper was presented before the Annual Meeting, American Association for the Advancement of Science, Joint Session, Sections K (Economics) and M (Engineering), December 27, 1954.

[2]See Luna B. Leopold and Thomas Maddock, Jr., *The Flood Control Controversy: Big Dams, Little Dams, and Land Management* (New York: The Ronald Press Company, 1954), 278 p. Raymond Moley, *What Price Federal Reclamation?* (New York: 1955), 72 p. (Series "National Economic Problems", No. 455.)

[3]See S. V. Ciriacy-Wantrup, "Cost Allocation in Relation to Western Water Policies," *Journal of Farm Ecnomics*, Vol. XXXVI, No. 1, February, 1954.

[4]These and other examples are discussed in greater detail in S. V. Ciriacy-Wantrup, *Resource Conservation, Economics and Policies* (Berkeley: University of California Press, 1952), 395 p.

[5]In order not to be indicted of subjective bias in favor of recreational resources, a recent attempt to evaluate another item—still more problematical but related, namely, leisure—may be cited: Simon Kuznets, "Long-Term Changes in the National Income of the United States of America Since 1870," in *Income and Wealth of the United States, Trends and Structure, Income on Wealth, Series II* (Cambridge: Bowes & Bowes, 1952). See especially pp. 63-69.

[6]Subcommittee on Benefits and Costs, *Proposed Practices for Economic Analysis of River Basin Projects* (Washington: May, 1950), 85 p. (Report to the Federal Inter-Agency River Basin Committee). See particularly pp. 8 and 9.

[7]The latter costs are called "associated costs," but this differentiation is not material for our present purpose.

[8]Ciriacy-Wantrup, "Cost Allocation in Relation to Western Water Policies," *op. cit.*

[9]Subcommittee on Benefits and Costs, *op. cit. Secondary or Indirect Benefits of Water-Use Projects* (Washington: June 26, 1952), 63 p. (Report of Panel of Consultants to Michael W. Straus, Coommissioner, Bureau of Reclamation.)

U. S. Congress, House, *Economic Evaluation of Federal Water Resource Development Projects* (Washington: Govt. Print. Off., December 5, 1952), 55 p. (82nd Cong., 2d sess., Report to the Committee on Public Works by the Subcommittee to Study Civil Works.)

Executive office of the President, U. S. Bureau of the Budget, *Reports and Budget Estimates, Relating to Federal Programs and Projects for Conservation, Development, or Use of Water and Related Land Resources* (Washington: Govt. Print. Off., December 31, 1952), 20 p. (Circ. A-47.)   M. M. Kelso, "Evaluation of Secondary Benefits of Water Use Projects," *Water Resources and Economic Development of the West* (Berkeley, California: March 2-3, 1953) pp. 49-62. (Proceedings, Committee on the Economics of Water Resources Development of the Western Agricultural Economics Research Council, Report No. 1, Research Needs and problems.)

[10]In the case of power, these benefits are sometimes subdivided further under the terms "savings benefits," "extended benefits," and "utilization benefits." See *Trinity River Division, Central Valley Project, California* (Washington: Govt. Print. Off., 1953), pp. 73-75 (83d Cong., 1st sess., H. Doc. 53.)   [11]For more details on this point, see Ciriacy-Wantrup, *Resource Conservation, Economics and Policies*, Chapter 17.

[12]In arriving at secondary benefits, it has become customary to apply standard percentages to the primary benefits. These percentages are derived from the statistics of average values added in processing. Thus, for cotton and other industrial raw materials produced by a public irrigation development the percentages are high (80 percent and more), and smaller for livestock products.

[13]For example, Subcommittee on Benefits and Costs, *op. cit.*, pp. 10 and 40.

[14]Ciriacy-Wantrup, *Resource Conservation, Economics and Policies*, Chapters 3 and 4.

[15]*Ibid*, Chapter 15.

[16]Kelso, "Evaluation of Secondary Benefits of Water Use Projects," *op. cit.*. p. 56.

A similar statement and illustrative graph appear in the Panel report itself (*Secondary or Indirect Benefits of Water use Projects, op. cit.*, pp. 31 and 32). However, these statements do not clarify how a positive factor is calculated.

[17]See, for example, *Economic Evaluation of Federal Water Resources Development Projects, op. cit.*

Chapter 9

CONCEPTUAL PROBLEMS IN PROJECTING THE DEMAND FOR LAND AND WATER*[1]

Demand in Long-Range Economic Projections

The last decade has brought a great increase in the literature dealing with long-range economic projections. This world-wide interest is explained by the attempt to apply economics as an operationally significant policy science and—in close relation—by greater emphasis on the quantitative character- ization of economic change. Conceptual problems encountered in these two important areas of current interest are the theme of the present paper.

Long-range projections of land and water use form a good part of the literature. The U. S. Department of Agriculture has released several studies.[2] The President's Water Policy and Materials Policy commissions and other groups have presented similar figures.[3] Numerous individual authors have used these projections with or without modification.[4] For individual states, there are detailed regional projections of land and water use.[5] Every benefit- cost analysis for public land and water development projects contains a section on future use of land and water.

Some of these projections are merely extrapolations of past trends in physical land and water use. Others focus on projections of the consumption of agricultural products. Land and water use is then determined on the basis of trends in average yields and water duties per acre. Projections of consumption of agricultural products are often interesting statistically.[6] Usually, a regression to gross national product or national income is employed. These, in turn, are projected through trends in population, labor force, and average productivity of labor, capital, or other inputs.

At the outset, one must emphasize that existing projections of land and water use are neither conceptually nor empirically identical with projections of land and water demand. In the literature, besides the word "use" similar

*Reprinted, with permission, from *Modern Land Policy*, Eds. Harold G. Halcrow, *et. al.,*(Urbana: University of Illinois Press, 1960), pp.41-67.

words with a physical-engineering connotation are employed. Such words are "consumption," "utilization," "requirements," "needs," "potential use," and "ultimate use." Commonly, however, the word "demand" is employed interchangeably, and the identity of projected demand with protected "use," "consumption," "requirements," and so on is clearly implied. In some cases, such identity is explicitly stated.[7] Nevertheless, projections of land and water use have two major characteristics which differentiate them from demand projections.

In the first place, use projections do not separate demand and supply conceptually or statistically. This lack of separation has operational advantages because—as will be shown presently—such separation is more difficult in land and water economics than in the economic analysis of most commodities. The conceptual defect is not too great if supply can be regarded as fixed—as, for example, the over-all regional supply of land—and if demand is not regarded as the "end" towards which use is oriented—as, for example, in military logistics, where orientation comes from outside of economics. On the other hand, if demand is to serve as a principle of orientation for public land and water policy—that is, to help in planning on the supply side— problems of demand and supply need to be separated conceptually and, in empirical investigation, variables pertaining to demand ("ends") must be differentiated from those pertaining to supply ("means").

In the second place, projections of land and water use do not consider sufficiently, if at all, the functional relation—and its changes over time— between prices (unit values) of land and water, on one side, and physical quantities, on the other. This relation is the foundation of demand and supply concepts. Its consideration is necessary in the analysis of many problems of land and water policy. Neglect of this relation is crucial even under conditions where lack of separation between supply and demand is no great conceptual defect. On the other hand, consideration of short-run and long-run price elasticity of use—and of its changes over time—would require differentiating between the significant variables which affect this relation and would induce a conceptual and empirical separation of demand and supply.

The demand by agriculture (the present paper is especially concerned with this "industry") for land and water is largely, but not exclusively, demand for productive factors and their services—for short, "inputs." It is derived demand. The consuming industry is agriculture. But can one define supplying industries for land and water? The term "industry" is employed in economic analysis as a useful fiction. In the application of demand and supply concepts to land and water, this fiction creates difficulties.

In order to reduce these difficulties with respect to land, the over-all supply is usually regarded as fixed for a given country or region. This means that man-made characteristics of land, which may affect microclimate, topography, soil, and economic location, are disregarded on the supply side. Instead, man-made characteristics appear in the demand function for land as inputs related to land in complementary or competitive fashion. More generally, a meaningful demand function for one input requires reference to the prices and quantities of related inputs.

Although this traditional definition of land makes it possible to disregard variations in the over-all regional supply of land, one must ask, "What about the supply of land to agriculture?" The price of land is not determined solely through the demand for land by agriculture even if over-all regional supply is regarded as fixed. Land is demanded for other uses besides agricultural. The most important of these uses are urban-industrial development; transportation, including highways, canals, and railroads; and what may be lumped together as "wild land" uses, that is, uses for forests, range, and recreation. These demands for land are frequently what Alfred Marshall would call "rival" or "competitive" demands.

From the standpoint of modern land and water policy, competitive demands pose one of the most significant issues. These issues can be referred to as the "allocation problem"; this means the allocation of given quantities of land or water among different uses. This terminology follows common usage that generally employs the words "allocation" and "development" of natural resources. The former term refers to the direction of the use vector. The latter term refers to length of this vector.[8]

In an economy like that of this country, in which land use is largely determined by the decisions of many individual users, the allocation of land among uses is related in many ways to the allocation among users, both public and private. For the purpose of a conceptual study, however, it is well to separate these two allocation problems. Such separation is also operationally significant for policy. There are some tools of policy—for example, zoning—which are aimed directly at the allocation among uses. There are other tools—for example, those concerned with land distribution between public and private ownership—which are aimed directly at the allocation among users.

The problems of defining the various industries that consume and supply water and of separating demand problems from those of supply are even more difficult than those incurred with respect to land. Decisions about the production and consumption of water are closely related. In most cases, these decisions are made by the same individuals or the same groups. This is true for the individual farmer who produces and consumes ground water or who diverts water from surface flow. It is also true for the hydroelectric and many individual industrial users who develop their own water supply. Finally, but most important, many water consumers develop their supply cooperatively through water management organizations with public characteristics and functions.

There are many varieties of these organizations. In agriculture, they are mainly irrigation and water conservation districts. In urban-industrial development, they are municipal water and utility districts. All of these organizations have in common that in their formation, operation, and growth, water consumers have a direct and significant influence that is outside the market demand-supply mechanism.

Even in those cases in which decisions about production and consumption of water are separated—for example, in water development by the federal government and individual states—one cannot speak of demand and supply and a resulting price. Consumers of water influence initiation of water projects by political, rather than economic, means. The public suppliers influence consumption in a number of ways other than through a supply price.

In water economics, the price per unit—for example, per acre-foot—is only a part of the total payment complex, which includes many forms of taxes and fees. This payment complex is always related to an institutional structure such as the rules of a public district, a contract with the Bureau of Reclamation, or the regulation of a public utility commission. Transfers of water among individuals and among water management organizations occur. But these transfers are generally in terms of water rights and are governed by water law more than by a water market. More research is needed on the economic terms of water transfers. But it is already fairly clear that there is little meaning in speaking of water demand, supply, and price in the sense of a market in which water-supplying and water-consuming industries meet.

Can these problems be simplified in a way similar to that for land—namely, by regarding the over-all regional supply of water as fixed? One may note in this connection that the concept of "ultimate use" occurs with increasing frequency in regional water projections.[9] The implication of this term is that the supply of water has physical, economically relevant limits.

Simplification through assuming regional supply as fixed or ultimately fixed is not meaningful for water. Water, in contrast to land, is a highly mobile productive service. Modern technology tends to increase the economic significance of physical mobility. The history of water institutions indicates considerable adaptability to the physical facts and the economic potentialities of regional water mobility.

Modern technology tends to make the assumption of ultimately fixed regional water supply questionable on several other grounds. Purification of mineralized waters is already economical under special conditions; it is only a question of time until existing knowledge makes more general application economical. The implications for regions with economical access to the ocean—for example, for southern California—are great. Modification of weather conditions with the objective of increasing precipitation and of reducing evaporation can no longer be regarded as a scientific dream. Management of the vegetative cover of watersheds to influence evapotranspiration, infiltration, and snow storage may greatly affect the volume, quality, and timing of water yield. Technological developments in geological exploration, well drilling, and pumping are constantly increasing ground water supplies. Control over new sources of energy, at present through fission of heavy elements and in the future through fusion of light elements, will greatly accelerate all these developments—and greatly increase the problems of waste disposal.

Although one cannot speak of a water market in the usual sense and cannot regard supply as fixed or ultimately fixed, application of demand and supply concepts to water may still be helpful in several important problem areas. First, water use is greatly influenced through the *ex ante* values of water employed in planning and constructing and the *ex post* payments for water employed in operating projects undertaken by water management organizations. The *ex ante* values imply a marginal social-benefit function. Such a function can be regarded as a species of demand function. For setting *ex post* payments for water, consideration of the price elasticity of water demand cannot be neglected. Second, the prices of inputs related to water are an important influence in water use regardless of whether they are conceptually considered in a demand or in a supply function of water. These price influences are neglected in existing use projections. An outstanding example is the price of electric power consumed in pumping ground water. Third, economic criteria may be applied to the functioning of the system of law which governs the transfer of water rights. Demand and supply concepts enter into these criteria.

Thus, instead of abandoning the application of demand and supply concepts to problems of land and water economics, let us inquire in what way these concepts might be used in economic projections. This involves an inquiry into the validity of economic projections in terms of the logic of inductive inference and into their relevance in terms of policy decisions in the land and water fields.

Validity and Relevance of Economic Projections in Policy Decisions

Projection over time is a special problem of inductive inference. In such projections, all undetermined cases of a hypothesis or of a system of hypotheses—a theory—are future cases. A projection is then called a prediction.

Predictions will differ with respect to the degree of articulation in the formulation of hypotheses and with respect to the degree of quantitative precision. On the basis of these differences, a projection is sometimes differentiated from a "forecast" and an "estimate." Without necessarily endorsing such differentiation, it may be noted that "projections," "forecasts," and "estimates" must be classed as predictions as far as the criteria for their logical validity are concerned. On the other hand, a prediction is not a prophecy. The only criterion that can be applied to a prophecy is the eventual outcome. In contrast, the eventual outcome of an individual case is not, in itself, a sufficient criterion of validity for a prediction. A prediction, in order to be valid, requires tested theories in the sense of "law-like" generalizations.

Criteria to decide whether a generalization deserves or does not deserve the designation law-like and, therefore, can be used for prediction, have occupied formal logic for a long time. In a recent small book, little known among economists, Nelson Goodman has made a suggestion which has attracted some attention in the philosophy of science.[10] His contribution is of interest for our present purpose.

In short, for establishing a criterion for "law-like," Goodman proposes not only to examine the predictive record of a theory but also to investigate how well this record is "entrenched" in scientific language. Like Hume, Goodman appeals to past recurrences, but to recurrences in the explicit use of terms as well as to recurrent features of what is observed. Inductive validity thus depends not only on the facts that are observed but also on how they are organized through language.

Such an approach may be called "semantic" because language rather than anything in the nature of human cognition becomes the principle through which predictive theories are separated from those that are not. Such separation does not, of course, imply that theories with predictive power will be confirmed by all or any future observations. As just emphasized, facts that are as yet unobserved cannot be used as criteria for predictability.

A semantic criterion for predictability may appear weak. Basically, however, Goodman's concept of "law-like" is similar to the concept of a law in modern physics and in other natural sciences. This latter concept of a law is merely stochastic.

Goodman is not specific about the meaning of the terms "entrenched" and "scientific language." Apparently, he is thinking primarily about the natural sciences, where agreement among competent men on the meaning of these terms may not be too difficult. In the social sciences there are few theories that could be called "entrenched" through agreement of competent men. This difference between the natural and the social sciences does not render the Goodman criterion unhelpful for our purpose. Rather, this difference indicates that the term "theory" does not have the same meaning in the natural and social sciences. It is increasingly recognized—among economists, at any rate—that most theories in the social sciences are, strictly speaking, "models."[11] The relations between theories and models will be considered presently.

In studying the linguistic terms of law-like generalizations, it becomes apparent that quantitative precision is not a requirement. On the contrary, most law-like generalizations are phrased on a rather low precision level (degree of quantification). For example, confirmed and unexhausted statements about the relations between variables are better entrenched if they refer to less quantified characteristics—such as general direction of change (increase, decrease), ordinal characteristics of change (greater, smaller, equal, proportional, and so on), sequences in time, reversibility, tendencies toward correction (equilibrium), or cumulation (disequilibrium)—than if they refer to cardinal characterization of parameters. This holds primarily for the social sciences, which are of concern here, but can be observed in many natural sciences as well. On the basis of the semantic criterion adopted, we may say that predictive power of a theory and degree of quantification are not correlated positively. Demand theory may serve as an illustration.

If by demand theory one means the broad generalizations in the Marshall-Henderson-Hicks formulation, they will pass Goodman's predictivity test.[12] Their language is couched in terms that refer only to general characteristics of change, that is, increase or decrease of prices and quantities. Elasticities, if mentioned at all, are stated in terms of ordinal characteristics. By the authors themselves and by most economists these generalizations are referred to as "the" demand laws.

On the other hand, there is little possibility of passing the Goodman predictivity test if by demand theory one means a demand function with a quantitative characterization of parameters that would allow demand projections comparable in precision to existing projections of land and water use.

Existing projections of land and water use may be regarded as a species of economic model. However, even the best of this particular species are incomplete in the sense that the most significant dynamic variables, namely, changes of technology, preferences, and institutions, are not included or only to a small extent. Furthermore, the relations between this species of model and theories are not conr predictability.

A semantic criterion for predictability may appear weak. Basically, however, Goodman's concept of "lawsidered or are poorly articulated.

What are the general relations of models to theories and law-like generalizations? Models are not substitutes for theories. Models are designed for better understanding of individual cases—past or future—and may be used for testing theories. Models, however, carry no predictive power in the sense just discussed. This holds for economic models generally but especially for existing projections of land and water use.

Against this lack of predictive power of models must be weighed the fact that for the individual case for which a model is designed they give a far more precise and frequently a "better"—in terms of outcome—projection than a prediction based on law-like generalizations. This superiority of modals, however, depends on their completeness. In this respect, as just noted, existing projections of land and water use are especially deficient. One may add that a prophecy also may be a more precise and "better" projection than a prediction based on law-like generalizations.

To question the validity of existing projections of land and water use in terms of criteria for predictability implicitly raises a question of relevance: If the attempt were made to base projections on law-like generalizations—for example, on the demand laws referred to—would such projections be relevant for the purpose for which the projection is made in spite of a precision level far lower than that of existing use projections?

One may postulate that the main purpose of projections of land and water demand is to serve as basis for public land and water policy. One may submit, then, that some of the most important decisions in modern land and water policy are a kind which, on their predictive basis, do not require a high degree of quantification. Stated positively, significant policy decisions are concerned with successive incremental improvements in social welfare that can be projected only in terms of direction of changes, their relative speeds, and their sequence in time.[13]

Frequently, one aspect of direction, speed, and sequence is of particular importance: It is important for policy to know whether an observed or planned change sets in motion corrective counterchanges tending toward a dynamic balance of the initial change, or whether a change sets in motion other changes which are circular and cumulative and tend to reinforce the initial change. Myrdal's well-known thesis about the nature of economic change is an example of a circular and cumulative system.[14] Likewise, relations between soil depletion, incomes, and population may involve such a system.[15] On the other hand, in the United States during the last 50 years relations between changes of relative prices of land, agricultural inputs other than land, and technological change in agriculture can be regarded as a corrective system.

For analyzing further how far quantitative precision in projection, or lack of it, is relevant for policy decisions, a particular area of policy decisions may be selected. Competition in demand for land and water, or what was called the "allocation problem," is of special interest here. Is the objective of policy decisions to "optimize" allocation of land and water? What is the meaning of optimizing? How relevant are quantitative projections of social optima in land and water allocation? These questions will be taken up in the following section.

Allocation Decisions in Modern Land and Water Policy

In modern Western society, land and water allocation among uses and users is accomplished largely through decentralized decision-making of many individual agents, both private and public. These agents are the subsectors in organizing and operating Western economies. Individual, federal, and state projects in land and water development may be regarded as subsectors in this sense, subject to "rules of the game" not greatly different from those applying to other subsectors. These rules become operational largely through property institutions and the price system. The design, performance, breakdown, and malfunctioning of these two systems are, therefore, of special interest in allocation. The ground rules and their constant adjustment are the domain of policy decisions.

In identifying the objectives of policy decisions in land and water allocation, one encounters what might be called the problem of unity of social objectives and criteria. Objectives in allocation policy cannot, in principle, be divorced from the objectives of other economic policies. Such objectives are interrelated, and social welfare criteria are no different in allocation policy than anywhere else.

Since Pareto,[16] economists have taken a special interest in optimizing social welfare and in the criteria of such optimizing. The present occasion is not suited for discussing the pros and cons of this literature. It must be noted, however, that optima of social welfare and formal criteria for optimizing are constructs in the sense of useful scientific fictions.[17] Optimizing is not and cannot be an actual policy objective.

These fictional constructs are useful as organizing principles for the great number of variables and kinds of relations that must be considered in welfare economics—to decide which ones to bring into the analysis explicitly, which ones to neglect, which ones to combine with others, and which ones to take into account as constraints. Information about these variables and relations is insufficient for projecting an optimum expansion path of social welfare over time in a dynamic framework.

For policy decisions of a limited scope—for example, evaluating a watershed project—incremental improvements in social welfare can be determined cardinally. This may be done in terms of comparing hypothetical changes of aggregate national or regional income that can be attributed to alternative projects or parts of them. For policy decisions of broader scope, incremental improvements in social welfare can be appraised only ordinally in terms of direction of changes, the relative speed of changes, and their sequence in time.

Having stressed the unity of objectives and criteria in public policy one must now make a suggestion which, to a few, may at first sight appear inconsistent: In natural resource economics, and particularly in allocation of land and water, there are some significant conditions which induce characteristic divergencies in the actual welfare performance of the economy from fictional welfare optima. This situation makes it permissible to focus on these significant conditions and their changes when considering policy objectives.

As implied above, the most significant of these conditions in land and water allocation is the performance of property institutions and the price system. Public policy is not so much concerned with quantitative optimizing of land and water allocation among uses and users at particular instants of time as with the direction and speed of continuous reallocation.

In water allocation, direction and speed are influenced more by water law than by the price system. Water law, and its changes over time, can be appraised by economic criteria.[18] These criteria, however, are mostly qualitative. If they are quantitative, they are ordinal rather than cardinal. Western water law in particular does not show up too badly under such an appraisal.

In the arid and semiarid regions in this country and elsewhere, water allocation among uses and users has always been a vital decision problem to society even when the quantity of water actually used was very small. In the beginning of water development—for example, in gold-rush days in the Mother Lode country of California—water allocation was such a decision problem when all uses including agriculture were small. In present-day California, water allocation is such a decision problem even though other uses are a small fraction of a great agricultural use. Since water allocation is always vital for societies in arid and semiarid regions, effective institutional tools have evolved. The result is a body of water law[19] which cannot be understood by taking its provisions one by one. It is a true system which functions as a whole. Each state is a laboratory in which this system has developed and is still developing.

If one wants to undertake an economic appraisal of the allocative function of this system, one cannot be content with appraising quantitative allocation prevailing at a particular instant of time. The purpose of this system is not to optimize water allocation in particular instants. What needs to be appraised is the direction and speed of reallocation. As indicated earlier, incremental improvements in these respects are the main policy objectives in water allocation. The first step toward such improvements is an understanding of the existing system and of the process of its change. When individual provisions are modified, such changes must be fitted into the whole system. If the system as a whole is judged inadequate, a better substitute must be offered. Only too often criticisms of water allocation at a particular instant are voiced by economists without regard to the nature of the decision problems that water allocation poses for policy. Optimizing as a fictional construct is confused with an actual policy objective.

In contrast to water policy, quantitative economic optimizing has not yet been proposed as an actual objective of land policy. However, highly quantified projections of changes in land allocation among various uses—to the year 2000 and beyond—are common.

There are two margins where direction and speed of reallocation are of special interest. The first is the margin between agriculture and urban-industrial development. The second is the margin between agriculture and wild lands.

A number of quantitative projections of the losses of land by agriculture to urban-industrial development are available. On the basis of these projections, the losses in food and fiber production are predicted. Concern is shown, especially in the West, because the acreage lost contains a high percentage of irrigated land. The level alluvial valleys are the most desirable land for both the irrigator and the subdivider.

In some regions, urban expansion may well be directed toward alternatively available land that is topographically unsuited for agriculture. But the transfer of irrigated land to urban-industrial development does not, in itself, create the need for policy measures. This need is created rather by the fact that reallocation of land between agriculture and urban-industrial development does not, in itself, create the need for policy measures. This need is created rather by the fact that reallocation of land between agriculture and urban-industrial development proceeds, at present, in a haphazard, leapfrogging manner involving high costs, both to agriculture passed over in the leapfrogging and to the resulting sprawled-out urban communities. There are several measures of land policy, mainly in the fields of taxation and zoning, by which these costs can be reduced through temporarily retarding reallocation of land in some areas and accelerating it in others. But projections of land losses by agriculture and of economic optima in land allocation at particular instants are not relevant for these policy decisions.

The literature also contains quantitative projections of losses of wild lands *to* agriculture. On this margin, in contrast to the urban-industrial margin, the problem of reversibility of allocation is involved. This problem is not even considered in existing projections, although it gives rise to the main policy issue on the wild-land margin. There is considerable evidence in this and in many other countries pointing to social costs of resource depletion brought about by cycles of expansion and contraction of agriculture.[20] These cycles can frequently be observed in regions where agriculture faces obstacles of climate, soil, and topography.[21] These regions are usually identical with the wild-land margin.

Public policy concerned with the conservation of soil, range, forests, and fish and game can do a great deal to reduce the social costs caused by expansion and contraction of agriculture on the wild-land margin. But projections of various land uses and of allocational optima at particular instants are of little help in this. Such projections merely beg the question. The approaches and tools of institutional economics, with particular emphasis on tenure, taxation, and credit, can be effectively applied without such projections.

The foregoing illustrations suggest that a discussion of land and water demand that does not aim at highly quantified projections may still have some relevance for land and water policy. For such a discussion, the modest and old-fashioned heading of "factors affecting the demand for land" may be forgiven.[22]

Factors Affecting the Demand for Land

Setting aside for the moment factors relating to uses other than agricultural and regarding agricultural demand entirely as derived demand, we might consider as variables in a demand function for land the value of agricultural land per acre, the net returns per acre, and the interest rate buyers of agricultural land might employ in capitalizing net returns. This simple set of variables has the advantage that statistical information relating to them is easily accessible (Fig. 1).[23]

Agricultural land values follow the movement of agricultural net returns with smaller amplitude and a lag. The lag is especially pronounced after land values have moved in one direction for a considerable period. Such movements in a downward direction took place between 1920 and 1933 and in an upward direction from 1940 to date. Net returns began to drop in 1918 and 1947, respectively.

The relation between land values and net returns, together with the lag in this response, makes net returns a fair predictor for major changes in the direction of land-value movement. (This is also true for gross returns. The turning points of gross and net returns are identical because movements of prices of productive services employed in agriculture are mostly more sluggish than the movements of prices of agricultural products.) This predictive power, however, is rather short-range, that is, does not extend further than the lag.

Changes of net returns per acre reflect changes of quantities and prices of agricultural outputs and quantities and prices of agricultural inputs related to land. One may inquire, therefore, about generalizations concerning the relations between these variables and land values.

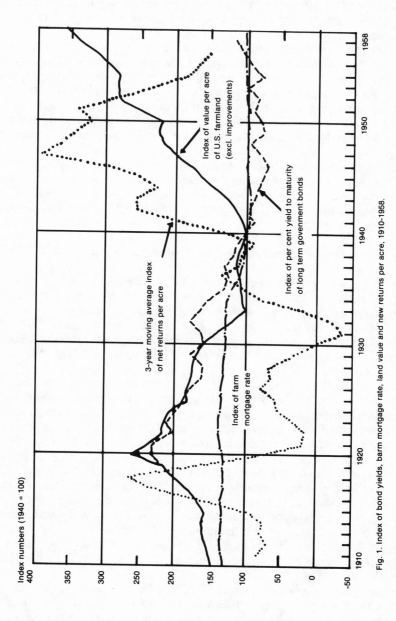

Fig. 1. Index of bond yields, barm mortgage rate, land value and new returns per acre, 1910-1958.

A comprehensive treatment of quantities and prices of agricultural outputs cannot be attempted in this paper. Such treatment would require a thorough discussion of the demand for agricultural products and of its changes over time. It need not be emphasized that changes in agricultural outputs have significant effects upon the demand for land absolutely and relatively to the demand for other inputs. This is true both for changes in the length of the output vector and for changes in its direction.[24]

An example of the latter changes may be noted in passing because it has played an especially significant role in the past and may again do so in the future. Changes in the demand for animal products have, other things being equal, much greater effects upon the demand for land than changes in the demand for food grains, potatoes, or, generally, for directly consumed vegetable products. This is due to the conversion losses incurred when final consumption of agricultural products is in the form of animal products. Changes of demand in favor of animal products have occurred during the last several decades in many countries under the influence of increasing per-capita incomes. If these changes should be reversed in the future, this would tend to decrease the demand for land. It is not impossible that such a reversal may take place under the influence of recent progress in the knowledge of certain aspects of human nutrition—largely connected with the role of saturated fatty acids—and the rapid and wide dissemination of this knowledge. The possibility, like other changes of consumer preferences, is not considered in existing projections of land use.

Prices and quantities of agricultural inputs reflect several changes which may be regarded here as conceptually different factors affecting the demand for land. First, there is technological change in agriculture in a narrow sense, that is, changes through discovery and invention of new kinds of inputs and changes of productivity coefficients, both affecting the inventory of known individual agricultural production functions. Second, there is technological change in a wider sense, namely, the gradual adoption of new techniques by the population of agricultural producers, which affects aggregate agricultural production functions. Third, there are changes of relative prices of agricultural inputs because of technological change in industries supplying such inputs or because of other changes in supply schedules. By some authors, the substitutions among agricultural inputs resulting from these relative price changes are also included in technological change. This terminology will not be employed here.[25]   In generalizing the relations between these factors and land values, two different views predominate. One view, which may be called the "modern," is held by many agricultural economists. This view emphasizes the significance of technological change in agriculture. Such emphasis leads to the expectation of increases in output per acre *and* in over-all output-input ratios of inputs other than land, and to the projection of minor increases or even decreases in land values relative to prices of other inputs. Some authors expect that land values will decrease relative to the prices of all commodities. The second, "classical," view puts less emphasis on technological change. This view also foresees increased output per acre but not so much through increased productivity of inputs as through increases in their quantities accompanied by decreases in their over-all output-input ratios. This view leads to the projection of a large increase in land values relative to the prices of other inputs.

The available evidence in the United States during the last 50 years does not give unqualified support to either of these two views. To this observer, at any rate, it seems that changes of relative prices of agricultural inputs because of changes in their supply schedules has far greater significance for the demand for land than they are accorded in these views.

The prices of the most important agricultural inputs, such as labor, machinery, improvements, fertilizer, and materials for the control of diseases in plants and animals, are determined largely by economic forces outside of agriculture and especially by technological change in nonagricultural industries. In relation to substitutions among agricultural inputs, these changes are the independent variables.

In the relation between changes of relative prices of inputs in a given industry and technological change in that same industry, the former are conceptually not always the independent variables. In the present case, however, there can be little doubt that changes of relative prices of agricultural inputs must be regarded as independent variables in relation to technological change in agriculture. Since this is not a matter of conceptual necessity but of historical fact, we need to take a short look at the actual changes of relative prices of agricultural inputs in the United States during the last 50 years. In Fig. 2, prices of agricultural inputs are shown relative to the prices of land with 1940 = 100.[26]

All price ratios show a pronounced general tendency which is upward from 1910 to World War II and downward since then. There appear, also, less pronounced fluctuations which are related to general price movements and indicate a somewhat less violent movement of land prices.

The pronounced general tendency in all price ratios suggests that it may be misleading to lump the prices of land and of improvements together in the prices of agricultural real estate. Likewise, the common practice of lumping the value of land together with that of improvements, machinery, and fertilizer as "capital" inputs hides significant differences in price movements.

The upward general tendency of the price ratios is especially pronounced for labor. The index of this ratio stood at 50 in 1910 and 160 at the end of World War II. This is a continuation of a trend that can be observed over several decades before 1910. Although the price ratio of labor to land shows the greatest secular change, the price ratios of labor to improvements, machinery, and fertilizer show changes in the same
direction. These changes in the relative price of agricultural labor must be explained by increased demand for labor in nonagricultural industries. Agriculture must be regarded as passive in this respect.

Under the influence of these changes in relative prices, one would expect that technological change in agriculture during the period between 1910 and World War II would have had a labor-saving and land-consuming accent.

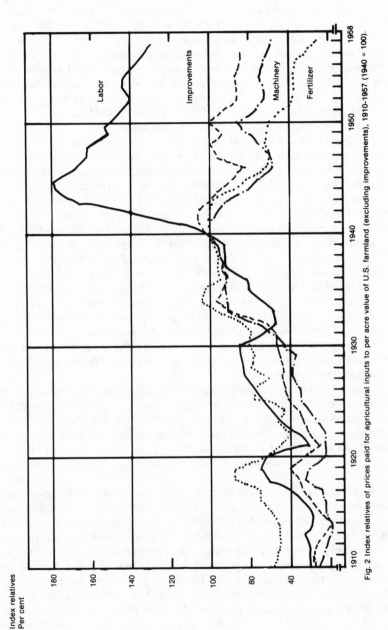

Fig. 2 Index relatives of prices paid for agricultural inputs to per acre value of U.S. farmland (excluding improvements), 1910-1957 (1940 = 100).

The words "saving" and "consuming" are, of course, meant figuratively and refer to substitution effects. In some cases, however, "land consuming" may be taken quite literally when effects on soil depletion are considered.

The outstanding illustration of labor-saving technological change is, of course, the mechanization of American agriculture and, connected with it, increased skill of farm operators and many organizational improvements. This is not to say that no aspect of this broad technological change was land-saving. One aspect—the replacement of draft animals by tractors— involved saving of labor *and* land. But the land-saving effects were incidental to the labor-saving orientation of mechanization.

From the land-consuming effects of this technological change, one would have expected corrective influences on the upward tendency of our price ratios. In view of the continuation of the economic forces outside of agriculture that affect the prices of labor and other inputs in agriculture, however, one would not necessarily have expected a reversal of this tendency. Yet such a reversal since World War II can be observed (Fig. 2). There is also some further corroborating evidence pointing to a sustaining and countercyclical influence on land values since World War II. The smaller amplitude and the lag in the movement of land values was observed previously (Fig. 1).

Thus, there is the possibility that the change in the general direction of the movement of the price ratios, which is noticeable since World War II, is the reversal of a long-time trend. In that case, one might expect a reversal in the character of technological change in agriculture. In other words, since World War II, this country might have entered a period in which technological change in agriculture would have a land-saving rather than a land-consuming accent—with continuation of labor-saving tendencies. There is some evidence to support this hypothesis.

Indications of an increasingly land-saving agricultural technology are the following: improvements in the use of fertilizer and other man-made components of soil fertility; improvements in the transformation of soil fertility into food and fiber through better strains of plants and animals, hybridization, artificial breeding, weed and pest control, plant hormones, and finally, beyond the horizon of practical adoption, hydroponics and algae culture.

A trend break after World War II in the movement of our price ratios is admittedly somewhat speculative. As mentioned before, cyclical variations in these ratios are normal. Furthermore, during and after World War II prices of most agricultural inputs were under administrative control which did not apply to the price of land. Still, one may mention several factors affecting the demand for agricultural land which support a trend-break hypothesis. These factors are well known to land economists.

One factor is the increase, since World War II, of the demand for agricultural land for uses other than agriculture. Another factor is the increase in the demand for agricultural land (for agricultural uses) by nonfarmers with relatively little interest in current net returns. In some cases, agricultural land is brought merely as an inflation hedge. The long period of price inflation since the beginning of the 1940's has made the American people especially asset-conscious. As an inflation hedge, investment in agricultural land has proved about as effective as investment in high-grade stocks. A further important influence in this investment demand is the increase in the rates and in the progression of income taxes during and after World War II. Agricultural land provides good opportunities for internal investment with low current income or even with losses. Income is then realized through capital gains, which are taxed at special rates. Finally, one important economic motive for nonfarmers to buy agricultural land is simply better and more secure living conditions (against automobiles and missiles) in the country.

Whether or not one accepts the hypothesis of a trend break in our price ratios and its effects on the character of technological change, there is one fairly safe conclusion that can be drawn from the interaction over time of changes in relative prices of agricultural inputs and technology in agriculture. It appears that this interaction tends to cushion changes in land values both in economic fluctuations and in secular perspective. Such a tendency injects a tempering note into the optimistic or pessimistic—depending on the two viewpoints discussed above—projections of land "scarcity" and its implication for policy decisions. The relations between changes of relative prices of agricultural inputs and technological change in agriculture can be called a "corrective system."

Demand in Water Economics

Consideration of demand is needed in three important areas of water economics: first, in determining *ex ante* values of water and *ex post* payments for water in public resource development projects; second, in understanding the effects on water use of changes in prices of related inputs and, in close connection, the effects of technological change; third, in appraising systems of water rights with respect to their effectiveness in allocating water in response to changes of water demand.

Demand considerations in determining values of water for the purpose of project planning are a part of an analytical procedure known as benefit-cost analysis. Admittedly, the various kinds of benefit-cost analysis now in use have shortcomings in dealing with water demand. These shortcomings were discussed in previous publications and suggestions for improvements made.[27]

Present trends are toward substitution of linear programming for benefit-cost analysis. The programming techniques presently in use are static, even though dating may be employed. The basic mathematics of dynamic programming have been known for a long time. They have been used in the conceptual clarification of the economics of conservation.[28] As yet, no operational applications of dynamic programming are available in water economics. It will be interesting to see, when actual results become available, whether the particular advantages of the technique are sufficient to overcome its particular limitations.

Benefit-cost analysis is essentially an informal but flexible programming technique. The informal technique leaves considerable latitude to its user in exercising judgment, professional competence, and integrity—or absence of these qualities—in selecting and stating his assumptions. In formal programming, the assumptions are largely "built in" and concealed from those who are not thoroughly familiar with the technique. Formal programming is superior to benefit-cost analysis in the sense that it can determine cheaply and precisely an optimum optimorum. As already implied, the significance of this superiority in time and uncertainty economics is at least doubtful. The numerical precision in determining optima may actually become harmful if it induces greater confidence in them. Calculations must be projected for instants of time beginning 15 to 20 years in the future. Such a gestation period is unavoidable between the planning stage and that of operation. The subsequent pay-out period cannot well be set at less than 40 years; usually it is longer. Programming for subsectors necessitates great detail in "activities" and "processes." While the conceptual defects of optimizing as an aid in the management of subsectors are less than those encountered above in optimizing for purposes of policy decisions, the problems posed by availability of data for smaller statistical aggregates are greater. Subsectors also will frequently find incremental analysis sufficient.

Project planning is only one of three important problem areas in which benefit-cost analysis may be useful. The other two areas comprise the broad problems of repayment of project costs, including problems of cost sharing and financing, and the related problems of pricing those products of a project that are sold. One may submit that the contribution of economics as an operationally significant policy science is potentially greater in the areas of repayment and pricing than in that of project planning. My reason for this proposition is that problems of repayment and pricing remain important after a project has been selected and constructed. This means that benefit-cost analysis can operate in the areas of repayment and pricing with a more complete and better-identified set of conditions that can be specified more accurately after the construction phase of the project has been completed.

Demand considerations involved in the pricing of water after a project has been constructed are different from those involved in arriving at water values for the purpose of project planning. The value per unit of water employed in project planning and the price used in project repayment are rarely the same. They are related in many ways, but there is no convincing reason why they should be identical conceptually or operationally.

Although a water price charged to individual consumers within a water management organization is only a part of the total payment complex, such a price may have effects similar to those of a market price. These effects are on the allocation of inputs, on prices and quantities of related inputs, on income distribution—especially through a creation of rents—and, over time, on technological change.

In understanding these effects and in applying efficiency criteria to water pricing practices, one has to keep in mind that the payment complex is an essential feature of the functioning of the water management organization that employs it. Formation, operation, and growth of water management organizations, individually and collectively, must be considered when appraising their pricing practices from the standpoint of the public interest. For example, when studying whether water prices should receive greater significance in water allocation and whether uniform or discriminatory pricing practices should be employed, instantaneous efficiency criteria are conceptually defective.

This is not to say that the efficiency of pricing practices within water management organizations should not be appraised in relation to the marginal-value productivity of water under the influence of crops grown, soil, time of water application, and so forth. Such "within" studies are rather neglected in water economics.[29] The effects of pricing practices on water use in the past is not even mentioned in existing projections which extrapolate such use. Beyond the efficiency of allocation at an instant of time, however, one has to appraise the efficiency of water management organizations as a system. The social function of the system is to develop additional water and to allocate water within each organization in response to changes over time of over-all water demand and of water demand by individual uses.

Water management organizations together with a water rights system functioning in combination largely replace the market system in water economics. These systems introduce characteristic discontinuities and rigidities. If, for example, water rights are allocated to an irrigation district, the district charter—that is, the state law under which it operates—may restrict water development and allocation by the district to agricultural uses. In some western states—for example, California—irrigation district law has been "loosened up" to broaden the purposes of irrigation districts. In addition, new laws permit the setting up of multiple-purpose water development and conservation districts.[30] Such discontinuities and rigidities and methods for their amelioration are promising subjects for economic analysis.

In considering changes of water demand under the influence of changing prices of related inputs, one must mention the pumping of ground water and the relation between ground water and surface water as a most important example from the standpoint of water policy. The effects on ground water pumping of a regressive rate schedule for electric power and of decreases over time in these schedules—relative to the prices of other inputs—has been studied for the Antelope Valley in California.[31] These changes of relative prices are closely related to technological change toward improvements in deep-well drilling and deep-well pumps. The great increase in the use of ground water during the last generation in the western United States, in spite of lowering of water tables through overdraft, can be directly traced to these interrelated changes of relative input prices and of technology. In some states—again, California is an example—more than half of total water use now consists of ground water. More recently, a similar increase has taken place in other arid and semiarid regions of the world—for example, Mexico, North Africa, and the Near East. New sources of energy for producing cheap electric power will give even greater impetus to these changes.

The relations between ground water and surface water are complex and of great interest to the resource economist. At the initial stages of development, ground water and surface water are frequently substitutes or, in the sense defined elsewhere, they are natural resources that are competitive in demand.[32] This situation changes with increased development. Ground water is so easily developed economically and institutionally that rapid depletion of this resource creates a strong demand for replenishment. Replenishment can come only from surface flow. Surface flow, on the other hand, is so variable in arid and semiarid regions, within the year and over a period of years, that storage is the essence of surface water development. Surface storage is limited, expensive, and subject to evaporation. Storage under ground is frequently an economically superior alternative. One may say, therefore, that surface water and ground water—and particularly ground water storage capacity—are natural resources that are complementary in demand. This change from competitiveness to complementarity with increasing length of use vectors is interesting because changes from complementarity to competitiveness are more common in natural resources development. This complementarity in demand increasingly requires integration of the use of ground water and surface water. The economic and institutional problems of this integration are a challenge to the social sciences.

From these relations between ground and surface water follow some conclusions with respect to long-range projections of water use. Projections through extrapolating past use are open to question because the rapid increase of water use during the last generation was, to a considerable extent, based on ground water mining and on the changes of relative prices and technology that gave rise to it. It is no less questionable to project water use on the basis of available nonirrigated irrigable land or population growth. To a considerable extent, future increases in the demand for surface water will be for replenishing ground water with the purpose of making the present agricultural and urban-industrial civilization, built on ground water, permanent. Economically and politically, this demand will have to be satisfied before that from new uses. The point in time when this replenishment demand will occur and its magnitude can be projected on the basis of existing knowledge regarding ground water depletion.

Again, an illustration from California may help to clarify the implication for water policy: The economic rationale of the Feather River Project is largely to firm up already existing water uses in the San Joaquin Valley and in southern California. New water uses may be regarded as by-products of this main objective. Quantitative projection of ultimate water use is not relevant for determining when and what additional quantities will be needed for replenishment, what the payment should be for these quantities, and under what economic arrangements the water not needed for replenishment should be disposed of. Present state water planning, on the other hand, is mainly concerned with the idea of projecting ultimate water requirements for each region of the state. In fairness to the planning officials, one should add that a legislative mandate relating to the determination of ultimate water requirements of certain areas of the state is partly responsible for this emphasis on projection. This mandate, known as the "area of origin laws," has been discussed elsewhere.[33]

Quite aside from the relation between ground and surface water just discussed, development of surface water can frequently be regarded as a by-product of projects the main purpose of which is the development of other resources, especially of hydroelectric power. Such projects range from relatively small developments undertaken by private electric companies to large federal developments as, for example, the Upper Colorado River Project. In these cases, one may say that the project creates and determines future water requirements rather than the reverse. Here, again, the task for water economics is an analysis of water values employed in planning individual projects and of the payment complex employed in water disposal. A similar situation exists when agricultural water use is—sometimes only temporarily— the by-product of water development for municipal and industrial use. The Colorado River Aqueduct of southern California is an example of this situation.

As a final example of areas in water economics where demand considerations are needed, we mentioned the economic appraisal of systems of water rights which govern the allocation of water between users and uses. An economic appraisal of these systems has been attempted elsewhere.[34] Space does not permit a detailed statement here.

This area of water economics is a promising field for cooperative research between the resource economist and the student of law. Help from the legal profession is needed because, as previously implied, the effectiveness of a system of water rights in taking into account changes of water demand has two aspects. The first is the provisions of the system as it exists at any instant of time that facilitate transfers of water rights between users and uses. An appraisal of the effects of these provisions is a task for the economist. The second aspect is the adaptability of the system over time to take into account changes of water demand. Greater adaptability of the system cannot be worked out by the economist alone.

Summary

Existing projections of land and water use have two major characteristics that differentiate them from demand projections. First, they do not separate demand and supply conceptually or statistically. If demand is to serve as a principle of orientation of public land and water policy, that is, to help in planning on the supply side, such separation becomes necessary. Use projections beg the question in this respect. Second, projections of land and water use do not consider sufficiently, if at all, the functional relation—and its changes over time— between prices of land and water and physical quantities. This relation is the foundation of demand and supply concepts. Its consideration is necessary in the analysis of many problems of land and water policy.

Existing projections of land and water use have no validity as predictions.

This, at least, follows from the logical criterion for predictive validity discussed in this paper. Projections of land and water use are not based on theories with predictive power. They are economic models, which have no such power. Furthermore, even the best of existing models in this area are incomplete in the sense that the most significant dynamic variables, namely changes of technology, preferences, and institutions, are not included or only to a small extent.

Existing projections of land and water use, like many economic models, are on a high precision level (degree of quantification) as compared with projections that could qualify as predictions in terms of the logical criterion adopted here. Generally, in projections, predictive validity and prediction level are not correlated positively. This situation poses the basic questions with which this paper is concerned: What precision level is required for projections in order to be relevant for decisions in public land and water policy? How is this precision level related to the actual objectives of policy decisions? What is the relation of such actual objectives to "optimizing" of social welfare? In view of the lack of predictive validity and the incompleteness of existing projections of land and water use, it is imperative that these questions be answered before statistical efforts to increase the number, temporal range, and quantitative precision of use projections are accepted as necessary or even useful.

The most important decisions in modern land and water policy are of a kind which, on their predictive basis, do not require a high degree of quantification. Stated positively, significant policy decisions are concerned with successive incremental improvements in social welfare that can be projected only in terms of direction of changes, their relative speed, and their sequence in time. Optimizing of social welfare is a scientific fiction, a construct useful as an organizing principle for the many variables and kinds of relations that must be taken into account in welfare economics. But such a functional construct should not be confused with the actual objectives of policy decisions. Thus, in allocation of land and water, policy decisions are not so much concerned with quantitative optimizing of allocation among uses and users at particular instants of time as with the direction and speed of continuous reallocation. Direction and speed can be appraised by economic criteria. These criteria, however, are mostly qualitative. If they are quantitative, they are ordinal rather than cardinal. Continuous reallocation is governed by several allocative systems—for example, the price system, water law, public districts, and water contracts—operating simultaneously. The design, performance, breakdown, and malfunction of these systems is the concern of allocation decisions in land and water policy. But quantitative projection of particular allocations or of optima in allocation at particular instants of time is of little relevance for these decisions.

In applying the foregoing analysis to current problems of land policy, one aspect of direction, speed, and sequence is of particular interest: whether an observed or planned change sets in motion corrective counter changes tending toward a dynamic balance of the initial change, or whether a change sets in motion other changes that are circular and cumulative and tend to reinforce the initial change. Relations between soil depletion, incomes, and population frequently involve a circular and cumulative system. On the other hand, the evidence indicates that in the United States during the last 50 years relations between changes of relative prices of land, of agricultural inputs other than land, and technological change in agriculture can be regarded as a corrective system. This system tends to cushion changes in land values both in economic fluctuations and in secular perspective. Such a tendency injects a tempering note into the optimistic or pessimistic—depending on the two predominant viewpoints in the literature that are discussed in this paper—projections of land "scarcity" and its implications for land policy.

In current problems of water-policy, those aspects of direction, speed, and sequence are of particular interest that are connected with the relation of ground and surface water. Projections of water use on the basis of the past are open to question because the rapid increase of water use during the last generation was, to a considerable extent, based on ground water mining and on the changes of relative prices and of technology that gave rise to it. It is no less questionable to project water use on the basis of available nonirrigated irrigable land or population growth. To a considerable extent, future increases in the demand for surface water will be for replenishing ground water with the purpose of making the present agricultural and urban-industrial civilization built on ground water permanent. Economically and politically, this demand will have to be satisfied before that from new uses. The point in time when this replenishment demand will occur and its magnitude can be projected on the basis of existing knowledge regarding ground water depletion. An illustration from California clarifies the implications for water policy: The economic rationale of the Feather River Project is largely to firm up already existing water uses in the San Joaquin Valley and southern California. Other water uses may be regarded as by-products of this main objective. Quantitative projection of ultimate water use is not relevant for determining when and what additional quantities will be needed for replenishment, what the payment should be for these qualities, and under what economic arrangements disposal should be made of the water not needed for replenishment.

[1]Giannini Foundation Paper No. 176. *Modern Land Policy.* Edited by Harold G. Halcrow *et al.* Urbana: University of Illinois Press, 1960, pp. 41-67.

[2]USDA, Agricultural Research Service, *Farm Output, Past Changes and Projected Needs* (Washington: GPO, August, 1956), 44 pp. (Agricultural Information Bull. No. 162).

USDA, Agricultural Research Service, *Agricultural Land Resources* (Washington: GPO, June, 1955), 107 pp. (Agricultural Information Bull. No. 140.)

USDA, Agricultural Research Service, *Major Uses of Land in the United States, Summary for 1954* (Washington: GPO, January, 1957), 102 pp. (Agricultural Information Bull. No. 168).

USDA, Agricultural Research Service, *Changes in Farm Production and Efficiency, 1956 Summary* (Washington: GPO, August, 1957), 45 pp.

[3]U.S. President's Materials Policy Commission, *Resource for Freedom* (Washington: GPO, 1952), Vol. 5, 154 pp. (Selected Reports to the Commission).

U.S. President's Water Resources Policy Commission, *A Water Policy for the American People* (Washington: GPO, 1950), Vol. 1.

U.S. Forest Service, *Timber Resources for America's Future* (Washington: GPO, 1958), 713 pp. (Forest Resource Report No. 14).

Marion Clawson, Burnell Held, and Charles H. Stoddard, *Future Land Use in the United States*, 2 Vols., June, 1958 (review draft). Mimeographed.

[4]Sherman E. Johnson, "Prospects and Requirements for Increased Output," *Journal of Farm Economics*, 34 (December, 1952), 682-94.

Carl P. Heisig, "Long-Range Production Prospects and Problems," *Journal of Farm Economics*, 35 (December, 1953), 744-53.

Colin Clark, "Afterthoughts on Paley: A Comment," *Review of Economics and Statistics*, 36 (August, 1954), 267-73.

Edward S. Mason, "Afterthoughts on Paley: A Comment," *Ibid.*, pp. 273-78.

John D. Black, "Resources Needed in American Agriculture," *Journal of Farm Economics*, 39 (December, 1957), 1074-86.

[5]State of California, State Water Resources Board, *Water Utilization and Requirements of California* (Sacramento: State Print. Off., June, 1955), Vol. 1, 227 pp., and Vol. 2, 358 pp. (State Water Resources Board Bull. No. 2).

[6]National Bureau of Economic Research, Conference on Research in Income and Wealth, *Long-Range Economic Projection, Studies in Income and Wealth* (Princeton: Princeton University Press, 1954), Vol. 16.

[7]U.S. Forest Service, *op. cit.*, p. 12. "Consumption of timber products and prospective timber demand are very nearly the same thing except with respect to time. Consumption is what has happened, whereas prospective demand is a projection of what may happen in the future under assumed conditions."

[8]For an explanation of these terms see S. V. Ciriacy-Wantrup, "Economics of Joint Costs in Agriculture," *Journal of Farm Economics*, 23 (November, 1941), 771-818.

[9]State of California, State Water Resources Board, *op. cit.*

[10]Nelson Goodman, *Fact, Fiction, and Forecast* (Cambridge: Harvard University Press, 1955), especially pp. 63-120. R. Carnap, "On the Application of Inductive Logic," *Philosophy and Phenomenological Research*, 8 (September, 1947), 133-47. For the classical views, see John Stewart Mill, *A System of Logic* (London: Longmans, 1843; new impression, 1947), especially Book 3, Chapter 3.

[11]H. A. Simon, *Models of Man* (New York: John Wiley and Sons, 1957). H. G. Papandreou, *Economics as a Science* (Chicago: J. B. Lippincott Co., 1958).

[12]Alfred Marshall, *Principles of Economics*, 8th ed. (London: Macmillan

Company, 1930), especially Book 5. H. D. Henderson, *Supply and Demand* (New York: Harcourt, Brace, and Co., 1922), Chapter 2. J. R. Hicks, *A Revision of Demand Theory* (Oxford: Clarendon Press, 1956).

[13]For more details on this issue, see S. V. Ciriacy-Wantrup, *Resource Conservation, Economics and Policies* (Berkeley: University of California Press, 1952).

[14]Gunnar Myrdal, *Rich Lands and Poor: the Road to World Prosperity* (New York: Harper and Brothers, 1957), (World Perspectives, Vol. 16).

[15]S. V. Ciriacy-Wantrup, "Resource Conservation and Economic Stability," *The Quarterly Journal of Economics*, 60, (May, 1946), 412-52.

[16]Vilfredo Pareto, *Cours d'Economique Politique* (Lausanne: F. Rouge, Libraire-Editeur, 1897).

[17]"A fiction is permissible in science if its character is clearly unerstood. A fiction is a deliberate, conscious deviation from reality. A fiction, however, is not a hypothesis or theory. By itself, a fiction is not intended to be validated by testing with empirical evidence. But a scientific fiction should be useful as a stimulus for or as a part of hypotheses and theories which can be so tested. That means the test of a scientific fiction is its conceptual usefulness, its expediency, in understanding, explaining and predicting reality. A fiction becomes mere dogma and, therefore, unscientific, if its two characteristics—consciousness of its fictional nature and conceptual usefulness—are obliterated. There are many examples in the history of science of fictions changing into dogma." See S. V. Ciriacy-Wantrup, "Policy Considerations in Farm Management Research in the Decade Ahead," *Journal of Farm Economics*, 38 (December, 1956), 1301-11.

[18]S. V. Ciriacy-Wantrup, "Concepts Used as Economic Criteria for a System of Water Rights," *Land Economics*, 32 (November, 1956), 295-312.

[19]Water law will be interpreted here broadly to include contributions by the legislative, judicial, and executive branches of government.

[20]S. V. Ciriacy-Wantrup, *Resource Conservation, Economics...*, Chapter 15.

[21]Regional changes of acreage do not necessarily appear in large aggregates including diverse regions. Thus, the United States crop acreage has been fairly stable for several decades; but this stability hides a number of significant regional changes.

[22]The original assignment was "The Demand for Land by Agriculture." In the present version of the paper, the following two sections serve as an application of the analysis of the first three sections to current problems of land and water policy.

[23]This information is not entirely satisfactory from our standpoint. The value of agricultural land is lumped together with improvements. As variable for interest, the farm-mortgage rate is used, which shows little response to economic change. Still, after separating the value of land from that of improvements, smoothing the net-return series by three-year moving averages, and employing the yields of government bonds (in addition to the farm-

mortgage interest rate), our conclusions are not greatly different from those reached on the basis of the series presented in *Current Developments in the Farm Real Estate Market*, cited below,

Sources: Index of per cent yield to maturity of long-term government (nontaxable) bonds from Standard and Poor's *Security Price Index Record*, 1957, p. 4, and Standard and Poor's *Security Owner's Stock Guide*,, 1958, p. 197. Farm-mortgage rates, Agricultural Research Service, USDA, *Agricultural Finance Review*, Vols. 18-20, 1955-58. (These represent contract rates except on loans of Federal Land Banks, 1934-1944, and Federal Farm Mortgage Corporation, 1938-1945, which are included at temporarily reduced rates.) Index of per-acre value of United States farmland from Agricultural Research Service, USDA, *Current Developments in the Farm Real Estate Market*, Nov., 1957, and March, 1958, and building values as reported by Census of Agriculture for 1910, 1920, 1925, 1930, and 1940. Intercensal years for 1910-1940 derived from straight-line interpolations. Annual estimates since 1940 based on crop reporters' estimates of market values of land with and without improvements to extrapolate the 1940 census values. Three-year moving average of indices of net returns per acre, United States farmland from Agricultural Research Service, USDA, *Current Developments in the Farm Real Estate Market*, November, 1957, and March, 1958.

[24]Changes in the length of the output vector would not lead to relative changes in the demand for land if agricultural production functions were homogeneous and linear. These conditions are frequently not fulfilled in agriculture—the contrary assumption in the literature notwithstanding.

[25]Frequently, changes in some or all of these factors affecting the demand for land are lumped together as changes in the "quality" of inputs. Quality is measured by over-all output-input ratios, referring to aggregate agricultural production functions. For such measurement, relative prices of inputs must remain unchanged. Most statistical investigations merely assume such constancy. It will be shown presently that this assumption is not justified in actuality. Changes of relative prices of inputs may occur without changes in the price index of groups of inputs or even all inputs—corrected for changes in the value of the dollar. This situation favors the general tendency to "assume away" changes of relative prices.

The variables of aggregate agricultural production functions are broad heterogeneous groups of inputs. The most extreme case of such grouping is to differentiate merely between "labor" and "capital." This extreme case is the most common one, not only in economic theory but also in most current models aiming at a quantitative analysis of aggregate production functions. Changes in the various kinds of labor or the various kinds of physical counterparts of capital funds (machinery, equipment, improvements, seed, fertilizer, materials, etc.), changes in the productivity coefficients of a particular kind of labor through education and training or of a particular kind of physical counterpart of capital funds through discovery of new uses, the gradual adoption of innovations and discoveries by the population of producers and, finally, substitution caused by changes of relative prices of inputs which change output-input ratios, all become changes of quality of labor and capital.

[26]Source: USDA Agricultural Marketing Service, *Agricultural Prices* (Washington: USDA, October 15, 1957), 56 pp. Processed.

[27]S. V. Ciriacy-Wantrup, "Cost Allocation in Relation to Western Water Policies," *Journal of Farm Economics,* 36 (February, 1954), 108-29 (Chapter 10 in this volume.); "Benefit-Cost Analysis and Public Resource Development," *Journal of Farm Economics*, 37 (November, 1955), 676-89. (Chapter 8 in this volume.)

[28]S. V. Ciriacy-Wantrup, "Private Enterprise and Conservation," *Journal of Farm Economics*, 24 (February, 1942), 75-96.

[29]M. F. Brewer, *Water Pricing and Allocation with Particular Reference to California Irrigation Districts* (Berkeley, 1959). Thesis (Ph.D. in Agricultural Economics), University of California, June, 1959.

[30]On these problems, see Stephen C. Smith, "Problems in the Use of the Public District for Ground Water Management," *Land Economics,* 32 (1956), 259-69.

[31]J. Herbert Snyder, *Ground Water in California, The Experience of Antelope Valley* (Berkeley: University of California Agricultural Experiment Station, February, 1955), 171 pp. (Giannini Foundation Ground Water Studies No. 2.)

[32]S. V. Ciriacy-Wantrup, *Resource Conservation, Economics...*, Ch. 3.

[33]S. V. Ciriacy-Wantrup, "Some Economic Issues in Water Rights," *Journal of Farm Economics*, 37 (December, 1955), 875-85.

[34]S. V. Ciriacy-Wantrup, "Concepts Used as Economic Criteria for a System of Water Rights," *Land Economics*, 32 (November, 1956), 295-312. See also the discussion of this paper in *The Law of Water Allocation in the Eastern United States*, edited by David Haber and Stephen W. Bergen (New York: The Ronald Press Company, 1958). (Papers and Proceedings of a symposium held in Washington, D.C., October, 1958, sponsored by the Conservation Foundation.)

Chapter 10

COST ALLOCATION IN RELATION TO WESTERN WATER POLICIES*[1]

1. Focus of this Paper

Cost allocation in the sense of apportioning joint costs of multiple-purpose projects to individual products (purposes) has been of considerable significance for western water policies in the past.[2] It will be of even greater significance in the future: an increasing proportion of water resources development is taking place in the form of large, public, multiple-purpose projects. There has been an intimate connection between cost allocation and several basic and vital policy issues. These issues will be called here "economic feasibility," "repayment," "rate making," "yardstick," and "form of contract." It appears fitting that the spotlight of economic analysis be thrown on these issues.

Focusing on the connection between these issues and cost allocation entails some unavoidable sacrifices. These should be made clear at the outset in order not to arouse a reader's expectations which cannot be fulfilled.

First, not *all* important aspects of the above policy issues can be considered here. For example, the issue of "economic feasibility" has several crucial aspects—such as the definition and quantitative determination of so-called "secondary" or "indirect" benefits and costs—which have no necessary connection with cost allocation. These other aspects are in great need of economic analysis.[3] But such an undertaking cannot be embarked upon at this time.

A second sacrifice follows from the first. Since we cannot possibly analyze all important aspects of the issues mentioned, we cannot attempt to provide a detailed blueprint which would provide precise substitute procedures for those which are presently in use by public agencies operating in this field. For example, concerning the policy issue of "repayment," detailed proposals as to how payments under various conditions may be computed, assessed, and collected are beyond the scope of this study. However, we can clearly

*Reprinted, with permission, from the *Journal of Farm Economics*, Vol. XXXVI(1):108–129 (February, 1954).

indicate the connection between repayment and cost allocation and draw conclusions with respect to certain broad but important changes in present procedures.

Third, the connection of cost allocation with water policies touches upon some knotty problems of economic theory. This is not a paper on the economics theory of joint production but an economic analysis of policy issues closely related to each other through their connection with cost allocation in procedures now in use. It is unavoidable, therefore, that some conclusions based on the economic theory of joint production are supported by references to other publications which supplement the present analysis. Otherwise, the focus would be blurred.

2. Experience with Cost Allocation

The problems of cost allocation have been discussed in numerous committees and commissions. There is a voluminous literature on the subject written by engineers, lawyers, accountants, and economists. After lengthy arguments, sometimes reminiscent of medieval dialectics on ecclesiastical dogma, the conclusion is invariably reached that cost allocation must be more or less arbitrary.

As a consequence, total joint costs of a multiple-purpose project are allocated among the various products in such a way as to afford an acceptable compromise of the divergent interests of federal, state, and local governments and of municipal and private users of water, power, navigation, recreation (including fish and waterfowl), and other products.[4] Because of the existing connection between cost allocation and the important policy issues mentioned, these divergent interests are strong and sensitive. Reference is always made to existing laws, precedents, engineering data, and economic concepts. The initiated, however, will probably agree that "rationalization" is not too strong a word for the kind of economic reasoning used to justify cost allocations recommended to Congress or other bodies who make the final decisions on authorization and appropriation.

It may be submitted that this state of affairs will not change until it is clearly recognized by those who analyze, recommend, and authorize projects that the problems of economic feasibility, repayment, rate making, yardstick, and form of contract are quite different economic issues. They require different approaches and different sets of tools for their solution. These approaches and tools, in turn, have little relation to past and present practices of cost allocation.

After stating the main theme in these negative terms let us see what can be said positively to clarify the issues of economic feasibility, repayment, rate making, yardstick, and form of contract without falling into the semantic traps of cost allocation.

3. Cost Allocation and Economic Feasibility

Determination of economic feasibility in federal multiple-purpose projects is connected with cost allocation through statute—for example, through the important sections 9 (a) and 9 (b) of the Reclamation Act of 1939.[5] Statutes differentiate between reimbursable and nonreimbursable costs and stipulate different proportions between these two kinds of costs for different purposes, such as irrigation, power, municipal water, navigation, and flood control.

As interpreted by the most important public agency operating in this field, there are two standards for determining economic feasibility. Both standards must be met by a project. They may be stated in the words of Commissioner Strauss in his testimony before Congress:[6]

> The first, required by reclamation law, consists of an allocation of project costs among the purposes served and a showing that the anticipated project revenues will return all reimbursable costs. The second, although not required by reclamation law, is the showing of estimated benefits and costs, and is made as a matter of Bureau policy. Thus, a reclamation project must meet two standards of economic feasibility: The estimated benefits must exceed the estimated costs and the anticipated project revenues must provide for return of all reimbursable costs.

The first standard mentioned by Commissioner Strauss is a standard for the possibility of repayment under the requirements of present laws. Sometimes, this standard is referred to as "financial feasibility." In the statutory sense it is a necessary condition for feasibility. In the economic sense it is neither a necessary nor a sufficient condition for feasibility because, in multiple-purpose projects, reimbursable costs include only a portion of total costs and project revenues only a portion of total benefits. Moreover, which portion of costs is designated as reimbursable and which portion of benefits has to be repaid as project revenues are not determined on the basis of a functional relation between costs and benefits.

The second standard does not involve cost allocation. It is a necessary condition for economic feasibility, provided that benefits and costs are properly evaluated.[7] It is a sufficient condition for economic feasibility under three restrictive assumptions: (1) that the benefit-cost ratio of the project considered cannot be further improved; (2) that there are no alternative projects with a higher benefit-cost ratio on which available public funds could be spent; and (3) that it is desirable to make public funds available.

In order to determine economic feasibility, that is, to make a recommendation on economic grounds whether a public project should be undertaken and when, one must ascertain in the planning stage the optimum proportion of products for various time intervals and the optimum quantities of products at that proportion. In more technical language, we want to determine the direction and the length of an optimum product vector extending over time. In order to avoid a term that has been little used by economists, this vector will be called the "optimum product combination."

Neither the proportion of different products yielded by a multiple-purpose project nor the quantities of these products at given proportions are fixed and constant over time on the basis of engineering or other technological data. For example, the Central Valley Project in California can be planned, constructed, and managed to yield water, power, and flood control—to mention only the three most important products—in various proportions and in various quantities for each proportion. Construction can be delayed or speeded up, and the yield of products can be varied over time. Decisions in this sphere do not merely concern the consumers of these products, but also affect deeply the relations between federal, state, and local governments.

In focusing on these decisions, three broader aspects of economic feasibility, already alluded to are left out of consideration. This omission happens to be in accord with the political realities which at present determine authorization and appropriation. These aspects are the following—in increasing order of broadness.

First, there is the question whether a similar product combination could not be obtained more economically by alternative projects in different geographic locations—for example, by supplemental irrigation, drainage, clearing, and fertilizing projects in the humid portions of the United States.[8]

Second, there is the question whether alternative public projects with an entirely different product combination may not be preferable. For example, public investment in the conservation of natural resources may compete with public investment in slum clearance, schools, hospitals, and the like.

Third, there is the question to what extent funds should be withdrawn from the private sector of the economy and invested in public projects. An answer to this question depends on the type of project and on the phase of economic fluctuations; beyond that, problems of taxation, public credit, and the effectiveness of the whole system of private enterprise need to be considered.[9] To some extent, the answer to this question can be arrived at through appropriate practices in evaluating benefits and costs. This is not possible with the first two questions.

Economic analysis can make a contribution in clarifying these three aspects of economic feasibility. But joint-cost allocation is not immediately involved.

4. Determining the Optimum Product Combination

It is not necessary to treat the economic theory of joint production in detail at this time.[10] Cost allocation in the sense of obtaining the total costs of a project first and then apportioning them to individual products is meaningless for obtaining the optimum product combination. The approach is different. The optimum product combination yields the total costs, which need not be allocated for determining economic feasibility. What is needed are the marginal benefits and costs of various products in the sense of partial derivatives of total benefit and cost functions. The independent variables of these functions are the rates of production of various purposes planned for various time intervals.

Theoretically, such partial derivatives can be calculated. This possibility, however, has little practical relevance. In actuality, approximations must be used. It is practical to calculate the present value of the expected flow of total benefits and costs from a small number of alternative (dated) product combinations. For each of these alternatives, in turn, benefits and costs may be calculated for various assumptions with respect to evaluation—for example, for various interest rates and prices of products and cost factors. Superior product combinations can be selected on the basis of benefit-cost ratios.

Usually, economic feasibility of only one product combination constant over time and based on only one set of assumptions with respect to interest and prices is calculated and submitted to Congress. By the time the political decision about construction is made, prices (including interest) may have changed—for example, in the course of economic fluctuations. Mistakes can be reduced if the submitting agency has thoroughly considered alternative product combinations and price assumptions and if the decision-making political body has a clear idea of what such changes mean in terms of benefit-cost ratios.

State and local governments, universities, and private groups of potential beneficiaries should participate in—or at least should have an opportunity to scrutinize—the determination of the optimum product combination. The Columbia Basin Joint Investigations and the Central Valley Project Studies have pointed the way. However, these studies were started too late and were not concerned with *ex ante* economic feasibility. Such studies should be completed *before* a project is recommended. Differing opinions of state and local governments and of potential beneficiaries, together with appropriate material to substantiate such opinions, should be submitted to Congress with the report of the agency responsible for recommending.[11]

In determining economic feasibility, no consideration should be given to direct and indirect subsidies. At present, such subsidies are given—for example, in the form of interest-free funds to individual purposes (irrigation). If comparison is made between taxed and tax-free value flows, an appropriate correction for this difference becomes necessary. Likewise, no consideration should be given in determining economic feasibility to whether costs are reimbursable or nonreimbursable. The extent to which subsidies and tax exemptions are granted and costs are regarded as reimbursable are important policy decisions for determining repayment but not for determining economic feasibility (see Section 6).

5. More Liberal Standards of Feasibility?

As noted, determination of economic feasibility must be understood as a critical appraisal of whether a project should be undertaken at all, when, and with what product combination. The objective of such determination is *not* to find an economic justification for a project which appears desirable to an agency or to a pressure group. There is a tendency to focus on such a justification and on attempts to liberalize standards for appraisal. These attempts are not helpful in eliminating existing weaknesses of benefit-cost analysis.

Besides constituting a retrogression in analytical method, these attempts have undesirable practical effects. Usually, water development for municipal and industrial uses and for power has high benefit-cost ratios as compared with irrigation use. Attempts to liberalize standards of economic and financial feasibility are concerned with irrigation use. Thus, if competitive relations exist between municipal and industrial uses and power on one side and irrigation use on the other, liberalization of feasibility standards leads to a change in the optimum product combinations to the disadvantage of the former. In other words, multiple-purpose projects in which irrigation is the dominant use of water will be undertaken in preference to those in which municipal and industrial uses of water are more significant. From the standpoint of *future* water needs, such a development is especially questionable. In most western states, water needs for municipal and industrial uses are increasing rapidly.

The most extreme attempt to liberalize standards of economic and financial feasibility is the suggestion to replace economic analysis simply by objectives imputed to the reclamation laws, namely, "to settle the arid lands of the West and further the economic development of the nation."[12] It is claimed for these objectives that "the policy implications are clear."[13]

Even if one accepts these objectives, should no priority be given to economically feasible projects? In many parts of the West, projects and purposes compete not merely for public funds but, more importantly, for scarce water resources. The dispute over the water of the Colorado River is an outstanding example. Granted that such disputes are finally decided in the political arena—that is, in this case, through court decisions, compacts, and treaties—is it in the public interest to eliminate costs in the consideration of benefits? Can economic evaluation be discarded as a tool for taking into account the welfare of *all* groups and regions? Can the decision about what priorities and what product combinations are to be recommended to Congress be left entirely to subjective judgment? Or do those who use the above argument contend that there are no economically feasible projects in western water resources development and that there is no objective basis for making selections between alternative product combinations?

6. Cost Allocation and Repayment

Let us turn to the problems of repayment. Recommendations of multiple-purpose projects and studies like those mentioned for the Columbia Basin and the Central Valley have given a great deal of attention to cost allocation in connection with repayment. Statutes, executive orders, and traditions have made the allocation of total construction costs to various project purposes the basis of repayment. According to these same social institutions, costs allocated to some purposes need not be repaid at all; some purposes need not pay the interest portion; other purposes must repay all costs allocated to them including interest; for still other purposes, allocated costs include costs which other purposes cannot repay.[14]

This institutional situation would lead to strong and sensitive interest in cost allocation even if no connection between repayment and rate making existed. Beneficiaries who must repay allocated costs are interested that the largest possible proportion of total cost is allocated to purposes the cost of which need not be repaid. Navigation, flood control, recreation (wildlife), and national defense, for example, are often burdened with higher cost allocations than are warranted by their relation to costs and to benefits received. Generally, the Department of the Interior has been in favor of such shifting of cost allocations while the Corps of Army Engineers and the Federal Power Commission have been more conservative.[15]

Among beneficiaries, such shifting of cost allocations is favored mainly by users of water and power. Cost allocations to water and to power, on the other hand, are influenced by a more complex grouping of interests. Frequently, irrigation interests are in favor of high cost allocations to municipal water and to power. With respect to cost allocations to power, this tendency is supported by private power interests because of the connection between cost allocation and rate making. This connection will be discussed presently (Section 7).

If irrigation is based to a considerable extent on ground water and, therefore, on electric power, pressures exercised by beneficiaries become even more complex. The positions taken in these matters by California farm organizations and the political alliances formed are interesting for the student of western water policies.

To summarize: Cost allocation for purposes of repayment has been a much broader institutional problem than the term would seem to indicate. From the standpoint of future water policy, it would be desirable to recognize this situation frankly and to separate problems of repayment entirely from any reference to construction costs and their allocation. What, then, could be the basis for repayment?

It appears economically justified and politically equitable that beneficiaries from public resource development pay for the benefits received—provided such benefits are practically assessable and provided that enough incentive is let for beneficiaries to participate in resource development. Payments under these provisions are the best guarantee that the determination of economic feasibility will receive the most thorough scrutiny by state and local governments and by private groups of beneficiaries. As suggested above, such scrutiny appears necessary if all aspects of economic feasibility are to be considered in the planning stage.

For some projects, the principle just suggested, namely, that assessable benefits and not costs are to be repaid, may mean that more is paid by beneficiaries than the total costs of a project. For other projects, the principle may mean that only a small portion of total costs is repaid. For still other projects, it may mean that payments are about equal to total costs. Payments may go to a reclamation fund or, preferably, to the general treasury fund.

It may be noted that the principle suggested here is not identical with the various "benefit methods" used in cost allocation.[16] The principle has broader implications. It does not solve *all* problems of "speculation" and of "unearned" increments of income and capital caused by public projects. But it goes far enough in this direction to offer a more effective and economically more acceptable alternative to present policies designed to reduce speculation and unearned increments—for example, the so-called "160-acre limitation."[17] This is especially true if the water furnished by public projects is supplemental to other waters in already developed irrigation areas, as in the Central Valley of California.

As a matter of public policy, it may be desirable not to assess certain benefits even if it is practical to do so. Recreational benefits may fall into this class. Some benefits are not practically assessable to natural or legal persons. Benefits to national defense are an example.

As a corollary of this policy, it may become an important part of federal policy to induce state, local, and private agencies to plan and build their projects with full consideration of benefits to recreation and national defense. Various forms of "inducements" appear practical and have been used in other connections.[18] Besides making repayments for such benefits, the federal government may stipulate consideration of such benefits when the use of federal waters and land is involved. Under some conditions, tax incentives may also be used.

One important point regarding repayment needs to be mentioned at this time, although a more detailed discussion must be deferred until later (Sections 7-9): The assessment of benefits for repayment should not determine unit prices of products sold—that is, for example, water and power rates. On the other hand, assessment for repayment is usually dependent on such prices. The form of repayment may be directly connected with such prices (power and water revenues) or may be made in the form of various types of taxes and fees. Not only power and water users but as many other beneficiaries as can practically be assessed should participate in payments.

Evaluation for determining repayment is not necessarily identical with evaluation for determining economic feasibility. For example, some localized benefits which may be assessed for repayment may be offset in the determination of economic feasibility by costs elsewhere in the economy. On the other hand, as already mentioned, in the determination of repayment some benefits— for example, to recreation (wildlife) and national defense—which are important in the determination of economic feasibility may not be assessed for reasons of policy or practical expediency.

Determination of economic feasibility is strictly *ex ante. Determination of repayment is partly ex post.* That means repayment is subject to revision if actual benefits should prove different from expected ones. However, repayment is facilitated if methods of assessment, form of repayment, and expected quantities and values (rates, taxes, fees) are clear to all parties concerned at the time when economic feasibility is determined. For example, beneficiaries of power can enter into purchase agreements with the federal government with the understanding that rates will be set according to principles discussed in the next section. If payments are to be made by beneficiaries in the form of taxes and fees to local and state governments, agreements on methods of assessment can be formulated.

Such an early arrangement for repayment has two advantages: first, the determination of economic feasibility will be taken seriously by all parties concerned; second, less difficulty will arise in disposing of products and in repayment after the commitment for the project has already been made; such difficulty has arisen, for example, in the Central Valley Project. In other words, the federal government—and the taxpayers—will not be left holding the bag.

7. Cost Allocation and Rate Making

As suggested in the beginning, determination of water and power rates is an economic issue quite different from that of repayment. Problems involved in the determination of water and power rates may be considered next.

At present cost allocation is directly connected with rate making in the Bonneville Project Act of 1937.[19] In other legislation, the connection between cost allocation and rate making is indirect but nevertheless effective. Two factors are mainly responsible. First, net revenues obtained from the sale of water and power are by far the most important—and thus far have usually been the only—financial source of repayment. Second, in view of the statutory differentiation between reimbursable and nonreimbursable costs, all reports on public multiple-purpose projects contain implications or direct suggestions about rates "necessary" to support cost allocations to water and power or to make these purposes "self-supporting."

This connection between cost allocation and rate making is recognized by all federal departments involved.

General Lewis A. Pick, Chief of Army Engineers, stated in his testimony before Congress:[20] "Rates for sale of this power that is, power produced by projects built by Army Engineers are established by the marketing agency upon approval by the Federal Power Commission, and according to the law should return the cost of producing the power. Power rates are thus affected by the cost allocations made by the Corps of Engineers."

Secretary of Agriculture Brannan stated before the same congressional committee:[21] "The allocation of costs of multiple-purpose reservoir projects is important to agriculture insofar as it affects the charges to farmers for electric power and the reclamation of land by irrigation, drainage, and flood control."

Undersecretary of Interior Searles has this to say as a witness:[22] "Reasonable allocations are of the greatest importance because repayment requirements, which in turn govern power rates, are as dependent upon the allocations to reimbursable purposes as they are upon the actual construction costs."

Private power companies have taken a lively interest in this issue. This is explained by the frequent attempts to employ rates charged by private companies. So long as cost allocations in public multiple-purpose projects influence rate making, such allocations are indeed of concern to private power companies. On the other hand, if this connection between cost allocation and rate making did not exist, one important reason for private power companies to oppose public projects would disappear.

Before we can analyze the economic soundness of the yardstick idea, we must inquire about the principles on which rate making may be based and about the significance—in terms of these principles—of past costs of physical plant.

Theoretically, the problem of setting rates for water or power can be approached with tools similar to those used in determining the optimum product combination.[23] A demand and supply function for water and power must be constructed. From the standpoint of social economics, a demand function can be interpreted as a marginal benefit function, and a supply function, as a marginal cost function. On this basis, an optimum (dated) product combination can be calculated.

For public projects, the physical plant can be adjusted to yield the optimum product combination without regard to price incentives. Rates can be set in such a way that supply and demand in each time interval are in equilibrium. For private industry, rates must be set in a way, first, that the optimum product combination results and, second, that supply and demand are in equilibrium in each time interval. To obtain these two results, rate making may have to be supplemented by tax incentives—for example, by provisions regarding depreciation allowances.

Such theoretical rates are not necessarily equal to short-run or long-run marginal costs of instantaneous economics. Rates set must make allowance for maintenance and discontinuous changes of physical plant in accordance with changes of demand and of technological conditions. Determination of such rates is possible only in economic theory. In the present case, as in the preceding one, practical approximations to theoretical solutions must be found. A proposal for such an approximation will be considered next.

8. Rate Making and Public Utility Commissions

The potentially most useful approximation to a theoretical determination of rates for public water or power may be based on the procedures developed by public utility commissions. In regulating rates, some of the more progressive commissions attempt to take into account expected changes of demand, the physical plant needed to satisfy such demand, the costs of such plant, "normal" efficiency of management, and "normal" profits to give an incentive to provide such plant.[24]

It may be admitted that many, possibly most, public utility commissions still look more toward the past than the future in appraising demand and "allowable" cost of physical plant. However, the various proposals for incremental cost pricing have started some healthy discussion.[25] For our purposes, the direction of change in public utility regulations and the possibilities of further improvement are more interesting than past and present shortcomings. On the other hand, it would be naive to forget that in a field so exposed to political pressures—like the field of rate making—considerations based on economic theory will be only one (and decidedly a minor) factor in political decision making for some time to come.

Besides the realities of political pressures, another factor which limits the immediate relevance of theoretical considerations must be mentioned. In order to have the desired effects upon future supply, rates regulated by public utility commission must be realistic in terms of cost-accounting and budgeting practices used by private utility companies in planning maintenance and changes of physical plant. These practices differ from the techniques employed in the theoretical determination of the optimum product combination. Likewise, the practical definition of "normal" efficiency and profits poses some knotty problems. However, through give and take between public utility commissions and private utility companies over many years, cost-accounting and budgeting practices have been developed which are reasonably well suited as a basis for regulation.

Such practices are becoming required standards for private companies of the regulated industry. There is a tendency for these standards to become more uniform for jurisdictions of different utility commissions. There is also a tendency for these standards to improve. Modern cost accounting has become a highly skilled profession. Since the last war, cost accounting as a means of controlling prices and profits has been used on a large scale in negotiating defense contracts. A great deal of experience has been gained in this field.

9. Rate Making for Public Water and Power

Rates regulated by public utility commissions in a way that takes account of supply and demand functions extending over time, and a wealth of cost data in the regulated private industry, can be used for approximating a solution of our present problem, namely, of setting rates for water and power produced by public multiple-purpose projects—for short, "public" water and power. Such rate making can be divorced entirely from the problem of cost allocation.

In the western part of the United States, conditions of demand and supply are such that any practically relevant addition—through public projects—to otherwise existing supplies of water and power can be absorbed without substantial reduction in rates. For demand, changes point strongly upward. Increases of supply have to come from greater distances, poorer sites, or steam plants. The latter generally produce at higher costs than hydroelectric plants.

Under these conditions, water and power produced by public multiple-purpose projects can be disposed of at rates corresponding with or only slightly below the rate structure as regulated by public utility commissions.

Such a price policy is opposed, not only by preference customers of public water and power (see footnote 26), but also by many public-spirited citizens because of "indirect" and "intangible" benefits of lower public rates—regardless of supply and demand conditions. However, in social economics, the effects of lower rates upon public revenues need to be considered, and also the possibility that such rates, in combination with rationing, may change consumption patterns to the disadvantage of those "higher" social uses which could compete successfully for available water and power at higher rates. Moreover, increases in the total volume of water and power available from public *and* private sources is no less important in social economics than decreases in rates. In other words, effects of price on future supply cannot be neglected.

It should be emphasized that we are talking about rates at the points of production—that is, at or near the multiple-purpose dams. Generally, these rates will be wholesale rates. Appropriate correspondence between wholesale and retail rates can be arrived at on the basis of cost data available to public utility commissions. Obviously, the seasonal distribution or "firmness" of the quantities available for sale must be considered. Under western conditions, water and power available at different seasons are, economically speaking, quite different commodities. Differences in firmness and in load factor are generally taken into account in the existing rate structure.

There are some geographic differences in the relevance of rates set by public utility commissions from the standpoint of rate making for public water and power. Existing rates regulated by public utility commissions are relevant in those regions where new public resources development is to be integrated into a large, already existing private development. This is the case, for example, in California. In other regions of the country—for example, in the Missouri Basin—recent public development of water and power is so important relative to the existing private development that the rate structure of public projects is more relevant for private projects than the reverse.

If no regulated rates are geographically relevant for a public project, or if there are potential customers of a public project who are willing to pay higher than the regulated rates, preference in the sale of public power and water may be given to the highest bidder.[26] Price discrimination in the sale of large blocks of power and water is frequently possible. In the case of public projects, such price discrimination is not necessarily objectionable.

The principle of highest bidder must be qualified with respect to imperfections in the capital market when transmission lines and distribution facilities are not available. For most projects, some major transmission lines must be constructed in any event in order to connect the project with existing systems and to serve other project purposes—for example, pumping plants. Such transmission lines are an integral part of the project. In some cases, public credit may be given to groups of customers who want to construct their own distribution facilities—for example, more than two billion dollars has been lent through the REA to rural cooperatives. These and other means to overcome imperfections in the capital market are outside our immediate field of inquiry.

10. Cost Allocation and the Yardstick Idea

In returning now to the yardstick idea, it has already been implied, in the reasoning about the absence of any necessary connection between cost allocation and rate making presented in the preceding sections, that rates set for water and power produced by public multiple-purpose projects cannot be used as a yardstick to measure whether the rates charged by private utility companies are too high. Even if it is assumed that rate making for public water and power is not based on the principles just discussed, but on allocated costs, such costs would not be comparable with those of private companies: the latter are generally not favored by the economies of joint production and tax exemptions.

Rejecting the yardstick idea does not mean that rates charged by private utility companies are always justified. Economic possibilities for rate reduction exist largely with respect to retail rates. As already stated, we are concerned mainly with wholesale rates. The spread between the two types of rates is great—especially for power. Costs of transmission and distribution represent by far the greatest portion—around 80 percent and more—of total power costs at points of consumption.

If, in a given situation, rates charged by private power companies lead to monopoly profits, the most direct relief is brought not by using cost allocation as a means to justify lower rates for public water and power but by making existing public utility commissions more effective in their highly important regulatory functions. There are several practical possibilities of doing this. At present public utility commission fall short of fulfilling the important role assigned to them here. However, they are an institutional device, developed by a democratic society, which gives promise of further development.

11. Cost Allocation and Form of Contract

By separating repayment and rate making entirely from cost allocation—as advocated in the preceding sections—another problem of water policy can be clarified. This problem is the form of the contract entered into between the government agency responsible for construction and marketing—particularly the Bureau of Reclamation—and the water users—particularly the irrigation districts.

The two principal forms of contract have become known as the 9 (d) and 9 (e) contracts in reference to the relevant subsections on the Reclamation Act of 1939. The 9 (d) contract is a repayment contract; it provides for repayment of allocated reimbursable costs within time periods specified in the Act. The 9 (e) contract is a service contract; it does not provide for repayment but merely for water service over a number of years (40) under conditions also specified in the Act.

Construction costs of water distribution systems are covered by 9 (d) contracts. Construction costs of the main project works, on the other hand, can no longer be treated in the same way—or at least that is claimed by the

Bureau of Reclamation—because the resulting payments would exceed the financial ability of the districts. The 9 (e) contract, therefore, has become more and more common, since it became available through the 1939 Act, and is now frequently employed in large, multiple-purpose projects. For example, in the Central Valley Project, all contracts concluded so far are 9 (e) contracts, and according to announcements by the Bureau of Reclamation, this situation will not change in the future.

Although the 9 (e) contract is financially more attractive than the 9 (d) contract, it creates problems which are not presented by the latter. Without going here in detail into the somewhat controversial and legally complex nature of these problems, they may be summarized with respect to the most important point: the security of water rights.

A repayment contract leads to a definite transfer of administration and operation of physical works—and, therefore, of permanent control over water deliveries—to the water users themselves.[27] By contrast, under a service contract, the Bureau of Reclamation retains control over administration and operation indefinitely. The Bureau claims it is legally free to make changes in water deliveries from one group of users to another after the time period specified in the contract (40 years) has expired. No provision for renewal is contained in the contract nor provided for in present federal law.

It can be argued that changes in water deliveries would create so much opposition in Congress that the attempt would not be made. However, Congress is usually divided in such matters. Security of water rights is so important in irrigation farming that the present weak substitute for a renewal clause is not sufficient.[28] This is especially true of the Central Valley Project in view of the large expenditures by the irrigation districts in constructing distribution systems. It may be submitted that the rights of users of water produced by federal multiple-purpose projects should not be less secure than other water rights established and protected by the laws of each state.

There is no need to argue here the question of state law versus federal law so often referred to in this connection. For the purposes of this paper, the issue is primarily an economic one: an optimum development of irrigation farming in an institutional system based on private initiative cannot be expected if the security of water rights is uncertain. For the economist, such uncertainty would be relevant even if it were merely subjective. Subjective uncertainty influences the economic decisions of water users.[29]

Security of water rights under state laws does not mean that such rights cannot be transferred from one user to another. Water rights, being real property, are bought and sold—with land if they are "appurtenant" or without land if they are not—in all western states. By and large, such transfer of water rights through an open market gives sufficient flexibility for adapting to changing economic conditions. In come cases, water rights can be transferred through loss, forfeiture, condemnation, and in other ways also defined under state laws.

Likewise, security of water rights under state laws does not mean that service contracts for water are undesirable. Many western farmers obtain their water from water companies on a contract basis. However, these water companies are public utilities operating and regulated under state laws. Such utilities are not free to shift water service to other customers.

Although insecurity of water rights is the most important problem raised by 9 (e) contracts, it is not the only one. Perpetuation of direct controls by a federal agency over the affairs of public districts organized and operating under state laws and supervised by state agencies has led to difficulties.

Here, again, there is no need to argue whether local, state, or federal control is preferable in water resources development. Neither federal, nor state, nor local governments are inherently superior with respect to the competence and integrity of their civil servants and with respect to freedom from corruption and rule by pressure groups.

On the other hand, too much concentration of economic power in any single agency—federal, state or local, public or private—appears undesirable. Although one may argue that economic power can be controlled by political power, in the end a system of countervailing economic powers appears safer. On the basis of this value judgment, federal, state, and local governments, together with private agencies, may well participate in water resources development. Some duplication and conflict may result from such multiplicity. As discussed elsewhere,[30] there are several practical possibilities to reduce these results through better coordination. The irreducible minimum of inefficiency caused by the multiplicity of participating agencies is the price paid for avoiding too much concentration of economic power.[31]

Regardless of one's attitude toward the over-all issue of federal versus state and public versus private control, it may be submitted that the scrambling of federal, state, and local law and government as brought about by the 9 (e) contract is unnecessary and undesirable. The internal economic affairs of irrigation districts are intrastate. The 9 (e) contract contains provisions which are irritating, to say the least, to local and state governments. For example, the final decision in interpreting many important clauses is left entirely to the "contracting officer," that is, to the Federal Commissioner of Reclamation or his representative. Institutional machinery for consultation and arbitration would be more appropriate.

Let us assume that use of water facilities created by a federal project is entirely intrastate. If repayment of benefits is arranged for between federal, state, and local governments, water rights vested in the federal government and control over administration and operation of water facilities may well be transferred to the state and, under appropriate agreements, to the water users soon after the project is put into operation. If costs have no connection with repayment, as explained in the preceding sections, individual parts of projects are independent from each other with respect to repayment. The problems created by joint costs, by the gradual completion of large projects— like the Central Valley Project—and by the financial inability of districts to repay allocated construction costs would no longer prevent transfer of control. Such transfer would overcome present objections against a water service contract that are based on insecurity of water rights and on federal control over affairs which can safely be left to the control of state and local governments.

There is no implication in the foregoing statement that control *must* always be transferred. There are several intrastate projects now in operation in which irrigation districts have preferred that the constructing federal agency remain in control.

Likewise, there is no implication that control over *other* features of an intrastate multiple-purpose project—for example, over power or flood control—should be transferred to water users. Such control *may* be transferred under adequate agreements protecting federal and state interests if that is desired by the water users themselves, power users, and other beneficiaries.

With respect to federal projects which have important interstate or international implication, the situation is different. It is difficult to see how control of such projects could be turned over to state or local governments. Most large multiple-purpose projects have interstate or international implications. Thus, the federal government should remain an important factor not only in the development but also in the administrative control of water resources. This is in accord with the position taken above concerning the principle of division of economic power. How far the states can actively and harmoniously cooperate with the federal government in the administrative control of such projects—for example through federal-state compacts—needs to be explored further.

Although the federal government should remain important in the administrative control over interstate projects, secure water rights may still be acquired by the water users of each state. If use of water facilities is interstate, state allotments will have to be made in any event by state compact, international treaty, or supreme court decisions, or by a combination of these. Water users may acquire water rights in these allotments according to the laws of each state. If a service contract for water is used, regulations of each state can be applied to its allotment.

12. Theoretical Analysis Versus Practical Application

It may be felt that an economic analysis of water resources policies has the dry taste of theory and cannot be applied to the political and legal facts of life. Economists restrict their own usefulness severely if they consider water policies only within the framework of present statutes. In many cases it is relevant to view laws as tools or obstacles of policy, and economists should make proposals for such changes.

Existing reclamation laws are not entirely antagonistic to the principles suggested here. With respect to the determination of economic feasibility and the processes of rate making, existing laws are not specific. In any event, for the solution of these two problems, only broad principles could be stated by law. Detailed practices must be worked out by professional staffs and through agreement between agencies and governments.

The 1939 Reclamation Act is more specific with respect to repayment through water and power sales. I have tried to show elsewhere[32] that each paragraph of the relevant Section 9(a) is capable of an interpretation which is not in conflict with the principles suggested here. Obviously, it would be much better if economic reasoning were clearly expressed in the Act rather than read into it. A suitable interpretation is possible only because the economic terminology that appears in the Act is rather vague.

With respect to repayment in other form than through water and power sales, the present practice of regarding national defense and recreation as nonreimbursable may be continued. But benefits from flood control, salinity control, and navigation can, in part at least, be assessed for repayment. As already implied, this would have the advantage that these benefits receive closer scrutiny in determining economic feasibility. Further, in some cases, political opposition to desirable projects would be reduced. For example, the benefits of the Central Valley Project through flood control, salinity control, and navigation are geographically concentrated in the Central Valley. Taxpayers in other parts of the state, such as southern California, receive only small, if any, benefits from these purposes. In other regions of the country, a similar differentiation exists between upstream and downstream interests in a big watershed such as the Missouri and Mississippi valleys. A more equitable participation of different groups of taxpayers in the financial burden of a project might facilitate authorization by Congress.

The most practical way of assessing the benefits from flood control, salinity control, and navigation would be through public districts, equipped with taxing power, formed for that purpose under state law. In the case of navigation benefits, economic arguments in favor of tolls exist. This country is reviving this principle for some important freeways. But the tradition of toll-free navigation is strong, and there are also economic arguments in favor of paying for navigation (and road) benefits in other form than through tolls.

All western states have had experience with public districts in the field of irrigation. Most states, especially California, have a variety of laws under which districts concerned with water resources development other than irrigation can be organized and operated. Likewise, it is a well-established practice that public districts enter into repayment contracts with the federal government.

A considerable literature exists on assessment practices in irrigation districts. Several studies undertaken in the Columbia Basin and the Central Valley have a bearing on assessment practices in districts other than irrigation. Further studies in this direction are desirable, but there is little doubt that practical means to repay benefits in the way suggested can be found.

By and large, changes in repayment as suggested here would mean a simplification of existing laws. Most students and interested parties are in agreement that amendment of reclamation laws is sorely needed. A codification of reclamation laws by the House Judiciary Committee is now in progress.

[1]*Journal of Farm Economics*, Vol. XXXVI, No. 1 (February, 1954) pp. 108-129. (University of California, Division of Agricultural Sciences, Giannini

Foundation of Agricultural Economics Paper No. 186.) An earlier version of this paper was presented before the Conference on Western Water Resources Development, March 2-3, 1953, Berkeley, California, under the title "Economic Analysis of Water Resources Policies." Giannini Foundation Paper No. 136.

[2]The term "joint costs" as employed here is a shorthand for "costs in joint production." The logical corollary is "separate costs." In multiple-purpose projects, it is advisable to differentiate between production and distribution. The distribution of products—for example, of water and power—can generally be regarded as separate processes. However, in some cases, a part of distribution must be included in joint production.

The term "separable costs" is avoided here. This term is employed in current practices of cost allocation. It is defined as follows: "the separable cost for each project purpose is the difference between the cost of the multiple-purpose project and the cost of the project with the purpose omitted." In connection with these same practices, "joint costs" are defined "as the difference between the cost of the multiple-purpose project as a whole and the total of the separable costs for all project purposes." U. S. Federal Interagency River Basin Committee. Subcommittee on Benefits and Costs: Proposed Practices for Economic Analyses of River Basin Projects. Washington, D.C., 1950. 85 p. Quotations are from p. 54.

[3]Striking differences sometimes occur in the benefit-cost analysis of different federal agencies for the same project. For example, in the recent Trinity River report, the Bureau of Reclamation calculates a benefit-cost ratio of 3.26:1 and the Federal Power Commission, a benefit-cost ratio of 1.5:1. (Trinity River Basin, Central Valley Project, California. House Document No. 53, Washington, D.C., January 9, 1953.)

The Corps of Army Engineers does not use indirect benefits in the same sense as the Bureau of Reclamation. The Federal Power Commission has gone on record that "reliance should be placed upon the more direct or primary types of benefits and costs susceptible of being evaluated." Survey reports on upstream flood control by agencies of the Departament of Agriculture show an increasingly critical attitude in matters of evaluation. Reports on Bureau of Reclamation projects on the other hand sometimes show "indirect" benefits equal to or exceeding "direct" ones. The Federal Interagency River Basin Committee is experiencing difficulties in resolving these differences among the agencies in the field of evaluation.

[4]The various methods of cost allocation that have been used or considered need not be discussed here. The most important methods are reviewed in a recent congressional report. Subcommittee to Study Civil Works of the Committee on Public Works: The Allocation of Costs of Federal Water Resource Development. House Committee Print No. 23, December 5, 1952. Govt. Print. Off., Washington, D.C. This report will be cited henceforth as "Allocation Report."

[5]Act of August 4, 1939, Ch. 418, 53 St. 1187, 43 U.S.C. 485.

[6]Allocation Report, p. 11.

[7]As stated in Section 1, it is not possible at this time to go into the important problem of evaluating benefits and costs (including the use of

interest and uncertainty allowance). This problem is not peculiar to multiple-purpose projects. The principles involved in obtaining market and extra-market values have recently been discussed elsewhere. (S. V. Ciriacy-Wantrup, *Resource Conservation, Economics and Policies.* University of California Press, Berkeley, 1952. 410 p.) Some of the procedures presently in use have been critically reviewed in a recent congressional report. (Subcommittee to Study Civil Works of the Committee on Public Works: Economic Evaluation of Federal Water Resources Development Projects. House Committee Print No. 24, December 5, 1952. Govt. Print. Off., Washington, D.C. This report will be cited henceforth as "Evaluation Report.")

[8]For an interesting, although controversial, beginning toward a quantitativie analysis of "western" and "eastern" alternatives, see Rudolph Ulrich. "Relative Costs and Benefits of Land Reclamation in the Humid Southeast and the Semiarid West." *Journal of Farm Economics*, Vol. XXXV, No. 1, February, 1953, pp. 62- 73.

[9]On these points, see S. V. Ciriacy-Wantrup. "Taxation and the Conservation of Resources." *The Quarterly Journal of Economics*, Vol. LVIII, February, 1944, pp. 157-195. S. V. Ciriacy-Wantrup. "Resource Conservation and Economic Instability." *The Quarterly Journal of Economics*, Vol. LX, May, 1946, pp. 412-452.

[10]For a detailed treatment, see S. V. Ciriacy-Wantrup. "Economics of Joint Costs in Agriculture." *Journal of Farm Economics*, Vol. XXIII, No. 4, November, 1941, pp. 771-818. An application of this theory to problems of "time jointness" is offered in *Resource Conservation, Economics and Policies, op. cit.*

[11]In some legislation—in the Flood Control Act of 1944 and the River and Harbor Act of 1946—it is stipulated that individual projects planned by federal agencies must be submitted to the states for review and that the latters' comments must accompany requests for appropriations. (Sections 1 (a) and 1 (c) of Flood Control Act, 1944. Public Law 534, 78th Congress. In the Amendments of 1945 and 1946, these provisions were reemphasized.)

[12]J. Karl Lee, "Irrigation Policy for Arid Lands." *Journal of Farm Economics*, Vol. XXXII, No. 5, December, 1952, pp. 751- 755. Quotations are from p. 754.

[13]Policy implications are said to be these: "(1) the liberalization of existing policy with respect to repayment requirements, (2) the elimination of alternative opportunity or cost in the consideration of benefits, (3) repayment would become a secondary consideration, (4) acreage limitation would be continued, and (5) antispeculation would be continued."

[14]In the Act of 1937 authorizing the Central Valley Project of California, power is designated as "a means of financially aiding and assisting other functions." This role of power goes back to the Reclamation Act of 1906.

[15]For examples in the area of the Southwest Power Administration, see Allocation Report, pp. 15-26. For examples in the Missouri Basin, see Missouri Basin Survey Commission: Missouri, Land and Water. Washington, 1953, p. 92.

[16]The name "benefit method" is applied mainly to two methods of cost

allocation. The first allocates the total costs of a project among the purposes "in proportion to their estimated benefits." The second allocates to each purpose its "direct cost plus a share of the joint costs in direct proportion to the estimated net benefits." Allocation Report, p. 4.

[17]The quotation marks are used because the quantitative definition of acreage limitation is, to a large extent, left to the discretion of the Secretary of the Interior. By statute "160 acres" is mentioned as a maximum. It can—and has been—reduced by the Secretary of the Interior to as low as 40 acres for some projects. On the other hand, the limitation has been interpreted in such a way that man and wife may operate 320 acres. According to another interpretation, this figure can be increased even further by transferring land to other members of the family.

Sometimes, the pressure of economic and political change forces a change in the rulings of the Secretary. For example, the Orland Reclamation Project in California has been operated under a 40-acre limitation from 1916-1953 (from 1907-1916 a limitation of 160 acres was in force). In 1953, a uniform limitation of 160 acres was decreed.

[18]Ciriacy-Wantrup, *Resource Conservation, op. cit..*

[19]50 St. 731, Section 7 reads in part: "Rate schedules shall be based upon an allocation of costs made by the Federal Power Commission. In computing the cost of electric energy developed from water created as an incident to and a byproduct of the construction of the Bonneville Project, the Federal Power Commission may allocate to the costs of electric facilities such a share of the cost of facilities having joint value for the production of electric energy and other purposes as the power development may fairly bear as compared with such other purposes."

[20]Allocation Report, p. 9.

[21]Allocation Report, p. 9.

[22]Allocation Report, p. 10.

[23]The techniques and their difficulties and limitations are similar to those involved in determining the optimum state of conservation in social economics. For details, see Ciriacy-Wantrup, *Resource Conservation, op. cit.*, Chapters 16 and 17.

[24]In this connection, a statement by R. I. Mittelstaedt, President, California Public Utilities Commission, before the California Farm Bureau is of some interest. See *California Farm Bureau Monthly,* Vol. 34, No. 4, April, 1953.

[25]Harold Hotelling, "The General Welfare in Relation to Problems of Taxation and of Railway and Utility Rates." *Econometrica*, Vol. XI, No. 3, July, 1938, pp. 242-269.

Donald Wallace, "Kinds of Public Control to Replace or Supplement Antitrust Laws." *American Economic Review*, Vol. XXX, No. 1, March, 1940, supplement, pp. 194-212.

Temporary National Economic Committee. *Economic Standards of Government Price Control.* Monograph No. 32. Senate Committee Print, 76th Congress, 3d Session, 1941.

Emery Troxel, "Incremental Cost Determination of Utility Prices." *Journal of Land and Public Utility Economics,*, Vol. 18, No. 4, November, 1942.

Emery Troxel, "Limitations of the Incremental Cost Patterns of Pricing." *Journal of Land and Public Utility Economics*, Vol. 18, No. 1, February, 1943, pp. 28-39.

[26]With respect to public customers, this preference is regulated by law. A public-preference clause in some form has been in the Reclamation Law since 1906. It was reaffirmed through Section 9 (c) of the Reclamation Act of 1939. A discussion of the economics and politics of public preference would lead us too far afield.

[27]According to the reclamation laws, nominal ownership of the main dams and reservoir sites remains with the federal government.

[28]Frequent criticism of 9 (e) contracts in California has led in recent contracts to an addition to the preamble reading as follows: "and such future contracts as may be made between the United States and the District."

[29]For a more detailed discussion of the effects of uncertainty upon resource use, see Ciriacy-Wantrup, *Resource Conservation, op. cit.,* Chapter 8.

[30]See Ciriacy-Wantrup. *Resource Conservation, op. cit.,* Chapter 21.

[31]Even the much criticized duplication of *federal* agencies in water resources development—for example, of the Bureau of Reclamation and the Army Engineers—may be considered from the standpoint of the above paragraph. At present, state and local governments may obtain consideration of their objectives by working with one of these agencies if they feel that their viewpoint is not sufficiently considered by the other. Differences are brought into the open. The much needed consolidation of the two agencies would be in accord with a system of countervailing economic powers only under the condition that state and local governments play a strong independent role in water resources development.

[32]U. S. Bureau of Reclamation. Central Valley Project Studies: Allocation of Costs, Problems 8 and 9. Appendix J. Letters of Comment and Dissent Submitted by Committee Members. Govt. Print. Off., Washington, 1947, pp. 235-238.

Part IV

IRREVERSIBILITY, UNCERTAINTY, AND CONSERVATION

INTRODUCTION TO PART IV

by

William E. Phillips*

In his book *Resource Conservation: Economics and Policies*, Professor Ciriacy-Wantrup devotes the first fifteen chapters largely to the private economics of conservation (entrepreneurial decision making). The remainder of the book is devoted to the social economics of conservation (public policy). The first paper to appear in this part of the selected papers is a condensation of the main thoughts contained in his book and is organized in a similar fashion. Because it is an overview of his book on resource conservation, this first article, "Economics and Policies of Resource Conservation", provides an important and useful background to the subsequent articles which all relate to resource conservation policy and in particular to those aspects of conservation policy relating to irreversibility in resource use and conservation decisions under uncertainty. They address social issues relating to public resource conservation policies. While the emphasis is on the social economics of conservation, background in the private aspects contained in the first paper provides essential foundation material for these remaining papers.

The first paper in this part of the collection begins with Wantrup's own definitions of conservation (resource use rate patterns over time that favour the future), and depletion (resource use rate patterns over time that favour the present). Any given use rate pattern over time is referred to as a "state of conservation". Among the various alternative states of conservation facing a private resource user is the "optimum state of conservation" which maximizes the present value of net revenues. Private conservation decisions following this objective are generally approximated. However, there are a number of economic forces that influence private conservation decisions: interest and income, uncertainty, prices, property rights, tenancy, credit and taxation. Furthermore, manipulations of these forces by government entities in attempts to affect private resource use management decisions give rise to a group of policy tools which Wantrup categorizes as indirect tools of conservation policy. Publicly subsidized credit with low interest rates or increased availability to high risk resource use ventures, depletion allowances, severance taxes,

*Professor of Agricultural Economics, University of Alberta.

201

establishment of resource commodity futures markets and price support programs are but a few examples of such indirect policy tools. There is a second category which Wantrup labels as direct tools of conservation policy which affect private resource users directly rather than through the manipulation of economic forces. The direct tools include education, zoning, public ownership, resource user associations, municipal ordinances and state and federal statutes. It is important to understand both the economic forces and policy tools that influence private conservation decisions in order to explain past resource user behaviour, predict future behaviour, understand processes at work in molding the state of conservation and design appropriate social (public) conservation policies.

The objective of public conservation policy in terms of economic efficiency is to maximize the present value of social net benefits. While not practically attainable nor the sole objective of public decision-making policy, it, or a reformulation of it, is the main underlying criterion used in the subsequent papers in this part of the collection. Public conservation decision-making parallels the private determination of the optimum state of conservation, but uses a social accounting stance and struggles more with extramarket values and uncertainty. Such problems are particularly acute in dealing with renewable resources, such as fish and wildlife and other biological resources, that may become irreversibly depleted through human action, that is, used to a point beyond which a reversal through conservation is no longer economically possible. The future consequences of a current economic irreversibility are uncertain and, in fact, may result in significant and far-reaching social costs due to losses in valuable future resource use options. The establishment of safeguards at low to moderate costs, which are designed to avoid or minimize such irreversibilities, may be in society's best long-term interests. Wantrup's concept of the "safe minimum standard of conservation" is often an appropriate public policy objective in such cases. The objective is not to maximize social net benefits through attempts to determine an optimum resource allocation over time or, at least, incremental steps in that direction. Rather, it is to minimize the possibility of high irreversible losses by imposing constraints on resource use and thereby leaving considerable latitude in resource use pattern determination over time.

The paper "Conservation of the California Tule Elk: A Socioeconomic Study of a Survival Problem" illustrates in some detail how the safe minimum standard concept can be applied in practice. Conflicts among various interest groups, notably agriculture and wildlife interests, over resource use patterns are identified. Historical public decisions to resolve these conflicts have resulted in policies that do not minimize possible losses, or even extinction, of the rare California tule elk. A reformulation of policy in terms of the safe minimum standard concept with the aid of benefit-cost analysis indicates that the possible losses from following current policies are large in relation to the costs associated with the alternative safe minimum standard policies. The social benefits include both consumptive (hunting) and non-consumptive (viewing and photographing) tule elk wildlife values, scientific values and values of the elk as an adaptable gene pool. Both market (values determined by market prices) and extramarket values are involved. The social costs include elk protection and management costs and costs associated with displaced or foregone agricultural and other resource uses. The safe minimum standard oriented proposed policies call for elk population increases in one of the two existing free-roaming tule elk herds and the establishment of two additional free-roaming herds, thus reducing significantly the possibility of high irreversible losses (social costs).

A second illustration of the application of the safe minimum standard concept is contained in "The 'New' Competition for Land and Some Implications for Public Policy." The issue is the irreversible loss of prime agricultural irrigated land to urban and industrial land uses. In the paper Wantrup calls for a land policy to redirect urban and industrial encroachment on to less productive agricultural land. The cost of avoiding the irreversibility is reflected in the higher urban-industrial development costs when such development is directed to less agriculturally productive land and is considered small in relation to the benefits of minimizing possible high irreversible losses in the future through the retention of significant tracts of irrigated land. These land tracts have considerable food production capacity that could be exceedingly important in the future. In implementing such a policy, Wantrup opts for direct policy tools over the indirect policy tools referred to earlier. He examines three direct tools: (1) taxation-zoning approach; (2) controlled urbanization through social overhead; and (3) easements. For reasons he explores in some detail, the first has serious shortcomings, the second is of doubtful effectiveness and the third most applicable.

The optimum state of conservation may be determined, or at least approached, with the assistance of formal programming techniques. In his paper "Conservation and Resource Programming," Wantrup acknowledges the usefulness of such techniques. However, in the context of conservation policy, the use of such techniques is accompanied with difficulties including: (1) the problem of valuation (existence of extramarket values and unreliable prices as value measures); (2) the problem of institutional constraints (social institutions used as constraints become conceptually indistinguishable from social objectives and a new optimum must be calculated for each combination of constraints under consideration); and (3) the problem of uncertainty. Risk, which is probabilistic, can be accommodated in formal programming techniques whereas uncertainty, which is not probabilistic, imposes severe limitations on the relevance of quantitative optimizing for policy decisions. In cases involving uncertainty and irreversibilities, the safe minimum standard of conservation approach to conservation policy, whereby constraints on resource use are imposed, is more appropriate.

The fifth paper, "Social Objectives of Conservation of Natural Resources with Particular Reference to Taxation of Forests" begins with a restatement of the definition of conservation and the optimum state of conservation using a production economics analogy and a forestry example. Discussion then turns to six types of breakdown or malfunctions of the price system including extramarket values and distorted values (discussed under problems of valuation in the preceding paper) and the existence of price signals which are not received by the decision maker but by others. Turning next to taxation as an indirect public policy tool, Wantrup points out that taxation must be discussed in relation to public expenditure for various reasons given. He points out as well several features and advantages of the tax system as a conservation policy tool. In concluding the paper, he relates several implications for future research in the field of forest taxation including the need for models to test the applicability of theories to forestry, the effects of tenure relations and the need to value noncommercial forest use (extramarket values).

The final paper in this part of the collection, "Multiple Use as a Concept for Water and Range Policy" contains three objectives: (1) to consider the appropriateness of the multiple use concept in natural resource allocation theory and as a conservation policy objective; (2) to trace the past role of the concept in U. S. National Forests allocation policies; and (3) to appraise its potential usefulness in the future. In meeting the first objective, Wantrup suggests that "optimum use" is the appropriate concept in theory rather than "multiple use". It is also the appropriate starting point as a conservation policy objective as well. He discusses the role and limitations of formal programming techniques in the context of public conservation policy once again, but with the addition of a wildlife example and a discussion of the problem of rigidity under conditions of economic change. In meeting the other two objectives he begins by pointing out the historical importance of the multiple use concept in the administration of U. S. National Forests and indicates that the resource allocation system has performed well through the flexibility engendered by the multiple use concept in moving from a single use orientation (timber) to a multiple use orientation (timber, forage and recreation). Looking ahead Wantrup suggests that "in view of the uncertainty about future demands for the various types of recreation, the irreversible nature of depletion of wilderness areas, and their relative low value for other uses, the large degree of administrative discretion which was shown to be characteristic for the structure of the existing allocative system should, looking into the future, be supplemented by statutory provisions..." which he suggests should parallel certain other existing legislation.

While economists continue to find and improve means to measure extramarket values, there are also growing efforts to integrate nonquantifiable values with quantifiable ones into public resource use decision making. Applications of the safe minimum standard concept allow this integration to take place and have led the way for more recent applications using other similar approaches (critical value and dominance). Wantrup's distinction between direct and indirect policy tools is also noteworthy. In cases of resource use policy issues that do not involve irreversibilities, indirect tools, like taxes and subsidies, have merit. However, Wantrup tends toward direct tools, like zoning and other direct regulation, in irreversible cases which is contrary to much of what is advocated in the current literature. His arguments may give cause to further thought on the matter. This set of articles dealing with irreversibility, uncertainty and conservation are important extensions of Wantrup's book and lay important groundwork for continuing subsequent work by natural resource economists and others.

Chapter 11

ECONOMICS AND POLICIES
OF RESOURCE CONSERVATION*[1]

1. The Economic Meaning of Resource Conservation

In this country, the word *conservation* when applied to natural resources
has become a magic formula in the political process. Its power in rallying
support for a public policy or a private interest and in weakening opposition
is equaled by few and surpassed by none—except possibly the word *democracy*
itself. Political power of this kind is derived from an appeal to emotion
rather than to the intellect. Such an appeal suggests that there is a genuine
deeply felt public need which finds expression in the word, but also that the
meaning of the word is not clearly defined. If an attempt is made here to
define the economic meaning of conservation, the intent is not to weaken its
emotional appeal but to restrain its abuse in the political process and to
increase its usefulness for economic understanding.

Generally, conservation is regarded more as a subject of the natural
sciences or the domain of the idealist and the politician than as a vital and
theoretically interesting subject of economics. To this, someone might reply
that the economic meaning of conservation is of no concern to the conservation
movement and that economics as a discipline may well discard the concept
conservation and find a more neutral substitute. Such parting of the ways is,
of course, feasible but not helpful. Whether they like it or not, the interest of
the conservationist and the economist is directed at the same problem, or
more precisely, the essential problem of the former looms also large among
the problems of the latter. This problem is the concern for the future—the
relation of past and present to future use of natural resources. Hence, a
semantic bridge between the conservation movement and economics would
seem more helpful than strengthening the existing semantic barrier. In the
absence of such a bridge, the word conservation will continue to be used for
obtaining political support for policy objectives which in their effects upon
natural resources are frequently not understood. Conservation has lent

*Reprinted, with the permission of McGraw-Hill Book Company, from
Symposium on Natural Resources, Eds. Warren L. Flock and Martin R.
Huberty, 1959, pp. 500-526.

support to contradictory objectives such as "breaking of monopoly," "eliminating wastes of competition," "socialization of resources," "private ownership of resources," "birth control to ease population pressure on resources," and "population increase for resource development."

There is fairly general agreement that conservation by itself does not mean nonuse. Conservation in this sense would be meaningless both for nonrenewable or "stock" resources such as oil, coal, and metal ores and for renewable or "flow" resources such as solar and other radiation, precipitation, animals, plants, and scenery. If nonuse were adopted as an objective of conservation policy, the "conserved" portion of the environment would merely be eliminated from the list of resources.

Most definitions of conservation, therefore, are in terms of use. By some, conservation is defined as "continuous", "constant," or "sustained" use; by others, "as the greatest use to the greatest number over the greatest length of time"; and by still others, simply as "wise" use. Such definitions may enhance the emotional appeal of conservation, but they add little to understanding. It is of interest here, however, that these definitions and the many books and papers in which they are presented have one common characteristic. They are concerned with the future use of natural resources—whether the emphasis is on oil and metal ores or on water and wilderness areas. Nearly always, the stimulus for this concern comes from the experience with past and present use.

Economics is concerned with the relations between human wants and the means to satisfy them—especially with the limitations of means. Economics is the study of choosing between alternative courses of action to deal with "scarcity." Such study is based on understanding past choices by individuals and social groups but looks toward the future in order to predict or to plan. Economics has a Janus face. In such an *ex post* and *ex ante* study of choosing, alternatives involving time must be considered. The choice between use of natural resources at different times and the relation between past, present, and future use of natural resources—the concern of the conservation movement—are, therefore, highly significant economic problems. Thus, the concept conservation is tied to a particular aspect of the use of natural resources: its intertemporal distribution. Conservation is concerned with the *when* of use.

More specifically, "conservation" and its logical corollary but economic opposite "depletion" are defined in terms of *changes* in the intertemporal distribution of resource use. Such changes imply comparison of two or more alternative time distributions of resource use, that is, interrelated series of "rates of use" occurring at different "intervals" of time.

A rate of use is the first derivative of cumulative use with respect to time. In order to avoid cumbersome language, the term *use* will be employed here in this sense. Use is measured in physical units, for example, tons, calories, acre-feet, kilowatt hours, and man-days.

The term *interval* has a special meaning in time economics. It is defined as that extent of time within which changes of use and of other economic variables can be neglected in the analysis. The actual clock-time extent of an interval may be a day, a week, a month, a year, or a number of years according to the nature of the economic problem to be solved. For example, in the pumping of an oil well, use may be planned by the week or month; in wheat production, the interval is determined by the seasons; in hog production, it is the time required for breeding and fattening; and in forestry, a cutting cycle may extend over decades.

We may compare (*ex post*) actual time distributions of use during different periods of history or in different geographic locations. Or we may compare (*ex ante*) hypothetical time distributions through economic calculation. In either comparison a change from one time distribution to another is called *conservation* if the redistribution is in the direction of the future and *depletion* if the redistribution is in the direction of the present.

The terms *in the direction of the future* and *in the direction of the present* could be defined simply on the basis of the time sequence of increases and decreases of use. This is satisfactory provided that one is interested in a differentiation of conservation and depletion and provided that increases and decreases occur without alternations over all intervals considered, or as a special case, if all changes are of the same sign. These conditions are approximated in most practical applications of the words conservation and depletion. Otherwise, ascertaining the direction of change requires a weighing of each change by time and aggregation. These problems have been explained elsewhere.[2]

Any given time distribution of resource use may be regarded as the result of conservation or depletion and will be called a *state of conservation* in the sense of resulting from or with respect to conservation or depletion. State of conservation is merely a convenient shorthand expression for "a given state in the intertemporal distribution of resource use." An important special case of a state of conservation is the one which may be regarded the economically "best" for an individual resource user or for a social group. This is the *optimum state of conservation.* The optimum state of conservation is an economic maximum that is not necessarily identical with maximum cumulative use.

The above definitions have several advantages. In application they are not contrary to popular terminology, but they are more useful for economic analysis. They are neutral in terms of value judgments. They are not affected by the money veil; that is, changes in the monetary value of use do not affect the definition and measurement of conservation, depletion, and state of conservation. They carry no connotation of efficiency or waste. In the literature, the term *waste* is usually associated with the depletion of flow resources. But conservation of resources also may be wasteful. A few illustrations must suffice here.

Conservation that would try to hold agricultural productivity of a virgin soil with distant markets at the original level or try to restore it to that level may be wasteful in terms of other natural resources (lime, fertilizer, fuel), labor, and equipment. A forester who would hasten the recovery of a cutover forest in a young country through planting instead of waiting for natural revegetation may be wasteful because his efforts may better be directed toward fire protection, improved systems of logging, and the like over a larger forested area. A mine owner who installs expensive permanent equipment in order to increase his recovery rate or to extend the life of his mine may be wasting labor and capital which he could more advantageously employ in alternative enterprises. Under some conditions, depletion of local ground water may enable a community to grow strong enough to import distant surface water, whereas conserving ground water would necessitate limiting economic development.

Apparently, there is an economic criterion for conservation. Somewhere, in conservation, an economically optimum time distribution of use is reached. This distribution was called above the optimum state of conservation. The meaning of waste in resource use must be related to such an optimum. What are the economic issues in making decisions concerning this optimum?

2. Conservation Decisions in Private Economics

The economic and social issues in conservation are different in private and in public decisions. We may focus on conservation in private economics first, because most private issues are simpler and because, in a private enterprise economy like that of the United States, both the need and the possibilities for public action are based on an understanding of the objectives of individual resource users and of the way they respond to economic forces, especially those affected by conservation policy.

Such an understanding is required not only for those who make and execute policies. In conservation policy, where continuity is of utmost importance, a continuous public demand for legislation and enforcement is a requirement for action by a democracy. A continuous and articulate demand for conservation policy requires that the electorate become aware of the economic issues involved. Likewise, execution of conservation policy is aided if those immediately concerned, the individual resource users and their political representatives, understand the relations between their own behavior and the interests of the social group.

As stated in section 1, conservation and depletion are defined in terms of changes in the intertemporal distribution of use. Decisions concerning such changes may be called, for short, conservation decisions. They are part and parcel of all business planning. Farmers, foresters, mine operators, oil producers, and other resource users plan use for more than one interval. This must be done because use in one interval is related through revenues or costs or both to use in other intervals. This economic necessity for an integrated production plan extending over time and, therefore, the economic significance of conservation decisions may be explained by indicating the types of relations between use in different intervals through revenues or costs.

When we say that use in two intervals is related through revenues or costs, we mean changes of use in one interval will affect revenues or costs in the other. Obviously, in order to measure such effects, use in the other interval must be kept constant. Furthermore, we have to measure the changes in revenues and cost brought about by the last unit of the change in use that is considered. By this we mean, in the terminology of the economist, we have to measure changes in *marginal* revenues and costs. The reason for this requirement is that, at different levels of use, a given change may have quite different effects. For example, up to a certain level of use (in terms of tons of feed harvested or animal units pastured per acre), grazing in one year may not increase the costs of taking the same harvest next year. However, from a certain level onward, an increase of use will require costs for irrigation, fertilization, and other inputs if the harvest next year is to remain unchanged.

We may define relations between use in two intervals as complementary through revenues if an increase of use in one increases marginal revenues in the other; relations are defined as competitive through revenues if a decrease of marginal revenues occurs. Relations are defined as complementary through costs if an increase of use in one interval decreases marginal costs in another; competitiveness through costs prevails if the opposite is true. The relations are called neutral, or use in different intervals independent, if no change in revenues or costs occurs. A parallel set of definitions is used for the relations between different resources through demand and supply, for example, between coal and iron ore (complementary through demand), coal and oil (competitive through demand), silver and copper ores (complementary through supply), and coal and soil (competitive through supply in strip mining).

Relations through revenues depend on market form. Under pure competition, product prices expected in different intervals are identical with marginal revenues. From the standpoint of the individual resource user, prices are given. This is merely a different way of saying that use in one interval does not affect marginal revenues in another. This situation holds for most users of flow resources, for example, agriculture, forestry, grazing, and fisheries. In these instances, therefore, we are concerned largely with relations through costs and can disregard relations through revenues, at least in private economics.

On the other hand, in the utilization of stock resources, market form is frequently characterized by monopolistic conditions of various types. This is true, for example, for metal ores, oil, natural gas, precious stones, and fertilizer materials. Here, the relations through revenues may require an integrated production plan even if relations through costs could be neglected. Monopolistic conditions, therefore, are of considerable significance in the economics and policies of resource conservation. Space does not permit consideration of this problem here.[3]

Competitiveness through costs is implicitly recognized in a large part of the literature on conservation. Such competitiveness is the major reason why conservation can be accomplished through decrease of present use in favor of future use, that is, through "waiting." Actually, however, this relation is frequently not sufficiently realized in business planning. An increase of future costs caused by soil depletion, overgrazing, overcutting, or overpumping is generally taken too lightly. This is due partly to difficulties in evaluating future increase of costs and partly to the laws and customs existing in resource tenure, taxation, and credit. We shall return to these problems later.

Complementarity through costs is a result of what we may call *sunk costs*. They include, first, costs which in short-run instantaneous economic analysis are known as fixed and lumpy. These are the costs of productive factors such as buildings, machinery, trees, and breeding stock which cannot be used economically if such use were confined to any one interval. Sunk costs include, second, some costs which in instantaneous economic analysis (short run or long run) are termed variable. In agriculture, the costs of fertilizer, feed, and labor are sunk over periods of gestation. Considerable costs for labor and materials must be expended to open a mine or to drill a well before production can start. These inputs are potentially useful in obtaining revenues over more than one interval. Additional costs necessary to obtain these revenues may be called *recovery costs*. Sunk costs play a role in maintaining production over time as do fixed and lumpy costs over a certain range in instantaneous economics. Likewise, recovery costs have economic characteristics similar to that of variable costs of instantaneous economics.

Another cause for complementarity through costs is that it is often difficult for individual resource users to shift to other employment. In terms of opportunity costs, this influence may be regarded as a part of sunk costs; it has the same effects upon maintaining production over time. But indivisibility, immobility, and specialization of the resource user himself differ in their origin and their susceptibility to change from similar conditions affecting other productive factors. In the latter case, these conditions are largely technological, whereas in the former, they are largely institutional. We may now ask: What is the objective of conservation decisions? In other words, what is the optimum state of conservation in private economics?

3. The Optimum State of Conservation in Private Economics

The objective of economic decisions is usually formulated as maximization of some expected value or state of economic well-being—variously called "net revenues," "income," "profit," "utility," or "satisfaction."

If the maximization principle is applied to conservation decisions, a flow of net revenues extending over time must be maximized. Net revenues at different intervals are reduced to "present values" through discounting with the prevailing interest rate. The optimum state of conservation is that time distribution of use that maximized the present value of the flow of net revenues.

In economic theory, the optimum state of conservation can be determined in various ways. Revenue and cost functions and the joint-production approach may be employed; or net revenues may be formulated as an integral over a variable period of time and the calculus of variations employed for maximization.[4]

In economic reality, it is usually not practical to calculate many small changes of variables as is theoretically required for maximization. Only a few lumpy changes of irregular magnitude can be considered. The practical objective of conservation decisions is a step-by-step directional (conservation or depletion) change of the existing or some hypothetical distribution toward the optimum. The optimum state of conservation can be approximated only through trial and error. An increment of present net revenues rather than maximum present net revenues is the objective of conservation decisions.

In connection with this more modest objective, the concept of a *conservation practice* is helpful. When resource users make conservation decisions, they usually consider as alternatives whole combinations of interrelated inputs and outputs. Such a combination may be called a conservation practice. Usually, a given conservation practice involves interrelated changes of inputs in more than one interval. The same is true for outputs. For example, in soil conservation, the practice of terracing involves inputs of man-hours and machine-hours for construction, the expenditure of materials for preparing proper outlets, repair and maintenance over the years, variations in size and layouts of fields, changes in methods of cultivating and harvesting, changes in yields, changes in risks, and possible other changes.

Under such conditions, the present total additional value product of the conservation practice is compared with its present additional total costs. Usually, only a small number of alternative conservation practices is calculated. Although no one can accurately determine the optimum state of conservation in this way, save by accident, the modest but practical objective of approximating the optimum step-by-step can be effectively pursued.

Not all questions which can be raised concerning the optimum state of conservation as a concept can be considered here. Two of them, however, deserve at least some mention because they are especially significant for conservation policy. The first question concerns the existence of extramarket values and the second the influence of uncertainty.

There is no need to labor the point that conservation decisions are not solely influenced by positive and negative values which are easily expressed in monetary terms, that is, which are evaluated through and in the market place. The availability of leisure time and good working relations with family members, neighbors, employees, and government officials are common nonmonetary considerations in business planning. Prestige, power, pride in his own achievement, aesthetic appreciation of a well-kept farm or landscape may be as important as monetary rewards. To remain in exclusive control of one's business may be regarded as more essential than to increase pecuniary net revenues. Group-centered motives, such as patriotism and community spirit or envy and vengefulness, may influence conservation decisions.

These values are usually called "intangible" in economic analysis. The implication of this term appears unfortunate. They will be called here *extramarket values.*

For individuals, inclusion of extramarket values in revenues and costs does not prevent approximating the optimum state of conservation. It can be established that individuals are able to compare changes in their state of well-being connected with changes in the combination of extramarket and market goods. They are able to take account of both types of goods in their conservation decisions. The psychological mechanism of these subjective evaluations (for example, whether cardinal or ordinal differentiation of utility is involved) is neither accessible nor relevant for objective evaluation of extramarket goods.

Objective or "administrative" evaluation of extramarket goods can sometimes be accomplished by analogy, that is, by using market values in auxiliary calculations or by employing market criteria, such as equality of supply and demand. Sometimes rates of substitution between extramarket and market goods can be obtained objectively through observation of behavior in situations of choosing, either actual or hypothetical, in questionnaires, for example. Administrative evaluation is of interest for conservation policy.

It is commonly recognized that resource users frequently have only hunches and broad guesses with respect to the economic data necessary for determining the optimum state of conservation. Expectations are uncertain. In more technical language, expectations are not single-valued but appear in the form of a probability distribution. Resource users seldom have exact numerical knowledge of the statistical moments of this distribution. But they have, generally, some notion about the range of possible outcomes and, sometimes, about the most probable outcome. The question arises whether and in what way this situation affects the meaning of the optimum state of conservation.

On one side it can be argued that there is no such influence: resource users employ in their calculations the most probable value of expected net revenues and discount this value for uncertainty, that is, reduce it in proportion to dispersion. Thus, multivalued expectations are treated in production planning as if they were single-valued.

On the other side, it can be pointed out that uncertainty of expectations cannot effectively be taken into account in this way. Without disputing the actual extent of this practice, it has two serious limitations.

1. Discounting is ineffective if the most probably value of net revenues cannot be ascertained. Such situations are common in economic reality because, as just emphasized, expectations frequently consist merely in hunches and vague notions of the range of possible occurrences.

2. Discounting may be an ineffective allowance for uncertainty even if the most probable value of net revenues can be ascertained. This is true if the possibility of a highly unfavorable outcome exists—even though such an outcome may be much less probable than alternative, more favorable outcomes. Discounting the most probable net revenues for the possibility of high negative net revenues (losses) may not lead to decisions that would safeguard the enterprise against bankruptcy if the most unfavorable outcome is actually realized. This threat depends both on the magnitude of the loss and on the financial strength of the enterprise, which always has definite limits.

A contingency which threatens bankruptcy can be guarded against in various ways, for example, through hedging, pooling, and spreading arrangements or by avoiding commitments which would cause dangerous losses if the most unfavorable outcome should occur, that is, by keeping the production plan flexible. Flexibility is a way of allowing for uncertainty of expectations because most uncertainties increase with distance in time: resource users know that expectations about a certain interval will become less uncertain the nearer this interval is approached in the course of time.

Avoiding the possibility of the most unfavorable outcome involves either definite costs, for example, a risk premium for an insurance policy, or possible losses through flexibility. Losses occur with a more flexible plan, as compared with a less flexible plan that would bring maximum net revenues under the most probable expectation, if the most probable outcome is actually realized or, at least, if the most unfavorable outcome is not realized. Thus, the more flexible plan may not be the optimum plan as defined through maximizing the most probable net revenues. However, these more probable losses through greater flexibility are moderate as compared with the losses through smaller flexibility if the most unfavorable outcome is realized.

In other words, one important objective of conservation decisions is to avoid immoderate possible losses, although of small probability, by accepting the possibility of moderate ones, although the latter are more probable. For our purposes, a loss may be called immoderate if it threatens the continuity of a production plan.

Economic choices between losses of various magnitudes and probabilities exist not only in those special cases in which immoderate losses, in the sense just indicated, are under consideration. Such cases were mentioned, first, because they reveal clearly the insufficiency of taking account of uncertainty through discounting. Much more numerous are cases in which alternatives exist between larger but less probable losses and smaller but more probable ones, although the former need not be immoderate.

It may be concluded that multivalued decision problems are so common in economics that the objectives of conservation decisions are best formulated in a way which takes uncertainty explicitly into account. This can be done, for example, by subjecting the economic optimum to the restriction of avoiding immoderate possible losses or by formulating it as "minimizing maximum possible losses." For conservation policy, such an objective is called here a "safe minimum standard," which will be discussed later.

The preceding discussion of the optimum state of conservation does not by itself explain conservation and depletion in actual situations of resource use. But such a discussion provides the organizing principle by which actual situations may be understood.

The optimum state of conservation is a helpful concept not only for understanding the behavior of resource users on the basis of their objectives. The optimum state of conservation may also be employed as an *ex post* concept without imputing objectives, such as maximization or any other, to resource users. In this sense, observable changes in the state of conservation may be called "toward" and "away" from the optimum in terms of relative economic success (survival) in a given economic environment.

To use an analogy, the concepts "climax type" in ecology and "adaptive peak" in genetics do not explain an actual plant association or the developmental state of a species at a particular time and place; nor do they indicate that static states are realizable or that the system which is being considered is closed. Still they are helpful constructs in understanding the direction of ceaseless change, the resultant of environmental forces which can be observed at a given time and place.

Thus, the optimum state of conservation both as an *ex ante* and as an *ex post* concept is a construct which is helpful as an organizing principle in analyzing the result of economic forces which influence conservation. A study of these forces is the central theme of the economics of conservation.

4. Economic Forces Influencing Conservation

An economic study of conservation must explain how a state of conservation and its change come about. The variables involved in such a study may be called *economic forces*, including the economic effects of social institutions.

An understanding of these forces is necessary for the following four reasons: (1) for explaining the behavior of resource users in the past; (2) for predicting the behavior of resource users under given assumptions with respect to such forces; (3) for understanding the selective processes that operate among a statistical population of resource users and, over time, mold the state of conservation; (4) for designing appropriate conservation policies—economic forces may be obstacles or tools for such policies.

Interest, Income, and Conservation

Among economic forces affecting conservation, interest and related forces are among the most powerful, most consistent, and, from the standpoint of theoretical analysis and practical effects, among the most clear-cut.

Interest rates are used in production planning for making net revenues occurring in different intervals comparable in time. This means that future net revenues that are numerically identical but occur in different intervals are decreased in relation to their distance in time from that interval in which decisions are made. An increase in interest rates means, therefore, a progressive decrease (one that becomes greater with distance) in the present value of future net revenues. The result will be an attempt to change the time distribution of net revenues in the direction of the present. This can be accomplished through redistributing revenues in the direction of the present or through redistributing costs in the direction of the future or through both.

Except for the relatively minor possibilities of reducing storage, revenues are redistributed in this way through redistributing use toward the present.

Costs are redistributed in this way by substituting productive services with shorter periods of gestation for those with longer periods or, in the terminology used above, by reducing sunk costs. This also means a redistribution of rates of use in the direction of the present if the state of technology is assumed to be unchanged. Thus, an increase of interest rates tends to change the time distribution of use in the direction of the present. This means depletion. By the same reasoning, a decrease of interest rates leads to conservation.

The effects of interest rates just discussed are not necessarily dependent on the assumption of economic calculativeness. A rise of interest rates makes relatively more successful not only those resource users who calculatively respond to this change of environment by depleting their resources but also those who for any other reasons or for no particular reason (at random) have a lower state of conservation than others. Thus, over time, selection and imitation would bring about depletion, considering a population of resource users as a whole. Similarly, conservation would be brought about by fall of interest rates.

Interest rates determined in the market place are relevant for individual resource users if they can easily purchase and sell expected net revenue flows discounted on the basis of such rates. In the terminology of the economist, market interest rates are relevant if the market for the physical, personal, and money "assets" of individual resource users is perfect. In such a market, all individuals can purchase and sell any desired quantities at the prevailing prices.

In economic reality, markets for assets are frequently not perfect. It is often more economical to disinvest in resources through depletion than through sale or borrowing if there are no ready markets in which assets are capitalized or in which funds can be borrowed at interest rates lower than individual "time-preference" rates. Conversely, it may be more economical to invest in resources through conservation than through purchase or lending if there are no ready markets in which assets are capitalized or in which funds can be lent at interest rates higher than individual time-preference rates.

The concept of individual time preference is a marginal one. Time-preference rates, therefore, are affected by the numerical value of net revenues or, better for the present purpose, the level of individual income. Thus, in the economics of conservation, we are greatly interested in the way changes of income levels affect time-preference rates.

A unit of income, a dollar, becomes less and less effective in influencing economic decisions as income increases. In time economics, one must focus on the ratio between the effectiveness (in influencing economic decisions) of the identical amount of income in different intervals. This ratio must also decrease progressively with increasing income levels. This ratio is identical by definition with the rate of time preference. It follows that, in conservation economics, we are interested in those income-changing forces which affect different income levels differently, or in terms borrowed from the economics of taxation which are "regressive" or "progressive" with income, and those forces which do not vary with income during general income changes, as during depressions. The latter forces are called "fixed charges."

If markets for assets and loans are imperfect, a decrease in income levels will increase time preference and lead to depletion; an increase in income levels will lead to conservation. A given change in income levels, however, will have less and less effect on the state of conservation as income increases. In other words, the relations between income levels and conservation decisions are most important in the low-income groups and have more importance during depressions than during booms.

The relations between conservation decisions, interest rates, and income are of special significance for industrially less developed countries. In these, interest rates are high, markets for assets are especially imperfect, incomes are low, and fixed charges on income are increasing through monetization of taxes and substitution of cash rents for share rents.

Uncertainty and Conservation

As we know, allowance for uncertainty can be made through discounting, by keeping the production plan flexible, and through hedging, pooling, and spreading.

The most important uncertainties, namely, those created by changes of technology, of consumer demand and of social institutions, increase with time. Uncertainties of nature (drought, pests, hailstorms, fire, floods) increase with time up to a certain limit, for example, within the season. Conversely, resource users know that uncertainty at a certain future date will decrease as this date is approached in the course of time.

Because of these relations between uncertainty and time, changes in the uncertainty discount affect the state of conservation like changes of the time discount: an increase in the uncertainty discount means a progressive decrease in the present value of future net revenues. The result will be an attempt to change the time distribution of net revenues in the direction of the present. Why such an attempt leads to depletion need not be repeated. Conversely, a decrease in the uncertainty discount leads to conservation.

The effects of changes in flexibility are not so simple. First, we may ask how is an increase in flexibility accomplished? Assuming a given command over assets of all kinds, flexibility is largely a problem of keeping liquid funds (cash, government securities) and liquid inventories (finished goods or materials) and of reducing the time over which commitments in durable factors are made. The latter can be accomplished by securing durable factors through short-time leases rather than through long-term leases and through ownership. If durable factors are secured through ownership rather than through lease, flexibility can be increased by giving preference to factors which are less durable. In the terminology used above, periods over which costs are sunk are reduced. What do these changes mean in terms of conservation?

An increase in liquidity does not in itself mean conservation or depletion. On the other hand, a reduction of sunk costs means depletion. Likewise, tendencies to avoid ownership and to shorten leases generally result in depletion, as will be discussed presently. In other words, unless liquidity alone is the method of adaptation, changes of uncertainty, if allowed for through flexibility, tend to change utilization plans in the same direction as if such changes are taken into account through discounting for uncertainty.

Hedging is not very important in the economics of conservation because existing markets for "futures" do not extend far enough in time. Within the narrow limits of its effectiveness, hedging reduces the need for uncertainty discounting and for flexibility and, therefore, encourages conservation.

Through pooling, some uncertainties of nature can be effectively reduced. With pooling, in contrast to spreading discussed below, uncertainties are of the same kind but of random incidence among producers in the same statistical class, that is, operating under similar physical and economic conditions.

The most important condition for pooling is that the membership in the pool be sufficiently large. Since the precision of an average is proportional to the square root of the number of terms it contains, pooling enables the most probable value of expectations to be determined more precisely than is possible for individual members of the pool. As a corollary, the aggregate allowance for uncertainty in the pool is smaller than the aggregate of individual uncertainty allowances without pooling. In other words, the need for uncertainty allowance through discounting and flexibility is reduced, expenditure of sunk costs encouraged; hence, with some exceptions which cannot be discussed here, pooling tends toward conservation.

Some uncertainties are connected with unique nonrecurrent contingencies which affect all producers in the same statistical class, but those in different classes differently. Such uncertainties are connected, for example, with changes of technology and demand and with the discovery of new deposits in the case of stock resources. These uncertainties cannot be reduced through pooling by producers in the same class; often, however, they can be reduced by spreading. This is possible if different branches of a multiple-product firm, different firms, different industries, or different geographical areas are subject to uncertainties of different kinds. Aggregate uncertainty allowance for such a composite of uncertainties can be less than the aggregate allowance for individual kinds of uncertainties because the dispersion of possible around the most probable revenues and costs is less for the composite than for the individual components.

Spreading, like hedging and pooling, reduces the need for uncertainty discount and flexibility. Spreading generally favors conservation. Again, some important exceptions cannot be discussed here.

Prices and Conservation

We have seen how conservation decisions are affected by changes in two particular prices—time and uncertainty discounts. The effects of these price changes are clear-cut because they have definite relations to time. Time relations of other price changes are more complex.

In order to make conclusive statements about the effects of price changes upon conservation decisions, one would have to know (1) how expected price changes are distributed over time and (2) how interrelations between use in different intervals through revenues and costs are affected, that is, whether a given price change (in a product or a factor) encourages practices that are specifically conserving or specifically depleting. The complexity created by these two requirements can be reduced by making simplifying assumptions. Let us first observe the effect of price changes under the assumption that interrelations between use in different intervals are not affected.

An increase of product prices that is expected to occur at some future interval and to last indefinitely or one that is expected to become greater with time will induce a shift of use in the direction of the future, that is, will encourage conservation. An expected decrease of product prices under corresponding assumptions will lead to depletion. On the other hand, if a current increase of product prices is not expected to last for more than a few intervals, as during a war or the upswing of a business cycle, a shift of use toward those intervals is encouraged. Such a shift means depletion.

With price changes in factors, interrelations through costs cannot be disregarded. Some factors are employed in both conserving and depleting practices. In agriculture, for example, the same labor and equipment can be used for exposing slopes to water erosion and for building terraces. Bulldozers may be used for stopping gullies or for strip mining. For these factors, one can make no general statement about how price changes will affect conservation decisions. Some factors, on the other hand, are conserving under most technological conditions. In agriculture, for example, fertilizer and purchased feed, legume and grass seed are usually, but not always, conserving. Other factors such as mining machinery, the donkey engine in forestry, and hunting equipment are usually, but not necessarily, depleting. In principle, only the production plan and a practice are conserving or depleting.

The absence of hard and fast rules about the effects of price changes upon conservation decisions may cause disappointment. However, emphasis on this absence and on the importance of specific assumptions with respect to the time distribution of price changes and their effects on interrelations between use rates seemed necessary because these assumptions are frequently overlooked.

Price changes of products and of factors have far-reaching effects upon conservation decisions; but to ascertain the direction of these effects (that is, conservation or depletion) and to assess their quantitative significance requires caution. This is especially true if price changes are advocated as a tool of conservation policy.

Property Rights and Conservation

The economic forces discussed thus far—interest, income, uncertainty, and prices—are strongly affected by property rights. But these rights have additional effects on conservation decisions.

Property is a "bundle" of rights to control resource use. This bundle includes the rights an owner surrenders to a tenant when he leases or to a creditor when he borrows and such public rights of control as taxation. The specific influence upon conservation of the three "derived" property institutions will be considered subsequently. Here we will deal in general terms with the broad over-all relations between property rights and conservation. These relations will be discussed under indefiniteness, instability, and imbalance.

Indefiniteness of property rights exists in "fugitive" resources that must be captured through use, such as wildlife, high-seas fisheries, oil, natural gas, and ground water where control of subsurface resources is vested in the surface owner. Definite property rights belong only to those who are in possession. Deferred use is always subject to a great uncertainty: others may capture the resource in the meantime. Hence, every user tries to protect himself against others by acquiring ownership through capture in the fastest possible way; use tends to be concentrated in the least possible number of intervals near the present. Indefiniteness of property rights leads to depletion.

There are effective remedies for the wasteful depletion caused by indefiniteness of property rights: control over resource use may be defined through law and public regulations in such a way that the need for capture disappears. Such definition may vest control in individuals or in collective bodies. Examples are for oil and gas, regulation of well spacing and of proper gas-oil ratio in pumping, and the establishment of unitized pools. Unified control was established over the public range after the Taylor Grazing Act provided the legal and administrative basis. Several ground-water basins have been adjudicated in California, and uncertainty of water tenure is recognized as a major problem of water policy.[5]

Property rights may be well defined but unstable over time. This is another important cause of economic uncertainty and resource depletion. The instability resulting from short leases and from fear of dispossession by creditors will be taken up later. Here, we are concerned with a more widely dispersed type of instability. In periods of political change which threatens a sudden and radical redistribution of property rights, all resource users will hesitate to make investments with deferred yield. In such cases, resource users will adopt a utilization plan that they themselves would regard as wasteful depletion if their property rights were more stable.

Property rights are imbalanced if they lead to such a distribution of revenues and costs among the members of a social group that the individual resource user is not interested in taking into account all revenues and costs that are functionally related to his management. Generally, he will take into account only those revenues which accrue to him and those costs which he is required to pay. Revenues and costs incident on others will not affect his conservation decisions. The difference between the incidence of revenues and costs, on the basis of property rights and their allocation to functionally related use, is of special significance for conservation policy.

Tenancy and Conservation

Tenancy affects the state of conservation through uncertainty allowance for instability, through incidence of revenues and costs on owner and user, through fixed regressive rents, and through lessening the results of imperfections in the markets for assets.

Uncertainty allowance for instability of tenancy can be reduced through longer lease contracts, through renewal clauses requiring notification in advance about intentions to renew, and through provisions for compensation if either party refuses to renew without such notice. Longer lease contracts can be made more acceptable to both owner and tenant by sliding-scale cash rents varying with prices instead of the common fixed cash or share rents, by a fair determination of rent, and by clear and detailed setting forth of the rights and duties of both parties to avoid misunderstandings and frictions. Theoretically, if expected revenues and costs functionally related to a tenant's management were incident on him, he would have no reason to alter the utilization plan because he is not the owner. This result can be approached through fuller compensation for deferred revenues and costs at the time of severance of tenancy.

Economic conditions and customs vary so much from region to region that it would not be wise to enact and rigidly enforce detailed regulations about length of leases and compensation. But general rules can be laid down in state land-tenancy acts; and special courts of tenancy arbitration, composed of owners and tenants with an experienced judge as chairman, could be provided to administer them.

The depleting effects of fixity of rents can be avoided if cash rents are expressed as a percentage of net revenues. Such rents are rare, however, because of difficulties in ascertaining all costs. An approximation is a rent variable with gross revenues. The various sliding-scale cash and share rents are of this type. The worst effects of fixity of rents can be avoided by variable payment plans, a surplus over the fixed normal rent being accumulated in periods of high net incomes, and payments being reduced in periods of subnormal production and prices. From the standpoint of conservation, the common fixed share rent is usually, but not always, better than the common fixed cash rent.

If the system of tenancy were sufficiently improved, it would encourage conservation by counteracting the effects of imperfections in the markets for assets. In the absence of such improvement, attempts to transform tenants into owners, as in the Bankhead-Jones Tenant Farmers Purchase Act, tend toward conservation provided that the new owners are set up in economic units and without too great debts. Improvements in tenancy and attempts to increase the proportion of owners do not conflict with each other; both can be pursued at the same time.

Credit and Conservation

The credit system is related to conservation in much the same way as is tenancy, that is, through uncertainty allowance, through fixed and regressive charges, through lessening imperfections in the markets for assets, and through conservation clauses in the loan contract.

If the owner's equity is small in relation to his creditor's, then ownership does not guarantee tenure. Even if the owner succeeds in fulfilling the loan contract, the creditors may recall the loan before it actually becomes delinquent in order to safeguard their equity. Inability to fulfill a contract and recall of the loan usually happen at a time when refinancing or liquidation of assets through sale is difficult or impossible. The result is bankruptcy and foreclosure. Allowance for this threat results in depletion: the owner may find it advisable to liquidate through depletion as much as possible of the present value of his resources before foreclosure prevents him from saving his equity.

These undesirable effects of the credit system upon the state of conservation may be reduced by institutional arrangements for debt adjustments without foreclosure. Such arrangements may be set up like the special tenancy courts previously suggested or may be combined with them.

Generally, interest and amortization payments are fixed charges which, as we know, tend to discourage conservation under imperfect markets for assets. Furthermore, credit charges tend to be regressive with income; debtors in low-income groups often pay higher interest rates than those with larger incomes because risks are considered greater by lenders and because the cost of administering smaller loans is higher per unit.

The depleting effect of these charges can be reduced by making them vary with income. This may be done by variable payment plans previously suggested in connection with rent payments or by relating interest and amortization payments more directly to the prices of products. A decrease in the amplitude of income fluctuations brought about by making interest and amortization payments flexible not only has favorable effects upon the borrower's utilization plan but is also favorable for the lender: the need for moratoria, refinancing, and foreclosure in periods of depression is reduced, and the purchasing power of interest income is protected in periods of prosperity.

Thus, the undesirable relations between credit and conservation are to some extent avoidable. Further, they are more than balanced by the relations that are economically desirable: a well-functioning credit system reduces the effects (upon the state of conservation) of imperfections in the markets for assets. Such a credit system is an effective aid in conservation.

A not infrequent cause of imperfections in the market for loans is obsolete lending practices such as outdated methods of appraisal, failure to recognize increased stability in developing regions or enterprises and to reduce rates accordingly, and insistence on certain customary types of collateral despite changes in physical and economic institutions. An example of this last situation is frequently encountered on western ranges where the collateral for loans is often livestock and the number grazed is the basis for loan rationing. Lenders, failing to recognize the overgrazing problem, may object to having the number of livestock reduced even though the value of the collateral may be reduced by loss of weight on overgrazed ranges. A change in such practices would eliminate a cause of depletion that is serious both for the borrower and for the lender.

The credit system could encourage conservation by including conservation clauses in the loan contract. Some Federal land banks and some private banks have made proper soil conservation a condition for lending. Similarly, silvicultural practices might be introduced as a part of a public forest credit system.

Taxation and Conservation

Like the other derived property institutions, the tax system has significant but frequently unintended and unrecognized effects upon conservation decisions. Taxation is sometimes an important obstacle for conservation policy. On the other hand, the tax system can be employed more easily and effectively as a tool of conservation policy than can the tenancy or credit system.

Any attempt to make general statements about the effects of taxation upon conservation decisions faces the same difficulties encountered in discussing the effects of prices: when new taxes are levied or existing ones changed (in rates, methods of assessment, modes of payment), one needs to know how interrelations between use in different intervals are affected and how the tax changes are distributed over time.

Taxes are generally not imposed on specifically conserving or depleting factors or products. If they are, conservation will be affected by new or increased taxes in much the same way as by prices.

Variations of taxes over time may be expected because the government has implied or announced that a given change of taxes will be limited in duration or on the basis of extrapolating past experience or because of important present events such as a war or a depression which are known to lead to great changes of fiscal needs. If a given change in taxes is not expected to last over the whole planning period, rates of use tend to be redistributed in such a way that the tax base is increased in those planning intervals in which taxes are more favorable. Conservation or depletion will result according to the time distribution of the tax changes. More usual are situations in which the tax change is expected to last over the whole planning period. In the following discussion of the different types of taxes, we will make the simplifying assumptions that resource users base their plans on this expectation and that interrelations between use are not affected by the change in taxes.

Property taxes are among the most important taxes in resource utilization. Because taxes on personal property are largely evaded, the general property tax has become mostly a tax on physical assets—natural resources, improvements, and equipment. For our purposes, the value of physical assets is assumed to be identical with the sum of discounted future net revenues which these assets are expected to yield. Recurrent (annual) taxes on the present value of resources may, then, be regarded as a special type of taxes on net revenues. In each year in which the tax is paid, net revenues of all future intervals are taxed. The further, therefore, net revenues are distant from the present, the more often they are subject to the tax. This provides an incentive to redistribute net revenues in the direction of the present in order to reduce the number of times they are taxed. Since such redistribution can be accomplished only through redistributing use in the same direction, this means depletion. Property taxes, therefore, affect the utilization plan in much the same way as interest does. Property taxes, in contrast to income and yield taxes, are not automatically adjusted when income changes. Furthermore, properties in a low state of conservation, such as cutover forest land with poor natural vegetation, eroded farm land, and overgrazed ranges, tend to be overassessed relative to other properties. A vicious circle is set in motion: property taxes encourage depletion most on these properties which are already relatively more depleted. This effect is often increased by tax regression.

Sometimes the depleting effects of property taxes are desired by tax authorities in attempts to check speculation in resources withheld from use such as vacant city lots and deposits of minerals under monopolistic conditions. Property taxes, in contrast with income and yield taxes, produce tax receipts immediately and, provided it is economically possible to develop the resource after imposition of the tax, change the time distribution of use in the desired direction.

Income, profit, and yield taxes are taxes on current net revenues and are generally regarded as providing no incentive to change the pretax system of utilization. Aside from certain special problems discussed in the following paragraphs, the common view would be correct in time economics under the assumption that (1) they are expected to be constant over time, (2) no shifts of productive services into leisure or into less heavily taxed employments take place, and (3) income effects upon individual time preference are disregarded. Under these assumptions, proportional taxes on current net revenues are neutral with respect to the state of conservation.

Somewhat different effects upon conservation result from the fact that the legal definition of income and profits for tax purposes does not coincide with the meaning of net revenues in economic theory. Thus, in agriculture and forestry many expenses for permanent improvements can be charged, for income-tax purposes, to current costs of production, partly in conformity with income-tax laws and partly because segregation of investments from current costs, as required by law, is difficult. At a certain level of income-tax rates, it is economical to evade income taxes by making such investments; for taxpayers can sell their improved properties at a profit and are taxed on the latter only on the basis of their capital gains, a considerably lower tax in the higher-income brackets. Thus, a high income tax in conjunction with a lower capital gains tax may result in conservation.

Yield taxes are superior to most other taxes with respect to economy of administration and accuracy of assessment. Because costs are not taken into account, however, they are inferior to net revenue taxes from the standpoint of ability to pay. They are less flexible than income and profit taxes in periods of income changes caused by factors other than yield.

Estate and inheritance taxes are based on the present value of the estate. But if, as is generally the case, only one payment of these taxes is taken into account, they tax future net revenue only once. Hence, they would be neutral with respect to the state of conservation. However, such taxes may weaken a testator's motives for investment or induce him to disinvest. Under imperfect markets for loans and other productive services, disinvestment may take the form of depletion. The beneficiaries, in turn, are faced with payment of a tax that usually far exceeds current net revenues from the inherited assets. If they have no liquid reserve and if, again, markets for assets are imperfect, they may have to liquidate a portion of the inherited assets through depletion in order to pay the tax. This type of depletion is common in forestry and agriculture.

Direct Tools of Conservation Policy

The economic forces discussed so far may be called "indirect" tools of conservation policy because changes of interest, income, uncertainty, prices, property, tenancy, credit, and taxation are usually brought about with objectives other than changing the state of conservation. In contrast, "direct" tools of conservation policy are employed for conservation. Such direct tools vary in type from government-subsidized conservation education to zoning ordinances, the requirement of specific conservation practices (or the prohibition of depleting ones), and outright public ownership of natural resources.

The need for education in resource conservation has often been stressed and is uncontroversial. It is needed not only for resource users but also for the whole voting public, which is becoming more and more urban and, thus, less in contact with resource problems. It is needed not only in the technology of conservation but also in recognizing when conservation is economically justified. It can help both resource users and the general public understand why conservation policy is necessary.

Important as education is for conservation, however, it is no cure-all. If economic forces stand in the way, results from education alone will be small. Sometimes it is effective only if used in combination with other tools.

Zoning can be successfully applied in the conservation of several natural resources. Forest resources may be protected by zoning against agriculture, grazing, or year-round residence. Important infiltration areas for ground water may be zoned against urban development; as a joint product, flood-control problems may thereby be alleviated in what is sometimes the most economical way. Billboard zoning may be used to protect scenic resources.

Direct public regulation of practices is applied through county and city ordinances, by state and Federal statute, and by special districts. In resource utilization, such special districts are of particular importance. Regulation of practices has gone furthest with water both in social philosophy and in the development of control mechanisms. This is especially true for the semiarid states. Soil-conservation districts have been formed in many states, but regulations have been passed by only a few districts, and enforcement has not been tested in the courts. Some states have not granted these districts regulatory power, and in most states, they do not have taxing power, an important tool for cooperative action. Other resources for which regulation is common are forests, ranges, wildlife, oil, gas, and coal and other mineral resources.

Both zoning and regulation pose the problem of the limits of direct public interference with private enterprises. While they increase economic opportunities for some uses and individuals, they decrease them for others. Such an interference with private utilization plans through use of the police power must, according to the Constitution, be "reasonable" and not "arbitrary." Interpretation of these legal limits is greatly influenced by how much of an economic burden zoning or regulation imposes on private enterprise. The courts have been neither negative nor inflexible in defining a "reasonable" degree of interference. The principle of compensation can sometimes be utilized to expand the economic limits of these tools.

If restrictions are very severe, or if a large compensation is necessary for some time, public ownership may be more effective and cheaper. For example, to protect a watershed for a big city by zoning, most other uses might have to be prohibited. Such areas must be owned by the public or by public utility districts operating under close public control. Exercise of eminent domain contains fewer elements of confiscation than many zoning ordinances and regulations. Public ownership is an important tool of conservation policy.

After reviewing the most important indirect and direct tools of conservation policy, a few words may be said about its objectives.

5. Objectives of Conservation Policy

The economic objectives of conservation policy, that is, the optimum state of conservation in social economics, could be determined by criteria similar to those used for the private optimum, provided revenues and costs could be reinterpreted for social accounting in a meaningful way. Several problems are encountered in such a reinterpretation.

First, it may be regarded as axiomatic that all revenues and costs of resource use must be considered in social accounting regardless of who receives or pays them. Usually, only a portion of such social revenues and costs is incident on the resource user who is responsible for them. This problem was discussed under imbalance of property rights. If there are discrepancies between the revenues and costs considered by individual resource users and social revenues and costs, there will be differences between the private and social optimum in the state of conservation. One objective of conservation policy is to reduce such differences by inducing private conservation decisions to approach the social optimum more closely.

Second, difficulties are created for reinterpreting revenues and costs in social economics by the existence of extramarket values which was also discussed above. For policy decisions, in contrast to private decisions, it is necessary to obtain some objective yardstick for comparing market with extramarket goods.

Third, over time public policy may change the meaning of revenues and cost by changing income distribution, preferences, technology, and social institutions. The economic calculus has validity only under restrictive assumptions with respect to such changes. It can be employed in appraising conservation policies of more limited scope, for example, in appraising a particular project in public resource development. But for policies of broader scope, the restrictive assumptions needed for benefit-cost analysis and for other systematic attempts at a precise quantitative economic appraisal of policy become too burdensome.[6]

Finally, there is the difficulty posed by the existence of uncertainty. The importance of uncertainty for private conservation decisions was emphasized throughout this chapter. But it is even more important in social economics for that important class of flow resources which contain soil, water, plants, animals, and related resources. The flow of these resources is characterized by a "critical zone"; that is, the flow may be decreased by human action until the decrease becomes economically irreversible.

Sometimes such irreversibility is not only economic but also technologic. The decrease in the flow of animal and plant life, for instance, becomes technologically irreversible for a certain species if the flow reaches zero, that is, if the breeding stock is destroyed; or within a species, destruction of a gene system represented by an isolated population race is a technologically irreversible loss.

Even if the flow has not reached zero, economic reversibility may be lost if highly complex ecological relations are affected, for example, plant associations and successions on some grasslands and forests. If overdraft of ground water has led to compaction of clay aquifers, restoration of storage capacity becomes economically impossible. Such storage capacity is no less a resource than are good dam sites for surface storage. A decrease in soil productivity can sometimes be reversed relatively cheaply if it results from depletion of plant nutrients, but if deep gullies have been formed which interfere with farm operations, or if all soil has been destroyed through erosion to bedrock or hydraulic mining, the economic reversibility of soil productivity, at least in certain uses, for example, cultivated crops, may have disappeared. Some scenic resources, for example, wilderness areas, may be spoiled irreversibly.

Economic irreversibility is uncertain. It depends on future technology, wants, and social institutions. Furthermore, it is uncertain whether economic irreversibility, if it actually occurs, will lead to what was called above an "immoderate" loss, that is, in social economics, a loss that threatens the survival of a society. This outcome may well have a rather small probability. But according to some serious students of social development, this outcome has actually occurred in the past. Thus, avoiding the possibility of such a loss may well be regarded as an objective of conservation policy.

A decision to avoid the social risk of irreversibility is not dependent on whether or not the losses which threaten are immoderate. As we know, avoiding the possibility of immoderate losses is merely a special case of making choices between the possibility of larger but less probable losses and that of smaller but more probable ones. If the more probable losses are small in relation to the less probable ones which may be avoided by accepting the former, the economic choice between the two alternatives would not be difficult. What, then, are these smaller but more probable losses?

They are connected with maintaining a "safe minimum standard of conservation." In the resource class under consideration, a safe minimum standard of conservation is achieved by avoiding the critical zone, that is, those physical conditions, brought about by human action, which would make it uneconomical to halt and reverse depletion. A safe minimum standard of conservation involves losses if its maintenance necessitates costs (either use foregone or positive efforts) and if the contingency guarded against should not actually occur, that is, if depletion should eventually prove not to be economically irreversible. These losses are similar to the costs of flexibility in private economics. The similarity is more than formal: a safe minimum standard of conservation is essentially an increase of flexibility in the continuing development of society.

The costs of maintaining a safe minimum standard are absolutely small if proper action is taken in time and if the proper tools of conservation policy are employed.

In some practical situations, maintenance of a safe minimum standard necessitates that use is foregone. Use in the neighborhood of the critical zone is small and, in the alternative case, that is, if a safe minimum standard were not maintained, would continue only over a small number of intervals. It is well to remember that the safe minimum standard of conservation is far more modest than a theoretical social optimum. Frequently, such a standard corresponds to a state of conservation which is considerably lower than the private optimum. Under these conditions, the great majority of private enterprises will be operating above the safe minimum standard.

In many practical situations, maintenance of a safe minimum standard does not involve any use foregone; rather, it involves a change in the ways (not the quantities) of utilization. These changes may or may not necessitate costs in the sense of positive efforts (inputs) by individuals or by the public or by both. Sometimes a change of social institutions without any inputs is sufficient. Sometimes the costs are only public, for example, if education or a temporary subsidy is the most economical tool of conservation policy. If private costs are increased, for example, as a consequence of regulation by governments or public districts, only a few enterprises may be affected because, as already emphasized, the minimum standard of conservation is a rather modest objective in terms of the private optimum.

Costs of maintaining the safe minimum standard are not only small in absolute amount but very small relative to the loss which is being guarded against, a decrease of flexibility in the continuing development of a society. Costs of maintaining the safe minimum standard of conservation are also very small as compared with generally accepted expenditures of a social group for safeguarding its continuity in other fields. Such fields are, for example, public health and safety and national defense. In these fields, likewise, a safe minimum standard is frequently adopted as an objective of public policy. The reason is the same as in the field of conservation: it is impractical to determine a precise social optimum in the state of public health and safety or national defense because of uncertainty and because of the difficulties of valuating social revenues and costs. On the other hand, it is practical to set up standards which would avoid serious losses--threats to social continuity--in cases of epidemics, internal disorder, and foreign military involvements.

Thus, in the objectives of conservation policy, the emphasis is on minimum standards in resource use rather than on the optimum use, on establishing base levels rather than on locating peaks, and on reducing institutional obstacles to resource development rather than on the "best" development. This approach does not pretend to establish criteria for maximizing social satisfaction. But it offers effective direction signals to conservation policy for pursuing the public interest turn by turn.

[1]S. V. Ciriacy-Wantrup, *Symposium on Natural Resources* (Warren L. Flock and Martin R. Huberty, eds.). New York: McGraw-Hill Book Company, Inc, 1959, pp. 500-526.

[2]S. V. Ciriacy-Wantrup, *Resource Conservation, Economics and Policies*, University of California Press, Berkeley, Calif., 1952.

The author acknowledges permission by the University of California Press to make use of this publication in several places in this chapter. However, many significant issues in the economics of conservation could not be treated here. The reader is referred to the book for a more complete statement.

[3]*Ibid*, chap. 14.

[4]S. V. Ciriacy-Wantrup, "Taxation and the Conservation of Resources," *Quart. J. Economics*, vol. 58, no. 2, pp. 157-195, February, 1944. (University of California, College of Agriculture, Giannini Foundation of Agricultural Economics, Paper 110.)

[5]S. V. Ciriacy-Wantrup, "Concepts Used as Economic Criteria for a System of Water Rights," *Land Economics*, vol. 32, no. 4, pp. 295-312, November, 1956. (University of California, College of Agriculture, Giannini Foundation of Agricultural Economics, Paper 154).

[6]S. V. Ciriacy-Wantrup, "Benefit-Cost Analysis and Public Resource Development," *J. Farm Economics*, vol. 37, no. 4, pp. 676-689, November 1955. (University of California, College of Agriculture, Giannini Foundation of Agricultural Economics, Paper 146.) (Chapter 8 in this book).

Chapter 12

CONSERVATION OF THE CALIFORNIA TULE ELK: A SOCIOECONOMIC STUDY OF A SURVIVAL PROBLEM*[1]

Abstract

From the large original herds of the California Tule Elk, approximately 425 animals have survived. Conflict among different economic interests has resulted in a policy of holding the Tule Elk located in Owens Valley (Inyo County, California) to a population level of 250-300 head. An analysis of the socioeconomic habitat in Owens Valley indicates that the Elk population there could be increased and kept at a higher level indefinitely. Such expansion would provide a significant increase in human social benefits. The order of magnitude of this increase in social benefits is estimated in relation to social costs. Policy changes are recommended to make it possible to maintain the Owens Valley herd at the higher level and to safeguard the survival of the Tule Elk through the establishment of two additional free-roaming herds.

The Problem

The California Tule Elk (*Cervus elaphus nannodes*) currently only number some 425 animals.[2] Confined Tule Elk consist of a population of 32 animals maintained at Tupman Elk Reserve (Kern County, California), plus a few individuals in parks and zoos within the State and elsewhere. Free-roaming Tule Elk herds are found in two widely-separated locations. About 80 head are in the Cache Creek herd of Lake and Colusa Counties, California. The remainder of approximately 300 animals are found in the Owens Valley herd. Both herds are transplants from the Central Valley of California, but only the Colusa herd is on a part of the original range.

The allocation of natural resources, such as grazing land and wildlife, to

*Reproduced, with permission, from *Biological Conservation*, Vol. 3, No. 1, pp. 23-32, 1970

different human uses in different time-periods and different locations, involves
conflicts among different economic interests. These conflicts generally
have alternative solutions with different economic and social implications.
Socioeconomic study attempts to identify these conflicts and to recommend
courses of action for public policy.

From the early Spanish days onwards, and particularly since the gold-rush
and settlement by ranchers, Tule Elk were hunted ruthlessly because (1) of
their economic value as a source of meat and hides, (2) ranchers found it
profitable to replace Elk by domestic livestock, and (3) farmers wanted to
dispose of Elk as a source of damage to crops and fences. There was no
public policy with regard to Elk; and by 1873, when the Elk received legal
protection, only a few head remained. By 1895, as a result of protective
efforts by Henry Miller—an emigrant from central Europe who founded an
empire of cattle ranches in California—their number had increased to
where 28 head were counted. At present the Elk are managed by the
California Department of Fish and Game under policies set by the Fish and
Game Commission.

Free-roaming herds still compete with other wildlife and domestic livestock
for range resources and do damage to cultivated crops. The agricultural
interests owning or leasing land used by the Elk would, in general, like to see
the Elk moved elsewhere on the grounds that they displace livestock and
damage crops and fences. Opposed are many non-agricultural groups—
conservationists, hunters, and the tourist industry—who direct their efforts
towards removal of domestic livestock in favor of the Elk and towards an
expansion of the Elks' range.

Scientific effort to analyze this problem situation began in 1963 when
Resources for the Future, Inc., of Washington, D.C., offered a grant to the
University of California for undertaking a two-part study under the heading,
'Conservation of the Tule Elk in California.' One part, the ecological phase
of this project, has been completed and is described in a published Ph.D.
dissertation by Dale R. McCullough (1969), who did his research under the
supervision of A. Starker Leopold. The second part, the socioeconomic
phase, supervised by S. V. Ciriacy-Wantrup, involved two stages, the first of
which has been completed as described in a Ph.D. dissertation by William E.
Phillips (1967). This constitutes an examination of the current and alternative
use-patterns of land, water, and associated natural resources, of the Owens
Valley region where some 80 per cent of the free-roaming Tule Elk population
is situated. This broad-based study served as a prerequisite to the second
stage, which deals specifically with examination of the distribution of property
rights as they pertain to Elk on both private and public lands in California,
and the relation of this to current and alternative Elk management policies
in a socioeconomic framework. This stage, which also gives particular
attention to the socioeconomic problems of the Cache Creek herd—which
is almost entirely on private land—is near completion and will be published
later. The current report draws on all three studies.

The Socioeconomic Habitat

Owens Valley offers the key habitat regarding current and alternative management plans for the Tule Elk. It is important because it supports such a large proportion of the existing Elk population. Relocation of this population would be difficult because of the opposition of both private and public landowners. Historically, only two of numerous transplants have been successful. As mentioned above, these two led to the establishment of the Owens Valley and Cache Creek herds.

Within the Owens Valley region, the number of feasible alternative Elk management schemes are constrained by ecological factors and by resource-use patterns which are intricately tied to property rights over land and water, together with other institutional factors.

Owens Valley is a structural trough located approximately 200 miles (320 km) north of the City of Los Angeles on the east side of the Sierra Nevada. It is about 80 miles (128 km) long (in the north-south direction) and 6 miles (9.6 km) wide, with valley-floor elevations ranging from 4,200 feet (1,280 m) in the north to 3,550 feet (1,082 m) in the south. The Sierra Nevada scarp constitutes a 10,000-foot (3,048 m) wall along the west side of the Valley, while the more gradually ascending Inyo-White Mountains range borders the east side. To the west, there are some nine peaks with elevations exceeding 14,000 feet (4,267 m), the highest being Mt. Whitney (14,495 feet = 4,418 m), located 13 miles (21 km) west of the town of Lone Pine. The Inyo-White Mountains peaks are more typically 9,000-11,000 feet (2,743-3,353 m) in elevation although White Mountain Peak, located 20 miles (32 km) NNW of the town of Bishop, has an elevation of 14,246 (4,373 m).

Owens River, which flows through the Valley, is fed by snow-melt from the Owens River watershed via some 40 tributaries. The River begins about 34 miles (54 km) north-west of the town of Bishop and enters Owens Valley as regulated reservoir discharge 7 miles (11.2 km) north-west of the town. At a point 11 miles (17.6 km) north of the town of Independence, the flow is diverted from its natural course into the Los Angeles Aqueduct. Prior to diversion in 1913, the River emptied into Owens Lake; this is now dry. The climate of the Owens Valley floor is semi-arid to arid. Temperatures range from a winter low of about 5 degrees F. (-15 degrees C.) to over 100 degrees F. (38 degrees C.) in the summertime. Average annual rainfall in the Valley floor is approximately 5 inches (127 mm), well over half, and sometimes as much as 75 per cent, of which occurs during November to April. On either side of the Valley, precipitation increases with elevation, high elevations in the Sierra Nevada receiving around 40 inches (1,016 mm)—mostly in the form of snow. Plant communities on the Valley floor and on the lower mountain slopes are characteristic Great Basin and semi-desert shrub vegetation types.

The 10,500 or so residents of Owens Valley are mainly found in the four communities spaced throughout the length of the Valley.[3] However, there is little privately-owned land. The City of Los Angeles owns about 95 per cent of the some 300,000 acres (121,500 ha) of land in the Valley floor. These holdings were purchased prior to 1913 in order to acquire rights to Owens River water for export to Los Angeles. In recent years, the Department of Water and Power (DWP) of the City of Los Angeles has been importing approximately 80,000 acre-feet (99 million cu m) per year from Mono Basin to the north into Owens Basin, and exporting about 320,000 acre-feet (396 million cu m) per year from the southern end of Owens Valley for use in the City of Los Angeles. The DWP grants leases on about 200,000 acres (81,000 ha) for pasture and crop production. Of this, some 30,000 acres (12,150 ha) are irrigated.

Bordering the city's lands and reaching into the lower slopes of the mountains on either side of Owens Valley is a ribbon of land (approximately 150,000 = 60,750 ha) of the U. S. Bureau of Land Management (BLM). This federal land was withdrawn from homesteading during 1931-33 to protect the Owens River watershed. For the most part, it is leased for livestock grazing, although in recent years BLM, along with DWP, has developed several camping grounds and turned them over to the County for management.

Beyond BLM land, and reaching well into the mountain ranges on either side of the Valley, are Inyo National Forest lands. This federal land has been reserved for watershed protection since the turn of the century. About half of the Inyo National Forest's 874,000 acres (353,970 ha) is situated in the Owens Valley area, this land being used for dry grazing of domestic livestock and for outdoor recreation. This National Forest is among the most heavily visited in the United States, having had more than 4.5 million visitor-days of use during 1966.

In summary, Owens Valley is a region with an outdoor recreation-based economy. Two other major natural resource-based uses are water export and domestic livestock production. Virtually all the land is publicly owned.

Present Range-Capacity for Tule Elk

Currently, five separate herds of Tule Elk are distinguished in Owens Valley: The Bishop, Tinemaha, Goodale, Independence, and Lone Pine herds. The four bottom-land herds (that is, all except the Goodale herd) have existed as such for some time and, because of poor food resources surrounding these ranges, long-term changes in herd ranges are unlikely. The Goodale herd developed about 1962 when a portion of the Independence herd broke away and established itself on the Goodale range. As the Goodale herd expanded in size, it spread southwards. If this migration continues, it is probable that colonization of an area to the south could establish a sixth herd which McCullough already terms the Whitney herd (McCullough, 1969). Beyond this, herd range-expansion, either natural or induced by Man, appears unlikely because of the lack of suitable habitats.

Some competition occurs between Elk and cattle in foothill areas in dry years, but the competition between Elk and domestic livestock in the Owens

Valley floor is minor even during drought. Although the Elk-carrying capacity is not precisely known, the bottom-land Elk ranges cannot support significant increases in Elk numbers (whether with or without cattle). McCullough (1969) suggests that the bottom-lands should have the potential to support a total of at least 250 head which would be broken down as follows: Bishop herd, 65 head; Tinemaha herd, 40 head; Independence herd, 80 head; and Lone Pine herd, 65 head.

The physical capacity of the Goodale range is exceeded at present. The Elk winter-range overlaps with a Deer[4] winter-range to the point where Bitterbrush (*Purshia tridentata*), a vital Deer winter-food source, is being seriously depleted. No domestic livestock are permitted to graze in this area. McCullough suggests that the Goodale range will support between 50 and about 235 Elk, depending on the number of Deer in the area. Both Elk and Deer harvest would be essential to curb range depletion.

Should the establishment of the Whitney elk herd take place, and assuming no substantial increase in the few Deer in the area plus continued livestock allotments at current levels, some 80-100 Elk could be supported on this range. With the establishment of the Whitney herd, it would seem physically feasible to maintain total Elk populations in the Owens Valley region of at least 500, and possibly as many as 600, animals—if Deer numbers were kept down on the Goodale range as suggested by the benefit-cost analysis presented later. This total assumes an ideal distribution by herds. Expansion of some herds—for example, the Tinemaha herd—would cause serious conflicts. Management and cropping programmes should also be undertaken on a herd basis, as emphasized below.

Present policy of the California Fish and Game Commission calls for holding Elk numbers between 250 and 300 head (actual count). This is done through periodic, controlled public hunts using a warden-guide approach.

Future Resource-use Patterns and Tule Elk Management Possibilities

Two related but separate changes will largely determine the future shape of resource-use patterns in Owens Valley (Phillips, 1967). The first of these is water export development. The DWP has exported about 320,000 acre-feet (396 million cu m) of water annually from Owens Valley for use in the City of Los Angeles in recent years. DWP has just completed a $105 million development programme whereby an additional 152,000 acre-feet (188 million cu m) of water per year will be exported. The value of this water (considering conveyance costs) for export to Los Angeles is approximately 10 times the value of that used locally in Owens Valley. Water for Los Angeles prior to export (that is, f. o. b. Owens Valley) is valued at $15 per acre-foot (1 acre-foot equals 1,234 cu m) over cost; water for local use in Owens Valley is valued at $1.50 per acre-foot. By 1975, water in Los Angeles will be well over 20 times as valuable as in Owens Valley, assuming that no substantial change in local use takes place.

Clearly, the City of Los Angeles will hold on to its rights to Owens River water. In order to protect these rights, it will want to retain ownership of virtually all its current land-holdings in Owens Valley. With the new water export facility, land leased by DWP as irrigated acreage (30,000 acres = 12,150 ha in recent years) is expected to be cut to half. The remainder will probably be added to existing leased dry-grazing land. Hence the open space, which was preserved to the present day because of water development for export, is expected to remain so into the foreseeable future.

Most of the relatively little private agricultural land which exists in Owens Valley is concentrated in contiguous areas surrounding urban communities. Land values for urban and suburban uses are at least 10-20 times the value of existing private agricultural land. Recent subdivision developments, particularly around Bishop, where most of the commercial economic activity of the Valley area is centered, attest to this value relationship. There is no apparent reason why this trend should not continue so long as private agricultural land adjacent to these communities in the Valley is available, and so it seems reasonable to assume that all this land will eventually become urbanized. The Owens Valley human population is expected to be double the 1960 level by the early 1980's.

So long as water rights are sufficient to meet the needs of the increased urban population at current consumption rates, the prices (that is, marginal values) for water will remain about the same as at present. Beyond that limit, local urban values of water will tend to increase. As private land available for urban development becomes scarce, the opportunity cost (that is, the alternative value it would have in urban use) of keeping City of Los Angeles lands adjacent to Owens Valley communities from urban development will tend to increase and to approach values comparable to current urban-land values.

The second change which will determine the shape of resource-use patterns in Owens Valley is the continuing development of outdoor recreation facilities as a result of ever-increasing visitor-day use of the area. Visitation doubled from 1955 to 1965 and is expected to be 5 times the 1965 level in 1976 and 10 times that level in the year 2000. There appear to be no institutional constraints restricting such growth, as virtually no competition for water exists—water used for outdoor recreation purposes is essentially non-consumptive. Should current overcrowding of facilities continue, unauthorized camping and resulting water pollution and litter will be an increasingly significant problem. Less significant but still important is the fact that competition for land between recreation and agriculture is minimal, and should remain so as the only acreages that are used exclusively for outdoor recreation are occupancy sites. Probably a little more than 1 per cent of current grazing land will eventually be taken over by occupancy sites.

In the last very few years, recreation users have injected approximately $20 million per year of first-round expenditures into the Owens Valley economy (cf Phillips, 1967). Social gross benefits from outdoor recreation have been about double its social costs. That the Owens Valley economy will become almost exclusively recreation-based seems clear. What is not entirely clear, however, is the effect this will have on the Tule Elk.

While it appears that little or no range-land that is currently used by Elk will be given to exclusive outdoor recreation use through establishment of occupancy sites, nevertheless a great increase in the number of visitor-days may disrupt the present pattern of range use by Elk. The question is not so much how new recreation facilities are developed but, rather, where they are developed. If recreational facilities were located in those areas where they would not interfere with Elk management, such restriction on location of occupancy sites would not materially affect the area-wide capacity of Owens Valley to accomodate currently foreseeable increased recreational visitation.

The implication of these changes may be summarized as follows: the economic incentive of the City of Los Angeles, stemming from water export, to maintain its extensive land-holdings in Owens Valley (largely used for livestock grazing by DWP lessees), plus the sizeable area of federal lands withdrawn from entry (committed mainly to watershed protection, outdoor recreation provision, wildlife management, and livestock grazing allotments), means that the present and potential Tule Elk herd ranges discussed earlier will remain intact into the foreseeable future. Some degree of disruption of Elk movements is possible if outdoor recreation developments, inducing persistent intense human activity, are permitted to take place in current and possible future Elk concentration areas. However, assuming that problems of this nature are avoided, there appears to be no reason why the future socioeconomic habitat could not support the increase in Tule Elk numbers suggested earlier. Let us, therefore, look at the criteria for this increase from the standpoint of public policy.

The "Safe Minimum Standard" of Conservation as an Objective of Public Policy

The general objectives of public policies are usually expressed in terms of maximizing some value or quantity, such as national income, social benefit, or public interest. The apparent simplicity of such formulation, however, hides significant complexities. In order to maximize a quantity—such as the contribution to social welfare—it must be expressed in measurable and comparable units. For some of the social benefits associated with Tule Elk, values are established in monetary terms in the market-place. This is the case for example with meat, hide, and other benefits resulting from hunting. But the system of market prices has several basic defects which make prices unreliable as indicators of social welfare. These defects are not simple; they are difficult to remedy and cannot be discussed in detail here (Ciriacy-Wantrup, 1960b, 1961).

Aside from these defects, market prices are frequently difficult to obtain. For example, how can one measure the contribution to social welfare of the Tule Elk as an object of scientific interest, of enjoyment to visitors through viewing and photography, and as a valuable gene-pool developed over long periods of time under semi-arid conditions?

In addition, there is the issue of the extent of contributions to social welfare over time. The public policy is not concerned so much with the contribution of natural resources to social welfare in the present or even the next decade as in the long-run future. This brings immediately to mind the problem of irreversibility of resource use in relation to projections of future social needs. The latter are so uncertain that only the directions of change and possibly the rates of change in ordinal terms can be projected (Ciriacy-Wantrup, 1960a). In view of this difficulty, added to the ones mentioned earlier, one may suggest that the objectives of conservation policy should be reformulated in a way that takes these difficulties explicitly into account.

There is no need to go into the technical aspects of such a reformulation, which lie in the field of uncertainty economics and game theory (Ciriacy-Wantrup, 1952-68). Suffice it to say that the objectives of conservation policy—and of many other public policies—can often be compared with the objectives of an insurance policy against serious losses that resist quantitative measurement. Here the objective is not to maximize a definite quantitative net gain but to choose premium payments and benefits in such a way that maximum possible losses are minimized. As a special case of this strategy, a "safe minimum standard" of conservation, specified in such a way that maximum possible future losses are minimized, is frequently a valid and relevant objective of policy.

With this reformulation of the objectives of public policy, we are mainly interested in the order of magnitude of maximum possible losses as compared with that of the insurance premium that must be paid to guard against them. It will be shown in the following section that the maximum possible losses which would result from not adhering to a safe minimum standard of conservation in managing Tule Elk are large in relation to the costs which must be expended in order to guarantee such a safe minimum standard.

Benefit-cost Analysis in Relation to the Safe Minimum Standard of Conservation

Social Benefits

The maximum possible loss in Tule Elk management is the extinction of the species. As stated in the preceding section, most of these losses or, in other words, social benefits foregone—are not evaluated in the market-place and are difficult to measure quantitatively. But there can be little question that they are important.

For many people, both in California and elsewhere, the loss of the opportunity of merely viewing and photographing Tule Elk would be large. That this is true, even if such an opportunity is enjoyed only vicariously, is evidenced by the existence of an active nation-wide "Committee for the Preservation of the Tule Elk." Additionally, disappearance of this interesting animal would involve a loss for several natural sciences—although the scientific community has not shown much active interest in the preservation of the Tule Elk.

As economists, the present authors believe that the greatest loss of social benefits from extinction of the Tule Elk would be the irreversible disappearance of a valuable gene-pool. The Tule Elk is the only one of the many forms of Elk currently in existence which is well adapted to a semi-arid environment, with great variations in climate and topography, such as ranges from the coast of California in the west to the foothills of the Sierra Nevada in the east, and from the headwaters of the Sacramento in northern California to the Tehachapi Mountains in the south. The variations in climate in this large area are especially great with respect to rainfall between different years and between "cycles" of years. That the Tule Elk has prospered in Owens Valley far from its original range is in itself an indication of the adaptability of this sub species. Another indication is that the Owens Valley herd has apparently been able to adjust itself to year-to-year and cyclical fluctuations in rainfall and forage conditions; this it has done especially well, and indeed better, than the local Deer which are in their original range. This last observation holds also for the Cache Creek herd where Elk and Deer are both in their original range.

In summary, Tule Elk are an especially effective means of converting, into valuable animal protein, the forage of semi-arid regions having large year-to-year and cyclical variations of rainfall and great variations in topography. There may well be a strong demand in the future for such an animal—as a converter of forage in large areas of the world which have similar climatic and topographic variations.

In addition to the "extra-market" social benefits just considered, there are others to which market evaluation can at least partially be adapted. These are the social benefits resulting from the availability of Tule Elk as a game animal for public hunting.

The first legal public hunt was held in Owens Valley in 1944. There have been six subsequent ones, including the one held in the Fall of 1969. Excluding the last one, for which statistics are not yet available, over 40,000 applications were submitted for permits costing $25 each (increased to $50 in 1969). In all, 371 permits were issued, and clearly their price was not used as an economic rationing device. Permits were issued on the basis of a "lottery."

In the market-place, the price of permits would be determined not by lottery but by bidding, and the limited number of permits would be allocated to the highest bidders. In this case, the price of the permit would be approximately equal to the costs of comparable hunting alternatives available to California hunters elsewhere. These economic alternatives are the following.

During 1966 there were an estimated 10,000 hunters from California who hunted Elk elsewhere in the United States. Total expenditures per hunter attributed directly to Elk hunting were (in 1968 dollars) Colorado, $522; Idaho, $568; Montana, $605; and Wyoming, $594. Comparable expenditures to hunt Owens Valley Elk would be of the order of $60-85, depending on the amount of travel involved. Thus, on the basis of this difference, hunting in

Owens Valley would involve a benefit of approximately $500 per hunter if success ratios and other conditions of out-of-state hunts were similar to those of the Tule Elk hunt. These conditions are, however, far from similar.

Elk hunting areas in North America outside of California typically show only a 30-40 per cent success ratio per annual permit. In the Owens Valley, on the other hand, the success ratio of those hunters receiving permits is very close to 100 per cent because of the use of the warden-guide system. Second, there is a considerable difference in the relative ease of attaining success. Elk hunting outside of California is on the average a five- to nine-day effort for California hunters. In the Owens Valley, a one-day hunting effort is sufficient. Third, a trophy of Tule Elk has a rarity value compared with that of the more abundant Roosevelt and Rocky Mountain Elk in other states.

We have not attempted to make monetary adjustments for differences in success ratios, ease of success, and trophy value, between hunting Tule Elk and hunting other Elk in Colorado, Idaho, Montana, and Wyoming. To do so would have required a costly in-depth study of the preferences of different classes of hunters, and in any case such a study would have been of limited relevancy because the class of hunters who prefer the type of Tule Elk hunt offered in Owens Valley is sufficiently large for an auction system—this in spite of the fact that many hunters would not be interested in having their Elk "served on a silver platter".[5] We believe, therefore, that, if market forces would be allowed to operate, Tule Elk permits could be sold for a minimum of $500 per head and probably for considerably more. In addition to the charge per animal regardless of trophy, it is recommended that an additional charge be made for the quality of trophy—based on a point system, as is done in many big-game areas in Europe, Africa, and elsewhere.

Two broad policy questions arise in connection with letting market forces determine the price of permits. First, should an excess (in terms of range capacity) number of Elk be removed through public hunting and, second, is it socially desirable to use price as a rationing device for limiting the number of hunters permitted to participate in this removal?

As suggested above, the Owens Valley herd should be allowed to increase and extend southwards to a higher figure than is permitted at present. Removal should be constrained by this objective. Still, if the higher figure suggested is reached, some removal will become necessary in order to avoid range deterioration. In this removal, transplanting should have priority over hunting. In terms of our objective of minimizing possible losses or even extinction in view of unforseeable contingencies caused by Man or Nature, it would be desirable that the minimum standard of conservation be not based mainly on the existence of one (Owens Valley) herd. Even assuming that the Cache Creek herd will be preserved, it would be prudent that at least two additional herds be established. One possibility is a potential San Luis Island herd which has frequently been suggested (most recently by McCullough, 1969). We are in accord with this suggestion but have some reservations because of the relatively small size of the proposed area which is already surrounded by highly intensive agriculture. The total area of San Luis Island is about 14,000 acres (5,670 ha). Of this, the U. S. Fish and Wildlife Service controls only about one-half. This is the proposed area; but it would have to be surrounded by an Elk-proof fence, as there are no natural barriers separating it from the surrounding agricultural areas. We suggest, therefore, that, in addition, serious consideration be given to reintroducing Tule Elk into the Point Reyes National Seashore after the purchase of this area has been completed. The Point Reyes peninsula is relatively isolated, being surrounded largely by the ocean and Tomales and Bolinas Bays, and it is a highly favourable part of the original Tule Elk range. It is no accident that, in spite of the closeness to the Bay area, the Point Reyes peninsula was one of the last entirely natural strongholds of the Tule Elk in California. This National Seashore will eventually comprise some 55,000 acres (22,275 ha), with additional public lands in close proximity. For viewing and photography, this location is more favourable than San Luis Island because of its proximity to large population centres and the fact that its immediate neighborhood—western Marin County— has an economy that is, and will remain, oriented largely towards recreation.

With respect to the second question, there appears no sound reason why the California taxpayer should underwrite the windfall benefits which a few lucky hunters, who are successful in the lottery, now derive from Tule Elk hunts. On the other hand, if the suggested drastic increase in permit fees should yield a net income for the State, such income could be paid into a Tule Elk conservation fund and used for establishing and maintaining new herds as suggested above.

Social costs

Costs associated with Elk protection and management are borne largely by the State of California. These costs include expenditures for public hunts, for aerial census surveys, and for game wardens. Excluding the costs of the public hunts, an estimated total expenditure of $7,800 per year (1968 dollars) appears conservative in the sense that it is on the high side. In addition, three land management agencies (Inyo National Forest, BLM, and DWP) incur some costs for habitat management. These, however, are small; and overall current direct costs of Elk management plus habitat management are certainly not more than $10,000 per year. Should the expansion of the herd suggested above take place, direct costs will increase but not in proportion to an increase in Elk population. It is doubtful that costs, excluding costs of public hunts, under full expansion conditions would exceed $15,000 annually.

With respect to the costs of public units, fairly accurate figures are available for 1964 when permits were issued to 50 hunters to take 50 Elk under a warden-guide system. The total costs for permits and for salary and expenses of the guiding personnel were $3,500. The costs of issuing and processing applications for permits, conducting a lottery, and issuing the permits, account for over half of the total costs. As indicated earlier, the permits brought in $1,250.

The question may be raised as to whether the costs of public hunts could be reduced by eliminating the warden-guide system. Past experience of where such elimination was tried shows an average "crippling loss" (of seriously wounded animals) of 12 per cent. This compares with only 5 per cent under the warden-guide system. Evaluation of this alternative involves a comparison of added crippling losses against reduced costs from not using the warden-guide system. Aside from the ethical issues involved, such a difference in crippling loss would amount to a minimum of $1,750 per 50 Elk harvested, assuming a value of the animals to the State of $500 per head and not considering the value of meat and trophy. The cost reduction from eliminating the warden-guide system would amount to less than that minimum. This alternative must, therefore, be rejected. Another alternative would be to have the Department of Fish and Game personnel harvest the Elk. This would eliminate the costs of public hunts but would also eliminate the benefits to the hunting public. Assuming that our recommendation of increases in permit fees is followed, this alternative does not appear economical.

Additional to the costs just discussed are opportunity costs associated with land used by Elk, and costs from damage to crops and fences. The former arise where Elk compete with domestic livestock and deer for forage. The virtual absence of competition between Elk and domestic livestock on bottom-lands, pointed out earlier, means that no opportunity costs exist there. Establishment of the Goodale herd involved displacement of domestic livestock to the extent of approximately 150 animal-unit months, amounting to a cost of $270 in all per year in 1967 dollars (Phillips, 1967). Elsewhere, similar displacements could result during very low-rainfall periods, but the costs involved would not exceed $90 per year in 1967 dollars. Additional opportunity costs of increasing the Elk herd on the Goodale range under sustained range conditions are the loss of the Deer replaced by Elk. Under the conditions of Owens Valley, under proper range management, the average rate of substitution between Elk and Deer is on the average 1 to 0.46. In other words, for the production of two Elk slightly less than one Deer would need to be eliminated. The explanation is, as stated above, that the Elk is a relatively more efficient converter of forage than Deer, and that there is no year-round competition between Elk and Deer for the bulk of the forage. In terms of biomass produced per acre, Elk are superior to Deer. On the other hand, overgrazing of Bitterbrush by Deer during a relatively short winter period is significant for the Elk. Opportunity costs caused by the replacement of livestock and Deer on the entire Goodale range would certainly not be more than $500 per year.

Attempts to obtain a measure of the extent of damage to Alfalfa and fences caused by Elk have been largely unsuccessful in spite of some complaints by ranchers. The damage is obviously minor—if it is present at all—even during dry periods (Phillips, 1967; McMullough, 1969).

In summary, the annual costs in 1968 dollars associated with Tule Elk under present conditions and under full expansion are as shown in Table 1.

Conclusions

We can now draw some conclusions from a comparison of social benefits and social costs of Tule Elk conservation in terms of the overall objectives of conservation policy stated earlier. It is clear that the social costs of Tule Elk conservation—that is, the insurance premium that must be paid in order to protect the Elk from extinction—is small in relation to the loss of social benefits which would occur. Furthermore, if our recommendations regarding expansion of the herd and regarding changes for hunting are followed, Tule Elk management can be made to yield a net income to the State of California. This net income should be paid into a Tule Elk conservation fund, to be used for improving Elk habitat in Owens Valley and to establish at least two additional free-foaming herds of Tule Elk.

Because of lack of natural predation, Elk harvesting by Man is essential in maintaining a viable Elk population in Owens Valley. Periodic public hunts should continue along the same lines as in the past. It is recommended, however, that the harvest of Elk by hunting be constrained first by allowing for full occupation of the potential habitat in Owens Valley and, second, by making transplants available for establishing two new herds.

A few policy changes would have to be made in order to make these recommendations operational. The most central change would be an amendment to the California Fish and Game Commission policy whereby the present requirement of holding the Elk at 250-300 animals would be increased to involve at least 500 animals. Cropping should always be determined on an individual herd basis, with special emphasis on developing and managing the Whitney herd.

Particular attention must be given to the Goodale range if further deterioration is to be checked. This would mean immediate harvest of at least 45 Deer, though the actual number would depend on the number of Elk available to replace the Deer. To assure an ecological balance, the Department of Fish and Game and the public land management agencies must have the cooperation of the officials of Inyo County. Should the present constraints on the management of the Deer herd be relaxed, the problem of determining the optimum combination of Deer and Elk on the Goodale range would arise. The uniqueness of the Elk on the one hand, and the ubiquitousness of the Deer on the other, argue that any action taken should be in favour of the Elk.

An implication of the results of our research concerns a conflict between agricultural and wildlife interests. Their efforts to change the status of the Tule Elk in Owens Valley have largely cancelled each other in the past. In our view, the various positions taken in support of removal of domestic livestock in favour of Elk, and those taken in support of the reverse, have little relevancy to the ecological and economic aspects of the situation.

TABLE 1

Cost	Present conditions	Full expansion
Management and protection	$10,000	$15,000
Harvest		
40 Elk	3,000	
75 Elk*		5,500
Opportunity cost	500	500
Total	$13,500	$21,000
Average cost per Elk	$ 50	$ 42
Average cost per Elk harvested	$ 340	$ 280

* Assumes warden-guide system continues to be used with hunters selected on the basis of a draw. Since a large portion of such costs is fixed, that is, independent of the number of Elk harvested per public hunt, the actual figure will vary with the frequency over time and resulting magnitude of such hunts.

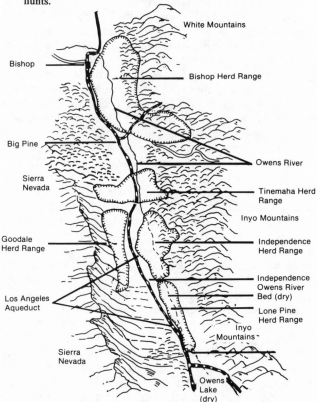

Fig. 1 Location map of Tule Elk herd ranges, Owens Valley, California. After McCullough (1969). The scale is approximately 15 km to 1 cm.

Competition between domestic livestock and Elk under current and foreseeable conditions is so minor that it can be disregarded in deciding on policy.

The California Tule Elk is a significant wildlife resource. The social benefits from its continuous use and management are larger than the social costs. There is a good possibility that net social benefits can be increased further, thereby strengthening the socioeconomic basis for Tule Elk survival.

Acknowledgements

The authors gratefully acknowledge their indebtedness to the many individuals and agencies who rendered assistance and cooperation during the course of this study. In particular they wish to thank Mr. Frank Bollman, Mr. Paul Lane and the Department of Water and Power of the City of Los Angeles, Professor A. Starker Leopold, Mr. R. Ken Miller, Mr. Wallace MacGregor and the California Department of Fish and Game, Dr. Dale R. McCullough, Dr. James J. Parsons, Mr. Douglas Powell, Mr. P. Dean Smith, Dr. J. B. Stevens, the County of Inyo, and the US Forest Service authorities in Inyo National Forest. The content of the article is, however, the sole responsibility of the authors.

[1]S. V. Ciriacy-Wantrup, Ph.D. and William E. Phillips, Ph.D. *Biological Conservation*, Vol. 3, No. 1, October 1970. Giannini Foundation Research Paper No. 297. Elsevier Publishing Company Ltd., England. Printed in Great Britain. pp. 23-32.

[2]The designation *nannodes* (from *nannos*, means "dwarf" in Greek) was given by C. H. Merriam, 1905. These Elk are one of three subspecies of Elk in North America, the other two being Roosevelt or Olympic Elk (*Cervus elaphus roosevelti*) and Rocky Mountain Elk (*Cervus elaphus nelsoni*). According to Webster's Dictionary, "tule" is Spanish and comes from the Nahuate word *tollin* or *tullin*, signifying either of two large bulrushes (*Scirpus lacustris* or *S. acutus*) which grow abundantly in the southwestern United States and adjacent Mexico, and especially in California at the junction of the Sacramento and San Joaquin Rivers. This area was an important portion of the original habitat of the Tule Elk.

[3]According to the U. S. Bureau of the Census, populations of the four communities in 1960 were as follows: the Bishop area, 6,553 persons (with 2,875 persons in Bishop itself); Big Pine, 863 persons; Independence, 891 persons; and Lone Pine, 2,467 persons.

[4]There are six kinds of Mule Deer in California, all considered to be members of the same species, *Odocailelus hemionus*. The Deer in Owens Valley are known as Inyo Mule Deer.

[5]In order to save time and costs, the Elk are driven by helicopter to the line of hunters accompanied by game wardens.

References

Ciriacy-Wantrup, S. V. (1952-68). *Resource Conservation: Economics and Policies.* Division of Agricultural Sciences, University of California, Berkeley, 1st edn., 1952, xiv + 395 pp.; 2nd rev. ed., 1963, xvi + 395 pp.; 3rd edn., 1968, xvi + 395 pp.

————. (1960*a*). Conceptual problems in projecting the demand for land and water. Pp. 41-67 in *Modern Land Policy, Papers of the Land Economics Institute,* Ed. Harold G. Halcrow *et al.* University of Illinois Press, Urbana, 449 pp. (Chapter 9 in this book.)

————. (1960*b*). Philosophy and objectives of watershed policy. Pp. 1-12 in *Economics of Watershed Planning,* Ed. G. S. Tolley & F. E. Riggs. Iowa State University Press, Ames, 339 pp. (Chapter 6 in this book.)

————. (1961). Conservation and resource programming. *Land Economics,* 37, 105-11. (Chapter 14 in this book.)

Merriam, C. H. (1905). A new elk from California, *Cervus nannodes. Proceedings of the Biological Society of Washington,* 18, 23-5, illustr.

McCullough, Dale R. (1969). *The Tule Elk: Its History, Behavior, and Ecology.* University of California Publication in Zoology No. 88. University of California Press, Berkeley & Los Angeles, v + 209 pp., illustr.

Phillips, William E. (1967). *Regional Development of the Owens Valley, California: an Economic Base Study of Natural Resources.* Unpublished Ph.D. dissertation, Department of Agricultural Economics, University of California, Berkeley, xi + 225 pp., illustr.

Chapter 13

THE "NEW" COMPETITION FOR LAND AND SOME IMPLICATIONS FOR PUBLIC POLICY*[1]

I. Changes in the Competition for Land

One of the central problems for public land policy is economic change. Of particular interest at the present juncture are changes in the competition for land that are related to urbanization and industrialization.

In the West, demands for land by urban-industrial development and by irrigated agriculture must be regarded for economic analysis as "rival" or "competitive" demands.[2] The level alluvial valleys and plains are the only—and usually scarce—location for irrigated agriculture. Agriculture has created and supported high land values relative to the surrounding areas not suited for irrigation because of topography and soils. Still, in terms of private economics, under the existing ground rules set by public land policy, these same valleys and plains are the most desirable location for subdivisions—especially those consisting of assembly-line dwellings—and for industry, transportation, and communication. In net value product per acre, these are "higher" land uses than irrigated agriculture—except greenhouses and certain horticultural enterprises. Thus, at the margin of urban-industrial development, irrigated agriculture is quickly priced out of the land market.

Since World War II, only a small part of the rapid urban and industrial expansion in California has taken place on the five least productive land classes, which are not suited for irrigation.[3] Most of the expansion has taken place on the three best land classes, which are suited for irrigation, and especially on Class I—the prime irrigable land. On this land, the leapfrogging of subdivisions has rendered far more land unusable for irrigated agriculture than is actually used for urban development.

A good illustration is the Santa Clara Valley, just south of San Francisco Bay. Until recently, this valley was famous for its production of high-quality fruits and vegetables. It is estimated that if urban expansion since 1947 were placed in one continuous parcel, that parcel would consist of twenty-six

*Reprinted, with permission, from 4 NAT.RES.J.252-67 (1964), published by the University of New Mexico School of Law, Albuquerque NM 87131.

miles. In actuality, there exists not a single square mile in a 200-square mile valley that has not been invaded by at least one subdivision.[4] Irrigated agriculture has largely been replaced. The impact on the organization of water management has recently been investigated.[5]

Most irrigated coastal valleys and plains between San Francisco and San Diego are in a state of development similar to that of the Santa Clara Valley. The Central Valley, backbone of California's irrigated agriculture, is in the initial stages of urbanization, especially around Marysville, Sacramento, Fresno, and Bakersfield. Even the irrigated desert valleys, such as the Antelope and the Coachella, have become susceptible to urbanization because of the rapid growth and improvement of air conditioning.

Freeways and airports are increasingly important competitors for irrigated land—both directly in terms of their own land requirements and as factors encouraging the leapfrogging of urban and industrial development. Freeways and airports have a strong preference for level topography. In California, such level land exists as alluvial valleys and plains. Efforts which have been made by agricultural interests to locate the main freeways in the Central Valley outside the prime irrigable land have not been successful.

Irrigated land is significant for the economy of California because of the high productivity per acre possible through irrigation as compared with other types of agriculture. The net value product per acre of irrigated land is about four times that of cultivated nonirrigated land and about twenty times that of rangeland.[6] Through feed production, and in several other ways, irrigated agriculture contributes to the productivity of nonirrigated land. Irrigated land is the foundation for California's highly developed processing industries.

In addition to increasing the competition for land between irrigated agriculture on one side and subdivisions, freeways, and airports on the other, urbanization and industrialization have brought about a great increase in the demands for land for various types of outdoor recreation. Potentially, this demand for land has complementary, as well as competitive, relations to the demand for land by agriculture, forestry, and grazing.[7] Under present land policies, competitive relations predominate.

One implication for land policy of these changes in the competition for land relates to the needed type of land-use planning. Planning for urban development can no longer be separated from planning for agriculture, forestry, water, and other natural resources. There is little contact and no co-ordination, either academically or administratively, between urban and natural-resources planning. A new breed of planner needs to be added who is not merely concerned with the internal problems of metropolitan regions but also is fully cognizant of the problems of the nonurban hinterland. By the same token, those concerned with natural-resources planning must first consider the land hunger of the megalopolis. This new breed of planner is already emerging. They may come from various backgrounds in the applied natural sciences, such as landscape design, engineering, architecture, and geography, but their common denominator is a thorough understanding of the tools of the social sciences—especially economics and law.

Another implication for land policy which follows from the increasing competition for land by urban and industrial uses is the irreversibility of the results. Previously, when competition for land meant merely that one agricultural use replaced another, or that agriculture replaced grazing, or that grasslands replaced forest and chapparal, these results were not necessarily irreversible. Before the large-scale use of concrete in subdivisions, freeways, and airports, the landscape was not irreversibly changed even by settlements and roads.

Irreversibility in the results of the "new" competition for land raises some interesting and significant questions for land policy: Do the public and the private interests coincide in the replacement of irrigated agriculture by urban-industrial development? Are social losses involved in the irreversible urbanization of prime irrigable land? If a decision were made by public land policy to divert urban-industrial development away from the prime irrigable land, what would be the costs? What about the allocation of such costs among the public and the private sectors of the economy? Are there tools of land policy to bring about and guide such diversion? An attempt to answer these questions requires a careful examination of the framework, the objectives, and the tools of land policy.

II. The Framework of Land Policy

Let us start with the framework, the basic assumptions of land policy. Control of California's 100 million acres is divided equally between private and public land managers.[8] However, nearly all urban and agricultural uses and use of the most productive forest and grassland lie within the private sector. We may assume that this state of affairs will continue. It follows that land policy must operate to a large extent through influencing the decisions of private land managers. Such influence can be accomplished in two major ways:

Land policy can operate through the economic forces which determine private decision making. Such forces are, for example, the price system, credit, taxation, highway and water development, and the institutions governing the ownership, selling, and leasing of land. Purposeful modification of these forces will be called here the "indirect tools" of land policy. At present, these economic forces are too often obstacles rather than tools of land policy.

Apart from these "indirect tools," the policy maker has available other devices which, as a shorthand expression, we will call "direct tools." These do not operate through the profit motive of private land managers, as do the indirect tools, but through laws, ordinances, and regulations which constrain or directly compel private decisions. Zoning, easements, pest-control regulations, and eminent-domain proceedings are examples. Administration of public lands in federal, state, or county ownership can also be regarded as a direct tool of land policy.

Frequently, when land policy is discussed, attention is focused on the direct tools and especially on the fee-simple acquisition and the administration of public land. Such a narrow point of view amounts to an abdication of land policy because it neglects the most important sector of land-use decisions and the most important set of policy tools. On the other hand, the significance of indirect tools requires that the motivation and behavior of private land managers be thoroughly understood. This is why familiarity with the social sciences was suggested above as a prerequisite in the training of the modern land-use planner.

III. The Objectives of Land Policy

Let us turn now to the objectives of land policy. The general objectives of all public policies are usually expressed as maximizing of some value or quantity such as national income, social net benefit, or public interest. As a first approximation, we may say that the basic objective of California land policy is to maximize the contribution of *all* land uses to the social welfare of the state.

The apparent simplicity of such a formulation, however, hides significant complexities. In order to maximize a quantity—the contribution to social welfare—it must be expressed in measurable and comparable units.

For some of the social benefits associated with land use, values are established in monetary terms in the marketplace. But the system of market prices has several basic effects which make prices unreliable as indicators of social welfare. These defects are not simple; they are difficult to remedy and cannot be discussed here.[9]

Frequently, market prices are difficult to obtain. For example, how can one measure the contribution to social welfare of outdoor recreation and compare it with that of types of housing or systems of communication?

The public interest in one area may conflict with that in another. For example, the maximum income from all land uses may not be obtainable with the income distribution and size of farms which may be desirable. To deal with this problem, a policy objective is usually maximized under institutional, technological, and other constraints. But this device has conceptual and operational weaknesses.[10]

The problem of quantitative definition and measurement of a policy objective is an area where more research is badly needed. Such research should ascertain to what extent various forms of social benefit-cost analysis, which have been applied to water-resources development, can also help in problems related to urban development. The planning of communication systems and of recreational opportunities are prime examples.

Apart from the difficulties inherent in quantitative definition and measurement of the social contribution by various alternative patterns of land use, there is the issue of the extent of such contributions over time. We are concerned here not with the contribution of land policy to social welfare in the present or the next decade but with the 1980's and beyond.

This brings immediately to mind the problem of irreversibility in relation to projections of future social needs. The latter are so uncertain that only the directions of change and possibly the rates of change in ordinal terms can be projected.[12] In view of this difficulty, added to the ones just mentioned, one may suggest that the objectives of land policy should be reformulated in a way that takes these difficulties explicitly into account.

There is no need to go into the technical aspects of such a reformulation, which lie in the field of uncertainty economics and game theory.[13] Suffice it to say that the objectives of land policy—and of many other public policies— can often be compared to the objectives of an insurance policy against serious losses that resist quantitative measurement. Here the objective is not to maximize a definite quantitative net gain but to choose premium payments and benefits in such a way that maximum possible losses are minimized. As a special case of this strategy, a "safe minimum standard" of present performance specified in such a way that maximum possible future losses are avoided is frequently a valid and relevant objective of policy.[14] Such an objective is equally well suited for the private as for the public sector of the economy.

IV. An Illustration: The Conservation of California's Prime Irrigable Land

An illustration may help to clarify this reformulation of the objectives of land policy. The land-policy problem with which this paper is mainly concerned is the irreversible loss of prime irrigable land when agricultural use is replaced by subdivisions, industries, freeways, and airports. Some questions were already raised regarding whether and in what way the conservation of prime irrigable land for agricultural uses should be regarded as an objective of land policy. The answers are by no means self-evident.

At the outset, one needs to make assumptions with respect to future water supply. It is very difficult to make meaningful statements about California land policy without considering, at the same time, water policy. Let us consider two alternative assumptions regarding future water supply.

First, we may assume that, in view of limited water supply, agricultural use of water will have to be curtailed in favor of urban and industrial uses. It has long been recognized that the marginal value product of water in these latter uses is higher than in irrigation uses. Under this assumption, the gradual encroachment of urban development on irrigated agriculture can be regarded as a self-regulating adjustment to water scarcity. Average per-acre water requirements of irrigated crops and of subdivisions are not greatly different. This adjustment is also painless to individual irrigation enterprises. In fact, they generally will make a capital gain in the adjustment process. The gain per acre will tend to increase as use of the remaining irrigable land is intensified. In conclusions, under our first assumption, land policy must be concerned not so much with the conservation as with orderly transformation of irrigable land into urban and industrial uses.

Alternatively, we may assume that future water supply will be sufficient for urban-industrial development *and* for the maintenance of agriculture on the prime irrigable land. This assumption is in accord with the projections of future water supply by the California Department of Water Resources.

There is some doubt whether such projections can be based solely on the transfer of northern California water to the south—even if such transfer is regarded as desirable and politically feasible.[16] But in view of other sources—especially the Columbia River—and technological developments in desalinization and reuse of water, and in view of the increasing popularity of a "public utility concept" of water development, we may accept here this alternative assumption regarding future water supply.

Acceptance of this assumption does not imply acceptance of some existing projections regarding the *timing* in the construction of future water-supply systems. On strictly economic grounds, deferment of some features of these systems may well be desirable. But because of the irreversibility already stressed, conservation of prime irrigable land is a *present* issue for land policy. A decision on this issue cannot be deferred.

Under our second assumption, a continuing or, more likely, accelerating disappearance of prime irrigable land will lead to an avoidable social loss—or benefit foregone—which would seriously affect the economy of the state. The loss consists of the direct and indirect social net value product of California's irrigation economy. A valid quantitative estimate of this loss, decade by decade, until a saturation point of urbanization and industrialization has been reached, would be rather difficult. But, in accordance with our reformulation of the objectives of land policy, we are mainly interested in the order of magnitude of maximum possible losses as compared with that of the "insurance premium" that must be paid to guard against them. There can be little doubt in this case that the maximum possible losses are high.

The insurance premium consists of the higher construction costs necessitated if urban-industrial development is diverted from the alluvial plains, to the benches, to the foothills, and to rocky and otherwise inferior soils. Irrigated valleys in California are surrounded by ample land of this type. Higher construction costs on these lands may be partly or fully offset by savings in social overhead for flood control, drainage, and sewage disposal. Other important offsets are the greater amenities made possible by the "poorer" sites for many aspects of urban life. Here also a quantitative estimate of costs and offsets over several decades would be of questionable validity. There is, however, some evidence that, in balance, the costs are not too high and are likely to decrease in the future.

In California, some of the better housing developments on the benches and in the foothills have proved quite profitable for subdividers. Admittedly, the alluvial valleys will remain the most profitable land for the dismal sprawl of cheap, assembly-line, individual dwellings. But in other parts of the country, private enterprise has successfully provided attractive low-cost housing of a land-saving type.

In a special case which the author had occasion to study recently, conservation of prime irrigable land is the deliberate result of private decision making. Land-use planning on the 90,000-acre Irvine Ranch in southern California involves conservation of a contiguous large tract of prime irrigable land for agriculture. On the same ranch, urban development is intensified on the benches, the foothills, and the inferior soils. Such planning appears profitable from the private viewpoint. But most private enterprises in land management are not large enough to plan "as if" they were a public body.

Planning for urban development on the Irvine Ranch includes industrial parks. These parks of light, technologically highly developed industries are located on the benches and foothills not suited for irrigation. If present trends continue, future industrial development in California will emphasize this same type of industry. Its location outside of the prime irrigable land presents no difficulties and many advantages.

Equipment and techniques to move earth cheaply and on a large scale are rapidly developing. Sometimes this technological development has not resulted in conservation—for example, when scenic values are destroyed in highway construction. But through lowering the costs of diverting subdivisions and freeways away from the prime irrigable land, conservation benefits will accrue from this development—as has already occurred through lowering the costs of terracing and leveling, both of which are important aids in soil conservation .

In conclusion, under our second assumption, one may suggest that the insurance premium to be paid is of such an order of magnitude as compared with that of benefits that it can well be considered a rational present and continuous social investment.

In order to avoid misunderstanding, it may be well to add that the reasoning presented here does not necessarily favor conservation of agricultural or wildland islands within metropolitan regions. This is a problem of "green belts" and other types of "lungs" as an integral part of urban development. It is an entirely different objective of land policy, which should be supported by a different kind of economic reasoning and carried out by a different set of tools. We are concerned here with the conservation of large contiguous blocks of prime irrigable land as one of the permanent economic foundations of the state. Such conservation need not interfere with continuing urbanization and industrialization; California has abundant land resources for these uses. Prime irrigable land, on the other hand, is scarce.

If a land-policy decision along these lines is made, the question arises: "Which sector of the economy should pay the insurance premium?" To what extent, for example, should increases in construction costs be allocated to the subdivider, the homeowner, or the tenant? What about equity to the owner of irrigable land who may have to forego a private capital gain? Is there justification for public participation in bearing the burden of the insurance premium? Which public should be involved—federal, state, or local—and in what proportions? These are questions to which research by competent people should be directed immediately.

To a large extent, the answer to these questions depends on the type of tool employed by land policy to influence the location of urban and industrial development. Therefore, let us turn our attention next to the tools of land policy.

V. The Tools of Land Policy

Within the space limits of a single paper, it is clearly impossible to consider thoroughly all tools of land policy or even merely those which have been mentioned as examples.[17] I should like, therefore, to take up two tools which appear especially significant for the present purpose. Taxation, one of the most important of the indirect tools, and easements, a promising direct tool, will be appraised with respect to their helpfulness for influencing the allocation of land between agricultural and urban-industrial uses.

A. Taxation in Combination with Zoning

Many attempts have been made in California and elsewhere to use taxation as a tool to prevent, to slow down, and to direct the transformation of agricultural land into subdivisions. The general procedure is to set up special tax districts in connection with zoning ordinances. More recently, deferment of taxes on agricultural properties for a certain number of years, under certain conditions, has been proposed without relation to zoning.[18] This proposal was defeated at the polls.

The best-known example in California for the taxation-zoning approach is Santa Clara County, comprising the valley of the same name. Santa Clara County was the first county in California that adopted a master plan (1934). Zoning ordinances with the objective of maintaining green belts were enacted in 1953 and 1955 on the basis of the then existing state enabling laws. In 1955, the state enacted the more specific "Green Belt Exclusion Law"[19] and in 1957 the closely related "Agricultural Assessment Law."[20]

The main objective of these measures of land policy in the Santa Clara Valley was not the conservation of prime irrigable land but an orderly transition from agricultural to urban land use. Still, several conclusions can be drawn from this experience with respect to the taxation-zoning approach to the conservation of prime irrigable land.

First, constitutional provisions make it difficult to assess at a lower level those agricultural properties which are most affected by the increase in land values due to urbanization. In California, the general constitutional provisions requiring uniformity in taxation are applied in the laws through the "no reasonable probability" limitation. This limitation provides that land in order to qualify for lower assessment must have no reasonable probability of changing from agricultural to urban use. Some states—Connecticut, Florida, Maryland, and New Jersey—have recently tried to remedy this situation by statute or constitutional amendment. Similar proposals have been discussed in California. It is difficult, however, to define permanent, bona fide agricultural use in such a way that lower assessment does not merely reduce the carrying charges for land speculators.

Second, zoning does not prevent eventual urbanization because farmers themselves usually favor a repeal of zoning ordinances when expected capital gains from urbanization become attractive. In other words, zoning has proved a politically unstable protection of agricultural use in the path of urban expansion. While zoning ordinances are in effect, they encourage leapfrogging if the zoning districts are discontinuous.

Third, the burden of property taxes is only one factor among several others which make it difficult to continue irrigated agriculture in the rural-urban fringe. Impending urbanization reduces the incentive to invest in proper maintenance of irrigation systems. In surface irrigation, each individual enterprise is a part of a larger system. This system is disrupted by leapfrogging, urban scatteration, and roads. An urban neighborhood puts serious limitations on the use of insecticides and fertilizers. Crops suffer from smog, trespass, and vandalism. Tax relief, therefore, is a necessary but not a sufficient condition for continuity of agriculture. Taxation at present is an obstacle to the objectives of land policy we are discussing. This obstacle should be removed, but it would be an illusion to expect that such removal by itself would bring about the desired objectives.

In conclusion, the experience with taxation and zoning in the Santa Clara Valley is not encouraging if the land-policy objective is the conservation of prime irrigable land for agricultural uses.

B. Social Overhead: Dependent or Independent Variable in Urbanization?

It is sometimes suggested that the effects of zoning can be strengthened by withholding social overhead such as roads, schools, and public utilities from areas for which urbanization is not desired. Social overhead is part of a master plan. There is no indication that withholding of social overhead is politically more stable than zoning or other features of the plan. Under the American systems of local government and of providing public utilities largely through private enterprise, the supply of social overhead is highly responsive to the demand by organized local groups. Such supply must be regarded as a dependent rather than an independent variable in urbanization.

The question may be raised of whether this situation holds also on the state level. It is sometimes suggested that California's urbanization problems should be attacked through the State Water Plan. Proposals are made in all seriousness to "control" the urbanization of southern California through limiting the southward transportation of northern water.

There can be little disagreement that for an undeveloped region, the provision of social overhead, if boldly undertaken under propitious conditions, is strategic for economic development. Many illustrations for this could be cited. But for a highly developed region with strong metropolitan areas and important urban nuclei outside of these areas, development of water-supply systems must be regarded economically and politically as a dependent rather than independent variable in urbanization. Furthermore, for the objectives of land policy we are discussing, it is meaningless to suggest that urbanization could be controlled through the water supply; as shown elsewhere, the water supply available through displacement of agriculture is one of the major economic attractions for the urbanization of prime irrigable land.[21]

C. Easements

Let us turn, therefore, to another tool of land policy which provides tax relief, which is politically more stable than zoning, and to which constitutional and other limitations apply in different ways than to taxation. This tool is the acquisition of public easements over private land.

Use of easements in connection with communication systems, airports, and public utilities is well established. Easements for open space, parks, and highways are common.[22] Some states, especially Wisconsin, have pioneered with recreational easements for hunting and fishing.[23] Conservation easements are mentioned in the literature in connection with open-space easements.[24] But, so far as I am aware, such easements have not been used for the conservation of large blocks of prime irrigable land. Such easements may be acquired by the state or by local governments under state enabling laws. For the purpose under discussion, the planning and guidance of acquisition are best undertaken on the state level.

Conservation easements may be acquired through voluntary sale or through eminent domain. In California, voluntary sale is open to challenge because the constitution prohibits the legislature from making gifts of public funds.[25] In both cases, therefore, a public interest must be shown to exist. It is the argument of this paper that a public interest exists if the purpose of land policy is the conservation of prime irrigable land for agricultural uses.

It is sometimes suggested by urban planners that the acquisition of the fee-simple right is less complicated, of greater advantage to the public later on, and not much more expensive than the acquisition of easements. This is quite true if the acquisition concerns permanent open space without much private development (green belts) or space to be developed later under public control. In the latter case, the fee-simple acquisition would assure effective control and simplify the problem of compensation. Furthermore, the increase in land value due to the development would accrue to the public. In the present case, however, important private uses will continue. High land values are created and supported by these uses. In our case, therefore, it is more economical for the public to acquire easement rather than fee-simple rights.

For the objective of land policy under discussion, easements must be purchased in perpetuity. Experience tends to indicate that the purchase price per acre of a perpetual easement is not significantly higher than that for a twenty-year easement.

Conservation easements would go a long way to solve the tax problem for individual irrigation enterprises when land values are affected by potential urbanization. Since development rights would be no longer vested in the private owner, he could not constitutionally be assessed for them. This, in itself, will constitute a strong inducement toward voluntary sale of conservation easements.

Voluntary sale would, of course, be influenced by the economic value placed on the development rights which are given up. This is the most crucial problem of conservation easements. It poses a real challenge to economics as an academic discipline, to the legal profession, and to the practical administrator.

Appraisal of individual strands of the bundle of private property rights that relate to an acre of land is not uncommon. Special problems, however, are created by the fact that conservation easements must be acquired simultaneously for large blocks of irrigable land. Should allowance be made for different dates at which individual parcels would have become ripe for urban development? Should geographical factors, such as distance to existing urban centers, be taken into account in combination with market transactions as benchmarks? In what way should other basic factors—climate, soils, and groundwater supply—be taken into account in valuation? What legal, political, and administrative safeguards should be built into the procedures of appraising and taking conservation easements? Should such safeguards be developed in analogy to those already existing in the procedures used to establish special public districts with the powers of taxation and eminent domain? Research by the social sciences is badly needed to answer these questions.

Such research would also benefit the use of other types of easements. Recreational easements are an example. It would be rather wasteful if California should neglect the contribution private lands could make in satisfying the increase in the demand for outdoor recreation that can be expected during the coming decades. Such contribution will not be forthcoming without reimbursement to the private land manager. The purchase or lease of recreational easements by the state is one of several alternative approaches to this problem. The state could recover these costs through fees charged for recreational uses. California has been backward in this area of land policy as compared with other states such as Wisconsin.

Conclusion

In the West, a "new" competition for land is becoming of far-reaching social significance. This is the competition for prime irrigable land between agriculture on one side and subdivisions, industries, freeways, and airports on the other. At the margin of urban-industrial development, irrigated agriculture is quickly priced out of the land market by these "higher" land uses. This change in land use is irreversible. In California, the replacement of irrigated agriculture has progressed farthest and raises some acute and interesting problems for public land policy.

If the general objectives of land policy as formulated in these pages are accepted, and if the more optimistic of two alternative assumptions regarding future water supply discussed here is fulfilled, conservation of large contiguous blocks of prime irrigable land for agriculture appears in the long-run public interest. The social costs for diverting urban-industrial development to land classes not suited for irrigation are of such an order of magnitude as compared with that of maximum possible social losses threatened by the continuation and probable acceleration of present trends that these costs can be regarded as a rational present social investment for avoiding such losses in the future. Under our assumption regarding water supply, conservation of large contiguous blocks of prime irrigable land for agriculture does not interfere with urban-industrial development.

Several tools of land policy are appraised with respect to their effectiveness in diverting urban-industrial development from the prime irrigable land. The usual taxation-zoning approach has several serious shortcomings for this purpose. Likewise, controlling urbanization through social overhead appears of doubtful effectiveness in the present case. Thus far, conservation easements have not been used for the particular objective of land policy discussed here. But the economic-legal characteristics of conservation easements and the experience with them in realizing other objectives of public policy suggest that they may be well suited for the objective of conserving large contiguous blocks of prime irrigable land for agriculture.

[1]*Natural Resources Journal* 4(2), pp. 252-267 (October, 1964). Giannini Foundation Paper No. 255. An earlier version of this paper was presented under the title, "Toward a California Land Policy for the 1980's" at the Conference on Man in California: 1980's, Sacramento, January 27-28, 1964.

[2]Because of the occasion for which this paper was first prepared, the focus is on California. But the problems dealt with are acute—or soon will be—in most other western states.

[3]Based on the eight land capability classes employed by the U. S. Soil Conservation Service.

[4]Wood & Heller, California Going, Going...Our State's Struggle to Remain Beautiful and Productive (1962).

[5]S. Smith, The Public District in Integrating Ground and Surface Water Management: A Case Study in Santa Clara County (University of California, Giannini Foundation Research Report No. 252, 1962).

[6]Ciriacy-Wantrup, *Major Economics Forces Affecting Agriculture with Particular Reference to California*, 18 Hilgardia 1 (Giannini Foundation Paper No. 121, 1947).

[7]Ciriacy-Wantrup, Multiple Use as a Concept for Water and Range Policy, in Water and Range Resources and Economic Development of the West 1 (Report No. 9, Conference Proceedings of the Committee on the Economics of Water Resources Development and the Committee on the Economics of Range Use and the development of the Western Agricultural Economics Research Council, 1961). (Chapter 16 of this book.)

[8]Federal government—47 million acres; state and local governments—3 million acres; private ownership—50 million acres.

⁹The implications for resource policy are discussed in Ciriacy-Wantrup, *Philosophy and Objectives of Watershed Policy*, in Economics of Watershed Planning 1 (Tolley & Riggs, ed., 1960) (Chapter 6 in this book); Ciriacy-Wantrup, *Conservation and Resource Programming*, 37 Land Economics 105 (1961). (Chapter 14 in this book.)

¹⁰For details, see the literature cited in this section.

¹²Ciriacy-Wantrup, *Conceptual Problems in Projecting the Demand for Land and Water*, in Modern Land Policy 41 (Land Economics Institute, 1960).

¹³For a discussion of this reformulation and its application, see Ciriacy-Wantrup, Resource Conservation: Economics and Policies (2d ed. 1963).

¹⁴*Ibid* at chapter 18.

¹⁶The problematic aspects concern the California "Area of Origin" legislation and the effects on fishery resources. Adequate solution of these problems will reduce the amount of water available for transfer.

¹⁷For a more comprehensive discussion, see Ciriacy-Wantrup, Resource Conservation: Economics and Policies, at chs. 7-15 (2d ed. 1963).

¹⁸Proposition 4 on the California state ballot of November 6, 1962.

¹⁹Cal. Gov't Code Section 35009.

²⁰Cal. Gov't Code Section 402.5.

²¹Ciriacy-Wantrup, *Projections of Water Requirements in the Economics of Water Policy*, 43 J. of Farm Economics 197 (1961).

²²In California, the "Open Space Act" of 1959 . Cal. Gov't Code Section 6950-54 authorized cities and counties to acquire land outright or the development right or easements to provide open-space areas. Such areas are defined as:

> any space characterized by (1) great natural scenic beauty or (2) whose existing openness, natural condition, or present state of use, if sustained, would enhance the present or potential value of abutting or surrounding development, or would maintain or enhance the conservation of natural or scenic resources.

²³Jordahl, *Conservation and Scenic Easements: An Experience Resume*, 39 Land Economics 343 (1963).

²⁴Whyte, Securing Open Space for Urban America: Conservation Easements 45 (Urban Land Institute, Technical Bulletin No. 36, 1959).

²⁵For a more detailed discussion of these problems, see *Preservation of ‘Open Spaces Through Scenic Easements in Green Belt Zoning*, 12 Stan. L. Rev. 638 (1959-1960).

Chapter 14

CONSERVATION AND RESOURCE PROGRAMMING*[1]

Definition of Terms

In order to avoid possible misunderstanding, the key terms of this paper require a few words of explanation.

The term *resource programming* has recently become popular in a broad informal sense—as a substitute for *resource planning* which has been in vogue since the early 1930's. This popularity can be traced to the impact, during the 1950's, of programming in its formal sense—as an operationally efficient mathematical technique for obtaining optimum solutions in planning problems.[2] This impact on problem-solving spread quickly from planning for the United States Air Force and similar large organizations to the applied phases of many natural and social science fields; for example, engineering, econometrics, and economic geography.

Some students, among them a well-known economic geographer, have compared the importance of formal programming to that of the atomic bomb.[3] Appraisal of this importance in the economics of conservation is a major part of my assignment. For this purpose I shall interpret the term *resource programming* as including but not as restricted to its formal varieties, such as linear, nonlinear, and dynamic programming.

Next, let us turn to the term *conservation*. Generally, conservation is regarded as a subject of the natural sciences or the domain of the idealist. But it is also a vital and interesting subject of economics. In essence, the concern of the conservationist and the economist focuses on the same problem. This problem is the relation of past and present to future use of natural resources. Hence, a semantic bridge between the conservation movement and economics would seem more helpful than strengthening the existing semantic barrier. In the absence of such a bridge, the term *conservation* will continue to be used to obtain political support for programs whose effects on natural resources are frequently not understood or are contradictory.

*Reprinted, with the permission of The University of Wisconsin Press, from *Land Economics*, XXXVII, No. 2, pp. 105–111, (May, 1961).

Economics is the systematic study of choosing between alternatives. In such a study of decision-making, alternatives involving time are among the most significant ones. Hence, the choice between different time distributions of the use of natural resources and the relation between past, present, and future uses are highly significant economic problems. By saying that they are economic problems, I did not imply that it is always meaningful or necessary to express them quantitatively in pecuniary terms or that the programming of aesthetic, educational, or scientific uses of natural resources can be neglected—as is so frequently alleged for economic analysis. I shall return to this problem presently.

To say that conservation is concerned with the relations of past and present to future use of natural resources is not a definition. There is no *best* definition for all purposes. Since 1941 I have been using a definition of conservation that has proved most useful for the purposes of economic analysis.[4] *Conservation* and its logical corollary *depletion* are defined in terms of changes in the intertemporal distribution of physical rates of resource use, implying comparison of at least two actual or hypothetical time distributions. Such comparison requires a weighting system in which distance in time is used as weight. The statistical problems encountered in weighting are similar to those in any index of physical output.

One aspect of a definition based on physical use rates is that it is neutral in terms of values and value judgments. Thus, it does not say anything about the economic objectives and criteria of conservation. An additional term is needed that involves valuation and refers to an economic optimum in the time distribution of physical rates of resource use. For short, this is called the *optimum state of conservation.*

The Optimum State of Conservation and Resource Programming

At first sight it appears that the techniques of formal programming would be highly useful for determining the optimum state of conservation. Such determination involves a time allocation of inputs and outputs in resource use which maximizes social welfare under constraints pertinent to the investigation. Formal programming is designed precisely to solve problems of this kind.

Since alternatives are characterized by differences in dating and since an optimum time path of resource use has to be determined, an extension of the technique becomes necessary. Such an extension, through use of Lagrange multipliers, is known as *dynamic programming.* The same device has been employed in the conceptual determination of the optimum state of conservation for many years.[5] Actual quantitative determination of the optimum state of conservation through dynamic programming has not yet been attempted. But resource economists should approach new techniques with an open mind and not see a "quantitative bogey man" behind every equation, as an editorial in *Economic Geography* has advised recently.[6] With this advice, I am in full accord.

On the other hand, it would be equally shortsighted not to recognize significant conceptual and operational difficulties that limit the usefulness of quantitative optimizing in economics—especially in the economics of conservation. These limitations apply no less to informal programming (for example, benefit-cost analysis) than to the formal kind. However, they are more concealed in the implicit assumptions of formal programming; and its comparative efficiency and the precision of its results have led to an enthusiasm that frequently overlooks the limitations.

These limitations are more severe for conservation decisions by federal, state, and local government—that is, for conservation policy—than for conservation decisions by subsectors of the economy such as individual farms and industrial firms, which operate within the framework of the "rules of the game" established by policy. This paper is mainly concerned with conservation policy. It should be mentioned that the difference in the usefulness of quantitative optimizing between decision-making by government and decision-making by economic subsectors is not confined to resource economics.[7]

The difficulties which I have in mind may be discussed as three interrelated problem areas which will be called here (1) the problem of valuation, (2) the problem of institutional constraints, and (3) the problem of uncertainty. These broad problems are present in the programming of all natural resources.

The Problem of Valuation

Quantitative optimizing in economics requires that commensurate indicators of value attach to all physical inputs and outputs of resource use—at least in relative terms. Market prices are taken as starting points and bench marks in valuation. While one may be in favor of judiciously expanding the area of pecuniary evaluation for purposes of public policy,[8] one should not forget that there will always remain a large portion of social benefits and costs for which such evaluation would be meaningless. Neglect of such *extramarket* benefits and costs introduces a systematic bias into quantitative optimizing.

Resource economists have stressed the significance of specific extramarket benefits and costs for some time.[9] In 1958 John Kenneth Galbraith called attention to them with special reference to affluent societies—like that of this country.[10] Emphasis is given to the increasing lack of what is called *social balance* between the products supplied by the market economy and products such as parks, playgrounds, and education, which are publicly supplied and financed by general taxation rather than sale. The supply of extramarket goods has an inherent tendency to lag behind the supply of market goods because modern advertising and emulation, which are largely responsible for demand shifts in affluent societies, operate exclusively in favor of market goods.

Extramarket goods, however, are only a part of the valuation problem. No less significant is the question: to what extent are present and projected market prices, where they exist, valid and relevant indicators for public policy? To what extent, for example, are the prices of agricultural products and of their cost factors relevant for programming public water resources development?

At this point I do not refer to the price and income effects of the development itself, to external economies and diseconomies, nor to economic fluctuation. Solution of these problems is often difficult but practical approximations can be found.

More basic difficulties are created by the fact that the functioning and results of the price system itself are profoundly affected by income distribution, market structure, and many public policies inside and outside agriculture. Formal programming looks at these influences as institutional conditions which—together with the technological ones—are introduced into the optimizing calculus as constraints. Only too often investigators are not aware of the severe limitations which this procedure imposes on the validity and relevance of quantitative optimizing if the results are to serve as a basis for decision making in public policy. To me at least, the implications seem so important that several of them need to be explored in the present context.

The Problem of Institutional Constraints

First, when social institutions are used as constraints, they become conceptually indistinguishable from social objectives. In this respect, they are different from technological constraints. As explained elsewhere,[11] in natural resource policy, changes of social institutions are among the most significant controllable variables and relations. In other words, in natural resource policy, social institutions must frequently be regarded as means rather than ends. Hence, the distinction in econometrics between the parts of the model that constitutes the *objective function* to be maximized or minimized and the part that constitutes the constraints describing the structure of the operation and the relations between variables becomes misleading if the conceptual difference between technological and institutional constraints is not sufficiently recognized.

Secondly, when social institutions are used as constraints in a quantitative optimizing calculus, a new optimum must be calculated for each combination of constraints that is considered. The optima calculated for different sets of constraints are then compared. Recently, a whole literature has grown up around this approach known as *the theory of second best.*[12] This term merely indicates that there is at least one constraint additional to the ones existing in the so-called *Pareto optimum.*[13] The exponents of this theory claim that the major contribution is a negative one: If a deviation from one of the Pareto optimum conditions prevails, the best course of action is not an attempt to attack this deviation and keep all others intact. On the contrary, a second-best solution is usually obtained only be departing from all other Pareto conditions. To apply only a part of the Pareto conditions would move the economy away from, rather than toward, a second-best position. In consequence, the exponents of this theory direct their criticism against what they call *piecemeal welfare economics.*

If this criticism is valid—I believe it has some merit—does it not point to a basic weakness in the logic of quantitative economic optimizing itself? If one tries to avoid the futility of piecemeal welfare economics and strives for bold changes in the combination of constraints, can one be sure that quantitative optima are comparable in a meaningful way? Is it not unavoidable that such bold changes affect some structural elements of the optimizing calculus— among them especially preferences, technology, and the motivation of human agents in their various functions in the economy? Are we not confronted with a problem of identification, in the econometric sense, on a grand scale?

In view of these questions, I should like to submit that optima of social welfare are constructs in the sense of useful scientific fictions.[14] Such constructs are not operational policy objectives. There is danger that the two are confused when formal programming is used to obtain quantitative optima for large social aggregates.

On the other hand, as fictional constructs, social optima are useful as organizing principles for the great number of controllable and uncontrollable variables and kinds of relations that must be considered in welfare economics—to decide which ones to bring into a particular investigation explicitly, which ones to neglect, which ones to combine with others, and which ones to take into account as constraints. In policy investigations, special care is needed to decide whether social institutions should be treated as constraints. An alternative treatment, just implied, will be sketched later.

The Problem of Uncertainty

Let us now turn to our third set of problems. Uncertainty is especially important in those areas of economic decision-making where time is a significant element in differentiating alternatives. This, as we know, is especially true of the economics of conservation.

The most important uncertainties, those created by changes of technology, of preferences, and of institutions, increase with time. The probability of such changes is not amenable to precise quantitative measurement. At best, the direction, the relative speed, and the range of such changes can be vaguely projected. Other uncertainties, for example, the occurrence of drought, floods, and hail storms, do not increase with time and their probability can be measured quantitatively. Economists frequently refer to these uncertainties as *risk* in order to differentiate them from the former. Techniques to allow for uncertainties of the latter kind are being developed in formal programming. The former kind of uncertainty imposes severe limitations on the relevance of quantitative optimizing for policy decisions.

Practitioners of formal programming who are also competent economists are aware of these limitations. Robert Dorfman, for example, in a recent appraisal of operations research states: "Another important limitation, in which less progress has been made, is that linear programming formulations do not allow for uncertainty."[15] On the other hand, one may wonder whether the enthusiasm of many less critical practitioners might not delay acceptance of formulations that would allow for uncertainty.

In the economies of conservation, allowance for uncertainty is best made, I believe, through the formulation of the policy objective itself. Such a formulation I have called *the safe minimum standard of conservation*. A detailed explanation of the theoretical development of this concept and its operational application is found elsewhere.[16] Space limitations permit merely stating that one aspect of the economic rationale of the safe minimum standard of conservation as a policy objective is to minimize maximum possible social losses connected with avoidable irreversibilities. In this respect the safe minimum standard of conservation may be regarded as a conceptual relative of the well-known min-max solution or *saddle-point* in a two-person, strictly determined game.[17] This is not to suggest, however, that all aspects of the economics of conservation should be forced into the framework of modern game theory—as "man playing against nature" in an almost literal sense.

Conclusion

It may be concluded from this sketch of three important limitations that formal programming is most useful when the model is little concerned with values, when the treatment of social institutions as constraints is logical, and when the influences of time and uncertainty are small. Stated differently, formal programming is more useful in engineering than economics, more for private than for policy decisions, and more under static than under dynamic assumptions. Usefulness for natural resource policy is limited on all three counts.

It is interesting to observe that the more sophisticated practitioners of formal programming design their models in such a way that the three limitations are involved as little as possible. The resulting models are engineering rather than economic ones. An engineering model, however, can throw light on some aspects of the economic issues. Examples in water resources programming are Dorfman's "Simple Valley" and Tolley's "Optimal Water Allocation."[18] The former model is purely hypothetical, designed to illustrate the technique. The latter model deals ex post with an actual allocation through existing social institutions. Under assumptions most favorable to formal programming, allocative efficiency is improved by no more than five percent. Careful comparative studies of this kind are only too rare.

On the positive side, it may be concluded that resource programming in the informal sense must include the programming of social institutions. Resources programming must be pragmatic; that is, it must regard institutions as means (tools) as well as ends (objectives), depending upon the purposes of the analysis.[19] In natural resource policy, an analytically-oriented institutional economics is by no means obsolete.

In such an approach, institutions are regarded as structured systems, each with particular patterns of change over time. These systems can be analyzed in structure, functioning, performance, and change over time. Their purpose is not to obtain quantitative optima of social welfare at given points in time under conditions projected for these points. Rather, their purpose is to increase social welfare continuously under constantly changing conditions that at any point in time can be projected only vaguely and are always uncertain with respect to actual occurrence. Responsiveness of these systems to economic change is more important than their efficiency in optimizing under particular sets of projected conditions.

Hence, appraising the performance of these systems by introducing arbitrary temporal cross-sections of them as alternative constraints in formal programming is inappropriate. Performance can be appraised only by criteria applied to alternative systems as they function over time. Such criteria need not always be pecuniary. As has been shown elsewhere, nonpecuniary criteria can be effectively employed.[20] Such an appraisal is an integral part of the field of economics, which includes econometrics but is not restricted to it. A restriction of this kind would be especially unfortunate in programming the use of natural resources.

[1]*Land Economics*, Vol. XXXVII, No. 2 (May, 1961), pp. 105–111. This paper was presented at the Symposium, "Programming the Use of Natural Resources," annual Meeting of the American Association for the Advancement of Science, Section E (Geography and Geology), New York, December 30, 1960.

[2]The origin of formal programming—as *linear* programming—is generally dated with the unpublished papers by Jerome Cornfield (1941) and G. B. Dantzig (1947). The latter paper was published as "Maximization of a Linear Function of Variables Subject to Linear Inequalities" in T. C. Koopman's (Ed.) *Activity Analysis of Production and Allocation* (New York, New York: John Wiley and Sons, 1951). The title of the Dantzig paper can serve as a definition of linear programming.

[3]William L. Garrison, "Spatial Structure of the Economy," *Annals of the Association of American Geographers*, June 1959, p. 232. See also, Merrill M. Flood, *American Scientist*, December 1958, p. 358 (book review).

[4]S. V. Ciriacy-Wantrup, "Private Enterprise and Conservation," *Journal of Farm Economics*, February 1942. Paper presented before the Annual Meeting of the American Farm Economic Association, New York City, December 27-30, 1941.

[5]Harold Hotelling, "The Economics of Exhaustible Resources," *Journal of Political Economy*, April 1931, pp. 137-175. See also, S. V. Ciriacy-Wantrup, "Private Enterprise and Conservation," *op. cit.*, pp. 82 and 83.

[6]Brian J. L. Berry, "The Quantitative Bogey Man," guest editorial, *Economic Geography*, October 1960.

[7]While the conceptual limitations of quantitative optimizing for subsectors are less than for policy decisions, the problems posed by the availability of data for smaller statistical agregates are frequently greater.

[8]S. V. Ciriacy-Wantrup, "Benefit-Cost Analysis and Public Resource Development," *Journal of Farm Economics*, November 1955. Paper presented

before the Annual Meeting of the American Association for the Advancement of Science, Joint Session, Section K (Economics) and M (Engineering), December 27, 1954. (Chapter 8 of this book.)

[9]S. V. Ciriacy-Wantrup, *Resource Conservation, Economics and Policies* (Berkeley, California: University of California Press, 1952), 381 pp.

[10]J. K. Galbraith, *The Affluent Society* (Boston, Massachusetts: Houghton, Mifflin and Co., 1958).

[11]S. V. Ciriacy-Wantrup, *Resource Conservation...*, especially chapters 16-21.

[12]R. G. Lipsey and R. K. Lancaster, "The General Theory of Second Best," *The Review of Economic Studies*, 1956-1957, pp. 11-32. The earlier literature is cited in this article.

[13]Wilfredo Pareto, *Cours d'Economique Politique* (Lausanne: F. Route, Libraire-Editeur, 1897). An excellent bibliography of welfare economics is appended to: E. J. Mishan, "A Survey of Welfare Economics, 1939-1959," *The Economic Journal*, June 1960, pp. 197-265.

[14]The usefulness of scientific fictions was discussed on a previous occasion: S. V. Ciriacy-Wantrup, "Policy Considerations in Farm Management Research in the Decade Ahead," *Journal of Farm Economics*, December 1956, pp. 1301-1311. Presented before the Annual Meeting of the American Farm Economic Association, Asilomar, August, 1955.

[15]Robert Dorfman, "Operations Research," *The American Economic Review*, September 1960, pp. 575-623.

[16]S. V. Ciriacy-Wantrup, *Resource Conservation...*, especially chapters 17 and 18.

[17]Johann von Neumann and Oskar Morganstern, *Theory of Games and Economic Behavior* (Princeton, New Jersey: Princeton University Press, 1944), 625 pp. See also, Robert Dorfman, Paul A. Samuelson, and Robert M. Solow, *Linear Programming and Economic Analysis* (New York, New York: McGraw-Hill Book Co., 1958), chapters 15 and 16.

[18]Robert Dorfman, "Simple Valley," *Economics of Watershed Planning*, edited by G. S. Tolley and F. E. Riggs (Ames, Iowa: Iowa State University Press, 1960); and G. S. Tolley and V. S. Hastings, "Optimal Water Allocation," *Quarterly Journal of Economics*, May 1960.

[19]On the schism between *orthodox* and *pragmatic* attitudes toward social institutions, see: F. O. Sarent, "A Methodological Schism in Agricultural Economics," *Canadian Journal of Agricultural Economics*, 1960, pp. 45-52.

[20]S. V. Ciriacy-Wantrup, "Concepts Used as Economic Criteria for a System of Water Rights," *Land Economics*, November 1956, pp. 295-312. Also published in *The Law of Water Allocation in the Eastern United States*, edited by David Haber and Stephen W. Bergen (New York, New York: The Ronald Press Co., 1958), pp. 531-552.

Chapter 15

SOCIAL OBJECTIVES OF CONSERVATION OF NATURAL RESOURCES WITH PARTICULAR REFERENCE TO TAXATION OF FORESTS*[1]

If you permit, I shall dispense with a formal paper. My assignment is to be informal and provocative in order to have a lively discussion afterward. I should like, however, to mention a formal paper on a very similar subject—although published 15 years ago.[2] If my remarks this morning are too general and do not spell out sufficiently the qualifying conditions, you may wish to consult this paper.

As the chairman has told you, my assignment is to emphasize the theoretical aspects of my theme. In itself, I find such an assignment a rather pleasant one. Theories, however, must be tested. In conservation policy, as in other fields of economic policy, theories are employed to understand and to predict the behavior of various classes of resource users with the objective of evaluating and influencing behavior in relation to the objectives of conservation policy. In other words, if one theorizes, one must think about testing and about the operational aspects of theories. I shall move on a fairly theoretical level, but it will be necessary to come down from the clouds occasionally!

The first point of my assignment is to define the term "conservation." There is no absolutely best definition. Definitions are used in science for a particular purpose, and my own[3] definition is presented here, not because I think it is the best for all purposes, but because I find it best for economic analysis and because you and I have to use a common language. It would be a waste of time if there were misunderstanding on a purely semantic basis. I should like to warn you, however, that the very reasons why I like my definition make it disliked by others. Most writers on conservation define the term in such a way that it means something "good." Conservation is defined as "wise use," as "the avoidance of waste," and in similar ways.

*Reprinted, with the permission of the University of Oregon College of Business Administration, from *Taxation and Conservation of Privately Owned Timber*, Bureau of Business Research, 1959.

Regardless of its scientific usefulness, a definition must explain the meaning of words and concepts. The above definitions do not fulfill this requirement. Furthermore, by defining conservation as something *a priori* "good" economic analysis is prejudiced.

I prefer to define the term "conservation" in terms of physical characteristics of resource use—specifically the changes of rates of use occurring during various intervals throughout a time period. "Conservation" and its corollary "depletion" describe changes from an initial state weighted according to the time incidence of changes. In contrast to this definition, it is necessary to specify an additional term, involving valuation and value judgments. This I have called the optimum state of conservation. One essential aspect of my definition is differentiation between the terms "conservation" and "depletion" on one side as neutral in terms of valuation and value judgment and the concept of "optimum state of conservation" on the other.

Let me use an analogy: In production economics we talk about output. We may consider changes—increases or decreases—of output. This, in itself does not necessarily involve values. Values may enter into the weighting system needed in order to combine different kinds of output in an output index. But values enter into that index quite differently than in a discussion of the optimum output vector. The problem of the optimum output vector, on the other hand, is one that is intimately related to values and to value judgments and is basic when the objectives of private and social decision making are discussed. My differentiation between "conservation" and "optimum state of conservation" is similar.

In conservation, we have outputs of the same kind distributed over different intervals of time. If we are using time as a weight, we get a weighted index of the time distribution of output. Conservation means merely an increase, depletion, a decrease of that index. It is a physical term in the same sense as an index of the volume of output.

Each of these two concepts, conservation and depletion on the one side, and optimum state of conservation on the other, has certain uses. Here, again, we have a parallel in general production economics. Nobody would contend that a volume of output index is useless for policy purposes, although it does not say anything about the optimum pattern of output. My proposal is merely to do the same in conservation economics. The conceptual difficulties in constructing an index of time distribution of output are not greatly different from those which are incurred in constructing a volume of output index. For example, what particular time weights we want to use is to some extent an arbitrary decision, much as in the weighting of a volume of output index.

Conceptually, my definition of conservation is fairly clear; operationally it is sometimes tricky. A practical example from the field of forestry may be helpful. Here on the West Coast we have a timber conservation problem that is very interesting to the economist. We may ask, is deferment in the cutting of virgin timber conservation? Most people would probably reply in the affirmative. According to my definition, however, such deferment is not necessarily conservation. Whether it is will depend not only on what happens to the mature timber during the period of deferment—mature timber may deteriorate—but on the comparison of two or more whole alternative utilization plans. These plans extend into the future far beyond the planned cutting dates of the virgin timber. In ascertaining whether or not a utilization plan means conservation as compared with an alternative plan, we are comparing physical outputs. That is quite different from the problem of the optimum rate of cutting the virgin timber. It is useful to ascertain what happens in physical terms quite aside from the question of the optimum rate of cutting in value terms. Let us now turn to these value problems, that is, to the objectives of private and social decision making.

In trying to identify the optimum time distribution in the use of resources from the standpoint of welfare economics, one encounters what might be called the problem of unity of social objectives and criteria. It is difficult to define objectives for individual aspects of the economy. One cannot state independently, "this is the optimum state of conservation, this is the optimum state of employment, this is the optimum state of foreign trade." In considering social welfare objectives, one cannot, in principle, split conservation away from other aspects of the economy. They are all interrelated. Welfare criteria are not different in conservation economics than in other sectors of the economy.

For the last 20 years, economists have worked intensively on these criteria. I have not the time to go into the pros and cons of this literature in order to evaluate the "new" welfare economics. Operational approximations to theoretical social optima have been suggested elsewhere.[4] They need not be repeated here.

Having stressed the unity of objectives and criteria in social decision making, I must now make a suggestion which, to some of you, may at first blush appear inconsistent. I should like to suggest that in natural resource economics there are some significant conditions which induce characteristic deviations of the actual state of conservation. This situation makes it permissible to focus on these significant conditions and their changes—as obstacles or tools of policy—when considering policy objectives. Some of these conditions are just as important for other aspects of the economy as for conservation. Others may be called special conditions because they affect natural resource economics to a far greater degree than other aspects of the economy.

We may ask, then, what are these significant conditions? They can be systematized in several ways. In my book,[5] for example, I have differentiated between various classes of social benefits and costs, and tried to explain why their allocation to decision-making agents and their incidence among other members of a social group lead to characteristic deviations of the actual state of conservation from the theoretical social optimum.

This morning I should like to systematize these conditions in a different way because I think it might make a contribution to the clarification of forest taxation problems, which come in at the end of my discussion. What I should like to do today is to differentiate between types of breakdown or malfunctioning of the signaling system of our Western economy, namely the price system. In the absence of such breakdowns and malfunctioning, it may be—and frequently is—contended that this signaling system steers Western economies toward the welfare optimum.

Allow me to differentiate between six types of breakdown or malfunctioning in sequence. Then I shall briefly discuss each of these points:

1. Price signals do not exist on the benefits or on the cost side or on both.
2. Price signals are "distorted" in a defined sense.
3. Price signals vary so much over time that the response is abortive.
4. Price signals are not received by the agent who makes the decisions about resource use, but are received by others.
5. The price signals are misunderstood or ignored by the decision-making agent.
6. Price signals cannot be followed by the decision-making agent.

Price signals do not exist for that important group of benefits and costs of resource use which I like to call "extra-market" benefits and costs. A large portion of them relate to collective goods, that is, goods that are not divisible in consumption. Another portion relates to goods that are divisible in consumption but are not evaluated in the market because of institutional conditions. Resource economistst have been stressing extra-market benefits and costs for a long time. Recently, John Kenneth Galbraith has called special attention to them in his best seller, *The Affluent Society*.[6] Among the special conditions mentioned above, the importance of extra-market benefits and costs is one of the most important.

Next, what is meant by "distorted" price signals? One may differentiate three types of such distortions. To begin with, the price system is obviously dependent on income distribution. An existing income distribution may not be the "ideal" from the standpoint of welfare economics. The ideal distribution may be an equalitarian one, or it may be some other distribution—for example, one favoring an "elite." Further, economists have long been familiar with necessary conditions regarding market form which must be fulfilled if the price system is to steer the economy toward a welfare optimum. The existence of monopolistic competition, of duopoly, and other deviations from pure competition, have been discussed at great length over the last several decades. Finally, the price system may be called distorted if social institutions have lost the identity of "concept" and "structure."[7] Social institutions influence the price system directly and indirectly—through income distribution—in many pervasive ways. These influences must be considered when social institutions are regarded as "constraints" in identifying social optima conceptually or statistically. Distortion of price signals is important for many resource problems, but not any more so than for other aspects of the economy. The conceptual significance of this point and the difficulties of dealing with it through policy measures makes it necessary to emphasize it in any discussion of social optima.

Our third point, namely that price signals vary so much over time that response becomes abortive, is one of the special conditions affecting natural resource economics.[8] There is, for example, the influence of the business cycle and other economic fluctuations upon the depletion of stock resources. For agriculture, there is the problem (which is of interest for forestry too) of acreage fluctuations during booms and depressions on the "extensive" margin between agriculture on one side and range and forests on the other. In good times, agriculture advances upon the range and forest lands, in bad times, it retreats. Sometimes an individual operator may make short-run profits in responding to these price variations. In the long run, however, the response from the standpoint of groups of operators and from the standpoint of society, gives rise to significant social losses through resource depletion. Finally, the economist calls to mind the "explosive" cobweb and other situations of a similar nature where the response to price signals becomes abortive for groups of producers.

Now for "point four:" Price signals are not received by the decision-making agent but by others. In classical and neoclassical economics, these problems appear largely as "external economies and diseconomies." Over the last two or three years, these externalities—or, with a new and rather inappropriate name, "spillover effects"—are becoming popular again in economic writings. Externalities are of many kinds. They may be pecuniary or nonpecuniary, static or dynamic, reversible or irreversible. For public policy, it is necessary to ascertain in each particular case what kind of externality is involved. The term itself has little explanatory value. For this reason, I usually try to avoid it. There is still, in spite of the classical article by Ellis and Fellner,[9] much confusion between externalities which are relevant for national or regional policies and those which are not. In some cases, price signals affect the firm but may affect various decision-making levels differently. In farming, for example, price signals may affect landlord but not tenant—or vice versa. In such cases, the term "external" becomes inapplicable. That price signals are not received by the agent who makes conservation decisions is one of the most important special conditions in natural resource economics. Public conservation policy is largely concerned with these conditions.

The fifth point, that price signals are misunderstood or ignored, occurs in agriculture, grazing, and forestry to the same extent as in other industries. In the past, many writers on conservation have focused on the "ignorance" of resource users—especially in agriculture. One may wonder whether or not many resource problems are explained by "ignorance." A kind of subheading under this point is what may be called "habitat patterns." Decision-making agents may not try to calculate optima or may not even calculate, but, instead, follow patterns of economic behavior which have proved successful for their fathers or neighbors or community leaders. To the extent that decision-making agents behave in this way, they ignore price signals. This type of ignoring price signals is not always detrimental from the standpoint of public policy. Habit patterns may even be used as a tool of policy.

The final point: Price signals are understood but cannot be followed. One important problem in natural resource economics under this point is lack of financial liquidity, which may prevent resource users from following price signals. Likewise, laws, regulations, and customs which exist for quite different social purposes, may prevent a response to price signals.

Let us turn now to the relation of these six points to forest taxation. Taxation is significantly related to all points. Taxation can be used as a substitute for the price system and as a supplementary or countermanding system. The reason for expressing this view regarding the broad usefulness of taxation as a tool for obtaining social objectives of conservation policy is the closer conceptual and operational connection between taxation and public expenditure. Institutionally, also, taxing and spending powers are intricately related. To define social welfare optima in taxation without considering public expenditure is neither conceptually nor operationally meaningful.

First of all, public expenditure is related to taxation because the size of the expenditure budget determines the size of the taxation budget. The size of the taxation budget influences the type of taxes, tax rates, and assessment. We cannot, for example, finance government expenditure by death taxes alone. An increasing portion of national income received by the government tends to shift taxation more and more toward those taxes, such as gross income and turnover taxes, where a relatively small individual bite yields a large total return.

Under fairly restrictive assumptions, one can design, theoretically, a system of taxation which is neutral in terms of the conservation complex; by that, I mean a tax system that does not result in a redistribution of use rates over time. A description of such a system—largely based on net income taxes—would require a detailed discussion of the various types of taxes. This is outside my assignment. You may, however, wish to consult the article which I mentioned at the very beginning. The effect of the various types of taxes on conservation is dealt with there.

Neutrality of the tax system is not necessarily an objective of conservation policy. Taxation has certain features which make it a powerful and effective tool of policy—for good and for bad.

Taxes represent a cash cost. Because of this, taxes are potentially more powerful than the interest rate, which is the most effective "price"—in relation to conservation—of any cost factor.[10] (If all assets are owned free of debt, interest does not create a cash outgo. In this sense, the influence of interest on conservation is not enforced.) As already noted, conservation policy can use this feature of taxation in various ways: it can be used to take the place of the price system; or it can be used to supplement and countermand the price system.

In conservation policy, special emphasis needs to be given to "negative taxation," that is, tax bonuses. Such bonuses may consist of depletion or depreciation allowances, reduction or deferment of taxes, and outright supports and subsidies. All these bonuses may be made dependent on fulfillment by the taxpayer of certain conservation requirements.

Another feature which makes the tax system an effective policy tool is that constitutional and political obstacles against changes are probably less than in making changes in other fields. For example, in the tenure field, the status of private property is involved. The constitutional safeguards in this field are especially strong and political sensitivity is great.

Another advantage of the tax system as a policy tool is its great variability over time. One cannot change property institutions or credit institutions from year to year. Stability over time in these fields is needed for the functioning of western economics. Changes of tax rates from year to year are common. Even changes in assessment and in types of taxes are not infrequent.

By the way of conclusion, let me point out a few implications for future research in the field of forest taxation. What we know about the effects of taxation in resource use is based largely on theory under fairly restrictive assumptions. We know much less about how far the forest owner and operator actually lives up to our theoretical schemes. How far does he maximize? What does he maximize? How does a time enter into his calculations? How does he respond to changes of prices and taxes?

There might be considerable differences in these aspects of economic behavior between different types of forest owners and operators. A large family corporation like Weyerhaeuser, for example, may behave differently than a large nonfamily-owned stock company like International Paper. These two types in turn may behave quite differently than a smaller enterprise or a farmer who merely manages his woodlot. I feel a very important aspect of further research in this whole field is to build appropriate models. There is some confusion in recent literature with respect to the function of models in economics. Economic models are no substitution for economic theories. They are reconstructions of concrete situations of real life designed to test theories. There is a great need for such testing in the area of forest taxation. We have an excellent body of taxation theory and a fair body of public expenditure theory. These theories need to be confirmed or rejected. Such testing involves building models for various types and sizes of forest owners and operators.

Another problem for research which I have encountered frequently, in water economics and agriculture and, I suppose, is present also in forestry, is the effect of various tenure relations between the decision-making agent and the resource. It probably makes a difference, for example, whether processors of trees own the land or whether they buy stumpage standing, as in this country, or cut, as in Central Europe. Models should be designed to take these and other aspects of tenure into account when theories are tested.

A special problem for forest land tenure is created by the gestation period over which land must be held in order to mature a forest crop. Some land may never reach this state. In many ways, such land which, in terms of acreage, forms a large part of "wild" lands, presents more difficult research and policy problems than the commercial forest lands. How do owners and operators of these lands respond to taxation and tax changes? How are responses related to the argument for or against public ownership? Wild lands other than commercial forests are becoming increasingly important for public policy because they yield significant extra-market benefits. The non-commercial wild lands are a field for further research where few attempts have been made to test existing taxation theories through appropriate models.

[1]*Taxation and Conservation of Privately Owned Timber.* University of Oregon, Bureau of Business Research, 1959, 95 pp. (Proceedings of a Conference held at the University of Oregon.)

[2]Ciriacy-Wantrup, S. V., "Taxation and the Conservation of Resources," *The Quarterly Journal of Economics*, Vol. LVIII, February, 1944.

[3]Ciriacy-Wantrup, *Resource Conservation: Economics and Policies* (Berkeley, University of California Press, 1952) Chapter 4.

[4]Ciriacy-Wantrup, *Resource Conservation . . .*, Chapter 18; and Ciriacy-Wantrup, "Economic Criteria for a System of Water Rights," *Land Economics*, Vol. XXXII, No. 4, November 1956.

[5]Ciriacy-Wantrup, *Resource Conservation . . .*, Chapter 17.

[6]J. K. Galbraith, *The Affluent Society* (Boston, Houghton-Mifflin, 1958).

[7]Ciriacy-Wantrup, *Resource Conservation . . .*, Chapter 16.

[8]Ciriacy-Wantrup, "Resource Conservation and Economic Stability," *The Quarterly Journal of Economics*, Vol. LX, May, 1946.

[9]H. S. Ellis and William Fellner, "External Economies and Diseconomies," *The American Economic Review*, September, 1943.

[10]Ciriacy-Wantrup, *Resource Conservation . . .*, Chapter 7.

Chapter 16

MULTIPLE USE AS A CONCEPT
FOR WATER AND RANGE POLICY*[1]

Multiple Use: A Perennial Topic

My assignment covers what may be called a perennial topic in natural resource policy both in the academic and in the political arena.

In looking back over the many contributions of the Water and Range Committees of the Western Agricultural Economics Research Council, the multiple-use theme recurs in a number of variations from the meeting of the Water Committee in 1951 up to the meeting of the Range Committee in 1959. The papers by Drs. Kelso and Upchurch at the latter meeting deal explicitly with today's topic.[2]

For me, the topic is an especially hardy perennial. One of my first papers after coming to California was under the title "Multiple and Optimum Use of Wild Land under Different Economic Conditions."[3] Although published 23 years ago, I was tempted to read it today. I was afraid, however, that my colleagues present here would not let me get away with such an easy discharge of my obligation.

Shifting our backward glance from the academic to the political arena, the multiple-use topic is even older. It seems to have arisen as a reaction to the narrow-use policy implicit in the U. S. Forest Reserve Act of 1897. Since that time, the concept has been one of the most significant ones for the administration and management of the U. S. National Forests. It has been continuously and hotly debated inside and outside the Forest Service.

In view of this perennial nature of the topic, it is not easy to say something that has not been said before. In any event, I should like to confine myself to three selected aspects that still appear interesting and relevant at the present juncture.

First, multiple use will be considered as a concept in the economic theory

*Reprinted from *Water and Range Resources and Economic Development of the West: Economic Analysis of Multiple Use. The Arizona Watershed Program—A Case Study of Multiple Use.* Report No. 9, Western Agricultural Economics Research Council. Tucson, 1961, pp. 1-11.

of natural resource allocation. A question will be raised regarding the logic of using the concept as an objective or a criterion for public allocation policy. The conceptual and operational usefulness of "optimum use" will be appraised as an alternative to "multiple use." Second, the history of the multiple-use concept will be traced in public policy affecting resource allocation in the U. S. National Forests. This history is of interest for the third aspect, for appraising whether the multiple-use concept can serve for public policy as a part of allocative systems irrespective of its usefulness in the economic theory of resource allocation.

Multiple Use as a Concept in the Economic Theory of Natural Resource Allocation

In economic theory, multiple use of natural resources is the actual or hypothetical result of economic conditions, including those influenced by public policy. That multiple use is a common result of economic conditions does not mean, however, that such an outcome is always necessary economically or desirable for policy. To regard multiple use as a general objective or criterion for policy is not warranted logically—it puts, if you permit, the cart before the horse.

Whether or not multiple use actually occurs is determined by the economics of joint production. These have been discussed elsewhere.[4] Economists know that relations between uses may be complementary, competitive, or independent. These relations are defined through marginal benefits and costs or, more precisely, through the second cross partial derivatives of benefit and cost functions. The occurrence of multiple use depends, therefore, on levels ("intensity") of uses under static assumptions and on changes of cost and benefit functions over time. Thus, multiple use may be merely a passing phase following upon or being followed by single use, both in terms of levels of uses and in terms of time.

To analyze under what conditions multiple use replaces or is replaced by single use is one of the most important tasks of resource economics. Such an analysis is identical with an investigation of changes in the optimum combination of uses. For a given resource, for example, the scenic qualities of an area of land, a population of plants or animals, a flow or stock of water or oil, we are dealing with the problem of optimum resource allocation among uses. Differentiation between resources and uses is not merely semantic. A part of some current confusion in the economic analysis of outdoor recreation, for example, is due to the fact that recreational resources and recreational uses are not distinguished. Since uses are frequently different between private and public users, and since private users are frequently specialized with respect to uses, the problem of optimum resource allocation among uses is intricately related to that among users.

Quantitative determination of optimum resource allocation is a goal of many current studies in economics. Encouragement for such attempts comes from the impact of formal programming during the last decade.[5] In resource economics, judicious expansion of quantification is desirable for reasons often not sufficiently appreciated.[6] On the other hand, quantitative optimizing involves serious difficulties that are often overlooked. Time does not permit dealing with them in detail. But exploration of the concept "optimum use" is unavoidable here in order to appraise its significance as an alternative of "multiple use."

The difficulties are more severe for optimizing in public policy than for optimizing in subsectors of the economy such as individual farms and firms. My assignment is to focus on the former. It may also be mentioned that these difficulties apply no less to informal programming, for example, benefit-cost analysis, than to the formal kind. However, they are more concealed in the implicit assumptions of formal programming and its comparative efficiency, and the precision of its results tends more toward overlooking its limitations.

Difficulties of quantitative optimizing in public resource allocation may be discussed as three interrelated problem areas which may be called: (1) the problem of valuation, (2) the problem of institutional constraints, and (3) the problem of uncertainty.

The problem of valuation has recently been discussed elsewhere.[7] For this problem area, therefore, I can be brief. Absence of market prices leads to a systematic bias if optimum use is calculated on the basis of market prices. Recreational uses are especially affected. A good illustration is the repeated refusal (withdrawn only recently) of the U. S. General Service Administration to sell military surplus land in the Bay Area to the state of California and the City of San Francisco for development as a park. The explicitly stated reason was that such land is "too valuable" for recreational use and should be used for subdivisions instead. No attempt was made to investigate what the comparative value for recreational use actually would be. The statutory discount from existing market prices that applies when surplus land is sold for public use was regarded as sufficient support for classifying use for subdivisions as optimum.

Absence of market prices, however, is only a small part of the difficulties. More significant is the question: To what extent are market prices, where they exist, valid and relevant indicators for public policy? The functioning and the results of the price system are profoundly influenced by public policy through income distribution, market structure, taxation, property rights, and in many other ways. Quantitative optimizing looks at these influences as institutional conditions that— together with the technological ones—are introduced into the optimizing calculus as constraints. The implications are so important that two of them need to be mentioned in the present context.

First, when social institutions are used as constraints, they become conceptually indistinguishable from policy objectives. In this respect, they are different from technological constraints. In natural resource policy, changes of social institutions are among the most significant controllable variables and relations. In other words, in natural resource policy, social institutions must frequently be regarded as means rather than ends of policy. Hence, the distinction in quantitative optimizing between the part of the model that constitutes the "objective function" to be maximized or minimized and the part that constitutes the constraints describing the structure of the operation and the relations between variables becomes misleading if the conceptual difference between technological and institutional constraints is not sufficiently recognized.

Secondly, when social institutions are used as constraints in a quantitative optimizing calculus, a new optimum must be calculated for each combination of constraints that is considered. The optima calculated for different sets of constraints are then compared. Recently, a whole literature has grown up around this approach, known as "the theory of second best."[8] This term merely indicates that there is at least one constraint additional to the ones existing in the so-called "Pareto optimum."[9]

The exponents of this theory claim that the major contribution is a negative one: If a deviation from one of the Pareto optimum conditions prevails, the best course of action is not an attempt to attack this deviation and keep all others intact. On the contrary, a second-best solution is usually obtained only by departing from all other Pareto conditions. To apply only a part of the Pareto conditions would move the economy away from rather than toward a second-best position. In consequence, the exponents of this theory direct their criticism against what they call "piecemeal welfare economics."

If this criticism is valid—I believe it has some merit—does it not point to a basic weakness in the logic of economic optimizing itself? If one tries to avoid the futility of piecemeal welfare economics and strives for bold changes in the combination of constraints, can one be sure that quantitative optima are comparable in a meaningful way? Is it not unavoidable that such bold changes affect some structural elements of the optimizing calculus— among them especially preferences, technology, and the motivation of human agents in their various functions in the economy? Are we not confronted with a problem of identification, in the econometric sense, on a grand scale?

In view of these questions, I should like to submit that "optimum use" is a construct in the sense of a useful scientific fiction.[10] Such a construct is not a quantitatively specifiable policy objective. In the strict mathematical sense, "optimum use" is not operational. There is danger that the two are confused when attempts are made to use quantitative optimizing as a basis for decisions in public allocation policy.

The conceptual usefulness of optimizing in the analysis of the private and the social economics of natural resources has been explained in detail elsewhere.[11] No repetition is needed here. The following discussion is not concerned with the construct but with the quantitative specification of an optimum allocation of natural resources in policy decisions.

Let us turn, first, to the difficulties in quantitative optimizing created by uncertainty. The probability of some uncertainties, for example, the occurrence of floods, drought, and hailstorms, can be measured quantitatively. Economists frequently refer to these uncertainties as "risk." Techniques to allow for uncertainties of this kind are being developed in formal programming.

On the other hand, the probability of the most important uncertainties, those created by changes of technology, of preferences, and of institutions, is not amenable to precise quantitative measurement. At best, the direction, the relative speed, and the range of such changes can be vaguely projected. This kind of uncertainty imposes severe and, as far as I can see, insurmountable limits on the validity and relevance of quantitative optimizing for policy decisions.

Practitioners of formal programming who are also competent economists are aware of these limitations. Robert Dorfman, for example, in a recent article appraising operations research, states: "Another important limitation, in which less progress has been made, is that linear programming formulations do not allow for uncertainty."[12]

In the economics of flow resources, allowance for uncertainty is best made through the formulation of the policy objective itself. Such a formulation I have called "the safe minimum standard of conservation." A detailed explanation of the theoretical development of this concept and its operational application is found elsewhere.[13] Time limitations permit merely stating that one aspect of the economic rationale of the safe minimum standard as a policy objective is to minimize maximum possible social losses connected with avoidable irreversibilities. In this respect, the safe minimum standard of conservation may be regarded as a conceptual relative of the min-max solution or "saddle-point" in a two-person, strictly determined game.[14] This is not to suggest, however, that all aspects of the economics of flow resources should be forced into the framework of modern game theory—as "man playing against nature" in an almost literal sense.

It is interesting to observe that the more sophisticated practitioners of formal programming formulate their models in such a way that the three difficulties just reviewed are involved as little as possible. The resulting models, however, are engineering rather than economic ones. Examples in water resources programming are Dorfman's "Simple Valley" and Tolley's "Optimal Water Allocation."[15] The former model is purely hypothetical, designed to illustrate the technique. The latter model deals ex post with an actual allocation among users through existing social institutions. Under assumptions most favorable to formal programming, allocative efficiency is improved by no more than five per cent. Careful comparative studies of this kind are only too rare.

Quantitative allocation may actually be harmful because it introduces an element of rigidity into public policy. Such allocation is based on detailed and usually expensive studies that cannot be repeated year after year. This becomes important under dynamic conditions when demands for different uses are changing rapidly over time at different rates or even in different directions. Let me illustrate this point by an example from range resources.

In 1947, after several years of detailed study through the California-Oregon Interstate Deer Herd Committee, optimum allocation of forage on the deer winter range, used by livestock during the spring and summer, was determined on a 50-50 basis. The logic of this particular ratio as an optimum allocation has never been satisfactorily explained to me. But I am more concerned now with the problem of rigidity.

During each season, livestock has the first crack at the forage; the deer have to take what is left. During dry years, it is largely the deer that suffer. Faced with a series of dry years during the 1950's, game managers, constrained by the 50-50 ratio, had no other choice but to reduce the herd through opening the season for does. During the same period, demand for hunting increased at a rate far greater than the demand for livestock. Hunting pressure on the bucks increased correspondingly. At the present juncture, measures will be necessary to conserve the remnants of the interstate herd. Game managers are under heavy public criticism. This criticism appears not entirely just. The crux of the matter is that, under conditions of economic change, a quantitative allocation tends to become a harmful constraint for policy.

On the positive side, it may be concluded that resource programming must include the programming of social institutions. Resources programming must be pragmatic; that is, it must regard institutions as means (tools or obstacles), as well as ends (objectives), depending on the purposes of the analysis.[16] In natural resource policy, an analytically oriented institutional economics is by no means obsolete.

In such an approach, institutions are regarded as structured systems, each with particular patterns of change over time. These systems can be analyzed in structure, functioning, performance, and change over time. In the jargon currently in vogue, such systems may be called "optimizing systems." Their purpose, however, is not to obtain quantitative optima of social welfare at given points in time under conditions projected for these points. Rather, their purpose is to increase social welfare continuously under constantly changing conditions that at any point in time can be projected only vaguely and are always uncertain with respect to actual occurrence. Responsiveness of these systems to economic change is more important than their efficiency in optimizing under particular sets of projected conditions.

It follows that to appraise the performance of these systems by introducing arbitrary temporal cross-sections of them as alternative constraints is inadequate. Performance can be appraised only by criteria applied to alternative systems as they function over time. In this functioning, direction, speed, and range of changes brought about by them are especially important. Criteria need not always be pecuniary. For a system that is of special interest for water allocation, namely, water law, it has been shown elsewhere that nonpecuniary criteria can effectively be employed.[17] Such an appraisal is an integral part of the field of economics, which includes econometrics, but is not restricted to it.

Multiple Use as a Concept in Public Policy Affecting Resource Allocation in the U. S. National Forests

If the foregoing reasoning is correct, it may not be a waste of time to take another look at the concept "multiple use." True, as a theoretical construct, it must be replaced in the economic theory of resource allocation by the concept "optimum use." Still, in view of the difficulties just reviewed in applying the latter concept in public policy in terms of quantitative allocations, one may ask whether the concept "multiple use" can serve as a part of allocative systems in spite of lack of usefulness in economic theory. As already mentioned, there is evidence concerning such a role of the multiple-use concept. This evidence is available over many years in public policy affecting resource allocation in the U. S. National Forests.

Following the legislation of 1891, establishing the National Forests, the Forest Reserve Act of 1897 limited their expansion to areas where water flow and timber were the dominant uses. Land more valuable for agricultural purposes and minerals was specifically excluded. Forage and recreation were not mentioned as important uses. The emphasis on water flow, of course, was necessary because it made establishment of federal forests constitutionally possible on the basis of the Interstate Commerce clause. In essence, however, the 1897 Act favored a single use, namely, timber.

In 1905, administration of National Forests was transferred from the Department of the Interior to the Department of Agriculture under the leadership of Gifford Pinchot. Immediately after this transfer, the concept "multiple use" was inaugurated, not in name but in fact. All important potential uses, besides timber, were referred to in the first issue of a booklet that, in its later issues, became known as the *Forest Service Manual*. This emphasis was repeated in all subsequent revisions of the *Manual*—the first being issued in 1906. At least since the beginning of the 1930's, the term "multiple use" has become generally accepted.

One important structural aspect of this development needs emphasis. The *Forest Service Manuals* did not spell out a criterion by which potential uses could be quantitatively combined. This left a great deal of discretion to administrative officers at different levels. This administrative discretion was not defined by later statutes. Even the "Multiple-Use, Sustained Yield Act" of 1960[18] still leaves essential decisions to administrative discretion. Thus, the multiple-use concept was essentially developed by and for the administration of the National Forests. The concept, therefore, must be appraised as a part of an *administrative* system of resource allocation.

In appraising the social performance of this allocative system, one must note that the multiple-use concept gave the administration of the National Forests the flexibility needed to counteract the single-use philosophy of the 1897 Act. The concept facilitated administration and expansion of the National Forests under western conditions where forage was and still is a significant use. The concept made possible the gradual acceptance by the Forest Service and by economic interests of recreation as an important and, in many areas, a dominant use. Here again, such acceptance, for example, through setting aside areas in the various categories of "wilderness," "wild," "primitive," and "roadless," was and is an administrative, not a legislative, decision. Generally speaking, administrative discretion is less objectionable in the structure of an allocative system if a competent and devoted civil service exists. In this respect, the Forest Service is one the the best in the country.

One may conclude that this administrative system of resource allocation, with the multiple-use concept as an important part, has responded well to changes of economic conditions when such changes favored replacing a single use, namely, timber, by multiple use, including timber, forage, and recreation. In such a situation, the multiple use concept gave flexibility to the allocative system for responding in a socially desirable direction with adequate promptness and extent.

I am well aware, of course, that the administration of the Forest Service is frequently criticized for responding to pressure by economic interests too much or not enough—depending on who does the criticizing. For example, the Forest Service policy of gradually reducing grazing permits has been criticized by grazing interests. I believe this policy is a more adequate response to changing economic conditions than the "optimum" quantitative allocation of the range between livestock and deer referred to previously.

The extent and the administration of the various categories of wilderness areas have been criticized from all sides. The timber, grazing, and some water interests wish these areas reduced and their administration liberalized. Some influential recreation interests wish them protected more securely and enlarged. Here again, the response of the allocative system to changing economic conditions has been adequate. But I should like to confine this statement primarily to past performance. The reason is the following.

In the past, as just shown, the multiple-use concept imparted flexibility to the allocative system in the right direction; namely, when replacement of a single use—timber—through multiple use was economically and socially desirable. The question arises: Will the multiple-use concept impede flexibility of the allocative system when a change in the opposite direction is desirable, that is, when multiple use should be replaced by single use? This question is posed by economic changes that point to recreational use as the dominant use on large areas under the administration of the Forest Service. The characteristics of these economic changes were analyzed 23 years ago in the paper mentioned in the beginning.[19] Politically, this question has already become acute.

In some quarters, multiple use is being used as an argument in favor of reducing wilderness and other areas devoted largely to recreational use. Strong interests on the other side believe that administrative classification by the Forest Service is not a sufficient protection for wilderness areas. They argue that special statutory protection must be given to such areas. Some go even so far as to advocate transfer of wilderness areas from the National Forests to the National Parks. In the National Parks, recreational uses are established as dominant by statute. The last Congress saw the introduction of a bill generally known as the "Wilderness Bill" (S. 1123) that would give statutory protection to all wilderness areas in a National Wilderness Preservation System. In such a system, wilderness areas in National Forests, National Parks, National Wildlife Refuges, and National Ranges would be included. But, otherwise, this bill would not interfere with existing administration. The same or similar legislation will, no doubt, be introduced in the 1961 Congress.

It is not easy to take a definite position in these controversial matters without being misinterpreted by some interested group. On the other hand, resource economists have some responsibility here in terms of the topic of this paper. Let us not shirk this responsibility.

It is fairly obvious, I believe, that the increase in the demand for recreational uses relative to the increase in the demand for all other uses will be so great that ways must be found to make other uses such as timber and grazing compatible with recreation in areas where one of these other uses is now dominant. The technological problems are not too difficult. Compatibility is largely a question of economics and of enforcing appropriate regulations of lumbering and grazing practices. Such practices should first be firmly established on public land. In the future, however, a good portion of both public *and* private land used for timber and grazing will also be needed for recreation. In this perspective, multiple use will remain a useful concept in natural resource policy.

But compatibility with wilderness recreation is a different question. To preserve wilderness values, regulations must be so strict that grazing and lumbering will usually be uneconomic.

There are three economic factors to consider in deciding whether wilderness areas should be reduced or preserved: first, the uncertainty of future changes in demand for various types of outdoor recreation; second, the irreversibility of depletion of wilderness resources, and the consequent permanent loss of flexibility if such areas are once developed; and third, the low value of wilderness areas for timber, grazing, and readily accessible recreation. These considerations have been developed in detail elsewhere, with emphasis on the uncertainty and irreversibility problems.[20]

On the basis of these considerations, the "Wilderness Bill"—or a bill similar to it—should be enacted now. Those who fear that a change from administrative to statutory protection is contrary to the principle of flexibility stressed above should not forget that the *direction* and *speed* of change are no less important considerations for structuring an allocative system than the provision for change *per se*.

A transfer of wilderness areas to the Park Service would not seem desirable. Park Service policy is a rigid, single-use policy even with respect to different recreational uses, and even if potential additional recreational uses are complementary to existing ones. The wilderness areas of the National Parks are closed to all hunting and to those hikers and friends of nature who object to keeping their dogs on a leash at all times. Serious wildlife problems have arisen in some parks because of lack of hunting. If a National Wilderness Preservation System is established, a transfer of wilderness areas from the National Parks to the National Forests would seem sounder than a transfer in the opposite direction.

Conclusions

What are the conclusions of this survey of "multiple use" as a concept for water and range policy? They have already been implied, but a short summary may be helpful.

First, as a theoretical construct in the determination of objectives or criteria of public policy, the concept "multiple use" must be replaced by "optimum use." This conclusion is not surprising to professional economists. But it needs emphasis at the present juncture because powerful economic interests are insisting that "multiple use" *per se* constitutes an objective or a criterion for public policy.

Second, "optimum use," although superior to "multiple use" as a theoretical construct, is limited in its quantitative specification by three difficulties called here the problems of valuation, of institutional constraints, and of uncertainty. The concept should not be applied in allocation policy in terms of quantitative optimizing under particular sets of projected conditions. Instead, it should be interpreted in terms of direction, speed, and range of continuous reallocation in response to constantly changing conditions that can be projected only vaguely and are always uncertain with respect to actual occurrence.

Third, for applying the concept "optimum use" in the latter interpretation, social institutions and their changes are of paramount interest. Historically, the multiple-use concept has been an important part of such an institution, namely, the legislation and administration affecting allocation of forest and range resources within the U. S. National Forests. Administration of the federal forests constitutes an allocative system for forest and range resources that is reviewed here with respect to structure, functioning, and performance. For water resources, likewise, an allocative system exists that has been studied elsewhere.

Fourth, in the past, the allocative system, of which multiple use has been an important part since the beginning of the century, has performed well. The multiple-use concept gave flexibility to the system for responding in a socially desirable direction with adequate promptness and extent. During this period, changes of economic conditions favored replacing a single use, namely, timber, by multiple use, including timber, forage, and recreation.

Fifth, in view of the uncertainty about future demands for the various types of recreation, the irreversible nature of depletion of wilderness areas, and their relatively low value for other uses, the large degree of administrative discretion which was shown to be characteristic for the structure of the existing allocative system should, looking into the future, be supplemented by statutory provisions similar to the "Wilderness Bill" (S. 1123) introduced in the 1960 Congress. This supplement is needed in order to insure an adequate response of the allocative system when changing economic conditions favor one particular use, namely, recreation. Still, the multiple-use concept will remain an important and useful part of the system. Extension of the concept to similar systems, for example, the administration of the national parks and of the national game ranges, would seem desirable.

[1]*Water and Range Resources and Economic Development of the West: Economic Analysis of Multiple Use. The Arizona Watershed Program — A Case Study of Multiple Use.* Report No. 9. Conference Proceedings of the Committee on the Economics of Water Resources Development and Committee on the Economics of Range Use and Development, Western Agricultural Economics Research Council. Tucson, 1961, pp. 1-11.

[2]M. M. Kelso, "Objectives of Public Resource Allocation," and M. L. Upchurch, "Resoure Allocation Under Conditions of Multiple Use of Land," *Economic Research in the Use and Development of Range Resources, Economics of Range and Multiple Land Use* (Logan, Utah, 1959), pp. 117-129 and 135-147. (Report No. 2, Conference Proceedings of the Committee on the Economics of Range Use and Development, Western Agricultural Economics Research Council.)

[3]S. V. Ciriacy-Wantrup, "Multiple and Optimum Use of Wild Land under Different Economic Conditions," *Journal of Forestry,* Vol. XXXVI, no. 7, July 1938, pp. 665-674.

[4]S. V. Ciriacy-Wantrup, "Economics of Joint Costs in Agriculture," *Journal of Farm Economics,* Vol. XXIII, No. 4, November, 1941, pp. 771-818. See also: S. V. Ciriacy-Wantrup, *Resource Conservation: Economics and Policies* (Berkeley: University of California Press, 1952), Chapter V.

[5]The origin of formal programming — as *linear* programming — is generally dated with the unpublished papers by Jerome Cornfield (1941) and G. B. Dantzig (1947). The latter paper was published as "Maximization of a Linear Function of Variables Subject to Linear Inequalities" in T. C. Koopman's (ed.) *Activity Analysis of Production and Allocation* (New York: John Wiley and Sons, 1951). The title of the Dantzig paper can serve as a definition of linear programming.

[6]S. V. Ciriacy-Wantrup, "Benefit-Cost Analysis and Public Resource Development," *Journal of Farm Economics,* Vol. XXXVII, No. 4, November, 1955. (Chapter 8 in this book.)

[7]S. V. Ciriacy-Wantrup, "Philosophy and Objectives of Watershed Policy," *Economics of Watershed Planning,* ed. G. S. Tolley and F. E. Riggs (Ames: Iowa State College Press, 1960), pp. 1-14. (Chapter 6 in this book.)

[8]R. G. Lipsey and R. K. Lancaster, "The General Theory of Second Best," *The Review of Economic Studies,* Vol. XXIV (1), No. 63, 1956-1957, pp. 11-32. The earlier literature is cited in this article.

[9]Vilfredo Pareto, *Cours d'Economique Politique* (Lausanne: F. Route, Libraire-Editeur, 1897). An excellent bibliography of welfare economics is

appended to: E. J. Mishan, "A Survey of Welfare Economics, 1939-1959," *The Economic Journal*, Vol. LXX, June, 1960, pp. 197-265.

[10]The nature of scientific fiction as a class of constructs was explained elsewhere: "A fiction is permissible in science if its character is clearly understood. A fiction is a deliberate, conscious deviation from reality. A fiction, however, is not a hyothesis or theory. By itself, a fiction is not intended to be validated by testing with empirical evidence. But a scientific fiction should be useful as a stimulus for or as a part of hypotheses and theories which *can* be so tested. That means the test of a scientific fiction is its conceptual usefulness, its expediency, in understanding, explaining, and predicting reality. A fiction becomes mere dogma and, therefore, unscientific, if its two characteristics—consciousness of its fictional nature and conceptual usefulness—are obliterated. There are many examples in the history of science of fictions changing into dogma." See S. V. Ciriacy-Wantrup, "Policy Considerations in Farm Management Research in the Decade Ahead," *Journal of Farm Economics*, Vol. 38, No. 5, December, 1956, pp. 1301-1311.

[11]S. V. Ciriacy-Wantrup, *Resource Conservation, op. cit.*, especially chapters 6, 17, and 18.

[12]Robert Dorfman, "Operations Research," *The American Economic Review*, Vol. 50, No. 4, September, 1960, pp. 575-623.

[13]S. V. Ciriacy-Wantrup, *Resource Conservation, op. cit.*, especially chapters 17 and 18.

[14]Johann von Neumann and Oskar Morganstern, *Theory of Games and Economic Behavior* (New Jersey: Princeton University Press, 1944), 625 pp. See also: Robert Dorfman, Paul A. Samuelson, and Robert M. Solow, *Linear Programming and Economic Analysis* (New York: McGraw-Hill Book Co., 1958), chapters 15 and 16.

[15]Robert Dorfman, "Simple Valley," *Economics of Watershed Planning,* ed. G. S. Tolley and F. E. Riggs (Ames: Iowa State College Press, 1960), 352 pp., and G. S. Tolley and V. S. Hastings, "Optimal Water Allocation," *Quarterly Journal of Economics*, Vol. 74, No. 2, May, 1960.

[16]For an interesting statement on the schism between "orthodox" and "pragmatic" attitudes toward social institutions, see: F. O. Sargent, "A Methodological Schism in Agricultural Economics," *Canadian Journal of Agricultural Economics*, Vol. 8, No. 2, 1960, pp. 45-52.

[17]S. V. Ciriacy-Wantrup, "Concepts Used as Economic Criteria for a System of Water Rights," *Land Economics*, Vol. XXXII, No. 4, November, 1956, pp. 295-312. Also published in *The Law of Water Allocation in the Eastern United States*, ed. David Haber and Stephen W. Bergen (New York: The Ronald Press Co., 1958), pp. 531-552.

[18]Public Law 86-17, 86th Cong. H. R. 10572, 74 Stat. 215, June, 1960.

[19]S. V. Ciriacy-Wantrup, "Multiple and Optimum Use of Wild Land under Different Economic Conditions" *op. cit.*

[20]S. V. Ciriacy-Wantrup, *Resource Conservation, op. cit.*, especially chapter 18.

Part V

NATURAL RESOURCES
IN ECONOMIC DEVELOPMENT

INTRODUCTION TO PART V

by

Terrence Veeman*

Wantrup was keenly interested in the roles of natural resources and institutions in the growth process. Toward the latter stages of his career, he became involved in supervising several doctoral students who were engaged in analyzing agricultural and resource problems in less developed nations. Wantrup's theoretical and policy insights, drawn from his European background and his many years of study of resource problems in the United States, proved valuable in the analysis of natural resource issues, especially water and land issues, in poor nations. Many renewable resource problems which are emerging in Third World regions—questions of surface water development and allocation, ground water depletion, salinity control and drainage, and land use—posed analytical and policy challenges that were similar to ones he had faced in his home state of California. Wantrup was always sensitive, however, that institutional and policy solutions in other nations would have to be adapted to their particular socio-economic conditions and historical traditions.

In the paper which follows, Wantrup expresses skepticism about the validity and relevance of the supposed declining role of natural resources in the growth process. His cautionary note pre-dates the "energy crisis" and the decade of the 1970's in which rural land may well have been a rising proportion of national wealth in nations such as the United States and Canada. Moreover, his unease foreshadows our current concerns of trying to deal more adequately with growth and productivity accounting. We cannot merely deal with the role of measured inputs in measured GNP growth; our conceptual horizons must be widened to include the increasingly important extra-market services provided by amenity resources as well as the extra-market costs imposed through pollution and the transformation and loss of natural environments.

Wantrup argued that the most significant resource conservation and public policy problems were likely to involve renewable resources with critical zones, rather than non-renewable or stock resources for which changing technology had been such a dominating force historically. Since

---

*Professor of Economics, University of Alberta

1973, much public and academic attention has focused on the scarcity of fossil fuel and mineral resources. In fact, many economists now tend to think that the essence of natural resource economics is the Hotelling problem of husbanding natural resource stocks over time. Such preoccupation should not blind us to the fact that the management of renewable resources poses equally important problems for mankind.

The second major theme of the following paper is the role of institutions and institutional change in the growth process—a subject close to Wantrup's heart. The failure of institutional reforms to provide a strong engine of economic growth in the agricultural sectors of poor nations in the 1950's led to the conventional wisdom of the 1960's that technological change was the dominant influence in economic and agricultural development. During the last fifteen years, economists have continued to struggle to sort out the complex roles of technological and institutional change in the development process. In Wantrup's eyes, institutions—such as property rights in land or water—should be regarded as social decision making systems or rules. He saw institutional change occurring primarily in the political arena rather than the market place—the outcome of the relative pressures of conflicting interest groups in the political process. It is probably fair to say that Wantrup would be skeptical of the theory of induced institutional innovation which has arisen in the 1970's in which changing relative factor prices are seen to play a leading role in inducing changes in institutions. Rather, Wantrup's challenge to the profession would be to place the element of conflict of various interest groups closer to the heart of the analysis of institutional change. In practical economic terms, this often implies analyzing the incidence of the benefits and costs of institutional (and technological) change.

Wantrup's general approach to resource management problems in poor nations is clearly illustrated in his comments on the design of appropriate water institutions in Northern India under the impact of the green revolution. The full potential of high-yielding variety technology would never be realized, he felt, unless suitable water policies were implemented. Public water policy, in turn, could only be implemented through changes in water institutions. The research which I completed under his direction pointed to the conclusion that the existing system of ground water rights in Northern India would prove inefficient, inequitable, and increasingly unsuited to the environmental and economic conditions of that region. A system of correlative rights, based on the common property concept, could be helpful in the solution of emerging ground water problems such as excessive depletion. India and many other poor nations also need improved water organizations such as water users' associations or public districts. Since institutional change typically creates differential gains for some and losses for others, Wantrup was under no illusion that the introduction and modification of water institutions would be an easy task. Neither policy analysts nor government could take merely a passive role in implementing changes in water institutions. Wantrup's legacy of thought on resource conservation and on institutions and institutional change remains relevant and useful in analyzing resource problems in less developed nations.

Chapter 17

NATURAL RESOURCES
IN ECONOMIC GROWTH:
THE ROLE OF INSTITUTIONS AND POLICIES[*][1]

Focus of this Paper

During the last ten years, it has become the fashion among economists to emphasize the decreasing importance of natural resources in economic growth. This applies especially to the renewable resources used by agriculture (21, 23). Use of these resources is strongly influenced by economic institutions, both in developed and underdeveloped economies. It is not surprising, therefore, that there has been, in recent literature, a de-emphasis of the role of institutions paralleling that of natural resources. In the current mathematical models of economic growth, the role of institutions is not explicitly considered (11, 14, 10). In a well-known book on transforming traditional agriculture (24), the author devotes the only two pages on the influence of economic institutions to land tenancy.[2]

Emphasis has shifted from natural resources and economic institutions to technological change or, in production function terminology, to "new" or "modern" factors of production. If institutions are considered at all, they are treated as factors furnishing services like other factors of production. Changes in the kind and quantity of institutional services are regarded as determined by an economic demand-supply scheme (22).

In accordance with my assignment, I should like to focus on this doctrine of the decreasing importance of natural resources and the relatively insignificant and passive role of institutions in economic growth. I should like to analyze its validity, inquire into its relevancy, and show its implications for policy in developing countries.

Decreasing Importance of Natural Resources
in Economic Growth?

The doctrine of the decreasing importance of natural resources in economic growth is based on the observation, documented largely for the United

*Reproduced, with permission, from the *American Journal of Agricultural Economics* 51(5):1314–1324 (December 1969).

States, that the shares of agriculture and of agricultural land in the national income have decreased in the course of economic growth. Two questions arise with respect to this observation.

First, does the fact that the income shares of agriculture and agricultural land have decreased in the United States since the last quarter of the nineteenth century mean that the income shares of all natural resources used by agriculture, including those used also by the rest of the economy, have decreased? Further, can the experience with the agricultural sector in the United States during a particular period of economic history be extrapolated to other sectors, other time periods, and other national economies?

Second, even if the first question can be answered in the affirmative, what is the meaning of a decreasing income share in terms of the "importance" of natural resources in economic growth? What are the implications for explaining, projecting, and influencing economic growth?

Let us turn to the first question. The natural resources used by agriculture are mainly land, water, and climate. All three are used also by industry, transportation, urban settlements, and recreation. For this reason, referring to differences in demand elasticities for the products of agriculture on the one side and those of the industrial, transportation, urban, and recreational sectors on the other and then equating agriculture with natural resources are not permissible.

Shifts of these natural resources out of agriculture into other uses proceed at different rates and with different geographical impact. In California, for example, the shifts of agricultural land and water into industrial, transportation, urban, and recreational uses is a relatively recent phenomenon but has progressed further than in other parts of the country (7). This shift involves price increases for natural resources that are frequently a multiple of prices prevailing in agriculture. Admittedly, the quantities of land and water used in agriculture are still large compared with those used in other sectors.[3] But this relationship is changing in favor of nonagricultural uses.

Next, we may note that the decrease in the income share of agriculture in the United States took place in a period of history when the terms of trade moved against agriculture internationally for a number of specific historical reasons which are not likely to recur in the same combination. Terms of trade were affected by the expansion of agriculture into less-developed regions, the mechanization and intensification of agriculture in more developed regions, and, cyclically, by economic fluctuations—especially during the 50-year "cycle" connected with the name of Kondratieff (3). Cyclical effects are distorting when income shares of sectors and factors are compared for periods, such as census years, falling into different phases of economic fluctuations.

With respect to climate and the increasingly important group of amenity resources—such as scenic attractions, public parks, clean water and air, and wilderness areas—it is difficult or impossible to evaluate shares in national income and wealth because the market system furnishes prices only incompletely or not at all. Still, there is little doubt that the significance of these resources for the location of industry and nonagricultural residence—including second homes—and for the income shares going to transportation, communication, and other services has greatly increased in the United States during the same period for which a decrease in the importance of natural resources is being claimed. There is also little doubt that the price society must pay for safeguarding the quality of these resources is increasing greatly and will continue to do so in the future.

With respect to natural resources originating and mainly used outside of agriculture, such as minerals and energy resources, there is evidence that their income shares have increased in the United States in some periods and decreased in others (19). Here, also, the effect of economic fluctuations is significant.

In summary, then, we should be cautious in extrapolating an observation that applies to agriculture and agricultural land in the United States during a particular period of its economic history to all natural resources, time periods, and economies. On the basis of the available evidence, the validity of such extrapolation appears at least questionable. The possibilities for such extrapolation depend on the type of natural resource considered, on the type of technological change that interacts with the resource, on factors affecting the terms of trade of the products of the resource, and, last but not least, on the degree to which the resource is integrated into the market system.

Let us now turn to our second question and disregard for a moment the cautionary remarks just made. What does the alleged decreasing "importance" of natural resources in economic growth mean for explaining and projecting economic growth and for public policy aimed at generating and influencing economic growth? The reply, I am afraid, must be that it is irrelevant.

A decreasing income share may be due to greater efficiencies in a sector favored by technological change, making its product cheaper—especially if demand elasticities are low—and/or releasing factors for other employment. Are we to argue that such a sector or the services employed in it have become less important for economic growth? The opposite would seem more plausible.

A decreasing income share of a sector, on the other hand, may be due to the growth of other sectors producing substitutes for particular uses. Historically, this has been the case in many minerals and energy resources (charcoal, bituminous coal, sperm oil, etc.). Still, this does not indicate that the individual natural resources replaced in particular uses and the larger groups of the natural resources to which they belong have become less important in economic growth.

The whole question of the importance or unimportance of natural resources in economic growth to which so much attention has been devoted in the last ten years, generously financed by some research foundations, appears rather banal. In the relation that one may call the resources function, all relevant variables are important (5, Ch. 3). Nobody has yet claimed that natural resources are irrelevant in economic growth. In the continuously changing interplay of challenge and response between natural environment and human culture, it is meaningless to say that the challenge is less important than the response. Both are a part of the same system—that of human ecology. If there were no challenge, there would be no response. And, I may add, challenges may yet appear that will prove overwhelming to the response.

The Role of Economic Institutions in Economic Growth: Factors or Decision Systems?

The remainder of my allotted time will be devoted to a more meaningful subject—the role of economic institutions in economic growth. In this connection, the mathematical models of economic growth need not be considered because, as stated above, economic institutions are not a part of their input. The output from a mathematical-statistical formulation depends on its input. If one is interested in explaining economic growth as a historical phenomenon and in development policy in the political reality of today, such models have little to offer. Good critiques by economists concerned with development policy are already available.[4] Rather, I should like to focus on the treatment of economic institutions in the book on traditional agriculture mentioned earlier.

To avoid misunderstanding, the main theses of the book are not under discussion. Within the assumptions and terminology employed, traditional agriculture can be regarded as efficient; and its marginal productivity of labor is greater than zero. Neither is it my main criticism that technological change is segmented into "new" factors in order to speak of "shifts" of a global production function—although understanding is scarcely advanced by such terminology.[5] Historically, technological change has proceeded through packages of interrelated changes of many factors. The nature of these interrelations over time, the *Gestalt* of technological change, if you like, is the phenomenon that needs understanding rather than the appearance as a *deus ex machina* of quantities of "new" individual factors. I mention this merely because institutions are subjected to the same segmentation as technological change. My main criticism is that the book presents a conceptually insufficient model of economic growth because the role of institutions is left out.

Sometimes the author himself seems vaguely aware of this insufficiency. He is "puzzled" by economic decisions under a fuedal land-tenure system and "baffled" by the economic behavior of plantation owners under a system of slavery.[6] Still, none of the economic institutions that are significant for resource use—such as the systems of owning and using property, the systems of water rights, taxation, collective and cooperative organizations and quasi-governmental agencies like public districts—is mentioned, much less systematically treated. Economic growth proceeds in an institutional vacuum as far as natural resources are concerned.

Is this vacuum filled by the belated admission of institutions as factors (22, p. 117), the services of which are supplied in kind and quantity in accordance with the demand for them until a demand-supply equilibrium is reached?[7] This comforting notion is presented as a "theory" in a field in which it is claimed that "there are virtually no terms of reference, concepts with specifications that can be identified, and no economic theory to guide the analysis" (22, p. 1114). The facts are quite to the contrary. Institutions have been the central focus of the study of social organization for more than a century, both by adherents of the theory of economic determinism of institutions and by its opponents.

While Marx, Engels, and Kautsky emphasized the role of technological change in economic growth and the economic determinism of institutions, they, as well as non-Marxian adherents of economic determinism, were too aware of the relations between economics and social organization to press institutions into a simplistic demand-supply scheme.[8] They recognized that the demand for changes of institutions is always opposed by demand for the status quo or demand for change in the opposite direction. They recognized also that a new equilibrium between conflicting demands on the one side and institutional change on the other is a long and hard struggle and is brought to conclusions by political rather than economic forces and tools.

The position of scholars who do not accept the theory of economic determinism of institutions—like Emile Durkheim in France; Max Weber, Werner Sombart, and Eduard Hahn in Germany; and W. I. Thomas and Talcott Parsons in the United States—is not affected by this recent oversimplified version of economic determinism (10, 13, 18, 25, 26, 27, 28).

What, then, is the essence of economic institutions? We may conceptualize an institution as a social decision system that provides decision rules for adjusting and accommodating, over time, *conflicting* demands (using the word in its more general sense) from different interest groups in a society. A change in the demand from one interest group, therefore, rarely effects a change in institutions. A feudal land-tenure system does not change merely because serfs or tenants demand it. A water-right system based on the riparian doctrine does not change simply because non-riparians demand it. A system of taxation does not change because one or even the majority of taxpayers demand it. It all depends on the effectiveness of different demands, that is, on the relative weight of the interest groups from which demands originate. The locus where conflicting demands meet and where the relative weight of interest groups is determined is the political arena rather than the marketplace. For this reason, changes in economic institutions are usually slow and often require political changes and sometimes outright revolution. Changes in the fuedal land-tenure system in Europe took centuries. In South America the change of similar land-tenure systems is still in progress. A hundred years after abolition, the economic effects of slavery in the United States are still present. It took half a century and required a constitutional amendment for the appropriation doctrine to obtain co-equal status with the riparian doctrine in the water-rights system of California. Tax reform in the United States is talked about for decades; but as every newspaper reader knows, accomplishments are slow.

Demands for institutional change may not even originate from those groups directly involved, such as the landlords and tenants in tenure systems. The demand may come from other groups because of what one might call the externalities of land tenure—that is, the benefits and costs incident on social groups other than landlords and tenants. This is frequently true for the collectivization of agriculture in order to promote industrial growth and the stability of a socialist political system. Other examples are tenure changes in fugitive resources—such as fisheries, range, oil, and gas—to further the social objectives of conservation. We are presently studying a case of this kind for a nomadic group of tribes in East Africa—the Masai. Here, tenure changes are demanded by the government in order to conserve the range resource and the game herds sharing use of the resource with the Masai livestock. The game herds, in turn, are important for economic growth as the basis for a flourishing tourist trade and large foreign-exchange earnings. If the demand for institutional change originates outside the groups directly involved, the changes required are even more clearly political and sociological and usually involve various degrees of "persuasion."

Economic institutions conceptualized as social decision systems provide decision rules both for the use of resources and for the distribution of the income stream derived from such use. This distribution has strong effects on the demand for institutional change. But such income effects are frequently just the opposite of those claimed by the doctrine under discussion. In other words, the demand for institutional change is increased if the income stream of a social group is decreased absolutely or relatively. The demand for changes in the feudal system in Central Europe was increased through dispossession of the peasants in the course of enclosures, and the demand for labor legislation in England was sparked by the misery of the working class during the first stages of the industrial revolution.

Our conceptual framework is not complete by designating economic institutions as social decision systems. I have tried to show elsewhere that economic institutions operate on the second level of a three-level hierarchy of decision systems (9). Understanding of the relations between the three levels is necessary for devising public policies. On each level, the structure, the functioning, and the performance of the decision system can be studied both conceptually and observationally. For economic institutions affecting private conservation decisions, that is, decisions on the first level, such a study has long proved its usefullness (5). Water institutions likewise have been analyzed within this framework (4, 8).

To bring this framework closer to the realities of development policy, I should like to illustrate it by some observations regarding the role of water institutions in northern India under the impact of the green revolution—the rapid spread of a new cereal technology based on varieties with greater capacity to combine with complementary inputs, such as labor, fertilizer, and especially water. Because of time limits and because our study is not completed, I can only sketch the main issues.

The Role of Water Institutions in Northern India
under the Impact of the Green Revolution

The results of the green revolution, expressed in yields per acre, increase in acreage of high yielding varieties, and total production, need not be recounted here. This revolution has spread so rapidly in northern India, Mexico, and several other countries because it requires the least institutional change of any new technology that I know of—at least in the initial stages. In subsequent stages, however, institutional changes will become necessary. Of these, changes in water institutions will be the most essential and the most difficult to bring about.

My concern is that the doctrine discussed in the preceding sections will lead to complacency regarding the institutional difficulties that lie ahead in realizing the full benefits of the green revolution and avoiding serious setbacks. According to this doctrine, there are no such difficulties because farmers themselves will accomplish those changes of water institutions that become necessary.[9] Let us take a closer look at this projection.

In northern India, irrigation has been based for centuries on groundwater lifted from open wells by the Persian wheel, a simple but ingenious device to develop groundwater resources where they are available in large quantities not more than some 40 feet below the surface. This is the situation in large parts of the extensive Indo-Gangetic Plain.

Groundwater use is usually possible on a more individualistic basis than surface water use. This is especially true for the relatively small, low-capacity development of groundwater based on the Persian wheel. The farmer can build, maintain, and operate the water facility himself or with the help of a small number of villagers. Water is available to the individual farmer where he wants it, when he wants it, and in quantities and over time periods that are under his own control.

An irrigation economy dominated by the Persian wheel differs greatly from one that is based on diversion from large rivers, such as in ancient Egypt and Mesopotamia, or, in modern times, from large multipurpose reservoirs. Here, the individual farmer is dependent on other farmers for building, maintaining, and operating the diversion facilities and the canal system that distributes the water. He must take this water at certain points on the canal. He must take his turn as to when the water is available to him. Quantities of water are rationed to him, and these rations may vary over time for reasons outside his own control. What is the effect of these fundamental differences in the irrigation economy on the development of water institutions?

In a diversion economy, water institutions—such as water rights, water districts, a water master, and public agencies engaged in building, maintaining, and operating facilities—are a necessary condition from the beginning. In a water economy based on the Persian wheel, such institutions are not needed and do not develop. Groundwater institutions become a necessity only when water use by one farmer affects his neighbor. This happens when the Persian wheel is replaced by modern deep-well pumps. Here the neighbor is affected by the pumping cone and by the seasonal and often secular depletion of the resource because of high-capacity pumps.

In countries where an irrigation economy based on diversion preceded the need for modern groundwater institutions, these institutions could be built on the experience and mental attitudes already formed. These relations between groundwater institutions and surface water institutions I have traced elsewhere (6). But such experience and such attitudes are not available in northern India. There, water institutions must be created from scratch.

The green revolution has created a need for more water. Groundwater tables are beginning to fall and will force the replacement of the Persian wheel by deep-well pumps. Increasing size of farms, related to the green revolution, will operate in the same direction because of the Persian wheel's relatively low capacity and high labor requirements. Increased irrigation will increase the need for drainage. Water allocation problems between users, between uses, between states and regions, between areas of origin and areas of destination, and between state and federal jurisdictions loom on the horizon.

To solve these problems, groundwater laws are needed to regulate the number and spacing of wells, the quantities pumped per well, the periods of pumping, and the provision and operation of recharge facilities. This will require adjudication of water rights and integration of groundwater and surface water development, and thus, an integrated water-rights and management system.

As a key element of such a management system, the water district has proved its usefulness in the United States and elsewhere. It is flexible with respect to its role as a part of local and regional government. It is flexible also with respect to the participation of social groups outside of agriculture that need additional water supplies. Water districts, possibly with greater governmental participation and supervision that in this country, are needed.

Water institutions of this kind will develop over time. But the individualism of the farmer, the local community, and the region, shaped over centuries in an irrigation economy dominated by the Persian wheel, requires a special effort by researchers and policy-makers to create and to make acceptable the water institutions that are needed. Complacency based on a simplistic doctrine of the role of institutions in economic growth is not at all warranted and will become dangerous if effort in research and in public policy is thereby deflected from this important area. What India's agriculture needs most at the present juncture are competent economists, fully aware of the intricacies and the difficulties in the development of water institutions. Otherwise, the cornucopia of the green revolution may indeed prove Pandora's box, to paraphrase the title of a perceptive recent paper (29). A laissez-faire attitude toward institutions is no less inappropriate than regarding them as constraints.

[1]*American Journal of Agricultural Economics* 51(5)1314-1324 (December, 1969). Giannini Foundation Research Paper 294.

[2]According to Schultz, this influence operates solely through profitability of tenant farming. Profitability is regarded throughout as a "strong explanatory variable" (24, pp. 167 and 168). Edmundo Flores' emphasis on land reform as the basic issue in increasing Mexico's agricultural productivity is explicitly rejected (24, p. 19).

[3]Because of these weights, the study by Goldsmith, Brady, and Mendershausen (12) shows a decreasing share of *all* land in the wealth of the United States, but this study applies only to the period 1896-1956 and is subject to a number of statistical difficulties with respect to comprehensiveness and valuation.

[4]See the discussion of the Ranis and Fei and Jorgenson models by John W. Mellor (17). Also, see the discussion of institutional influences by John M. Brewster (2).

[5]Since multidimensional relations are involved, one must, strictly, speak of movements to production hypersurfaces.

[6]"Why many of the farmers who own and are responsible for the operation of very large farms, especially in some parts of South America, do not successfully engage in the search for modern agricultural factors is a puzzle" (24, p. 174). "Why better health and longer life were not realized (for slaves in the antebellum South) is baffling" (24, p. 180).

[7]The author must be aware that the economic definitions of demand, supply, and equilibrium do not apply in the cases he discusses. Clarity is not served by interchanging the more general sense of a word with its precise scientific connotation.

[8]Compared with Marx and Engels, Kautsky has not gained a wide reputation in this country. He was, however, an economic theorist of some stature, who was especially interested in the role of agriculture in economic growth (15, 16). Besides Marx, Engels, and Kautsky, a long list of non-Marxian works could be mentioned. The best known in the United States is probably Charles A. Beard (1).

[9]As Professor Schultz puts it, farmers "will join with neighbors to acquire tube wells and to undertake minor investments to improve the supply of water. Both tenants and landowners will also use whatever political influence they have to induce the government to provide more and better large-scale irrigation facilities" (22, p. 1118).

References

(1) BEARD, CHARLES A., *An Economic Interpretation of the Constitution of the United States,* New York, The Macmillan Company, 1913.

(2) BREWSTER, JOHN M., "Traditional Social Structures as Barriers to Change," *Agricultural Development and Economic Growth,* Ithaca, New York, Cornell University Press, 1967.

(3) CIRIACY-WANTRUP, S. V., *Agrarkrisen Und Stockungsspannen zur*

Frage der langen 'Welle' in der Wirtschaftlichen Entwicklung, Berlin, Paul Parey, 1936.

(4) _____, "Concepts Used as Economic Criteria for a System of Water Rights," *Land Econ.*, 32:295-312, November, 1956.

(5) _____, *Resource Conservation: Economics and Policies*, 3d ed., Berkeley, University of California Division of Agricultural Sciences, 1968.

(6) _____, "Some Economic Issues in Water Rights," *J. Farm Econ.*, 37:875-885, Dec. 1955.

(7) _____, "The 'New' Competition for Land and Some Implications for Public Policy," *Natural Resources J.* 4:252-267, Oct. 1964. (Chapter 13 in this volume.)

(8) _____, "Water Economics: Relations to Law and Policy," in *Waters and Water Rights: Eastern, Western, Federal*, ed. Robert Emmet Clark, Indianapolis, The Allen Smith Company, 1967, Vol. 1, pp. 397-431. (Chapter 5 in this book.)

(9) _____, "Water Policy and Economic Optimizing: Some Conceptual Problems in Water Research," *Am. Econ. Rev.* 57:179-189, May 1967. (Chapter 4 in this book.)

(10) DURKHEIM, EMILE, *De la Division du Travail Social; etude sur l'organisiation des societes superieures*, Paris, F. Alcan, 1893.

(11) FEI, JOHN C. H. and GUSTUAV RANIS, *Development of the Labor Surplus Economy: Theory and Policy*, a publication of the Economic Growth Center, Yale University, Homewood, Illinois, Richard D. Irwin, 1964.

(12) GOLDSMITH, RAYMOND W., DOROTHY S. BRADY, and HORST MENDERSHAUSEN, *A Study of Savings in the United States*, Vol. 3, Princeton, Princeton University Press, 1956.

(13) HAHN, EDUARD, *Die Entstehung der Pflugkultur*, Heidelberg, Carl Winter's Universitatsbuchhandlung, 1911.

(14) JORGENSON, DALE W., "The Development of a Dual Economy," *Econ. J.* 71:309-334, June 1961.

(15) KAUTSKY, KARL, *Die Agrarfrage: Eine Uebersicht ueber die Tendenzen der Modernen Landwirtschaft und die agrarpolitik der Sozialdemokratie*, Stuttgart, I. H. W. Dietz Nachf, Inc., 1902.

(16) _____, *Die Sozialisierung der Landwirtschaft*, Berlin, Paul Cassirer, 1919.

(17) MELLOR, JOHN W., "Toward a Theory of Agricultural Development," *Agricultural Development and Economic Growth*, Ithaca, New York, Cornell University Press, 1967.

(18) PARSONS, TALCOTT, *The Structure of Social Action; a study in social theory with special reference to a group of recent European writers.* New York, McGraw-Hill, 1937.

(19) POTTER, NEAL, and FRANCIS T. CHRISTY, JR., "Employment and Output in the Natural Resource Industries, 1870-1955," in *Output, Input and Productivity Measurement*, Studies in Income and Wealth, a report of the National Bureau of Economic Research, Princeton, Princeton University Press, 1961. Vol. 25 pp. 109-145.

(20) RANIS, GUSTAV, AND JOHN C. H. FEI, "A Theory of Economic Development," *Am. Econ. Rev.* 51:533-565, Sept. 1961.

(21) SCHULTZ, THEODORE W., "Connections Between Natural Resources and Economic Growth," in *Natural Resources and Economic Growth*, Papers presented at a conference held at Ann Arbor, Michigan, April 7-9, 1960, ed. Joseph J. Spengler, Washington, D.C., Resources for the Future, Inc., 1960, pp. 1-9. (Similar views are expressed in papers by Chandler Morse, Harold J. Barnett, John H. Adler, and others.)

(22) _____. "Institutions and the Rising Economic Value of Man," *Am. J. Agr. Econ.* 50:1113-1122, Dec. 1968.

(23) _____, "Land in Economic Growth," in *Modern Land Policy*, ed. J. B. Halcrow, Urbana, University of Illinois Press, 1960, pp. 17-39.

(24) _____, *Transforming Traditional Agriculture*, New Haven, Yale University Press, 1964.

(25) SOMBART, WERNER, *Der moderne Kapitalismus*, 3 vols. in 6, Munchen and Leipzig, Duncker und Humblot, 1928.

(26) THOMAS, W. I., *The Polish Peasant in Europe and America; monograph of an immigrant group*, 5 vols., Chicago, University of Chicago Press, 1918-1920.

(27) WEBER, MAX, "The Evolution of the Capitalistic Spirit," in *General Economic History*, trans. Frank H. Knight, Glencoe, Illinois, The Free Press, 1927, pp. 352-369.

(28) _____, *The Protestant Ethic and the Spirit of Capitalism*, trans. Talcott Parsons, London, George Allen and Unwin, Ltd., 1930.

(29) WHARTON, CLIFTON R., JR., "The Green Revolution: Cornucopia or Pandora's Box?" *Foreign Affairs*, 47:464-476, April, 1969.

Bibliography of S. V. Ciriacy-Wantrup

1. Ciriacy-Wantrup, S. V. *Die zweckmässigen Betriebagrössen in der Landwirtschaft der Vereinigten Staaten von Amerika.* Berlin: P. Parey, 1932, 149p. (Germany: Reichsministerium für Ernahrung u. Landwirtschaft. *Berichte über Landwirtschaft; Zeitschrift für Agrarpolitik und internationale Landwirtschaft,* Sonderheft 51, neue folge.)

2. ———. *Agrarkrisen und Stockungsspannen zur Frage der langen "Welle" in der wirtschaftlichen Entwicklung.* Berlin: P. Parey, 1935, 445p. (Germany: Reichs. und Pr. Ministerium für Ernahrung u. Landwirtschaft. *Berichte über Landwirtschaft; Zeitschrift für Agrarpolitik und Landwirtschaft,* Sonderheft 122, neue folge.)

3. ———. "Ziele und Ergebnisse der Landwirtschaftspolitik in den Vereinigten Staaten seit 1933." (In Germany: Reichs. u. Pr. Ministerium für Ernahrung u. Landwirtschaft. *Berichte über Landwirtschaft; Zeitschrift für Agrarpolitik und Landwirtschaft,* neue folge, Bd. 21, hft. 3, 1937, pp. 529–590.)

4. ———. "Die Bevölkerungskapazität Kanadas im Licht wirtschaftlicher Entwicklungstendenzen der Gegenwart." (In Germany: Reichs. u. Pr. Ministerium für Ernahrung u. Landwirtschaft. *Berichte über Landwirtschaft; Zeitschrift für Agrarpolitik und Landwirtschaft,* neue folge, Bd. 22, hft. 3, 1937, pp. 502–517.)

5. ———. "Soil Conservation in European Farm Management," *Journal of Farm Economics,* Vol. 20, No. 1 (February, 1938), pp. 86–101. (University of California, College of Agriculture, Giannini Foundation of Agricultural Economics Paper No. 66.)

6. ———. "Economic Aspects of Land Conservation," *Journal of Farm Economics,* Vol. 20, No. 2 (May, 1938), pp. 462–473. (University of California, College of Agriculture, Giannini Foundation of Agricultural Economics Paper No. 70.)

7. ———. "Land Use Planning or Land Use Policy in the United States," *Agricultural Engineering,* Vol. 19, No. 6 (June, 1938), pp. 261–263. (University of California, College of Agriculture, Giannini Foundation of Agricultural Economics Paper No. 69.)

8. ———. "Multiple and Optimum Use of Wild Land Under Different Economic Conditions," *Journal of Forestry,* Vol. 36, No. 7 (July,

1938), pp. 665-674. (University of California, College of Agriculture, Giannini Foundation of Agricultural Economics Paper No. 68.)

10. ⸺. "Multiple and Optimum Use of Wild Land Under Different Economic Conditions," *Journal of Forestry*, Vol. 36, No. 7 (July, 1938), pp. 665-674. (University of California, Giannini Foundation Paper No. 68.)

11. ⸺. *Problems of the "Long Cycle" in Economic Development Since the Eighteenth Century*. Berkeley: University of California, College of Agriculture, Giannini Foundation of Agricultural Economics, 1938, 10p. Abstract in Cowles Commission for Research in Economics, *Report of Fourth Annual Research Conference on Economics and Statistics*, July 5-29, 1938, pp. 72-74.

12. ⸺. "Land Conservation and Social Planning," *Plan Age*, Vol. 5, No. 4 (April, 1939), pp. 109-119. (University of California, Giannini Foundation Paper No. 77.)

13. ⸺. "Economic Aspects of Flood Control," *Forests and Other Vegetative Cover as Related to Runoff Retardation and Soil Erosion Prevention in Flood Control*. Berkeley: University of California, College of Agriculture, Agricultural Experiment Station, June 30, 1939, pp. 50-52. (Preliminary Review by the Flood Control Committee, College of Agriculture, University of California and the Division of Water Resources, California State Department of Public Works.)

14. ⸺. "Notes on the Significance of Trade, Legal, and Price Barriers in Relation to 'Social Progress,'" in Western Farm Economics Association, Proceedings, 1939, pp. 139-152.

15. ⸺. *Die Preisbildung der Landwirtschaftlichen Erzeugnisse, von Adolf Schilling*. (In Weltwirtschaftliches archiv, Bd. 49, hft. 2, März, 1939, pp. 82-83.)

16. ⸺. "The Relation of War Economics to Agriculture with Particular Reference to the Effects of Income and Price Inflation and Deflation," *American Economic Review*, Vol. 30, No. 1 (March, 1940), pp. 366-382. (University of California, Giannini Foundation Paper No. 85.)

17. ⸺. "Review of *Land Economics* by Richard T. Ely and George S. Wehzwein," *Journal of Land and Public Utility Economics*, Vol. 16, No. 4 (November, 1940), pp. 493-496.

18. ⸺. "Economics of Joint Costs in Agriculture," *Journal of Farm Economics*, Vol. 23, No. 4 (November, 1941), pp. 771-818. (University of California, Giannini Foundation Paper No. 99.)

19. ⸺. "Private Enterprise and Conservation," *Journal of Farm Economics*, Vol. 24, No. 1 (February, 1942), pp. 75-96. (University of California, Giannini Foundation Paper No. 102.)

20. ⸺. "A Discussion of 'Food Production Policies in Wartime' by

Sherman E. Johnson," *Journal of Farm Economics*, Vol. 25, No. 4 (November, 1943), pp. 869-874. Western Farm Economics Association, Proceedings, 16th, 1943, pp. 92-95.

21. _____. "Taxation and the Conservation of Resources," *Quarterly Journal of Economics*, Vol. 58, No. 2 (February, 1944), pp. 157-195. (University of California, Giannini Foundation Paper No. 110.)

22. _____. *Conservation of Natural Resources: An Inquiry into Economic Theory and Public Policy.* Berkeley: University of California, 1945, 349p.

23. _____. "Review of *The T. V. A.: Lesson for International Application* by Herman Finer," *Journal of Farm Economics*, Vol. 27, No. 1 (February, 1945), pp. 226-228.

24. _____. "International Cooperation in Conservation Policy," *World Economics*, Vol. 3, Nos. 9-10 (March-June, 1945), pp. 3-21. (University of California, Giannini Foundation Paper No. 112.)

25. _____. "Prepared Discussion: Natural Resources and International Policy," *American Economic Review*, Vol. 35, No. 2 (May, 1945), pp. 130-133.

26. _____. "Administrative Coordination of Conservation Policy," *Journal of Land and Public Utility Economics*, Vol. 22, No. 1 (February, 1946), pp. 48-58. (University of California, Giannini Foundation Paper No. 113.)

27. _____. "Resource Conservation and Economic Stability," *Quarterly Journal of Economics*, Vol. 60, No. 3 (May, 1946), pp. 412-452. (University of California, Giannini Foundation Paper No. 115.)

28. _____. "Review of *Food or Famine: The Challenge of Erosion* by Ward Shepard," *Political Science Quarterly*, Vol. 61, No. 2 (June, 1946), pp. 259-262.

29. _____. "State-Federal and Interstate Relations in Conservation Policy," *State Government*, Vol. 20, No. 4 (April, 1947), pp. 1-5. (University of California, Giannini Foundation Paper No. 117.)

30. _____. "State, Federal, and Interstate Roles in Conservation," *California Agriculture*, Vol. 1, No. 5 (April, 1947), pp. 1 and 3.

31. _____. "Capital Returns from Soil-Conservation Practices," *Journal of Farm Economics*, Vol. 29, No. 4, Part 2 (November, 1947), pp. 1181-1196. (University of California, Giannini Foundation Paper No. 122.)

32. _____. "Major Economic Forces Affecting Agriculture with Particular Reference to California," *Hilgardia*, Vol. 18, No. 1 (December, 1947), pp. 1-76. (University of California, Giannini Foundation Paper No. 121.)

33. _____. "Relations Between Agriculture and Industry in Economic Fluctuations," in California State Reconstruction and Reemployment Commission, *Suggested Agricultural Policies for California; Suggestions on Sixteen Subjects of Major Importance*

to the Future of Agriculture in California. A report presented by the California State Board of Agriculture, Joint Interim Committee of the California Legislature on Agriculture and Livestock Problems and California State Reconstruction and Reemployment Commission. Sacramento: California State Printing Office, 1947, pp. 153–180.

34. _____. "Booms, Depressions, and the Farmer; If Causes Are Understood, Steps Can Be Taken to Lessen Severity," *California Agriculture*, Vol. 2, No. 1 (January, 1948), p. 2.

35. _____. *Booms, Depressions, and the Farmer.* University of California, California Agricultural Experiment Station Circular 376. Berkeley, 1948, 24p.

36. _____. *Man and Resources in the Atomic Age.* Prepared for the Symposium on Man and the Atomic Age, University of California Medical School, San Francisco, California, 1949. Berkeley: Giannini Foundation of Agricultural Economics, University of California, 1949, 12 p.

37. _____. "Conservation of Renewable Natural Resources in Relation to Economic Instability," *Proceedings of the Inter-American Conference on Conservation of Renewable Natural Resources, Denver, Colorado.* U. S. Department of State Pub. 3382, International Organization and Conference Series II, American Republics 4, 1949, pp. 222–234. (University of California, Giannini Foundation Paper No. 123.)

38. _____. (with Bartz, Patricia M.). "Ground Water in California," *California Citrograph*, Vol. 35, No. 4 (February, 1950), pp. 138–163.

39. _____. "Factoree Económicos que Afectan la Conservación de los Recursos Naturales," *Trimestre Economico*, Vol. 17, No. 3 (July-September, 1950), pp. 455–478.

40. _____. *Land Use, The Basis of Western Economy.* Prepared for the Symposium on the Westward Migration and Its Consequences, American Association for the Advancement of Science, Salt Lake City, Utah, 1950. Berkeley: University of California, College of Agriculture, Agricultural Experiment Station, 1950, 12p.

41. _____. *Dollars and Sense in Conservation.* California Agricultural Experiment Station Circular 402. Berkeley, 1951, 39p.

42. _____. "Economic and Social Aspects of Utilizing Ground Water in California," *Water Resources and Economic Development of the West: Direct and Indirect Benefits.* Report No. 0, Conference Proceedings of the Committee on the Economics of Water Resources Development, Western Agricultural Economics Research Council. Ogden, Utah, 1951, pp. 77 and 78.

43. _____. "The Economics of Water Resources Development," *Water Resources and Economic Development of the West: Direct and Indirect Benefits.* Report No. 0, Conference Proceedings of the Committee on the Economics of Water Resources Development,

Western Agricultural Economics Research Council. Ogden, Utah, 1951, pp. 63–66.

44. _____. *Resource Conservation: Economics and Policies.* Berkeley: University of California Press, 1952, 395p.

45. _____. "Farmer Dollars and Horse Sense Conservation," *Farm Management*, Vol. 2, No. 2 (January, 1953), pp. 36–48.

46. _____. "Prepared Discussion: The Economic Development of Our Western Interior," *Journal of Farm Economics*, Vol. 35, No. 5 (December, 1953), pp. 713–715.

47. _____. "Economic Analysis of Water Resources Policies," *Water Resources and Economic Development of the West: Research Needs and Problems.* Report No. 1, Proceedings of the Committee on the Economics of Water Resources Development, Western Agricultural Economics Research Council. Berkeley, California, 1953, pp. 21–40.

48. _____. "Cost Allocation in Relation to Western Water Policies," *Journal of Farm Economics*, Vol. XXXVI, No. 1 (February, 1954), pp. 108–129. (University of California, Giannini Foundation Paper No. 136.)

49. _____. "Review of *The Flood Control Controversy—Big Dams, Little Dams and Land Management* by Luna B. Leopold and Thomas Maddock, Jr.," *American Economic Review*, Vol. XLIV, No. 5 (December, 1954), pp. 994–996.

50. _____. "Some Policy Aspects of Water-Resource Development," *Water Resources and Economic Development of the West: Institutions and Policies.* Report No. 2, Conference Proceedings of the Committee on the Economics of Water Resources Development, Western Agricultural Economics Research Council. Bozeman, Montana, 1954, pp. 75–78.

51. _____. "Benefit-Cost Analysis and Public Resource Development," *Journal of Farm Economics*, Vol. 37, No. 4 (November, 1955), pp. 676–689. (University of California, Giannini Foundation Paper No. 146.)

52. _____. "Some Economic Issues in Water Rights," *Journal of Farm Economics*, Vol. 37, No. 5 (December, 1955), pp. 875–885. (University of California, Giannini Foundation Paper No. 148.)

53. _____. "The Role of Benefit-Cost Analysis in Public Resource Development," *Water Resources and Economic Development of the West: Benefit-Cost Analysis.* Report No. 3, Papers presented at the December 27, 1954, meeting of Sections K and M of the American Association for the Advancement of Science, Berkeley, California, reproduced by the Committee on the Economics of Water Resources Development, Western Agricultural Economics Research Council.

54. _____. "Concepts Used as Economic Criteria for a System of Water Rights," *Land Economics*, Vol. XXXII, No. 4 (November, 1956),

pp. 295–312. (University of California, Giannini Foundation
Paper No. 154.) Also published in *The Law of Water Allocation
in the Eastern United States*. Edited by David Haber and Stephen
W. Bergen. New York: The Ronald Press Co., 1958, pp. 531–552.

55. ———. "Policy Considerations in Farm Management Research in the
Decade Ahead," *Journal of Farm Economics*, Vol. 36, No. 5
(December, 1956), pp. 1301–1311. (University of California,
Giannini Foundation Paper No. 156.)

56. ———. *Conservacíon de los Recursos, Economía y Politica, Traduccíca
de Edmunde Fiones*. Mexico-Buenos Aires: Fondo de Cultura
Economica, 1957, 397p.

57. Ciriacy-Wantrup, S. V, and Schultz, A. M. "Problems Involving
Conservation in Range Economics Research," *Journal of Range
Mangement*, Vol. 10, No. 1 (January, 1957), pp. 12–16. (University
of California, Giannini Foundation Paper No. 155.)

58. Ciriacy-Wantrup. "Criteria and Conditions for Public and Private
Ownership of Range Resources," *Journal of Range Management*,
Vol. 11, No. 1 (January, 1958), pp. 10–13. (University of California,
Giannini Foundation Paper No. 164.)

59. ———. "Objectives of Conservation Policy," *Business Organization
and Public Policy*. Edited by Harvey L. Levin. New York: Rinehart
and Company, 1958, pp. 373–382.

60. Ciriacy-Wantrup, S. V., and Smith, Stephen C. (eds.). *Economics of
California's Water Development*. Berkeley: University of
California, Committee on Water Resources Research, 1958,
180p. (Conference Proceedings of the Committee on Water
Resources Research.)

61. Ciriacy-Wantrup. "Review of *Perspectives on Conservation: Essays on
America's Natural Resources* by Henry Jazreti," *American
Economic Review*, Vol. 49, No. 3 (June, 1959), pp. 480 and 481.

62. ———. "Philosophy and Objectives of Watershed Development," *Land
Economics*, Vol. XXXV, No. 3 (August, 1959), pp. 213–221.
(University of California, Giannini Foundation Paper No. 178.)

63. ———. "Economics and Policies of Resource Conservation," *Symposium
on Natural Resources*. Edited by Warren L. Flock and Martin R.
Huberty. New York: McGraw-Hill Book Company, Inc., 1959,
pp. 500–526.

64. ———. "Social Objectives of Conservation of Natural Resources with
Particular Reference to Taxation of Forests," *Taxation and
Conservation of Privately Owned Timber*. Oregon: University
of Oregon, Bureau of Business Research, 1959, 95p. (Proceedings
of a Conference held at the University of Oregon.)

65. ———. "Conceptual Problems in Projecting the Demand for Land and
Water," *Modern Land Policy*. Edited by Harold G. Halcrow *et
al.* Urbana: University of Illinois Press, 1960, pp. 41–67. (University
of California, Giannini Foundation Paper No. 176.)

66. ———. "Philosophy and Objectives of Watershed Policy," *Economics*

of Watershed Planning. Edited by G. S. Tolley and F. E. Riggs. Ames: Iowa State University Press, 1960, pp. 1-12.

67. _____. "Conservation and Resource Programming," *Land Economics* Vol. XXXVII, No. 2 (May, 1961), pp. 105-111. (University of California, Giannini Foundation Paper 207.)

68. _____. "Projections of Water Requirements in the Economics of Water Policy," *Journal of Farm Economics,* Vol. XLIII, No. 2 (May, 1961), pp. 197-214. (University of California, Giannini Foundation Paper No. 193.)

69. _____. "Projections of Water Requirements in the Economics of Water Policy," *Western Resources Papers, 1960—Water: Measuring and Meeting Future Requirements.* Edited by Harold L. Amosa. Boulder: University of Colorado Press, 1961, pp. 211-226. (University of California, Giannini Foundation Paper No. 193.)

70. _____. "Multiple Use as a Concept for Water and Range Policy," *Water and Range Resources and Economic Development of the West: Economic Analysis of Multiple Use. The Arizona Watershed Program—A Case Study of Multiple Use.* Report No. 9, Conference Proceedings of the Committee on the Economics of Water Resources Development and Committee on the Economics of Range Use and Development, Western Agricultural Economics Research Council. Tucson, 1961, pp. 1-11.

71. _____. "Multiple Use as a Concept for Water and Range Policy," *Water and Range Resources and Economic Development of the West: Economic Analysis of Multiple Use. The Arizona Watershed Program—A Case Study of Multiple Use.* Report No. 9, A Reply to the Papers by Emery N. Castle and John A. Edward, Conference Proceedings of the Committee on the Economics of Water Resources Development and Committee on the Economics of Range Use and Development, Western Agricultural Economics Research Council. Tucson, 1961, pp. 19 and 20.

72. _____. "Water Quality, A Problem for the Economist," *Journal of Farm Economics,* Vol. XLIII, No. 5 (December, 1961), pp. 1133-1144. (University of California, Giannini Foundation Paper No. 212.)

73. _____. "Notes on Land and Water Economics Branch Seminar." Washington, D. C.: U. S. Department of Agriculture, Economic Research Service, Farm Economics Division, 1961, 6p.

74. _____. "Structure and Objectives of the Conference," *Water Resources Economics Conference,* Report No. 4. Berkeley: University of California, Water Resources Center, 1963, pp. 1-4.

75. _____. *Resource Conservation: Economics and Policies.* 2d ed. rev.; Berkeley: Division of Agricultural Sciences, University of California, 1963, 395p.

76. _____. "Toward a California Land Policy for the 1980's," *Proceedings*

of Statewide Conference on Men in California—1980's. Sacramento, January 27 and 28, 1964, pp. 23–30.

77. ————. "The 'New' Competition for Land and Some Implications for Public Policy," *Natural Resources Journal*, Vol. 4, No. 2 (October, 1964), pp. 252–267. (University of California, Giannini Foundation Paper No. 255.)

78. ————. "Benefit-Cost Analysis and Public Resource Development" (Chap. 2), "Cost Allocation in Relation to Western Water Policies" (Chap. 12), and "Concepts Used as Economic Criteria for a System of Water Rights" (Chap. 15), *Economics and Public Policy in Water Resource Development.* Edited by Stephen C. Smith and Emery N. Castle. Ames: Iowa State University Press, 1964.

79. ————. "Economic Analysis of Secondary Benefits in Public Water Resources Development," *Proceedings: Irrigation Economics Conference.* Edited by Travis W. Manning. Edmonton: University of Alberta, 1964, pp. 52–68.

80. ————. "Water Policy," *Handbook of Applied Hydrology: A Compendium of Water-Resource Technology.* Editor-in-Chief, Van Te Chow. New York: McGraw-Hill Book Company, 1964, Section 28, pp. 28-1 to 28-25.

81. ————. "A Safe Minimum Standard as an Objective of Conservation Policy," *Readings in Resource Management and Conservation.* Edited by Ian Burton, Robert W. Kates, and Lydia Burton. Chicago: University of Chicago Press, 1965, pp. 575–584.

82. ————. *Conflicts in the Creation of Water Policy.* Chapel Hill: University of North Carolina, Department of Environmental Sciences and Engineering Publication No. 98, 1965, 15p.

83. ————. "Water Resources and Economic Development: The Challenge to Knowledge," *Water Resources and Economic Development in the South.* API Series 16, Conference Sponsored by the Council of State Governments, Southern Land Economics Research Committee, and the Agricultural Policy Institute. Atlanta, Georgia, 1965, pp. 1–10.

84. ————. "Relations Between Ecology and Economics," *Proceedings: Fourth Annual Tall Timbers Fire Ecology Conference.* Tallahassee, Florida: Tall Timbers Research Station, 1965, pp. 3–5.

85. ————. "Water Economics: Relations to Law and Policy," *Waters and Water Rights.* Editor-in-Chief, Robert Emmet Clark. Vol. 1. Indianapolis, Indiana: The Allen Smith Company, 1967, pp. 397–430.

86. ————. "Water Policy and Economic Optimizing: Some Conceptual Problems in Water Research," *American Economic Review*, Vol. LVII, No. 2 (May, 1967), pp. 179–189. (University of California, Giannini Foundation Paper No. 272.)

87. Ciriacy-Wantrup, S. V., and Parsons, James J. *Natural Resources: Quality and Quantity.* Berkeley: University of California Press, 1967, 217p.
88. Ciriacy-Wantrup. *Resource Conservation: Economics and Policies.* 3d ed; Berkeley: Division of Agricultural Sciences, University of California, 1968, 395p.
89. ⸻. Response [to six basic questions relating to the problems of economic analysis as applied to public expenditure decisions]. U. S. Congress, Joint Economic Committee. *Guidelines for Estimating the Benefits of Public Expenditures.* Hearings before the Subcommittee on Economy in Government. 91st Cong., 1st Sess., May, 1969, pp. 219 and 220.
90. Kalter, Robert J., Lord, William B., Allee, David J., Castle, Emery N., Kelso, Maurice M., Bromley, Daniel W., Smith, Stephen C., Ciriacy-Wantrup, S. V., and Weisbrod, Burton A. *Criteria for Federal Evaluation of Resource Investments.* Ithaca: Cornell University, Water Resources and Marina Sciences Center, 1969, 11p.
91. Ciriacy-Wantrup. "Natural Resources in Economic Growth: The Role of Institutions and Policies," *American Journal of Agricultural Economics*, Vol. 51, No. 5 (December, 1969), pp. 1314-1324. (University of California, Giannini Foundation Paper No. 294.)
92. Ciriacy-Wantrup, S. V., and Phillips, William E. "Conservation of California Tule Elk: A Socioeconomic Study of a Survival Problem," *Biological Conservation*, Vol. 3, No. 1 (October, 1970), pp. 23-32. (University of California, Giannini Foundation Paper No. 297.)
93. Ciriacy-Wantrup. "The Economics of Environmental Policy," *Land Economics*, Vol. XLVII, No. 1 (February, 1971), pp. 36-45. (University of California, Giannini Foundation Paper No. 314.) Also published in *Pace in Maribus I*, Vol. 5: *The Ocean Environment; Proceedings of the Preparatory Conference on Ecology and the Role of Science, April, 1970.* Malta: The Royal University of Malta Press, 1971, pp. 116-126.
94. Ciriacy-Wantrup, S. V., and Bishop, Richard C. "'Common Property' as a Concept in Natural Resources Policy," *Natural Resources Journal*, Vol. 15, No. 4 (October, 1975) (University of California, Giannini Foundation Paper No. 336.)

INDEX